# THE HISTORY OF RELIGIONS
## Understanding Human Experience

American Academy of Religion
Studies in Religion

Editors
Charley Hardwick
James O. Duke

Number 47
THE HISTORY OF RELIGIONS
Understanding Human Experience

by
Joseph M. Kitagawa

# THE HISTORY OF RELIGIONS
## Understanding Human Experience

by
### Joseph M. Kitagawa

Scholars Press
Atlanta, Georgia

# THE HISTORY OF RELIGIONS
## Understanding Human Experience

by
Joseph M. Kitagawa

© 1987
The American Academy of Religion

**Library of Congress Cataloging-in-Publication Data**

Kitagawa, Joseph Mitsuo, 1915–
  The history of religions

  (AAR studies in religion ; no. 47)
  Bibliography: p.
  1. Religion. 2. Religion—Study and teaching.
I. Title.  II. Series: Studies in religion (American Academy of Religion) ; 47.
BL50.K55  1987  291          87-9545
ISBN 1-55540-127-9 (alk. paper)
ISBN 1-55540-128-7 (pbk. : alk. paper)

Printed in the United States of America
on acid-free paper

*In memory of*
*Joachim Wach (1898–1955)*
*and*
*Mircea Eliade (1907–1986)*

# TABLE OF CONTENTS

# PREFACE

I am by no means a predestinarian or a fatalist, but I cannot help feeling that there was something akin to destiny at work in the choice of the history of religions as my life's profession. Having a father who was a Confucian-turned-Christian minister and growing up in the Yamato area, the oldest district of Japan, with the children of Buddhist and Shinto clerics as my playmates, made me realize the importance of religion early in life. As an adult, and unlike my college professor, Kan Enkichi, who was originally a student of George Foot Moore but shifted to Ernst Troeltsch's philosophy of religion and arrived finally at the theology of Karl Barth, I found that my own academic pilgrimage moved in the opposite direction: from theology to the philosophy of religion to *Religionswissenschaft* (known as the history of religions, or *Shūkyō-gaku*).[1]

Having known so many different religious traditions, the Japanese are unusually sensitive to the academic study of religions. For example, when direct imperial rule was restored in 1867, a number of Buddhist scholars immediately went abroad to investigate the religious problems of the West. In 1876, Nanjio (Nanjō) Bunyū (1949–1927) and Kasaharu Kenju (1852–1883) were dispatched to Oxford to study with F. Max Müller, a leading spokesman for the scientific study of religions, or history of religions. It is not surprising that when the World's Parliament of Religions convened in Chicago in 1893 as part of the Columbian Exposition, Japanese scholars of various religious persuasions were most eager to participate. Since Max Müller himself so warmly endorsed it, some arrived under the mistaken impression that the Parliament would be a conference of scholars dedicated to the comparative study of religions and not the assembly of religious leaders that it actually was. Space does not permit me to discuss the Parliament's influence on religions and the study of religion in Japan; but I will say that in 1896, the Society for the Comparative Study of Religions *(Hikaku-shūkyō Kenkyū-kai)* was organized in that country.[2]

1905 saw the first chair of Religious Science *(Shūkyō-gaku)* inaugurated

---

[1] I have written about this in Mitsutake Suzuki, ed., *Theologia Ecumenica: Essays in Honor of Dr. Enkichi Kan* (Tokyo: Rikkyo Daigaku, 1958), p. 161.

[2] Earlier in 1896, the first Conference of Religionists *(Shūkyō-sha Kondan-kai)* was held in the villa of Viscount Matsudaira. It was commonly referred to as the Buddhist-Christian Conference *(Butsu-Ya Ryōkyō Kondan-kai)* because the predominant members of the conference were either Buddhists or Christians. As Notto R. Thelle states in his unpublished doctoral thesis, "From Conflict to Dialogue: Buddhism and Christianity in Japan, 1854–1899,"

at Tokyo Imperial University, with Anesaki Masaharu as its first occupant. It seems worth nothing that though much younger than the chairs at Leiden, Amsterdam, Utrecht, and Groningen (all established in 1876) and the chair in religious history at Uppsala (1878), the Tokyo chair preceeded those at Berlin (1910) and Leipzig (1912); and that Kyoto Imperial University established a second chair in Religious Science in 1906. In fact, the Kyoto program soon excelled in philosophy and the philosophy of religion to the extent that the study of religions at Kyoto became for all intents and purposes a supplement to the philosophy of religion.[3]

At any rate, scholarly inquiry concerned with religion and religions attracted support from both the government and private universities in Japan, so that by 1930, there were eighteen such chairs.

As I noted once before,

> . . . various factors . . . helped the growth of the scholarly study of religions in Japan, factors including (1) the Japanese propensity toward relativism in religious matters, no doubt from the historic coexistence of several religious and semi-religious traditions—this openmindedness favors a comparative study of religions; (2) the existence in Japan of closely related disciplines such as studies in Indian and Buddhist philosophy, Sinology, Shinto, Christianity, and folk religious traditions; (3) the rapid growth of studies in sociology, ethnology, psychology, folklore, and history; (4) interest in the religions and cultures of the Ainus as well as Formosan aborigines and Koreans.[4]

Ironically, these same factors also prevented the development of *Religionswissenschaft* as a unified, autonomous discipline. For instance, many of the private universities which taught *Shūkyō-gaku*, including my own alma mater, were sectarian institutions—or at least universities with a sectarian spirit—bound to view all religious phenomena from the perspective of a particular religious tradition, thus negating entirely the first principle of religious science.

I remember the 1930s in Japan as a very unhappy period. The 1920s,

---

Shaku Sōen and several of the most influential participants in the conference had attended [the World's Parliament of Religions in Chicago], and other participants and supporters had in various ways been involved in it. . . . It was even called "the little Parliament of Religions." The fact that John Henry Barrows, the General Secretary of the Parliament of Religions, was present as a guest of honor and the main speaker at the second meeting in April 1897 clearly demonstrated that the Buddhist-Christian Conference was regarded as a Japanese counterpart of the Parliament three years earlier. (University of Oslo, 1982, pp. 501–502)

[3] For the so-called "Kyoto School" of philosophy see, among many publications, Thomas Kasulis, "The Kyoto School and the West," *Eastern Buddhist* 15, no. 2 (1982): 115–44.

[4] J. M. Kitagawa, "Upon the Fiftieth Anniversary of the Nihon Shūkyō Gakkai," *Nihon Shūkyō Gakkai Gojūnen-shi* (Tokyo: Nihon Shūkyō Gakkai, 1980), p. 5.

which some scholars call the period of Taishō Democracy, had come and gone. Worldwide economic crisis followed and with it the rise of Fascism and Naziism in Europe; Japan's invasion of Manchuria and China proper, and an attempted coup d'etat in 1936. All of those things convinced us that the old world order was about to crumble under our feet. Some of my friends were attracted by extreme or uncompromising forms of piety, both Christian and Buddhist. Some people were lured to Marxist dialectical materialism and others wanted to explain away religion altogether by misusing, if I may say so, the social sciences. And again, some of us read with keen interest the solutions to the modern dilemma proposed by Ernst Troeltsch and the *Religionsgeschichte Schule* and by the philosophy of religion of Hatano Sciichi (1877–1950), who taught at Kyoto.[5] In the end, nothing came of our searching, for the world quickly plunged headlong into World War II.

*     *     *

Having crossed the Pacific Ocean in the spring of 1941, I found a very different world on the other side. Many of the new friends I made seemed to feel that as North Americans, they were exempt from the problems and anxieties that so troubled the rest of the world. During the war, I was forced to spend a total of three-and-a-half years in detention camp, an internment camp, and a war relocation camp successively, and so experience taught me otherwise. Practical concerns necessarily took precedence over my academic interest in religions, although I became deeply involved in what religious people and religious groups could do to alleviate the sufferings of minority groups in a so-called democratic society. At the same time, the war years taught me not to trust religions, however noble and intellectually satisfying they might be, except insofar as they can make men and women compassionate toward one another. (Some four decades later, I still recall with great admiration the activities of the Quakers and other peace-oriented groups, but I have since recognized the dangers of too moralistic an outlook as well.)

From 1947 to 1951, I had the good fortune to study the history of religions at the University of Chicago under Joachim Wach. Besides being a renowned scholar, Wach was also a superb human being. Having lost his teaching position in Germany under Nazi pressure in the 1930s, he was particularly sensitive to discrimination based on race or ethnic identity; and having been an ardent admirer of Cuzanus and Lessing, he was persuaded that all genuine religions are derived from a primary religious experience common to all. I joined the faculty of the University of Chicago in 1951 and worked closely with Wach until his death in the summer of 1955. In the autumn of that year, Wach's own teacher, Friedrich Heiler, came from Marburg to Chicago to help fill Wach's absence; and in 1956, Mircea Eliade

[5] For brief accounts of Hatano, see Gino K. Piovesana, S. J., *Recent Japanese Philosophical Thought 1862–1962: A Survey* (Tokyo: Enderle Bookstore, 1968), pp. 131–32.

began a tenure here that has lasted three decades. I was thus extremely fortunate to find myself, from the very beginning, in the company of some of the most important historians of religions this century has produced.

The 1950s and 1960s were exciting periods for the history of religions. It seemed that North Americans were finally waking from their Europo-centric dream and were beginning to be open to the non-Western world. Also during the 1950s and 1960s, many colleges and universities, both public and private, established programs in the study of religion as part of the standard curriculum, whereas before the war, only private institutions offered such programs of study. And, whereas religious studies before the war meant primarily the philosophy of religion, theology, and history, religious studies after the war engaged the social sciences—sociology, anthropology, and psychology—and Asian and African studies as new "conversation partners."

In this new climate, the history of religions, or the comparative study of religions, became extremely popular, although I fear that in North America, the nature of such studies continues to be greatly misunderstood. Wach and I, and later Eliade and other of our colleagues, have invested enormous amounts of time and energy interpreting the ideas and methods of the history of religions to others. We have written, lectured, attended conferences, and served on committees of all kinds. We have worked very hard to develop the program in the history of religions at Chicago and to place our graduates in leading educational institutions all over the world. In 1961, the *History of Religions* journal came into being under Mircea Eliade's passionate leadership and it has flourished ever since.

Our efforts notwithstanding, it is obvious that historians of religions make up only a tiny minority among those who study religions in a scholarly way. Unfortunately, young women and men today find that they cannot commit themselves to the long period of training required to become historians of religions; and of those few who do aspire to learn about the many religions and cultures that exist—including their own—many lack the language preparation and broad humanistic training needed to excel. Moreover, even one who possesses all the requisite skills and training must acknowledge limitations, including the finite time in which one has to work. I agree with Eliade that "a scholar regretfully finds himself becoming a specialist in *one* religion or even in a particular period or a single aspect of religion."[6]

It is always tempting to borrow the methodologies of disciplines other than the history of religions—of cultural anthropology or psychology, for example—to solve problems in the history of religions; and that makes it all the more difficult for historians of religions to persevere. To date, well over a hundred young scholars from various continents have been trained in the

[6]Mircea Eliade, "History of Religions and a New Humanism," *History of Religions* 1, no. 1 (Summer 1961):1.

history of religions at the University of Chicago.[7] My feelings about their placement in teaching are very mixed. On the one hand, most of our graduates have found jobs, thanks to the mushrooming growth of religion departments in colleges and universities across North America during the last thirty-five years. On the other hand, a discouraging number of young historians of religions cannot teach the history of religions. They are assigned to teach one of the historic religions they know well, simply because chairpersons and senior colleagues think of the history of religions as no more than a composite of studies concerned with specific religions, excluding somehow Judaism and Christianity. I do hope that the situation will improve before long and that historians of religions will hold more influential positions in the academy than they do now.

*   *   *

Most of the essays brought together in this volume have been published at different times and for diverse audiences during the past thirty-five years of my academic career. This may account for the number of unavoidable duplications and for the uneven coverage given to certain topics in the book. All of the essays, however, touch on various aspects of the history of religions (*Allgemeine Religionswissenschaft*). There does not seem to be much agreement as to the nature of this nebulous discipline, and certainly I do not claim to have resolved the many difficult problems involved in defining it. I have wished only to contribute in modest ways to the ongoing discussion of the history of religions, its aims, methods, and principal ideas.

It is only fair to state at the outset that my own understanding of the history religions owes a great deal to my mentor, Joachim Wach, who taught at the University of Chicago from 1946 to 1955, and to my senior colleague, Mircea Eliade, who spent the last three decades of his life (1956 to 1986) here. My thinking reflects Wach's dictum that the history of religion is neither theology nor philosophy but that it is, instead, a program for "understanding" the religious experience of humankind. Likewise, I am sure that readers will spot many Eliadean ideas and expressions throughout this volume.

Like Wach and Eliade (and like Raffaele Pettazzoni and many others), I hold that the history of religions has both a historical and a systematic dimension. The historical dimension rests on a dialectical relationship between the histories of specific religions—for example, one of the so-called "primitive" religions, or Islam, Hinduism, or any of the classical traditions of

---

[7] I am pleased to acknowledge here a recent volume of important contributions to the history of religions, all by former students of mine: *Transitions and Transformations in the History of Religions: Essays in Honor of Josseph M. Kitagawa*, edited by Frank E. Reynolds and Theodore M. Ludwig (Leiden: E. J. Brill, 1980). See also Carsten Colpe's generous review of that collection in *History of Religions* 24, no. 2 (November 1984): 174–78.

history—and the "history of religion", that is, the historical study of human-kind's specific religious modes: myths, symbols, and rituals. The systematic part of the discipline consists in organizing significantly, to paraphrase van der Leeuw, what the historical part can supply in the way of "religious data." Of course scholars have chosen to organize the data with different emphases in mind. Some refer to the "phenomenology of religion" (which, incidentally, is very different from philosophical phenomenology à la Husserl and which Eliade preferred to call "morphological" study). Wach stressed the sociological implications of the systematic task. Some emphasize the anthropological (especially in its classical sense) or cultural significance of the data, while others accentuate the psychological import.

Benedetto Croce held that "religion" does not constitute an autonomous activity of the mind, and that so-called "religious phenomena" are nothing but "historical phenomena" and thus can be approached only through history. By contrast, the history of religions begins by looking at certain human phenomena, which have been called "religious" by individuals, communities, and cultures, and then develops a generalized and systematized notion of "religion," much as linguists arrive at a notion of "language" based on studies of specific languages. What historians of religions call religious phenomena are descriptions of essential qualities of the human condition or the mode of being human in the world. The history of religions does not approach human phenomena only historically (as Croce urged us to); it depends also on comparative analysis, following Dilthey's principle that we must actively correct our understanding of human/religious phenomena and not simply confirm our suspicions about the intricate relations between lived experience, expression, and understanding. In this sense, the history of religions shares the objective of all human studies (Geisteswissenschaften), namely, "understanding"—not theological evaluation or philosophical speculation. For that reason, the history of religions also needs hermeneutics, which was advocated as "integral understanding" by Wach and "total hermeneutics" by Eliade.

As might be expected, there are all sorts of misunderstandings about the nature of the history of religions. Basically, it is a demanding and not so glamorous discipline, whereas many people hope and expect this discipline to solve a great many problems, some of those only remotely connected with religion(s). Also, some people equate certain aspects of the discipline, such as studies of individual religions or the task of developing phenomenological typologies, with the supreme objective of the history of religions. An amazing number of people equate religion(s) with morality and/or with doctrine and expect the history of religions to be a kind of ethical or theological discipline. Often very pious people want the history of religions to become their guide for viewing other religions and end up with no more than a distorted image of their own religious faith. In that case, what they want is a "theological history of religions," which has a very different aim from that of the history of religions. The recent attempt to develop religious concepts which are acceptable to the various religious traditions also betrays underlying theological concerns. When the methods of the history of religions are utilized for proselytizing purposes, what you have is *Missionswissenschaft* and not *Religionswissenschaft* (the history of religions, in our terminology).

Questions have often been raised as to whether the "history of religions" and "comparative religion" (or the "comparative study of religions") are the same discipline or not. Indeed, the latter two often are different names for the history of religions. Sometimes the comparative study of religions (or "comparative religion," which is more commonly used in the British Isles) sets up a kind of three-storied house. The first storey comprises the narrow historical study of various religions (for which some scholars utilize the term, "history of religion"), and the second storey tries to classify religious data to provide the basis for the third storey, which adjudicates religious data and provides an evaluation in terms of a "philosophy of religion" (or a "theology" in some cases). Obviously, this kind of three-storied scheme is very different from the history of religions as we use the term here.

As hinted earlier, the use of such expressions as "religious phenomena" may be very arbitrary. In reality there is only amorphous human experience, which is at the same time historical experience, cultural experience, religious experience, and so on. This means in turn that what we call religious experience is aesthetic, moral, psychological, cultural, and other experience. This also implies that what we call religious systems are cultural, artistic, philosophical, ethical, economic, psychological, social, and other systems, and that the meaning of religious systems can and should be pursued as such. In this situation, the discipline of the history of religions aims at "understanding" human experience as "religious experience," bracketing out theological evaluation, philosophical and other cultural speculations, depending on the phenomenological tool called *epochē* and basing its judgements on the historical and systematic dimensions of inquiry. In other words, what is left inside the phenomenological brackets *(epochē)* are the historical facts of religion as integral parts of human experience which are now integrated significantly into the whole of the history of the religions of humankind. Beyond that it is up to individual scholars to advance their own hypotheses so as to develop and refine our understanding of human religious experience.

\* \* \*

I have decided to divide my essays into three parts and to add an appendix. The first part deals with the main subjects of the history of religions, while the second part may be regarded as "applied history of religions." The third is a collection of portraits of scholars, some of whom, like Tillich and Suzuki, are not historians of religions. They have nevertheless influenced me greatly. For the appendix, I have chosen my lecture on the 1893 World's Parliament of Religions, held in Chicago. In the following, I have cited the sources of my essays and have given some rationale for their composition.

"The History of Religions in America" was taken from Mircea Eliade and J. M. Kitagawa, eds., *The History of Religions: Essays in Methodology* (Chicago: The University of Chicago Press, 1959), dedicated to the memory of Joachim Wach (1989–1955). In addition to the editors, contributors included W. C. Smith, Raffaele Pettazzoni, Jean Daniélou, Louis Massignon, Ernst Betz, and Friedrich Heiler. My article was written at a time when departments of religion or of religious studies were beginning to be established in liberal arts divisions of many North American colleges and universities. Many administrators asked us for suggestions on how to include courses on the history of religions and/or world religions; and I attempted to indicate that such concerns were not new to North America but had very checkered histories.

"Primitive, Classical, and Modern Religions" was included in J. M. Kitagawa, ed., *The History of Religions: Essays on the Problem of Understanding* (Chicago: The University of Chicago Press, 1967), dedicated to the memories of Joachim Wach and Paul Tillich. This volume includes Mircea Eliade's article, "Cultural Fashions and the History of Religions," and Paul Tillich's article, "The Significance of the History of Religions for the Systematic Theologian," both presented at the 1965 conference on the history of religions at the University of Chicago. My effort, which attempted to synthesize historical and phenomenological types, was presented earlier at Grinnell College, and its shorter version was included in Paul G. Kuntz., ed., *The Concept of Order* (Seattle: The University of Washington Press, 1968).

The article, "Ainu Bear Festival (Iyomante)," was published in *History of Religions* 1, no. 1 (Summer 1961), pp. 95–151. Despite uncertainties about actual Ainu identity, scholars believe that the Ainu inherited a form of religious belief and practice common to prehistoric peoples of the arctic area. Thus historians of religions can learn something from the Ainu about prehistoric arctic religion, to which we otherwise have no direct access. Historians of religions are motivated to study the religion of the Scandinavian Lapps for similar reasons.

"The Making of a Historian of Religions," taken from the *Journal of the American Academy of Religion* 36, no. 3 (September 1968), is in a way a sequel to my earlier essay, "The History of Religions in America."

"Humanistic and Theological History of Religions With Special Reference to the North American Scene" was presented as a plenary lecture at the opening of the quinquennial Congress of the International Association for the History of Religions held in 1980 at the University of Manitoba. The article was an attempt to interpret the criss-crossing trends of the history of religions in North America for the benefit of delegates from other countries. This essay was published in *NVMEN: International Review for the History of Religions* 27, fasc. C (December 1980).

"The History of Religions at Chicago" is published here for the first time. It chronicles the study of comparative religion, as it was once called, or the History of Religions *(Religionswissenschaft),* as it is called now, at the University of Chicago, the institution at which I have taught for the duration of my professional career.

"Religious Studies and the History of Religions" was presented at a conference on revisioning the study of religions held in Denver in 1982; it has never been published. In it, I have tried to portray the ambiguities of both religious studies and the history of religions, promising factors of both aside.

As I mentioned earlier, Part 2 may be characterized as a sort of "applied history of religions," if you will. The essays here do not address themselves to the main objectives of the discipline but discuss subjects closely related to it. Valued for their expertise, historians of religions are often invited to participate in discussions of allied areas; and I have come to realize the importance of articulating this kind of "second order discourse" even though the subjects are not the scholarly aims of our study.

"The World Has Many Centers" was a convocation address to the graduating class of the University of Chicago and was printed in the university's *Record* of 1972. I realize, of course, that not many students are aware of the breadth and scope of the history of religions; but it is my sincere hope that intelligent young men and women will come to understand the depth of the pluralism which is the hallmark of today's global situation.

"Religion as a Principle of Integration and Cooperation for a Global Community" was a paper presented at a conference in Kyoto and was published in *Proceedings of the First International Congress of Scientists and Religious Leaders on Shaping the Future of Mankind* (Tokyo: Kyo Bun Kwan, 1973). My message cautions religious leaders from making extravagant claims for religions as a focus for the intergration and cooperation of a global community.

"Western Understanding of the East" is the introduction to J. M. Kitagawa, ed., *Understanding Modern China* (Chicago: Quadrangle Books, 1969). This essay, with "Search for Self-Identity" *Divinity School News* 36, no. 4 (November 1959), warns against a Europo-centric or a West-centric view of the world and stresses the importance of dialogue as a genuine two-way traffic of ideas between East and West.

"Convergence and Prejudice in the United States" was the topic assigned to me at a conference in Princeton and was subsequently published in *The Graduate Journal* 7 (University of Texas) (1966). It gives a historian of religions' analysis of contemporary American society. Part of the same material later appears in J. M. Kitagawa, ed., *American Refugee Policy: Some Ethical and Religious Reflections* (Minneapolis: Winston Press, 1984).

"Theos, Mythos, and Logos," taken from *The Barat Review* 3, no. 3 (June/September 1968), is based on a lecture given at Barat College and attempts to clarify the relationships between religious experience and its expressions in terms of religious language.

"Experience, Knowledge, and Understanding" appeared in *Religious Studies* (London) 11, n. 2 (June 1975) and was originally presented as the Walter and Mary Touhy Lectures at John Carroll University in Cleveland. I stress here the influence of Eastern religions on the West today.

"Other Religions" was contributed to R. C. Raughley, ed., *New Frontiers of Christianity* (New York: Associated Press, 1962). Here I remind those who are committed to the Christian religion that adherents to other religions have equal rights to truth claims, hence the importance of a true dialogue.

In part 3 I have collected articles on some of the influential scholars I have known. I regret that I could not include portraits of many more.

The articles entitled "Joachim Wach" and "Mircea Eliade" have been written for the *Encyclopedia of Religion* issued by the Macmillan Publishing Company. Wach was my teacher and Eliade was my life-long colleague. I have learned much from them both.

"Joachim Wach and the Sociology of Religion" originally appeared in French in *Archives de Sociologie des Religions* 1, no. 1 (Paris: Janvier–Juin 1956); the English version was published in the *Journal of Religion* 37, no. 3 (July 1957). My main point is that the nomenclature of the sociology of religion notwithstanding, Joachim Wach was a historian of religions, and he considered the sociology of religion his systematic enterprise within the history of religions.

"Daisetz Teitarō Suzuki" was written as an obituary for *History of Religions* 6, no. 3 (February 1967) shortly after Suzuki's death. I have paid high tribute to him as both a scholar and a religious person.

"G. van der Leeuw and 'Worship'" originally appeared under the title, "The History of Religions and 'Worship,'" in *Shūkyō-bunka no Shosō* (Faces of Religious Culture), a Festschrift in honor of Professor Takenaka Shinjō of Taishō (Buddhist) University. Although the idea of "ritual" is familiar to us, that of "worship" is more problematical. This is especially true for historians of religions who live in the Buddhist orbit. I hoped to show how "worship" looks to the history of religions by examining van der Leeuw's conception of this difficult subject.

"Tillich, Kraemer, and the Encounter of Religions" was taken from James Luther Adams *et al.*, eds., *The Thought of Paul Tillich* (San Francisco: Harper and Row, 1985). I am interested in the contrast between Paul Tillich and Hendrik Kraemer, two Western Christian visitors to Japan in 1960. I also note the common habit of simultaneous monologues which are mistakenly considered dialogues.

"Eliade and Tillich" appeared in German in Hans Peter Duerr, ed., *Die Mitte der Welt: Aufsätze zu Mircea Eliade* (Frankfurt: Suhrkamp, 1984), I have always been intrigued by Tillich and Eliade, who were so different in age, origin, and academic discipline and yet shared such similar visions about religion(s), cosmos, and the future. No wonder that in their personal contacts and in their joint seminars they stimulated each other. They shared another quality as well: each died as he was moving into a new phase.

The Appendix to this volume, "The 1893 World's Parliament of Religions and Its Legacy," was delivered as the Eleventh John Nuveen Lecture at the University of Chicago. Although the Parliament has been practically forgotten, especially in America, I feel strongly that we cannot afford to ignore its mixed legacy to the history of religions in this country.

*   *   *

I am very grateful to Dean Franklin I. Gamwell of the Divinity School of the University of Chicago and to the publishers who generously gave their permission to reproduce my articles here. I also want to thank my secretary, Ms. Martha Morrow-Vojacek, and my research assistant, Mr. Peter C. Chemery, for their invaluable assistance. Owing to my slow recovery from surgery, Mr. Chemery kindly took over the chore of proofreading, and Ms. Jane Marie Swanberg contributed the index. My thanks to both of them.

Since the essays presented here span thirty-five years of my professional career, it is only fitting to dedicate this volume to Joachim Wach and Mircea Eliade, who have decisively influenced my understanding of the history of religions. For all these years they, as well as Wach's sister, Susi, and Eliade's wife, Christinel, have extended countless kindnesses to me, to my wife, Evelyn, and to our daughter, Anne Rose. I have also been blessed with many other thoughtful colleagues, students, assistants, and secretaries.

# PART I: THE HISTORY OF RELIGIONS

# 1

# THE HISTORY OF RELIGIONS IN AMERICA

## I

On the sixtieth birthday of Gerardus van der Leeuw, Joachim Wach dedicated to him an essay "On Teaching History of Religions."[1] In this essay, Wach noted that there was no one way or method which could be handed down from one generation of scholars and teachers to the next, because the approach will have to be adapted to the specific needs of each generation and different conditions prevailing in different countries. Considering the fact that increasing numbers of educational institutions in America are offering courses in the history of religions and related subjects, it may be worthwhile for us to reflect on the nature and the scope of the discipline, and discuss some of the relevant problems relating to the research and teaching in the field of the history of religions or *Religionswissenschaft* in America.

It is significant to note that the discipline of the history of religions, in the sense the term is used in the present article, did not develop in America until a relatively recent date. This may be due, in part at least, to the religious background of America. During the Colonial period, America witnessed the introduction of various types of European church groups. In the course of time American cultural experience, coupled with the influence of pietism, revivalism, and rationalism, resulted in the principle of religious liberty, which enabled Americans of diverse confessional backgrounds to live together in relative peace. In this situation the religious problems which were relevant to Americans centered around the relations among different ecclesiastical groups—between Protestantism and Catholicism, and between Christianity and Judaism. Tales were told of other religions in far-off lands, but religions other than Judeo-Christian traditions presented no real alternative and thus did not concern the citizens of the new republic. To be sure, there was one Bostonian, Hannah Adams (d. 1832), who wrote on such topics as "A Brief Account of Paganism, Mohometanism, Judaism, and Deism," and "A View of the Religions of the Different Nations of the World," but she was a rare exception.

---

[1] Joachim Wach, "On Teaching History of Religions," *Pro-regno pro sanctuario*, ed. Willem J. Kooiman (Nijkerk: G. F. Callenbach, 1950), pp. 525–32.

In the latter half of the nineteenth century, however, interest in religions of the world became rather widespread in America. Philosophers, theologians, philologists, historians, and ethnologists began to be fascinated by the so-called comparative approach. In the year 1867, James Freeman Clarke was called to the chair of natural religion and Christian doctrine in the Harvard Divinity School. His *Ten Religions: An Essay in Comparative Theology* dealt with the historical origin and development of individual religions as well as the historical survey of certain key ideas and doctrines, such as doctrines of God, man, and salvation. Another pioneer in this field was a Unitarian minister, Samuel Johnson, whose book *Oriental Religions and Their Relations to Universal Religion* was indicative of the cultural climate of his day. In 1873 Boston University invited William Fairfield Warren, author of *The Quest of the Perfect Religion*, to become its first professor of comparative theology and of the history and philosophy of religion. Crawford Howell Toy's *Judaism and Christianity* and Frank Field Ellinwood's *Oriental Religions and Christianity* were also read in the same period. Parenthetically, Ellinwood, who was professor of comparative religion at New York University, was instrumental in organizing the American Society of Comparative Religion in 1890. Other books which appeared in the latter part of the nineteenth century include James Clement Moffat's *A Comparative History of Religions* (1871), Samuel Henry Kellog's *The Light of Asia and the Light of the World* (1885), David James Burrell's *The Religions of the World* (1888), Edward Washburn Hopkins' *Religions of India* (1895) and *The Great Epics of India* (1901), William Dwight Whitney's *Max Müller and the Science of Language* (1892), George Stephen Goodspeed's *A History of the Babylonians and Assyrians* (1902), and William James's *The Varieties of Religious Experience* (1902).[2]

In the year 1881, Princeton Theological Seminary established a chair in the relations of philosophy and science to the Christian religion, and in 1891 Cornell University appointed a professor of the history and philosophy of religion and Christian ethics, and Harvard University called George Foot Moore to the chair of the history of religions. In 1892 the University of Chicago established the Department of Comparative Religion and called George Stephen Goodspeed to teach comparative religion and ancient history. In the same year Brown University inaugurated a chair in natural theology. Also in 1892 a committee representing Columbia, Cornell, Johns Hopkins, Pennsylvania, Yale, and other leading institutions established "The American Lectures on the History of Religions" for the purpose of encouraging scholarly presentation on various aspects of the religions of the world. It is also to be noted that in 1895 the University of Chicago established the Haskell (annual) and Barrows (triennial) lectureships, and in 1897 the Amer-

---

[2] Louis Henry Jordan, *Comparative Religion, Its Genesis and Growth* (Edinburgh: T. & T. Clark, 1905), pp. 197 ff.

ican Oriental Society formed a section for the historical study of religions. In 1899 Union Theological Seminary, New York, joined other institutions in establishing a chair in the philosophy and history of religions.

By far the most dramatic event to stimulate American interest in the religions of the world was the World's Parliament of Religions, held in Chicago in 1893 in connection with the Columbian Exposition. Its motto was:

> To unite all Religion against all irreligion; to make the Golden Rule the basis of this union; to present to the world . . . the substantial unity of many religions in the good deeds of the Religious Life; to provide for a World's Parliament of Religions, in which their common aims and common grounds of unity may be set forth, and the marvelous Religious progress of the Nineteenth century be reviewed. . . .[3]

The parliament had a far-reaching effect on the American scene. Something of the nature of the parliament is indicated by the fact that the general committee, under the chairmanship of John Henry Barrows (Presbyterian), included William E. McLaren (Episcopal), David Swing (Independent), Jenkin Lloyd Jones (Unitarian), P. A. Feehan (Catholic), F. A. Noble (Congregational), William M. Lawrence (Baptist), F. M. Bristol (Methodist), E. G. Hirsch (Jew), A. J. Canfield (Universalist), M. C. Ranseen (Swedish Lutheran), J. Berger (German Methodist), J. W. Plummer (Quaker), J. Z. Torgersen (Norwegian Lutheran), L. P. Mercer (New Jerusalem, Swedenborgian), and C. E. Cheney (Reformed Episcopal). In addition to the representatives of the Christian and Jewish bodies, representatives of Islam, Hinduism, Buddhism, and other religious faiths were invited to come and "present their views of the great subjects of religious faith and life." Each group was asked to make the best and most comprehensive statement of the faith it holds and the service it claims to have rendered to mankind. "All controversy is prohibited. No attack will be made on any person or organization. Each participating body will affirm its own faith and achievements, but will not pass judgment on any other religious body or system of faith or worship."[4] Significantly, at the last union meeting of the parliament, E. G. Hirsch spoke on "Universal Elements in Religion," William R. Alger on "The Only Possible Method for the Religious Unification of the Human Race," J. G. Schurman on "Characteristics of the Ultimate Religion," George Dana Boardman on "Christ the Unifier of Mankind," and Merwin-Marie Snell on "The Future of Religion."

Among the participants were many notable scholars, including historians of religions, but they attended the parliament as representatives of their

---

[3] The World's Religious Congress, *General Programme* (preliminary ed.; 893), p. 19.
[4] *Ibid.*, p. 20.

faiths or denominations and not of the discipline of the history of religions. Nevertheless, in the minds of many Americans, comparative religion and the cause of the World's Parliament of Religions became inseparably related. What interested many ardent supporters of the parliament was the religious and philosophical inquiry into the possibility of the unity of all religions, and not the scholarly, religio-scientific study of religions. Nevertheless, the history of religious and comparative religion, however they might be interpreted, became favorite subjects in various educational institutions in America. Even the established churches took keen interest in these subjects. For example, the conference of the Foreign Mission Boards of the Christian Churches of the United States and Canada in 1904 recommended that theological schools of all denominations provide for missionary candidates courses of instruction in comparative religion and the history of religions.[5]

Undoubtedly, the widespread acceptance of the study of comparative religion or the history of religions in American universities and seminaries from the turn of the century was greatly aided by religious liberalism. Professor George F. Thomas suggests two reasons for the popularity of these subjects. First, the history of religions was considered a science and was thus regarded neutral in the conflict between Christianity and other religions. Second, religious liberalism stressed the continuity of Christianity with other religions and preferred the philosophical to the theological approach to the subject of religion. Many liberals were convinced that the philosophy of religion could pronounce conclusions about religious questions without Christian presuppositions.[6] In short, Christian liberalism was "an expression of the Christian faith in the one human community under the reign of God."[7] Many liberals were naïvely optimistic about social progress as well as the "stuff of human brotherhood" crossing religious lines.

This tendency, favorable to the history of religions and comparative religion, has been reversed since the middle of the 1930's, partly under the influence of the theological renaissance and partly because of the change which has taken place in cultural and educational domains. Philosophers, theologians, and social scientists who formerly were fascinated by the comparative approach to the study of world religions have begun to question the validity of such an approach. Not a few of them go even so far as to deny the integrity of *Religionswissenschaft* or the history of religions as an academic discipline. At the risk of oversimplification, let us cite four major criticisms of the history of religions.

First, some philosophers of religion hold that historians of religions are

---

[5] Jordan, *op. cit.*, p. 375.

[6] George F. Thomas, "The History of Religion in the Universities," *Journal of Bible and Religion*, Vol. XVII (1949).

[7] Daniel Day Williams, *What Present-Day Theologians Are Thinking* (New York: Harper & Bros., 1952), p. 53.

essentially philosophers of religion, or they ought to be if they are not already. To them, the religio-scientific inquiry of the history of religions is an important tool to develop an adequate philosophy of religion, which transcends the regional and subjective elements involved in all religious systems. Or, to put it differently, they may say that all religions are manifestations of, or a search for, one underlying primordial "religion" and the task of the history of religions is, in co-operation with the philosophy of religion, to study the relation between religion and religions and to enlighten a confused humanity so that it will eventually move toward the absolute truth.

Second, there are those who hold that the so-called objective approach of the history of religions is not objective enough, because of the very nature of the subject matter. Thus they urge historians of religions to concentrate more on the historical, phenomenological, and institutional aspects of religions, depending heavily on the co-operation and assistance of anthropologists, sociologists, philologists, and universal as well as regional historians.

There is a third group who hold that the history of religions does not take seriously enough the subjective elements involved in the study of various religions. They sometimes compare historians of religions, uncharitably to be sure, to "flies crawling on the surface of a goldfish bowl, making accurate and complete observations on the fish inside . . . and indeed contributing much to our knowledge of the subject; but never asking themselves, and never finding out, how it feels to be a goldfish."[8] What is important, according to this line of thinking, is to let the adherents of each religion speak for themselves about the nature of their own religious experiences, their views of the world and of life, and their own forms of beliefs and worship.

Finally, there are still others who rule out the possibility of religio-scientific approach to the study of religions on the grounds that each investigator is incurably conditioned by his own religious and cultural background. On this basis they advocate the necessity of what might be termed a theological history of religions, be it Islamic, Christian, or Hindu, as the only legitimate discipline. Closely related to this perspective is that of missiology or *Missionswissenschaft*, which utilizes the data and findings of *Religionswissenschaft* for apologetic purposes from the standpoint of Islamic, Christian, Buddhist, or Hindu faith.

All these criticisms have been raised by men and women in all walks of life. However, what concerns us particularly is the fact that the basic unclarity of the discipline of the history of religions has created confusion regarding the place of the history of religions in the academic curriculum in this country. Generally speaking, there are three kinds of educational institutions which are concerned with the teaching of the history of religions. In the

---

[8] Wilfred Cantwell Smith, "The Comparative Study of Religion," *Inaugural Lectures* (Montreal: McGill University, 1950), p. 42.

undergraduate colleges and universities the question of the history of religions is discussed in connection with the problem of the teaching of religion. In the graduate institutions questions are raised as to the legitimacy of the history of religions as an academic discipline, and also the relations of the research method to other disciplines. In the theological schools and seminaries, the questions of the history of religions are invovled in the relations of Christianity to other religions.

## II

There are different kinds of undergraduate colleges in America, some private, some church-sponsored or church-related, and others are municipal or state institutions. Many of the state colleges and universities do not offer instruction in religion, while some of them provide courses dealing with the Bible, general surveys of religions of the world, and philosophical and ethical concepts of the Judeo-Christian traditions. The distinction between the private and church-related colleges is not always clear. A number of private colleges and universities were originally founded by church groups at the time when American religious life was strongly influenced by emotional revivalism. As a result, it was said in the last century that educated people had to choose between being intellectual and being pious, but found it difficult to be both simultaneously. In this historical context, one can appreciate the struggle of the educational institutions for the right of freedom of inquiry. Happily, today in most of the private colleges and universities teaching and research are free from ecclesiastical interference. At any rate, in some of the colleges there still remains an antireligious tradition, which began as a reaction against the earlier religious background of their institutions. It must also be remembered that until recently it was fashionable for intellectuals, both in the private and state institutions, to explain away religion.

Since World War II this situation has changed somewhat. The present religious scene in America is even described as an "Indian Summer of Religious Revival." In this situation, many educators, students, and parents ask: "What is the place of religion in the college curriculum?" Some people, while recognizing religion as a legitimate subject matter, maintain that religion is basically "caught" but not "taught," thus arguing against inclusion of courses in religion in the curriculum. Others, who admit the importance of religion in the curriculum, nevertheless have an instinctive fear that such a step might become the opening wedge of a wholesale invasion of religious groups into the academic institution. In this setting many questions are inevitably asked, such as whether or not the history of religions teaches religion, whether religions of the world can be or should be taught without value judgment, and finally whether the history of religions is to provide intellectual understanding about religions or contribute to the religious growth of students.

These questions are especially relevant to a program of general education. In many colleges, the first two years are devoted to general education and are followed by two years of a specialized program; in some others, both types of educational program are given side by side; in still others, the general education program is built in a pyramid fashion—for instance, three general education courses are taken in the first year, two in the second, and one each in the third and fourth years. In the specialized program, it is taken for granted that there are a number of courses dealing with the subject matter of religion in one way or another, such as courses in sociology, anthropology, history, philosophy, literature, and the fine arts. But the place of the study of religion as such in the general education program is a subject of heated discussion and controversy. The famous report of the Harvard Committee, published in 1945 under the title, *General Education in a Free Society*,[9] did not propose courses on religion as such. Instead, certain aspects of religion were included in the humanities and the social sciences. For example, in recommending a course on the study of the "heritage of philosophy in our civilization," the report said:

> Western culture may be compared to a lake fed by the stream of Hellenism, Christianity, science, and these contributions might offer an extremely valuable way of considering the conceptions of a life of reason, the principle of an ordered and intelligible world, the ideas of faith, of a personal God, of the absolute value of the human individual, the method of observation and experiment, and the conception of empirical laws, as well as the doctrines of equality and of the brotherhood of man.[10]

The Harvard Committee also proposed a course within the social sciences on "Western Thought and Institutions," which was designed to examine the institutional and theoretical aspects of the Western heritage. In the words of the Committee:

> The attempt is not to survey all history and all political and social thought but to open up some of the great traditions, to indicate the character of some attempted solutions of the past, to study a few of those topics and of the great statements of analysis or of ideals with some intensity.[11]

Columbia University's introductory courses on "Contemporary Civilization" are similar to the Harvard Committee's proposed course on "Western

---

[9] Harvard Committee, *General Education in a Free Society* (Cambridge, Mass.: Harvard University Press, 1945).

[10] *Ibid.*, p. 211.

[11] *Ibid.*, p. 216.

Thought and Institutions." Along this line, most colleges and universities in America offer courses in which the place of religion in Western history and culture is treated. It is a sound educational principle to discuss the writings of, say, Thomas Aquinas or Luther in the economic, social, and political context of their times, for in a real sense they were "great expressions of ideas which emanated from certain historical backgrounds."[12]

It is significant that today there is a definite trend toward offering courses in religion within the context of general education. A recent catalogue of Harvard University shows that all students are required to elect three elementary courses in general education, one to be chosen from each of three areas (humanities, social sciences, and natural sciences). The elementary courses in humanities include such titles as "Ideas of Good and Evil in Western Literature," and "Ideas of Man and the World in Western Thought." The second group of courses in humanities include such courses as "Classics of the Christian Tradition," "Classics of the Far East," "Introduction to the New Testament," "New Testament Thought and the Mind of Today," "Religion and Culture," and "Roots of Western Culture." The social sciences also offer an interesting variety of subjects, such as "Natural Man and Ideal Man in Western Thought" and "Freedom and Authority in the Modern World" in the elementary courses, and "History of Far Eastern Civilization," "Introduction to the Civilization of India," and "Introduction to the Civilization of the Middle East" in the secondary group.[13]

This is not an isolated development at Harvard. Many colleges and universities offer at least one course in religion. "Typically," says Professor Harry M. Buck, Jr., "it is a three-hour course in 'comparative religions' in which Christianity, Judaism and all the religions of Asia are surveyed in a single semester by lectures, textbook assignments and collateral readings." Buck points out that "developments in the methodology [of the history of religions] have quite outstripped the practices in most undergraduate institutions," and "the demands placed upon instruction in this area in our own day compel a radical reappraisal of aims and methods."[14]

Who teaches such courses, and how are they administered? Here, again, wide variety may be observed. Where there are scholarly talents in specific religions and cultural areas, their participation is solicited to form a team. More often than not, however, what is nominally known as teamwork in teaching a number of religions in a single course degenerates into a "cafeteria" system. On the other hand, a single teacher cannot be expected to keep up with all the important researches in reference to many religions and cultures. To make the matter more complex, in some institutions courses on

[12] *Ibid.*

[13] *Official Register of Harvard University,* LII, No. 20 (August, 1955), 19.

[14] Harry M. Buck, Jr., "Teaching the History of Religions," *Journal of Bible and Religion,* XXV (October, 1957), 279.

world religions are offered in the department of philosophy, in others in the departments of history or religion. In some cases, teachers with personal interests, say a historian, linguist, anthropologist, philosopher, biblical scholar, or a returned missionary, persuade the college administrators to let them develop courses on world religions under the titles of the history of religions or comparative religion. Although accurate statistics are not yet available, it has been estimated by some that two to three hundred teachers, full-time or part-time, are engaged in teaching the history of religions in America, and nearly a hundred more may be added if we include Canada. All these teachers are wrestling with the question how best to teach the history of religions in the undergraduate setting.

We agree with Wach that there is not one way or one method of teaching, because the approach will have to be adapted to specific needs and different conditions. However, Wach's seven suggestions seem to be sound as general principles. He states that instruction in the history of religions must be (1) integral, (2) competent, (3) related to an existential concern, (4) selective, (5) balanced, (6) imaginative, and (7) adapted to various levels of instruction.[15] Buck also makes helpful suggestions, emphasizing the importance of (1) selectivity, (2) thoroughness in context, (3) comprehensiveness, and (4) a balanced perspective.[16] Far more urgent, however, is the clarification of the nature, scope, and method of the discipline of the history of religions itself. This is the problem which is debated heatedly in the context of the graduate program as much as in the undergraduate setting.

In a real sense, the chaotic picture of the undergraduate teaching of the history of religions can be traced to the lack of adequate graduate training centers for *Religionswissenschaft* in North America. Thus, when teachers of world religions are needed at many undergraduate colleges, they usually appoint either philosophers of religion, historians, biblical scholars, or theologians who happen to have personal interests and perhaps have taken two or three courses in the history of religions or comparative religion. If and when a person is trained solely in the general history of religion, he will have difficulty in fitting into the undergraduate teaching program. In retrospect, one is struck by the fact that the vogue of comparative religion, which started in the latter part of the last century and lasted until the 1920's, did not penetrate graduate institutions to the point of establishing strong centers of research and training in the field. Even where the so-called graduate departments of comparative religion were instituted, they usually centered around one or two scholars, who offered courses with the assistance of scholars in related fields.

In today's academic world, especially in the graduate institutions, scholarship implies specialized knowledge and competence. Unfortunately, from

---

[15] *Op. cit.*, pp. 528–30.
[16] *Op. cit.*, pp. 280–85.

the standpoint of academic specialization the current teaching and research in the field of the history of religions appear to be ambiguous. The history of religions inherited the encyclopedic interest of the age of the Enlightenment. Its pioneers were interested and trained in several disciplines, such as philology, history, folklore, philosophy, and psychology. These "auxiliary" disciplines were regarded as necessary tools of research, to be called into service contemporaneously and employed by the same investigator. Today few, if any, can claim competence in all phases of the encyclopedic *Allgemeine Religionswissenschaft*. By necessity a historian of religions must concentrate on one or two of the auxiliary disciplines and also on special fields, such as primitive religion, antiquity, Middle Ages, modern period, or any one of the major religious systems. It is inevitable that those historians of religions majoring in specific areas are constantly rivaled by scholars outside the field of religion who are interested in the same areas. It has come to be taken for granted, for instance, that Islamicists, Indologists, Sinologists, and Japanologists are "specialists" of Islam, Hinduism, Chinese religions, and Shinto, respectively, and that anthropologists are "specialists" on primitive religion. Hence the "Memoirs of the American Anthropological Association" include such works as *Studies in Chinese Thought* (Memoir No. 75), *Studies in Islamic Cultural History* (Memoir No. 76), *Islam: Essays in the Nature and Growth of a Cultural Tradition* (Memoir No. 81), and *Village India* (Memoir No. 83). The scholars of these rival disciplines, equipped with adequate research personnel, facilities, and financial backing, are in a better position to pursue research in their endeavors than the historians of religions, and they often question the competence of the history of religions as an academic discipline.

It has also been observed that some disciplines are developing comprehensive outlooks, from their own perspectives, which often touch upon the problems that have been in the past dealt with in the systematic dimension of *Religionswissenschaft*. There is no denying that philosophers such as Hocking, Radhakrishnan, and Northrop, missiologists like Kraemer, and historians like Toynbee have much to say on the subject of religions. It is but natural that many people ask whether or not historians of religions have a special contribution to make which these scholars cannot make.

Thus it is that in both the undergraduate colleges and the graduate institutions questions have been raised concerning the nature of the discipline of the history of religions. Similar questions are also viewed with the perspective of theological schools and seminaries. One of the main features of American theological institutions is that the overwhelming majority of them are denominationally oriented and autonomous institutions, loosely related or unrelated to graduate universities. Although theological study itself is supposed to be graduate work, for the most part it tends to emphasize professional preparation, concentrating on ministerial training. The majority of seminaries, with the exception of interdenominational graduate theological schools, have little access to universities, and thus are more sensitive to the movements within the churches than to the trends in the academic world.

Most seminaries in America consider either comparative religion or the history of religions a tool for the Christian world mission. In this connection, it must be remembered that American denominations developed as missionary churches. While European churches generally depended on semi-autonomous missionary societies for the missionary work abroad, most American churches accepted the missionary obligation as a task of the total church body. Starting with the formation of the Baptist missionary society in 1814, most major denominations established their own denominational missionary societies in the nineteenth century, and American churches played increasingly important roles in the domain of the Christian world mission. Some of the American missionaries were well trained in comparative religion, and they made significant contributions to scholarship. It is also to be noted, as stated earlier, that comparative religion was a favorite subject of American seminaries from the latter part of the nineteenth century to the 1920's.

Today, however, under the impact of a theological renaissance, American theological schools and seminaries are preoccupied with theology. Professor Nels Ferré analyzes the recent theological trends in America into two major kinds, those that stress objectivity and those that emphasize the subjective response. Under the former, he lists Fundamentalism, the High Church wing, and "Barthian" biblicism; under the latter, he discusses liberalism and existentialism.[17] Here we cannot go into the analyses of each of these trends or the adequacy of Ferré's interpretation of the recent trends in American theology, except to say that theologians of different persuasions, with the possible exception of the so-called liberals, while recognizing the usefulness of the history of religions, nevertheless agree with Professor Hendrik Kraemer in stating that only theology "is able to produce that attitude of freedom of the spirit and of impartial understanding, combined with a criticism and evaluation transcending all imprisonment in preconceived ideas and principles as ultimate standards of reference."[18] Such assertions imply that only those who view religions "from within" are competent to understand them. They do not exclude the validity of the history of religions; they insist, however, that the history of religions must for its own sake be aided by a theology.

Confronted by such serious questions and criticisms in the undergraduate colleges, graduate institutions, and theological seminaries, the history of

[17] Nels F. S. Ferré, "Where Do We Go from Here in Theology?" *Religion in Life* (Winter, 1955/56).

[18] Hendrik Kraemer, *Religion and the Christian Faith* (Philadelphia: Westminster Press, 1956), p. 53.

religions is compelled to re-examine, from its own standpoint, its relation to other disciplines and in so doing to clarify the nature and scope of its own discipline.

### III

The term the "history of religions" means different things to different people. To some it is a sort of Cooke's tour in world religions, in the sense that various aspects of religions are depicted and studied, using the comparative method. To others it is essentially a philosophical study of "religion" as it underlies all historical phenomena of various religions. To still others it is a historical discipline, analogous to church history, dealing with not only one religion but a number of religions. Is the history of religions a discipline auxiliary to philosophy of religion or to a social science? Or is it an autonomous discipline? And, if so, does it belong to the theological curriculum or the humanities?

This apparent ambiguity of the nature of the discipline of the history of religions is reflected in the diversity of names by which it has come to be known, such as comparative religion, phenomenology of religion, science of religions, and history of religions. All these terms, with minor differences, refer to a general body of knowledge known originally as *Allgemeine Religionswissenschaft*. In the English-speaking world the imposing title of "general science of religions" has not been used widely, partly because it is too long and awkward, and partly because the English word "science" tends to be misleading. Thus, the world-wide organization of scholars in this field has recently adopted an official English title, "The International Association for the Study of the History of Religions." It is readily apparent that the term "history of religions" has come to be regarded as a synonym for the "general science of religions," and as such the nature of the discipline must be discussed in the total context of *Religionswissenschaft*.

It must be made abundantly clear that the history of religions is not proposed as the only valid method of studying religions. Actually, it is only one among many different approaches, such as philosophy of religion, psychology of religion, sociology of religion, and theology. Unlike philosophy of religion and theology, however, the history of religions does not "endorse" any particular system offered by the diverse religions of the world, nor does it advocate, as many ultra-liberals think it ought, any new universal synthetic religion. On the other hand, there are those who study other religions much as the commander of an invading army investigates enemy territory, and with much the same motivations. Such an approach is, of course, not acceptable to the history of religions, for this discipline does not prove the superiority of any particular religion over others.

There are three essential qualities underlying the discipline of the history of religions. First is a sympathetic understanding of religions other than one's own. Second is an attitude of self-criticism, or even skepticism, about one's own religious background. And third is the "scientific" temper.

Historically, the encounter of different peoples and religions has often resulted in serious conflicts and the subjugation of one group by another, but in some cases it has also fostered sympathetic understanding and mutual respect among individuals of different backgrounds. Sometimes, knowledge of other religions, or a crisis in one's life, leads one to question one's own religious faith.

For example, in sixth century B.C. Greece, the traditional faith in local gods began to be questioned for a number of reasons. Similar things happened in other parts of the world. In ancient times, however, questions about gods and religions were more often than not approached and solved "religiously" rather than "intellectually." Thus, the Hebrew god triumphantly challenged the skeptical man in the Book of Job:

> And the Lord said to Job:
> "Shall a faultfinder contend with the Almighty?
> He who argues with God, let him answer it."[19]

> Then Job answered the Lord:
> "I know that thou canst do all things,
> and that no purpose of thine can be thwarted,
> 'Who is this that hides counsel without knowledge?'
> Therefore I have uttered what I did not understand,
> things too wonderful for me, which I did not know."[20]

During the Middle Ages three monotheistic religions—Judaism, Christianity, and Islam—existed side by side in the Mediterranean area. The relationship among them was amazingly amiable in certain areas, and Christians, Jews, and Muslims had ample opportunities to "compare" their religions with others and ask serious questions. Indeed, some of them did ask fundamental questions, but their questions and answers were dealt with theologically and philosophically, not "scientifically" in the sense of *Religionswissenschaft*. This "scienfitic" temper in the study of religions developed only at the dawn of the modern period, namely, during the Enlightenment.

Few words are necessary to emphasize the importance of the fifteenth and sixteenth centuries, when the intellectual climate of Europe changed with the discovery of the non-European world. Knowledge of the sacred texts, rituals, and customs of non-European religions gradually became accessible to European intellectuals. Confronted by the diversity of religious

[19] 40:1–2.
[20] 42:1–3.

phenomena, thinkers like Lord Herbert, Berkeley, Locke, Hume, and others tried to reconcile the rival claims of religions by digging deeper into the nature of religion itself. The thinkers of the Enlightenment attempted to find the meaning of religion in terms of "reason," rather than depending solely on the authority of "revelation." Locke was hopeful that revelation would confirm the natural knowledge of God given by reason. Hume sought the meaning of religion in its origin, as evidenced in his book, *The Natural History of Religion*. Leibniz differentiated between "contingent truths" and "necessary truths" in religions.

The expression *Religionswissenschaft* was first used in 1867 by Max Müller. Like the Enlightenment thinkers, he was concerned with *religio naturalis*, or the original natural religion of reason, and assumed that "truth" was to be found in the most universal essence of religion and not in its particular manifestations. The process of differentiation of the original truth into diverse religions was seen in much the same way as the Old Testament described the origin of different languages in the legend of the Tower of Babel. Significantly, Max Müller's key to the scientific investigation of religions was philology. He and his disciples were hopeful that by studying the development of languages they could arrive at the essence of religion "scientifically." He used the term *Religionswissenshaft* in order to indicate that the new discipline was freed from the philosophy of religion and from theology, even though in actuality his "science of religion," embracing both comparative theology and theoretical theology, was not too different from philosophy of religion. A Dutch historian of religion, C. P. Tiele, also regarded the science of religions as the philosophic part of the investigation of religious phenomena. While Tiele held that philosophic doctrines of belief and dogmatic systems should not be dealt with in the science of religions, nevertheless this discipline remained a philosophy of religion in Tiele's view. Another Dutch scholar, Chantepie de la Saussaye, did not find a qualitative difference between the science of religions and the philosophy and history of religions, here using the term "history of religions" in its narrower sense.

In retrospect it becomes evident that the scientific study of religions was a product of the Enlightenment. In the study of religion the Enlightenment period accepted the deistic notion of reason and rejected the authority of revelation. The Enlightenment thinkers also accepted the concept of *religio naturalis* or a universal religiosity underlying all historic religions which was to be perceived by reason without the aid of revelation.

The rationalism of the Enlightenment was followed by romanticism, in which the doctrine of *religio naturalis* was again foremost. Van der Leeuw provides us with a careful analysis of the impact of the three romantic periods on the scientific study of religions. First, the period of philosophic romanticism "endeavored to comprehend the significance of the history of religion by regarding specific religious manifestations as symbols of a primordial revelation." Second, the period of romantic philology, while reacting against the unfettered speculation of romanticism, remained romantic "in its desire to comprehend religion as the expression of a universal mode of human thinking." Third, the period of romantic positivism, preoccupied with the principle of development, still accepted religion to be "the voice of human-ity." Thus, Chantepie de la Saussaye, for example, "sought to comprehend the objective appearances of religion in the light of subjective processes."[21]

The early historians of religions, notwithstanding their conscious "eman-cipation" from philosophy, had definite philosophical assumptions, be they rationalistic or romantic, and they dealt with religio-scientific data "philo-sophically." According to Joachim Wach, Max Scheler was probably the first scholar who made the distinction betwen philosophy and *Re-ligionswissenschaft*. Following Max Scheler, Wach held that the religio-scientific task must be carried out not "philosophically" or "scientifically" but "religio-scientifically," with its own methodology. While Wach acknowledged the necessary contributions of philosophy to the scientific study of religions, he rightly insisted that the point of departure of *Religionswissenschaft* was the historically given religions.

Obviously the history of religions or *Religionswissenschaft* does not monopolize the study of religions. Normative studies, such as theology and philosophy, and descriptive disciplines, such as sociology, anthropology, and others, are concerned with various aspects of religions and religious phe-nomena. At the same time it must be made clear that the history of religions is not merely a collective title for a number of related studies, such as the history of Islam, Christianity, Buddhism, Hinduism, and primitive religion, or the comparative studies of doctrines, practices, and ecclesiastical institu-tions of various religions. In short, the history of religions is neither a normative discipline nor solely a descriptive discipline, even though it is related to both.

Our thesis is that the discipline of *Religionswissenschaft* lies between the normative disciplines on the one hand and the descriptive disciplines on the other. Following Wach, we may divide *Religionswissenschaft* into histor-ical and systematic subdivisions. Under the heading of "historical" come the general history of religion and the histories of specific religions. Under the heading of "systematic" come phenomenological, comparative, sociological, and psychological studies of religions. All these subdivisions are regarded as integral parts of *Religionswissenschaft* or the history of religions, in the way we use this term.

While *Religionswissenschaft* is an autonomous discipline in the sense that it is not a composite of various disciplines concerned with the study of religions, it does not claim to be a self-sufficient discipline. That is to say, *Religionswissenschaft* depends heavily on other disciplines, including both

---

[21] Gerardus van der Leeuw, *Religion in Essence and Manifestation*, trans. J. E. Turner (London: George Allen & Unwin, Ltd., 1938), pp. 691–94.

normative and descriptive studies of religions. For example, the descriptive aspect of the history of religions must depend on the disciplines which deal with the historical delineation of each religion. Moreover, the analytical aspects of the history of religions must depend on psychology, anthropology, sociology, philosophy, philology, and hermeneutics in its study of various features of religions, such as scriptures, doctrines, cults, and social groupings. This does not mean, however, that *Religionswissenschaft* regards itself as the queen of all disciplines dealing with the study of religions. It simply means that from the standpoint of *Religionswissenschaft* other disciplines can be regarded as its auxiliary disciplines. On the other hand, from the standpoint of a normative or descriptive discipline, *Religionswissenschaft* may be regarded as one of its auxiliary disciplines.

Careful attention must be given to the relation between *Religionswissenschaft* and other disciplines. This is an important question in today's academic world, especially in America. The question of the sociology of religion may be cited as an example of the relation between *Religionswissenschaft* and another discipline. According to Professor E. A. Shils: "It is scarcely to be expected that American sociologists would make contributions to the sociological study of religion along the lines of Max Weber's *Gesammelte Aufsätze zur Religionssoziologie*. American sociologists are usually too poorly educated historically and their religious 'musicality' is too slight to interest themselves in such problems." Nevertheless, Shils cites such works as Kincheloe's *The American City and Its Church*, Niebuhr's *Social Sources of American Denominationalism*, Mecklin's *Story of American Descent*, and Pope's *Millhands and Preachers* as examples of American "sociology of religion."[22] The crucial question arises as to whether the sociology of religion must be viewed as a subdivision of *Religionswissenschaft* or of sociology.

It is our contention that there are two kinds of sociology of religion, one derived from sociology and the other from *Religionswissenschaft*, despite Wach's hope: "We would like to believe that, though there is a Catholic and Marxian philosophy of society, there can be only *one* sociology of religion which we may approach from different angles and realize to a different degree but which would use but one set of criteria."[23] Wach himself defined the task of the sociology of religion as "the investigation of the relation between religion(s) and society in their mutual ways of conditioning each other and also of the configuration of any religiously determined social processes."[24] Throughout his life, Wach tried to bridge the gap between the

[22] E. A. Shils, "The Present Situation in American Sociology," *Pilot Papers*, II, No. 2 (June, 1947), 23–24.

[23] Wach, "Sociology of Religion," *Twentieth Century Sociology*, ed. G. Gurvitch and W. E. Moore (New York: Philosophical Library, 1945).

[24] Wach, "Religionssoziologie," *Handwörterbuch der Soziologie*, ed. A. Vierkandt, No. 1 (1931), pp. 479–94.

study of religion and the social sciences from the perspective of *Re-ligionswissenschaft*. In his conclusion to *Sociology of Religion* he states: "The fact that this study is limited to a descriptive sociological examination of religious groups need not be interpreted as an implicit admission that the theological, philosophical, and metaphysical problems and questions grow-ing out of such a study of society have to remain unanswerable. They can and most certainly should be answered."[25] But the sociology of religion as a subdivision of sociology is interested in religion within the framework of the objectives of sociology, that is, "to gain a knowledge of man and society insofar as it may be achieved through investigation of the elements, pro-cesses, antecedents and consequences of group living." The sociologist, in his study of the sociology of religion, despite Wach's admonition not to view religion as a function of natural and social groupings and as one form of cultural expression, has to start from the fundamental assumption that "the conduct of the person—his ways of thinking and ways of acting—and the nature of the social order—its structure, function and values—are to be understood as a product of group life."[26] Thus, although both kinds of sociology of religion deal with the same data and may even utilize similar methods, one sociology of religion inevitably views the data "sociologically," whereas the other views the same data "religio-scientifically." Similar obser-vations can be made regarding the relation of *Religionswissenschaft* to other disciplines.

What does it mean to view the data "religio-scientifically"? This is not a simple question. Basically, the point of departure of *Religionswissenschaft* is the historically given religions. In contrast to normative disciplines, *Re-ligionswissenschaft* does not have a speculative purpose, nor can it start from an a priori deductive method. While *Religionswissenschaft* has to be faithful to descriptive principles, its inquiry must nevertheless be directed to the meaning of religious phenomena. Professor Mircea Eliade rightly insists that the meaning of a religious phenomenon can be understood only if it is studied as something religious. "To try to grasp the essence of such a phenomenon by means of physiology, psychology, sociology, economics, linguistics, art or any other study is false; it misses the one unique and irreducible element in it—the element of the sacred."[27] To be sure, Eliade is aware that there are no purely religious phenomena, because no phenom-enon can be exclusively religious. But we agree with him that this does not mean that religion can be explained in terms of other functions, such as social, linguistic, or economic ones. In saying this, however, historians of religions confront many serious methodological problems.

[25] Wach, *Sociology of Religion* (Chicago: University of Chicago Press, 1944), p. 374.

[26] Philip M. Hauser, "Sociology," *Encyclopaedia Britannica* (1957 ed.).

[27] Mircea Eliade, *Patterns in Comparative Religion*, trans. Rosemary Sheed (New York: Sheed & Ward, 1958), p. xi.

## IV

One of the fundamental problems confronting the history of religions is that traditional Western scholarship in the field of *Religionswissenschaft* has been too "European" and "Western" in basic orientation and framework. There are two implications of this problem. First, *Religionswissenschaft*, if it is to remain and grow as a religio-scientific inquiry of religions, has to reexamine its methods and categories of interpretation in the light of the criticisms of non-Western scholars in the field. Second, American historians of religions must articulate their unique tradition of scholarship so as to make significant contributions to the world-wide co-operative inquiry in the religio-scientific study of religions.

It is apparent that from the time of the Enlightenment *Religionswissenschaft* has been operating with Western categories in the study of all religions of the world, in spite of its avowed principles of neutrality and objectivity. We know, however, that world religions are developmental movements grounded in historic communities. Thus, the ultimate assumptions of each religion have been colored by decisions of human communities in particular historical and cultural situations. Yet the ultimate assumptions of each religion must be subjected to critical analysis if there is to be any *Wissenschaft* at all. The difficulty is that the assumptions and methodology of *Religionswissenschaft* are also products of Western historical culture. There is no denying that in practice the history of religions has acted too often as though there were such an objective frame of reference. Even those concerned with Eastern religions have asked, unconsciously if not consciously, "Western" questions and have expected Easterners to structure their religions in a way which was meaningful to Westerners. Admittedly, the Eastern emphasis on an immediate apprehension of the totality or essence of Ultimate Reality has been also conditioned by the Eastern historical communities. But the fact remains that the Western historians of religions, with their preoccupation with "conceptualization," have tended to interpret non-Western religious phenomena by attempting to fit them into their logical non-regional abstract systems of *Religionswissenschaft*.

The difference of outlook between Eastern and Western historians of religions seems to be magnified as time goes on in regard to the methodology, aim, and scope of the discipline. Historically, it was the Western scholars who made Eastern religions the subject matter of academic disciplines. They too were credited with training many Eastern scholars in Western universities. These European-trained Eastern historians of religions, upon returning to their native countries, faced precarious situations.

In the nineteenth century people in the East, under the strong impact of the West and modernity, reacted against the West in several ways. There was a small minority of those who, in their enthusiasm for everything the West stood for, became "denationalized" for all practical purposes. On the other hand, there was another minority who, looking back to their own religious and cultural traditions with a newly acquired Western-type national consciousness, became extremely conservative and rejected the West *in toto*. In this situation, those European-trained Eastern historians of religions became suspect in the eyes of conservative elements in the East because of their emphasis on "Western scientific methodology" in the study of traditional religions. At the same time, these newly trained scholars "discovered" afresh the meaning of the Eastern religions; consequently, they were not welcomed by the progressive people who rejected everything traditional. In fact, it took some time for the history of religions to become an accepted discipline in the East. In the course of time, Eastern historians of religions began to reconcile their Western scientific methodology and Eastern world view.

The Eastern attitude, borrowing Dr. Radhakrishnan's oft-repeated expression, may be characterized by the statement, "religion is not a creed or code but an insight into reality." Religion is understood as the life of the inner spirit, available anywhere and everywhere in the universe. Easterners are inclined to feel that religious truth is the sum total of all the religions of the world. This Eastern attitude and understanding of religions enables us to appreciate why the first- and second-generation disciples of Max Müller in Asia were such enthusiastic advocates of the World's Parliament of Religions and similar endeavors, and why some of them, such as Radhakrishnan and Anesaki, found their way into the International Committee of Intellectual Cooperation of the League of Nations, and later into UNESCO.

On the other hand, Western historians of religions implicitly feel that religion is not the sum-total of all religions, but rather that "religion" underlies all religions. A religion is thus understood as the particular expression of a universal mode of human reaction to Ultimate Reality. Even today, in the Western tradition of *Religionswissenschaft*, there is an undertone of a search for "universals in religion" or "pure religion" underlying all the empirical manifestations in various religions of the world. Characteristically, many Western historians of religions often suspect the Eastern cosmological outlook as "mystical or intuitive," and not worthy of systematic investigation. On the other hand, the Eastern scholars are becoming critical of the Western scholarship in the field. For example, Dr. D. T. Suzuki observes: "Formerly Buddhists were glad to welcome a scientific approach to their religion. But nowadays a reaction seems to have taken place among them. Instead of relying on scientific arguments for the rationalization of the Buddhist experience they are at present trying to resort to its own dialectics."[28] It might be

---

[28] Quoted in *Modern Trends in World-Religions*, ed. A. Eustace Haydon (Chicago: University of Chicago Press, 1934), p. 38.

added that such a development in the East has something in common with the Western development of a "theological history of religions."[29]

In the American setting, it is our fond hope that there will develop several centers of learning in the field of the history of religions. The European centers of learning, nearly all of which were affected by two world wars, continue to devote great interest to this discipline. But the practical difficulties under which they have to work place an increasing responsibility upon American scholarship and initiative. It is encouraging to note that since World War II facilities for the study of Eastern languages, histories, and cultures have been greatly expanded in the United States, but provisions for the study of Eastern religions are still far from adequate. The crucial problem is how to develop coordination and co-operation among (a) theoreticians of the systematic aspects of the general history of religions, (b) historians of religions who deal with regional cultures and specific religions, (c) historians of religions who are competent in auxiliary disciplines, as well as scholars in the related subjects. From this point of view the introductory address on "The Actual Situation of the History of Religions" by Van der Leeuw at the Seventh Congress for the History of Religions, held in 1950 at Amsterdam, is significant. In it he stressed two main tasks of the history of religions for the future: (1) the need of a friendly relationship between the history of religions and theology and (2) the importance of contacts with other branches of learning, such as philosophy, archeology, anthropology, psychology, and sociology.[30] His statement is particularly pertinent to the American situation. Furthermore, American scholars in the field are in a strategic position to mediate between European and Asiatic schools of thought.

In a comprehensive discipline such as *Religionswissenschaft*, communication among the scholars in the various subdivisions of the field does not develop automatically. For example, the historians of religions who are engaged in the religio-scientific inquiry into Buddhism or Hinduism tend to be preoccupied with their subject matters and do not always relate their findings to the generalists in the field. They would rather work with Budhologists or Indologists who have little interest in *Religionswissenschaft* as such. In reality, these specialists or those historians of religions engaged in the study of regional cultures or specific religions need informed criticisms both from, say, Buddhologists or Indologists, and from generalists in the field.

It is our observation that in the past both generalists and specialists have tended to be sharply split between inquiries into the theoretical or doctrinal

---

[29] Cf. Joseph M. Kitagawa, "Theology and the Science of Religion," *Anglican Theological Review*, Vol. XXXIX, No. 1 (January, 1957).

[30] *Proceedings of the Seventh Congress for the History of Religions* (Amsterdam: North-Holland Publishing Co., 1951), p. 20.

aspects and the historical, phenomenological, institutional, or cultic aspects. It goes without saying that both aspects are important, but what is more important is the study of interplay between theoretical, practical, and sociological aspects of religions. In order to understand the history of a specific religion integrally and religio-scientifically, one cannot ignore the problem of its origin, which, incidentally, fascinated the historians of religions of the nineteenth century. However, one must remember the admonition of Tor Andrae that the origin of religion is not a historical question; ultimately it is a metaphysical one. Thus, the popular theories of *Urmonotheismus* or the high-god, interesting though they may be, cannot be used as the basis of the religio-scientific study of religions with utmost certainty. What is probably most meaningful and fruitful is an approach toward a historic religion as a "wholeness." This task, however, is not an easy one. As a working hypothesis, we agree with Profesor Gibb that Islam, or any other religion for that matter, "is an autonomous expression of religious thought and experience, which must be viewed in and through itself and its own principles and standards."[31] In order to follow this principle, one must study the historical development of a religion, in itself and in interaction with the culture and society. One must try to understand the emotional make-up of the religious community and its reaction or relation to the outside world. Finally, there must be added a religio-sociological analysis, in our sense of the term, the aim of which is to analyze the social background, to describe the structure, and to ascertain the sociologically relevent implications of religious movements and institutions. One must be sensitive throughout to the internal consistency of the various aspects of the religious community. This is indeed a difficult task.

The term "internal consistency" is used advisedly in order to get away from popularly accepted genetic, causal theories, such as that Buddha rebelled against Brahmanism, therefore Buddhism rejects the caste system. Unfortunately, the field of the history of religions is plagued by many such dangerous oversimplifications. The pioneers in the field were largely responsible for this. Many of them had definite ideas about the so-called essence of each religion, such as its concepts of deity, of the nature and destiny of man and of the world, which have been handed down to us through manuals and handbooks that are abundant in the European tradition of *Religionswissenschaft*. These shorter treatises are useful and instructive, especially on the introductory level, but they must be used with great care. It is dangerous to explain, for instance, all the cultic and sociological features of Islam solely in terms of the religious experience of Muhammad. There is a gap between ideals and actual practices in all religions. At the same time,

[31] Sir Hamilton A. R. Gibb, *Mohammedanism, an Historical Survey* ("Home University Library" ed. [London, 1953]), p. vii.

what is happening in remote villages in Turkey or Indonesia cannot be understood without some reference to the life and teaching of Muhammad. Such is the problem of internal consistency.

Let us take another example. What does it mean when we say that the Vedas are central in Hinduism? If we accept the religious authority of the Vedic literature in the orthodox schools, we must also be aware of the fact that the Vedas have been interpreted, modified, believed, and abused by men throughout the ages. Or we may study the sacrificial system of Hinduism, but that again is not all of Hinduism. How, then, can we possibly understand the internal consistency despite these seeming contradictions which characterize historic and contemporary Hinduism? And yet, all aspects of Hinduism—theoretic, cultic, and sociological—are held together, and they are closely related to arts, literature, customs, politics, economics, and other aspects of Hindu history and culture. The task of the historian of religions is to try to feel and understand the "adhesiveness" of various aspects of historic religions.

But can we understand the adhesiveness and internal consistencies of religions and cultures other than our own? Here is the crux of the problem for the historian of religions. It is small comfort to know that other scholars, such as those who deal with intellectual history, confront similar difficulties.[32] The historians of religions, in order to understand other religions of various cultural areas and historic epochs, must think of themselves as observers and investigators. Their own assumptions inevitably prevent them from entering into the inner world of other peoples, to say nothing of the difficulties involved in the linguistic and cultural gap. Often, written records must be checked by oral traditions and "acted myths." Language is dynamic; it is always changing. It influences the culture, but men's thinking and experience also influence language. It is impossible to abstract such words as *moksha* and *nirvana* from the historical contexts of ancient and modern India, China, Burma, and Japan and expect those words to have the same connotations.

The religious commitment, or lack of commitment, of a historian of religions must also be taken into account. Regardless of his formal affiliation with any ecclesiastical institution or adherence to a faith, he is never free from commitments on various issues, partly because of his upbringing and partly because of his fundamental decisions about life. In the words of Professor Benjamin Schwartz: "While these commitments are bound to color his understanding to some extent, he can make an effort to distinguish in his own mind between his commitments and his attempts to understand the conscious response of others. On the other hand, the illusion of complete non-involvement, with all the self-deceptions it nourishes, is more detrimen-

[32] John K. Fairbank (ed.), "Introduction: Problems of Method and of Content," *Chinese Thought and Institutions* (Chicago: University of Chicago Press, 1957).

tal to objectivity than a lively sense of involvement controlled by the desire to understand."[33]

One's religious faith is both an advantage and a disadvantage in the religio-scientific inquiry. It is true that "the only and the best way to learn how to pray is to pray." We may recall Professor Hocking's account of Jesuits in Kurseong, who are "poised, unhurried, with firm judgment and far vision," dedicated to the study of the religions of India. More often than not, however, those who study other religions with firm conviction about their own faith are what Hocking calls "partly prepared men." He says: "It is as though the graduate level of adept preparation were out of tune with our sense of haste and scantiness of means. . . . The real lack . . . is a lack of perception; a certain triviality . . . a supposition that we already know enough, and that more thinking is a luxury that can be dispensed with."[34] Furthermore, it must be kept in mind that the historian of religions is engaged in the religio-scientific inquiry of religions for the sake of "understanding," and not for the service of the propagation of any particular faith. While we recognize the important role of a "theological history of religions," this is a theological discipline, and we must maintain a wholesome tension between the history of religions and a theological history of religions.[35]

Nevertheless, the religio-scientific inquiry of a historic religion cannot stop there. Any religion is man's experience of, response and commitment to, Ultimate Reality in a specific historic situation. No religion, however regional and ethnocentric, can be interpreted without reference to universal human themes, such as birth, death, love, marriage, frustration, meaninglessness, and beatific vision. Just as in intellectual history, the religio-scientific inquiry has to proceed in the manner of oscillation between the universal religious themes and particular religious systems, communities, and histories, because all religions, both lofty and superstitious, are integral parts of the universal history of religions. Even for the sake of understanding one specific religion, we must relate it to the larger framework. As Fairbank suggests, "each step in such an oscillation leads into problems," such as the problems of a text or a historic figure. "Inevitably we are faced with the broad question of the cultural circumstances, the social institutions and events. . . . In this stage of our process there is no logical stopping place short of the total historical comprehension of human history on earth; we must use our understanding of the whole historical process, such as it may be."[36] Here we enter the most difficult stage of the *Allgemeine Religionswissenschaft*. "It is less difficult to amass factual data, on the one hand,

[33] Benjamin Schwartz, "The Intellectual History of China," in Fairbank, *op. cit.*, p. 74.

[34] William Ernest Hocking, *Living Religions and a World Faith* (New York: Macmillan Co., 1940), pp. 206–7.

[35] Kitagawa, "The Nature and Program of the History of Religions Field," *Divinity School News*, November, 1957.

[36] *Op. cit.*, pp. 4–5.

and to understand generalized concepts, on the other, than to fit them all together in an integrated, articulate account."[37] Ultimately, such a synthetic systematization must depend on many years of research and the genius of individual scholars, whereas individual scholars must be engaged constantly in the co-operative inquiry with like-minded scholars, who can provide them with informed criticisms, insights, and suggestions.

We discussed earlier some aspects of the problems of teaching the history of religions in colleges, universities, and seminaries in America. Questions have been raised again and again as to the real significance of the history of religions. The answer is to be found, in part at least, in the aim of education itself. We agree with John Henry Newman, who held that the object of a university is intellectual and not moral, and we might paraphrase him by saying that the significance of the teaching of the history of religions must be intellectual and not "religious" in the traditional sense of the term.

This essay was written with the conviction that the curriculums of all institutions of higher learning should include courses in the religio-scientific study of a variety of religions, including some of the major religions of the East as well as the Judeo-Christian religious traditions of the West. While many institutions are consciously attempting to present alternative interpretations of significant religious and philosophical questions in the Western tradition, a surprising number of leading schools in America have as yet done nothing to acquaint their students with the questions which have been raised in the non-Western religious and cultural traditions. We are not advocating that all students must become experts in *Religionswissenschaft*. But certainly in this bewildered world of our time, students ought to be exposed to some of the deepest issues of life, as they have been experienced and understood by the noblest men and women through the ages, in the East as well as in the West.

The history of religions, if it is taught competently in the undergraduate colleges, universities, and seminaries, can widen the intellectual and spiritual horizons of students by bringing to them these deeper dimensions of life and culture in the dreams and faith by which men live.

[37] *Ibid.*, p. 5.

# 2

## PRIMITIVE, CLASSICAL, AND MODERN RELIGIONS: A PERSPECTIVE ON UNDERSTANDING THE HISTORY OF RELIGIONS

Is it shame so few should have clim'd from the dens in the
level below,
Men, with a heart and a soul, no slaves of a fourfooted will?
But if twenty million of summers are stored in the sunlight
still,
We are far from the noon of man, there is time for the races
to grow.
Red of the Dawn!
Is it turning a fainter red? so be it, but when shall we lay
The ghost of the brute that is walking and haunting us yet,
and be free?

TENNYSON

### PROBLEM OF UNDERSTANDING

Religion is a complex phenomenon, embodying within it diverse elements and different dimensions of relationship between man and the mysterious universe and among members of the human community. No one has as yet proposed a satisfactory definition of the term "religion" that is acceptable to everybody concerned, and obviously we cannot solve this matter in this article. However, the following assumptions pertaining to religion are generally accepted by students of the discipline of History of Religions (*Religionswissenschaft*).[1]

First, religion presupposes "religious experience," however this term may be interpreted, on the part of *homo religiosus*. Call it the experience of

---

[1]We are aware of the fact that not all the scholars of religions share our assumptions. For example, Wilfred Cantwell Smith is persuaded that the study of religion is the study of persons. He says: "The externals of religion—symbols, institutions, doctrines, practices—can be examined separately; and this is largely what in fact was happening until quite recently, perhaps particularly in European scholarship. But these things are not in themselves religion, which lies rather in the area of what these mean to those that are involved." (See his article, "Comparative Religion: Wither—and Why?" in *The History of Religions: Essays in Methodology*, ed. M. Eliade and J. M. Kitagawa [Chicago: University of Chicago Press, 1959], p. 35.) The same suthor elaborates this perspective in his *The Meaning and End of Religion* (New York: Macmillan Co., 1963).

the Holy, the Sacred, or Power, it is that something which underlies all religious phenomena.[2] According to Joachim Wach, religious experience is (1) a response to what is experienced as Ultimate Reality; (2) a total response of the total being to Ultimate Reality; (3) the most intensive, that is, the most powerful, comprehensive, shattering, and profound experience of which man is capable; and (4) the most powerful source of motivation and action.[3] The notion that religious experience underlies all religious phenomena has a serious methodological implication in the study of religions. In this respect, Mircea Eliade rightly reminds us that "to try to grasp the essence of such a [religious] phenomenon by means of physiology, psychology, sociology, economics, linguistics, art or any other study is false; it misses the one unique and irreducible element in it—the element of the Sacred."[4]

Second, religion is more than a system of beliefs, doctrines and ethics. It is a total orientation and way of life that aims at enlightenment, deliverance, or salvation. In other words, the central concern of religion is nothing less than soteriology; what religion provides is not information about life and the world but the practical path of transformation of man according to its understanding of what existence ought to be. That is to say, religion views social, political, economic, and all other aspects of life from the soteriological standpoint, and in this sense religion is concerned not only with what is usually regarded as "religious" but with the totality of life and the world.

Third, religions generally have three dimensions, to use Joachim Wach's schema, namely, (1) theoretical—beliefs and doctrines regarding the ultimate reality, the nature and destiny of man and of the world; (2) practical—rites of worship, sacramental acts, and forms of meditation; and (3) sociological—various types of religious groupings, of leadership, and of relations between specifically religious groups and society.[5]

These assumptions are descriptive statements, and they are not meant to be used as definitions of religion. They might enable us, however, to differentiate religious phenomena from pseudo- or semi-religious phenomena, such as communism and nationalism. On the other hand, with these characteristics of religion in mind we may include in the category of religion such traditions as Confucianism, which is often regarded as a system of non-religious ethical teaching, and Buddhism, which is considered by some to be essentially a system of philosophy.

[2] See Rudolf Otto, *The Idea of the Holy*, trans. John W. Harvey (London: Oxford University Press, 1923); G. van der Leeuw, *Religion in Essence and Manifestation*, trans. J. E. Turner (London: George Allen & Unwin, 1938); and Mircea Eliade, *The Sacred and the Profane*, trans. Willard R. Trask (New York: Harcourt, Brace & Co., 1959).

[3] See Joachim Wach, *The Comparative Study of Religions*, ed. J. M. Kitagawa (New York: Columbia University Press, 1958), pp. 30–36.

[4] Mircea Eliade, *Patterns in Comparative Religion*, trans. Rosemary Sheed (London and New York: Sheed & Ward, 1958), p. xi.

[5] See Wach, *The Comparative Study of Religions*, esp. chaps. iii–v.

Even such a brief sketch of the assumptions which are generally accepted by the students of *Religionswissenschaft* already suggests some of the difficult hermeneutical problems involved in our attempt to understand the nature of religious experience and its expressions. The diversity of opinions proposed on this question of "understanding" reflect the nature of the discipline of *Religionswissenschaft* itself, which must hold within it both "historical" and "structural" approaches and methodologies. To be sure, most scholars agree that "historical" and "structural" approaches are closely interrelated, and they try to combine them in one way or another. However, in actual practice most of them tend to stress, either by temperament or by training and perhaps by both, one of the approaches at the expense of the other. Thus, historically oriented scholars are sensitive to the uniqueness of the particular religious phenomenon or the specific religious tradition. They are inclined to inquire about "what has actually happened" and the actual "becoming" of religions, and to deal with "religious data in their historical connections not only with other religious data but also with those which are not religious,"[6] even though they may resort to structural inquiry in their effort to delineate the meaning of "what has happened." Structurally oriented scholars, on the other hand, are sensitive to the universal characteristics of diverse religious phenomena. They tend to look for similarities, analogies, and homologies, and to deal with religious data typologically and cross-sectionally, disregarding historic contexts and religious traditions in which these data are found, even though they acknowledge the fact that religious data themselves must be provided by historical inquiry.

It goes without saying that the problem of "understanding," which is the central task of *Religionswissenschaft*, requires a hermeneutical principle which would enable us to harmonize the insights and contributions of both historical and structural inquiries, without at the same time doing injustice to the methodological integrity of either approach. This is easier said than done, of course. Indeed, most of the scholars in the discipline accept, reluctantly to be sure, the methodological schizophrenia in this respect. It must be noted, however, that there have been some significant efforts to integrate the historical and structural concerns of *Religionswissenschaft*. Joachim Wach's concept of the "classical," for instance, is a case in point. According to him,

There are, to give examples, among the religious leaders of mankind certain figures who stand out as classical founders; of the deities of vegetation known to us from various regions of ancient Western Asia, we can single out some as "classical" representatives; the seemingly infinite

---

[6] Raffaele Pettazzoni, *Essays on the History of Religions*, trans. H. J. Rose (Leiden: E. J. Brill, 1954), p. 216.

number of mystics of all times and places is reduced by choosing "classical" figures. There are clasical forms of the institution of priesthood and classical patterns of sacrifice and prayer.[7]

In so stating, Wach, whose primary effort was directed toward structural understanding of religious experience and phenomena, attempted to preserve the historic character of religious data which are incorporated into his systematic, typological schema. Conversely, historically oriented students must also make serious efforts to integrate the insights of the structural inquiries into their perspectives and approaches. With this in mind, the present writer will attempt to depict three major types of religious experience and expressions that in some senses correspond to the historical development of religions of the human race. They are: (1) primitive religions; (2) classical religions; and (3) modern world religions.

## PRIMITIVE RELIGIONS

The emergence of man upon earth is a fascinating problem, which, however, will not be discussed at length since it has no direct bearing upon the development of religion. The discovery of *Zinjanthropus* places man's origins at a date at least a million and a half years ago. The so-called erect ape man (*Pithecanthropus erectus*) and the Chinese man of Peking (*Sinanthropus pekinensis*) can be dated to the Middle Pleistocene epoch (around four hundred thousand years ago). Then, there was the long age of Neanderthal man (*Homo neanderthalensis*) before the appearance of *Homo sapiens* somewhere in the Late Paleolithic period, which is roughly fifty thousand years ago. Although starting with the chance discovery of the cave of Altamira in Spain in 1879, several other prehistoric sites, such as the grotto of La Mouthe, the caves of Les Combarelles and Font de Gaume, the cavern of Niaux, the grotto of Tuc d'Audoubert, and the caves of Trois Frères, Montespan, and Lascaux, have been found and studied by scholars, our knowledge of the religious life of the paleolithic hunter is still very scanty. It is safe to speculate, however, that the development of agriculture—called "the food producing revolution" by V. Gordon Childe—must have brought about a major change in the religious outlook of prehistoric man. Unfortunately, we cannot go into the discussion of prehistoric religion, except to depict some of the major characteristics of the so-called primitive religions.

The term "primitive religion" is often used to refer both to archaic religion, that is, the religion of precivilized societies, and to the religion of present-day primitive societies, partly because our knowledge of the former depends heavily on speculations based on the study of the latter.[8] Under-

[7]Joachim Wach, *Types of Religions Experience: Christian and Non-Christian* (Chicago: University of Chicago Press, 1951), p. 51.
[8]E. E. Evans-Pritchard, *Social Anthropology* (Glencoe, Ill.: Free Press, 1952), p. 7: "The

standably, there are different kinds of religious beliefs and practices included in the broad category of "primitive religion." For example, the religion of food gatherers and hunters, characterized by belief in High-Gods, the Lord of Animals, and totemism, shows a marked difference from the religion of primitive planters, epitomized by the symbolism of the Great Mother. Nevertheless, there are enough structural similarities among them so that we can lump them together with some justification. Unfortunately, the term "primitive religion" connotes different things to different people, depending on their preconceived notions of primitive man. In fact, one of the mysteries of our time is how our image of primitive man has changed from one extreme to the other. As Evans-Pritchard points out, "first he was little more than an animal who lived in poverty, violence, and fear; then he was a gentle person who lived in plenty, peace, and security. . . . First he was devoid of any religious feelings or belief; then he was entirely dominated by the sacred and immersed in ritual."[9] Likewise, some people tend to think of "primitive religion" as a qualitatively inferior religion of lawless savages, whereas others consider it to be a pristine form of religion practiced by our innocent ancestors just outside the Garden of Eden. Obviously, both views miss the point.

As far as we are concerned, the term "primitive religion" does not imply a qualitative value judgment. Rather, it stands for a special kind of religious experience and apprehension indigenous to the archaic and primitive societies. In this connection, the statement of Robert Redfield is worth quoting. He said that "the primitive and precivilized communities are held together essentially by common understanding as to the ultimate nature and purpose of life," for, in both cases, the society "exists not so much in the exchange of useful functions as in common understandings as to the ends given."[10] And it is our intention to suggest that the ultimate purpose of life was understood by the archaic and primitive men as participation in the act of creation of a "cosmos" out of "chaos" by imitating the celestial model, handed down in various kinds of myths.

The importance of myth and ritual in primitive religion cannot be exaggerated. Myths, it should be noted, are not tales concocted by the undisciplined imagination. "Myth," says Mircea Eliade, "narrates a sacred

---

word 'primitive' in the sense in which it has become established in anthropological literature does not mean that the societies it qualifies are either earlier in time or inferior to other kinds of societies. As far as we know, primitive societies have just as long a history as our own, and while they are less developed than our society in some respects they are often more developed in others. This being so, the word was perhaps an unfortunate choice, but it has now been too widely accepted as a technical term to be avoided."

[9] *Ibid.*, p. 65.

[10] Robert Redfield, *The Primitive World and Its Transformations* (Ithaca, N.Y.: Cornell University Press, 1953), p. 12.

history; it relates an event that took place in primordial Time. . . . Myth tells us, through the deeds of Supernatural Beings, a reality came into existence. . . . Myth, then, is always an account of a 'creation'; it relates how something was produced, began to *be*."[11] In a similar vein, Charles H. Long states that myth, especially the creation myth, is an expression of man's cosmic orientation. "This orientation involves his apprehension of time and space, his participation in the world of animals and plants, his judgment concerning other men and the phenomena of the sky, the interrelationship of these dimensions, and finally the powers which have established and continue to maintain his being in the world."[12] In other words, the mythic mode, different from the rational and the scientific modes of apprehending reality, enables archaic and primitive men to grasp symbolically and simultaneously "man, society, and nature and past, present, and future" within a unitary system.[13] This accounts for the fact that to them the mythical world and this world interpenetrate to the extent that human activities are explained and sanctioned in terms of what gods, ancestors, or heroes did in primordial time.[14] To put it another way, by imitating the mythical accounts of supernatural beings, archaic and primitive men repeat and participate in the primordial act of creating cosmos out of chaos, which implies establishing and maintaining norms and forms as well as order.[15]

The primitive mode of religious experience is dramatically expressed in rituals. The close interrelationship between myth and ritual has been suggested by many scholars. For example, according to Robertson Smith, myths are derived from ritual, and in turn "every rite is originally basd on a myth."[16] It is also significant to note that, just as in the case of myth, every ritual in the archaic and primitive societies has a divine model. As Eliade states, man repeats the act of the Creation in ritual, "his religious calendar

---

[11] Mircea Eliade, *Myth and Reality,* trans. W. R. Trask (New York: Harper & Row, 1963), pp. 5–6.

[12] Charles H. Long, *Alpha: The Myths of Creation* (New York: George Braziller, 1963), pp. 18–19.

[13] W. E. H. Stanner, "The Dreaming," in *Reader in Comparative Religion: An Anthropological Approach,* ed. William A. Lessa and Evon Z. Vogt (Evanston and White Plains: Row, Peterson & Co., 1958), p. 516.

[14] For examples of myths, see Long, *op. cit.,* and Joseph Campbell, *The Masks of God: Primitive Mythology* (New York: Viking Press, 1959).

[15] Eliade suggests that settlement in a new territory, for example, is equivalent to an act of creation. When the Scandinavian colonists took possession of Iceland and cultivated it, "their enterprise was for them only the repetition of a primordial act: the transformation of chaos into cosmos by the divine act of Creation. By cultivating the desert soil, they in fact repeated the act of the gods, who organized chaos by giving it forms and norms." He suggests that "in Vedic India the erection of an altar dedicated to Agni, which implied the microcosmic imitation of the Creation, constituted legal taking possession of a territory." Mircea Eliade, *The Myth of the Eternal Return,* trans. W R. Trask (New York: Pantheon Books, Inc., 1954), pp. 10–11.

[16] Quoted in Joachim Wach, *Sociology of Religion* (Chicago: University of Chicago Press, 1944), p. 26.

commemorates, in the space of a year, all the cosmogonic phases which took place *ab origine*. In fact, the sacred year ceaselessly repeats the Creation; man is contemporary with the cosmogony and with the anthropogony because ritual projects him into the mythical epoch of the beginning."[17] Thus, marriage rites are recognized as the repetition and continuation of the union of heaven and earth that took place in primordial time. The New Year rites signify on the one hand the return to chaos and the creation of cosmos. In the initiation ceremonies, death signifies a temporary return to chaos; "hence it is the paradigmatic expression of the *end of a mode of being*—the model of ignorance and of the child's irresponsibility. Initiatory death provides the clean slate on which will be written the successive revelations whose end is the formation of a new man."[18]

There are two main characeristics of the rituals or cultus of the archaic and primitive societies. First, rituals are corporate acts of the whole tribe or the community; in a real sense, there is no distinction between performers and spectators. For example, a few years ago, the writer had an opportunity to participate in the Bear Festival of the Ainus in Hokkaido, Japan. We were impressed by the fact that man and animal as well as invisible divine beings called *kamui*, played their respective roles in the great ritual. We then wrote:

> The *Iyomate* was a long ritual, and as it slowly moved from one stage to the next, there was a gradual heightening of religious feeling among those who took part. As the ritual approached its climax, one could not help being drawn into a drama, recapitulating a religious experience from the most remote past. The ecstatic expressions of those who participated in the singing, dancing, and praying gave one every reason to believe that for the Ainus, at any rate, the memorable experiences of their ancestors had become real again in the performance of *Iyomante*.[19]

Second, ritual is not isolated from other human activities as the only "religious" act in the archaic and primitive societies. Van der Leeuw reminds us that to primitive man every act is both ritual and work: "Song was prayer; drama was divine performance; dance was cult."[20] In this sense, the attitude of modern man toward life is grossly different from the attitude of the primitive man. "When we dance, we do not pray; when we pray, we do not dance. And when we work, we can neither dance nor pray. . . . The culture of primitive man is at the same time sport, dance, concert, and much

[17] Eliade, *The Myth of the Eternal Return*, p. 22.

[18] Mircea Eliade, *Birth and Rebirth: The Religious Meanings of Initiation in Human Culture*, trans. W. R. Trask (New York: Harper & Bros., 1958), p. xiii.

[19] Joseph M. Kitagawa, "Ainu Bear Festival *(Iyomante),*" *History of Religions*, I, No. 1 (Summer, 1961), 98.

[20] G. van der Leeuw, *Sacred and Profane Beauty: The Holy in Art*, trans. David E. Green (New York: Holt, Rinehart & Winston, 1963), p. 11.

more."[21] To be sure, there are apparent differences in human activities—farming, fishing, cooking, and fighting, as well as art, witchcraft, oracles, and magic. But they are interdependent parts of a whole, or interpenetrating circles sharing a mid-point, which is the meaning and purpose of life, namely, participation in the divine act of creating and maintaining cosmos (order).

In this connection, W. E. H. Stanner observes that the mode, ethos, and principle of the Australian aboriginal life are "variations on a single theme—continuity, constancy, balance, symmetry, regularity, system, or some such quality as these words convey."[22] In such a situation, what life *is* as well as what life *can be* is determined, so that life is basically a "one-possibilty thing," to use his expression.[23] Although the aborigines are endowed with intelligence and rationality, these faculties are directed primarily toward the maintenance of the "given order" of life, as apprehended by myths. In such a situation, if an accepted belief fails to correspond to a particular experience, "this merely shows that the experience was mistaken, or inadequate, or the contradiction is accounted for by secondary elaborations of belief which provide satisfactory explanations of the apparent inconsistency."[24] Essentially, primitive religion provides no real alternatives in life. There is no enlightenment, deliverance, or salvation in the usual sense of the term. The soteriology, if we may introduce such a term to the context of primitive religion, implies the primitive man's initiation into the ancestral orientation of his tribal or communal life that is expressed in the mythical apprehension of cosmos. It follows, then, that the *summum bonum* of primitive religion is continuity and preservation of this type of cosmic orientation, which holds the inner unity of ritual, art, interhuman relationships, and all the rest. Understandably, there is no room for individual freedom in the archaic and primitive societies. However, the primitive people, as a people, have managed to attain an ontological freedom of a sort by defeating and overcoming what Eliade calls the "terror of history."[25]

## CLASSICAL RELIGIONS

Inasmuch as it is impossible to discuss all the historical religions of the world individually, we have adopted the two arbitrary and ambiguous categories of "classical religions" and "modern world religions" in order to portray, at least, certain differences in their religious perspectives. Under the cate-

22Stanner, *op. cit.*, p. 522.
23*Ibid.*, p. 517.
24Evans-Pritchard, *op. cit.*, p. 99.
25Cf. Eliade, *The Myth of the Eternal Return*, pp. 141–62; and Stanner, *op. cit.*, p. 521.

gory of "classical religions," we include religions of the ancient Near East, Iran, India, the Far East, and the Greco-Roman world, whereas more recent aspects of living religions are discussed under the heading of "modern world religions."

As far as archeological scholarship can ascertain, agriculture and stock-breeding developed as early as the eighth millenium B.C. in the Iranian plateau. This marked the beginning of the so-called food-producing revolution, which stimulated the rise of self-sustaining villages. The transition from the neolithic village pattern to a more advanced phase of the city and state was a long process. Around 3500 B.C. the first great civilization emerged in the Mesopotamian plain. Shortly afterward, other civilizations arose in Egypt, Crete, India, China, Mexico, Peru, and Palestine. All these civilizations were grounded in definite religious outlooks and orientations. Different though these religious traditions were, they shared these characteristics: (1)the emancipation of the *logos* from the *mythos;* (2) the negative attitude toward the phenomenal world and life coupled with recognition of another realm of reality; and (3) a high degree of sophistication and systemization of theoretical, practical, and sociological aspects of religion. In all these religious traditions, the existence of the cosmic order was taken for granted, variously known as *Ma'at, Themis, Ŗta, Tao*, and so on, although their understanding of the nature of the cosmic order varied greatly. Closely related to the question of the cosmic order is man's understanding of his own nature and destiny, which determines to a great extent the differences of various religious traditions, not so much in philosophical speculation as in soteriological outlook.

(1) One of the differences between the classical religions and the primitive religions is found in their attitudes toward myth. Earlier we pointed out that archaic and primitive men know only one mode of thinking, that is, the mythic, which enables them to grasp symbolically and simultaneously "man, society, and nature and past, present, and future" within a unitary system. In such a unified system, everything in this world is endowed with life, so that every phenomenon appears to be a "Thou," in the sense in which Martin Buber uses this term. "'Thou' is not contemplated with intellectual detachment; it is experienced as life confronts life, involving every faculty of man in a reciprocal relationship. Thoughts, no less than acts and feelings, are subordinated to this experience."[26] In observing certain movements of the planets, for example, the primitive mind "looks, not for the 'how,' but for the 'who,' when it looks for a cause . . . he does not expect to find an impersonal law regulating a process. He looks for a purposeful will committing an act."[27] Thus, in the primitive religions, everything is "Thou," and every event is a

---

[26] H. and H. A. Frankfort, John Wilson, Thorkild Jacobsen, and William Irwin, *The Intellectual Adventure of Ancient Man* (Chicago: University of Chicago Press, 1946), p. 6.

[27] *Ibid.,* p. 15.

concrete act by a certain "Thou." There is no effort to stand outside the world of myth and reduce different experiences to certain universal principles.

The classical religions, on the other hand, recognize the distinctions among "man, society, and nature" as well as among "past, present, and future," although their interrelations are explained in terms of myth. In Babylonia and elsewhere in the ancient world, the correct performance of the New Year ritual was considered essential to insure good harvest, but the importance of agricultural skill was also recognized. The great rivers—the Nile, the Tigris, the Euphrates, the Indus, the Yangtze, and others—were no doubt believed to be living beings having their own will and temperament, worthy to receive gifts and sacrifices from the people. And yet, the regularity of their movements was observed in terms of mathematical calculations. Thus the classical religions retained the language of myth, but speculative inquiry into causal principles and universal laws was no longer inhibited and stultified completely by the mythic mode of thinking. In other words, there was a certain degree of emancipation of the *logos* from the *mythos*. For instance, the ancient Near Eastern man

> recognized the problem of origin and the problem of *telos*, of the aim and purpose of being. He recognized the invisible order of justice maintained by his customs, mores, institutions; and he connected this invisible order with the visible order, with its succession of days and nights, seasons and years, obviously maintained by the sun. [He] even pondered the hierarchy of the different powers which he recognized in nature.[28]

(2) Probably, the difference between the primitive religions and the classical religions is most conspicuously demonstrated in man's own view of himself. In the former, there is no recognition of man apart from nature. Or, to put it another way, man is a part of society, which in turn is an integral part of nature and the cosmos. In the latter, however, man is recognized as something apart from society and the cosmos. Here again, various religious traditions developed different views of man.[29] Nevertheless, most of the classical religions accepted man as a psycho-physical-mental and spiritual being, a mortal endowed with memory, intelligence, and sexuality. There also developed speculations about the invisible inner self within man's physical being—atman, spiritus, anima, Seele, or pneuma. Undoubtedly the

[28] *Ibid.*, p. 8.

[29] Cf. Joachim Wach, *Typen religiöser Anthropologie: Ein Vergleich der Lehre von Menschen im religionphilosophischen Denken von Orient und Okzident* ("Philosophie und Geschichte," No. 40; Tübingen: J. C. B. Mohr [P. Siebeck], 1932); C. J. Bleeker, ed., *Anthropologie Religieuse* (Leiden: E. J. Brill, 1955); and S. G. F. Brandon, *Man and His Destiny in the Great Religions* (Toronto: University of Toronto Press, 1962).

most sophisticated analysis of man was attempted by Greek thinkers,[30] although other religious traditions also provided theories and answers to the riddle of man and his destiny.

Most of the classical religions held a belief in the existence of some sort of cosmic order that provides ultimate meaning for human existence. However, the regulation of the relationships among the cosmic, social, and human realms was a difficult problem. Human beings, then and now, look for answers to the suffering, failure, and frustration of their existence. For example, according to Jacobsen, man in ancient Mesopotamia

> no longer permitted his world to be essentially arbitrary; he demanded that it have a firm moral basis. Evil and illness, attacks by demons, are no longer considered mere happenings, accidents: the gods, by allowing them to happen, are ultimately responsible, for only when an offense has been committed should the personal god be angered and turn away. Thus in human moral and ethical values man had found a yardstick with which he presumptuously proceeded to measure the gods and their deeds. A conflict was immediately apparent. Divine will and human ethics proved incommensurable.[31]

Caught by the discrepancy between human experience and the idea of a just cosmic order, various religions offered different explanations and solutions. Hinduism and the mystics of all religions are inclined to affirm the essential oneness of the human soul with God or the cosmic spirit, and Buddhism holds that problems of the human condition have no ontological reality. Ancient Greek and Babylonian religions, on the other hand, put the accent on the essential differences between the divine and human natures. Thus, the recognition and acceptance of human mortality was considered as the first order of wisdom. At any rate, these classical religions tended to take negative attitudes toward the phenomenal world and tried to locate the meaning of human existence in another realm of reality, however it was conceived.

In this connection, it is significant to note that some of the classical religions wrestled with the problem of time and history. One should recall that for the primitive religions the only time that was meaningful was the primordial time, so that efforts were made to overcome and defeat the onslaught of empirical time and history. In a somewhat similar vein, a few of the classical religions adopted a cyclical view of time and taught men to live

---

[30] Joachim Wach, *Types of Religious Experience: Christian and Non-Christian* (Chicago: University of Chicago Press, 1951), pp. 66–70; see also James Luther Adams, "The Changing Reputation of Human Nature" (reprinted for private circulation in slightly revised form from the *Journal of Liberal Religion* [Autumn, 1942 and Winter, 1943], pp. 7–10).

[31] Frankfort *et al., op. cit.,* p. 213.

in an "eternal present." Some others like the ancient Egyptian and Chinese religions, on the other hand, stressed the normativeness of the golden past. It was the Persian religion of Zoroaster that interpreted the relation between the cosmic order and human experience in terms of a linear view of history. Accepting the cosmic dualism based on Ahura Mazdah and Angra Mainyu, representing Good and Evil respectively, Zoroastrianism viewed history as a battleground in which the divine will, order, and purpose are threatened by Evil. This concept of history had a profound significance for man in the sense that the individual was compelled to make a moral decision to join either the side of Good or that of Evil in a struggle that takes place in the temporal historical process without any thought for himself of "securing a good lot . . . in the *post-mortem* existence."[32] Zoroastrianism exerted a significant influence on Judaism, which stressed its god as the lord of the cosmic order who reveals his will through events in history. To the Jews, unlike the Egyptians and the Chinese, the locus of the meaning of history was to be found in its end (*eschaton*). No less important was the Christian view that amplified the Jewish notion of "history as the epiphany of God."[33]

(3) As to the third characteristic of the classical religions, namely, sophistication and systematization of theoretical, practical, and sociological expressions of their religious experience, we can discuss them only superficially.[34] Here again a brief comparison with primitive religions may be helpful. Earlier, we cited the view of Robert Redfield to the effect that the society of the archaic and primitive peoples—which he terms "folk society"—found its cohesiveness "in common understandings as to the ends given." It is significant to note that

> the ends are not stated as matters of doctrine, but are implied by the many acts which make up the living that goes on in the society. Therefore, the morale of a folk society—its power to act consistently over periods of time and to meet crises effectively—is not dependent upon discipline exerted by force or upon devotion to some single principle of action, but to the concurrence and consistency of many or all of the actions and conceptions which make up the whole round of life.[35]

In other words, according to the comprehensive world view of the primitive religions, not only is there no distinction between theory and practice, there is only one unified order that governs cosmic law, ritual law, and social law, so that the course of nature, of human life, and of society was seen as one

---

[32] Brandon, *op. cit.*, p. 287.

[33] Cf. Eliade, *The Myth of the Eternal Return*, p. 104.

[34] For Wach's explication of this threefold scheme, see his *The Comparative Study of Religions*.

[35] Robert Redfield, "The Folk Society," *American Journal of Sociology*, LII (January, 1947), 299.

harmonious whole. In the classical religions, however, the distinctiveness of three domains of religion—theoretical, practical, and sociological—was recognized, even though a high degree of correlation among these domains was maintained. In most religious traditions, theoretical development centered around theological, cosmological, and anthropological concerns that are expressed in terms of myth, doctrine, and dogma, although certain religions tended to be more theocentric, others to be more cosmocentric or anthropocentric.[36] In some cases, philosophy and ethics grew out of theology and religious doctrine. It was the Greek thinkers who developed the notion of *theoria*, and as Wach points out, "we find in Aristotle's system a scheme for the organization of knowledge, evidencing the first beginnings of the pursuit of a theory for its own sake ('science')."[37] At any rate, with the development of the theoretical aspects of religion, oral traditions tend to be replaced by written traditions and professional or semiprofessional interpreters of doctrines come into existence.

Side by side with the theoretical development, we find the gradual articulation of practical or cultic expressions of religion, such as ritual, symbols (images), sacraments, and various forms of sacrifices. In discussing the development of cults, it is well to remember that there is "the same continuous interplay between compulsion and tradition, on the one hand, and the constant drive for individual liberty, making for the emergence of new impulses and the creative activity of *homines religiosi*, on the other, which we observed in the development of thought patterns."[38] Equally important is the gradual stratification of religious groupings, leadership, and interhuman relations, based on the natural criteria of sex and age and/or the religious criteria of charismata, skills, knowledge, healing power, and training. In this connection it is to be noted that in the classical religions the structure of religious groups as well as their relations to sociopolitical order were believed to be based on, and sanctioned by, the cosmic order, whether it was understood to exist above the gods as in Hinduism or under a divine being as in the Judeo-Christian tradition. Moreover, various institutions such as the sacred king in the ancient Near East or the priestly cast in India came into existence ostensibly for the purpose of safeguarding the cosmic order from the destructive power of chaos. Thus, although there was some room for freedom and spontaneity exemplified by prophetic and reform movements, most classical religions were primarily concerned with the preservation of order in the cosmic, human, and sociopolitical realms. Inevitably, man's

[36] Wach, *Sociology of Religion*, p. 23: "The nature of God or gods, the origin and growth of deities (theogony), and their attributes, the relation of the deity to the world and its justification (theodicy)—all are delineated and expounded in theology. Cosmology is concerned with the origin, development, various phases and destiny of the world, while theological anthropology, including soteriology and eschatology, ponders over the origin, nature, and destiny of man."

[37] *Ibid.*, p. 24.

[38] *Ibid.*, p. 27.

soteriological yearning was subordinated to an overwhelming concern for the preservation of order, so that salvation was sought either as the acceptance of order or as the rejection of it. The dichotomy between "this worldly ethics" and "otherworldly spirituality" confronted all the classical religions.

MODERN WORLD RELIGIONS

The category of "modern world religions," as stated earlier, refers not to new forms of religion that have emerged in various parts of the world in recent decades but to the modern trends and ethos of historic religions that have been discussed in the previous section.[39] Unfortunately, the long and fascinating historical developments of the various classical religions cannot be discussed here. All we can do at this point is to remind ourselves that none of the historic religions has remained unchanged; each one has undergone numerous stages of transformation resulting from internal and external factors, even though some of the basic characteristics of each religion have been preserved.

Historians of religions today are greatly indebted to the structural inquiry of Gerardus van der Leeuw, who among other things attempted to depict the main characteristics of historic religions in terms of typology. For example, Confucianism and eighteenth-century deism are characterized by him as "Religions of Remoteness and of Flight," Zoroastrianism as "the Religion of Struggle," various forms of mysticism as "the Religion of Repose," certain features of Judaism, Christianity, and Islam as "the Religion of Unrest," a wide assortment of movements from polydemonism to polytheism as "Syncretism," some phases of Greek religion as "the Religion of Strain and Form," Hinduism as "the Religion of Infinity and of Asceticism," Buddhism as "the Religion of Nothingness and of Compassion," Judaism as "the Religion of Will and of Obedience," Islam as "the Religion of Majesty and of Humility," and Christianity as "the Religion of Love."[40] Van der Leeuw also depicted three approaches of the religions to the world in terms of creative domination, theoretical domination, and obedience, and the three different goals sought by various religions as man, the world, and God.[41] In all fairness to Van der Leeuw, we must bear in mind that his typological attempt, like similar efforts by other scholars, is not meant to portray historic religions in a monolithic and unidimensional manner. Each religion, at various stages of its historical development, often manifests contradictory features, as ably demonstrated by H. Richard Niebuhr in his discussion of the relation of Christ to culture, for example, Christ against Culture, the

---

[39] For discussion of individual religions, see Joseph M. Kitagawa, ed., *Modern Trends in World Religions* (La Salle, Ill.: Open Court Publishing Co., 1959).

[40] Van der Leeuw, *Religion in Essence and Manifestation*, pp. 597–649.

[41] *Ibid.*, pp. 543–87.

Christ of Culture, Christ above Culture, Christ and Culture in Paradox, and Christ the Transformer of Culture.[42]

What is significant from our point of view is that the modern ethos and trends in all major religions share, to a greater or lesser extent, (1) preoccupation with the meaning of human existence, (2) this-worldly soteriology, and (3) the search for "freedom" rather than the preservation of "order." These three features are closely interrelated, of course. Needless to say, we are not advocating these as religious ideals for our time; we are simply depicting them as significant characteristics of "modern world religions."

(1) Historically, the meaning of human existence (religious anthropology) has been one of the three main problems of many classical religions, the other two being the nature of Ultimate Reality or deity (theology) and the origin, structure, and destiny of the universe (cosmology). In various religious traditions, different doctrines have been formulated regarding these three major topics. In this connection we agree with Paul Tillich that all these doctrinal statements were formulated essentially as answers to "questions."[43] And the fact is that the traditional balance of the triple doctrinal formula is no longer meaningful to modern man, because his existential "question" is primarily concerned with the meaning of human existence and is rather indifferent to the topics of deity and the universe. In other words, the discussions of deity and the universe are meaningful only when they are related to the problem of man. This shift in accent or emphasis has profound implications for the ethos of modern world religions in the sense that various religious traditions can no longer preserve the traditional doctrinal formulations and the symbol systems intact however meaningful they may have been to premodern man. In this respect, the statement of Clement Webb is pertinent that "the idolatry of today is often the true religion of yesterday, and the true religion of today the idolatry of tomorrow."[44] In today's world, all religions are compelled to wrestle with modern man's question as to how man can realize his highest possibilities in the midst of the brokenness and meaninglessness of our time.

This does not imply, however, that traditional doctrines of man have become completely obsolete in different religious traditions. Modern Hindus still accept the ancient belief that man's inner self is an aspect of Ultimate Reality. Contemporary Buddhists would subscribe, just as most Buddhists of

[42] H. Richard Niebuhr, *Christ and Culture* (New York: Harper & Bros., 1951). See also Christopher Dawson, *Enquiries into Religion and Culture* (New York: Sheed & Ward, 1933); and S. Radhakrishnan, *Religion and Society* (London: George Allen & Unwin, Ltd., 1947).

[43] Thus he proposes for Christian theology the method of correlation that "explains the contents of the Christian faith through existential questions and theological answers in mutual interdependence." Paul Tillich, *Systematic Theology* (Chicago: University of Chicago Press, 1951), I, 60.

[44] Clement C. J. Webb, *God and Personality* (New York: Macmillan Co., 1918), p. 264.

all ages have done, to the notion that man is ever "becoming" and that what appears as a self is therefore impermanent and basically unreal. And both Jews and Christians in our time still hold that man is "equipped with a reverence for the majesty of God who created him and endowed him with a sense of obligation as well as a longing for forgiveness. Man is a sinner not only in the sense of his finiteness but by an act of the will."[45] However, these doctrines are no longer accepted just because they have been sanctioned by religious traditions; they are meaningful to modern man only when these historic beliefs can be tested by experience and restated in a form of language that makes sense. Thus, Daniel Day Williams states the "question" behind the contemporary theological renaissance in the Christian world as follows: "What is there in the Christian faith which *gives us such an understanding of ourselves* that we must assert our loyalty to the Holy God above all the splendid and yet corruptible values of our civilization?"[46] Similar observations can be made in regard to the serious effort of contemporary Jews, Muslims, Hindus, and Buddhists to discover the foundations of their faiths. Indeed, in today's world the primary concern of religious man, no less than of his secular counterpart, is man and the meaning of his existence.

(2) The second characteristic feature of modern world religions, namely, a "this-worldly soteriology," is closely related to the first. We might recall that all classical religions tended to take negative attitudes toward phenomenal existence and recognized another realm of reality, however differently it was conceived in various religious systems. Religious iconography in many parts of the world dramatically portrays the stages and grades of the heavenly state as well as of hell, purgatory, or the nether world. They were not invented merely to scare the ignorant masses as some skeptics and cynics think. To many adherents of the classical religions, the existence of other realms beside the phenomenal world order spoke with a compelling force. And man in his finitude was believed to be confined to this world which is permeated by suffering, sinfulness or imperfection. Thus, the religious outlook of the classical religions often had an overtone of "nostalgia for a lost paradise," to use Eliade's expression, or of longing for a heavenly reward in the afterworld. In this life, man was thought to be a sojourner or prisoner. In addition, there was a conviction that all these different realms of existence were either regulated by the cosmic order or dominated by an omnipresent personal deity. Thus, for example, the Hebrew Psalmist said:

> If I ascend to heaven, thou art there!
> If I make my bed in Sheol, thou art there!

---

45 Wach, *The Comparative Study of Religions*, p. 92.

46 Daniel Day Williams, *What Present-Day Theologians Are Thinking* (New York: Harper & Bros., 1952), p. 12 (my italics).

> If I take the wings of the morning
> and dwell in the uttermost parts of the sea,
> Even there thy hand shall lead me,
> and thy right hand shall hold me.[47]

It is important to note that a radical change has taken place in this respect in the thinking of modern people, in that they no longer take seriously the existence of another realm of reality. To be sure, they still use such expressions as paradise, Pure Land, Nirvana, and the Kingdom of God. These terms have only symbolic meaning for the modern mentality. The colorful imagery of Dante, Milton, Bunyan, and their counterparts in the Jewish, Muslim, Hindu, and Buddhist traditions no longer convinces modern man that the present world is only a shadowy reflection of a more real world that exists somewhere else. To the modern man, this phenomenal world is the only real order of existence, and life here and now is the center of the world of meaning. The rejection of pluralistic realms of existence, however, coincided with the widening and broadening of the present world order and cosmos. The single cosmos of the modern man, despite superficial resemblances, has very little in common with the undifferentiated cosmos of the primitive and archaic man, since the modern cosmos is no longer a sacred reality for the experience of contemporary man. Increasingly the mystery of outer space has been diminished, and even the deities have been robbed of their heavenly thrones.

The loss of other realms of existence has compelled modern world religions to find the meaning of human destiny in this world—in culture, society, and human personality. Never has there been any period in the history of the human race when the relation of religion or faith to sociopolitical, economic, and cultural spheres has been taken so seriously as it is today. This does not mean that today we are witnessing another example of the phenomenon of the "ecclesiastification of culture," as in medieval Europe, or of the "secularization of religion," as in the days of rationalism. What we find now is an increasing realization on the part of modern world religions that, just as religious man must undergo the experience of personal transformation or *metanoia*, culture and society must be renewed and revitalized in order to fulfill their vocation in the midst of the ambiguities and upheavals of this world. Thus, even in Theravada Buddhism, which has been regarded by some as one of the most otherworldly of the religions, advocates of a soteriology centered on this world argue that Buddhist leaders must pursue "not a will-o'-the-wisp Nirvana secluded in the cells of their monasteries, but a Nirvana attained here and now by a life of self-forgetful activity . . . [so that] they would live in closer touch with humanity, would better understand

---

[47] Psalm 139:8–10 (R.S.V.).

and sympathize with human difficulties. . . ."[48] Likewise, leaders of contemporary Judaism, Christianity, Islam, and Hinduism are deeply involved
in the building of new nations and in various spheres of social, educational,
political, and cultural activities because of their conviction that these areas of
life are the very arena of salvation.

(3) As has become apparent, the ethos and trends of modern world
religions reflect the questions and existential contradictions of modern man,
whose concern may be characterized as an almost pathological search for
"freedom" rather than as the preservation of "order." In today's idiom the
term "freedom" has two different, but internally related, meanings. On the
one hand, it refers to man's effort to be free from something, such as the
established order of society, an outmoded standard of morality, or an archaic
doctrinal system of religion. On the other hand, freedom refers to the
aspirations of man in discovering novelty and creativity in art, philosophy,
religion, and interhuman relations. Inevitably, modern man's search for
"freedom" has resulted in the rejection of the foundation of the classical
religions which believed that all aspects of the human, social, and natural
orders were grounded in, and regulated by, the cosmic order. What was
taken for granted by the classical religions was the notion of "order" or "law,"
not simply as a general descriptive formula depicting some specific complex
of observable facts, but as a self-evident normative principle that governs all
aspects of the universe. Thus, the effort was made by all the classical
religions to preserve the "givenness" of the cosmic order as mirrored in the
concrete structures of society and interhuman relationships. Such an understanding of cosmic order—its givenness and its normativeness—has been
rejected by modern man and to a great extent by the modern world religions
as well. In today's world, "order" simply means either a general descriptive
formula or something man must establish in order to avoid chaos and
disharmony.

The glory of modern man is his faith in his own capacity to transcend the
limitations which premodern man had accepted as the "givenness" of
finitude. To the premodern man, the dignity of man was found in his
finitude, precisely because finitude was the gift of the gods. Thus, the
ancient Psalmist could say:

When I look at thy heavens, the work of thy fingers, the moon and the stars
which thou hast established;
What is man that thou art mindful of him, and the son of man that thou
dost care for him?[49]

---

[48] *The Revolt in the Temple* (Colombo: Sinha Publications, 1953), p. 586. See also Ediriweera
R. Sarachandra, "Traditional Values and the Modernization of a Buddhist Society: The Case of
Ceylon," *Religion and Progress in Modern Asia*, ed. Robert N. Bellah (New York: Free Press of
Glencoe, Inc., 1965), pp. 109–23.
[49] Psalm 8:3–4 (R.S.V.).

But today finitude is regarded as a source of embarrassment for man, who seems to be determined to create freedom, overcoming the limitations of time and space. But the glory of the modern man is at the same time the cause of his tragedy, for he is caught in a new existential situation which he has created. In the words of Eliade:

> He regards himself solely as the subject and agent of history, and he refuses all appeal to transcendence. In other words, he accepts no model for humanity outside the human condition as it can be seen in the various historical situations. Man *makes himself*, and he only makes himself completely in proportion as he desacralizes himself and the world. The sacred is the prime obstacle to his freedom. He will become himself only when he is totally demysticized. He will not be truly free until he has killed the last god.[50]

Fortunately or unfortunately, the contemporary world religions are destined to address themselves to this tragic predicament of modern man, who is caught between his determination to gain freedom from the past with its transcendental sanctions, on the one hand, and his search for novelty, creativity, and freedom, on the other. In this connection it must be noted that bold reinterpretations of traditional doctrines have already been attempted by some theologians and philosophers in the various religious traditions. For example, according to a contemporary Christian philosopher, "the recognition that God requires the freedom of the creatures for his own life is the best way to insure against a false conception of omnipotence as suppressing that freedom. Divine power is an ability to deal with free beings, not an ability to suppress or avoid their existence or to manipulate them so thoroughly that they would not be free."[51] Similarly, a Buddhist existential philosopher, echoing the Kierkegaardian formula of "either/or," advocates the formula of "neither/nor" to reinterpret man's freedom for the Absolute Nothingness.[52] But for the most part, modern world religions have a long way to go before they can reinterpret their traditional doctrines in the light of modern man's existential situation.

The fact that the world religions are not adequately prepared to cope with the human situation today does not imply that the historic religions have become irrelevant or are dead. Undoubtedly, the challenge of the contemporary situation has released new energy that had hitherto been submerged in the tradition of the historic religions, as dramatically demonstrated by the

[50] Mircea Eliade, *The Sacred and the Profane*, trans. W. R. Trask (New York: Harcourt, Brace & Co., 1959), p. 203.

[51] Charles Hartshorne and W. L. Reese, *Philosophers Speak of God* (Chicago: University of Chicago Press, 1953), p. 234.

[52] Cf. Yoshinori Takeuchi, "Buddhism and Existentialism," *Religion and Culture: Essays in Honor of Paul Tillich*, ed. Walter Leibrecht (New York: Harper & Bros., 1959), pp. 291–318.

passive resistance movement (*Satyagraha*) of Mahatma Gandi in India, by similar movements on the part of Blacks in America, and by the active roles played by the Buddhists in South Vietnam and Muslims in Indonesia in social and political affairs. This energy is also evident in the dedicated efforts of adherents of other religions to establish a new order of society. However, the greater and a far more difficult task that confronts the modern world religions is that of relating modern man's search for "freedom," which demands an awesome responsibility on the part of man, to the cosmic source of creativity, novelty, and freedom—the Sacred itself.

# 3

## AINU BEAR FESTIVAL (IYOMANTE)

### INTRODUCTION

The descendants of an archaic tribe, the Ainus, now living in Hokkaido, Sakhalin, and the Kuril islands, have attracted the attention of travelers and scholars for many years. As early as the seventeenth century, two Roman Catholic missionaries, Girolamo de Angelis and Luis Frois, as well as a Dutch captain, de Vries, reported about the unusual customs of the Ainus.[1] During the eighteenth century, Russian travelers, Krasheinnikoff and Spanberg, the French explorer J. F. G. de la Perouse, and the British naval officer W. R. Broughton made references to the Ainus, while Russian colonists and missionaries in the Kurils came into direct contact with the Kuril Ainus.[2] In the last two centuries, more reliable data concerning various aspects of Ainu life have become available through the efforts of such Westerners as B. H. Chamberlain,[3] J. M. Dixon,[4] Edward Greey,[5] Romyn Hitchcock,[6] B. Scheube,[7] H. von Siebold,[8] W. Martin Wood,[9] and John Batchelor.[10] Also, a

---

[1] Girolamo de Angelis, *Relatione del regno di Iezo, relatione di alcune cose* (Milan, 1625); Sadakichi Shibata, "Kirisuto-kyo no Ezo Torai ni tsuite," *Hokkaido Kyodoshi Kenkyu* (Sapporo, n.d.); P. F. von Siebold, *Geographical and Ethnological Elucidations to the Discoveries of Maarten Gerritsz Vries, Commander of the Flute Castricum A.D. 1643*, trans. F. M. Cowan, 1859. (Other publication data not available.)

[2] Shinichiro Takakura, *The Ainu of Northern Japan: A Study in Conquest and Acculturation*, trans. and annotated by John A. Harrison ("Transactions of the American Philosophical Society," N.S., Vol. L, Part 4 [Philadelphia: The Society, 1960]), p. 49.

[3] Basil Hall Chamberlain's work includes: "A Catalogue of Books Relating to Yezo and the Ainos," in *Memoirs of the Literature College*, No. 1 (Tokyo: Imperial University, 1887); "An Aino Bear Hunt," *Transactions of Asiatic Society of Japan*, XV (1887), 126–29; "Reply to Mr. Batchelor on the Words 'Kamui' and 'Aino,'" *ibid.*, XVI (1888), 33–38; and "The Language, Mythology, and Geographical Nomenclature of Japan Viewed in the Light of Aino Studies," *Memoirs of the Literature College*, No. 1 (Tokyo: Imperial University, 1887).

[4] "The Tauishikari Ainos," *Transactions of Asiatic Society of Japan*, XI (1883), 39–50.

[5] *The Bear-Worshippers of Yezo* (Boston, 1884).

[6] "The Ainos of Yezo, Japan," pp. 429–502 in *Report of the U.S. National Museum*, 1889–90 (Washington, D.C.: Smithsonian Institutiion, 1891).

[7] B. Scheube, "Die Bärencultus und die Bärenfeste des Ainos, mit einigen Bemerkungen über die Tänze derselben," *Mittheilungen der Deutschen Gesellschaft für Natur- und Völkerkunde Ostasiens*, Book 22 (1880), 44–51; "Die Ainos," *ibid.*, III (1882), 220–45.

[8] *Ethnologische Studien über die Aino auf der Insel Yesso* (Berlin, 1881).

number of able Japanese scholars have contributed a great deal to Ainu studies; the philological research of Kyosuke Kindaichi alone has been invaluable.[11] More recently Mashio Chiri, himself an Ainu and an eminent professor of linguistics at Hokkaido University, has written extensively on the culture and tradition of the Ainus.[12]

Scholars of various disciplines, especially history of religions and ethnology, have been fascinated by the fact that the Ainus have preserved to this day a bear ceremonial (*Iyomante*) of an archaic religious type practiced widely among arctic and subarctic peoples scattered from Finland to North America. While the various accounts of *Iyomante* recorded by different observers evince basic agreement regarding the structure and meaning of the ritual, they inevitably betray differences in detail. There are many reasons for this, of course. For example, most field workers or scholars have had of necessity to rely on interpreters or informants who were not always consistent in their explanations. We must bear in mind, too, that not only are the rituals of the Sakhalin Ainus somewhat different from those of the Hokkaido Ainus, but also that various tribes among the Hokkaido Ainus have their own peculiar local customs and traditions. Furthermore, with the passage of time some parts of *Iyomante* have come to be modified in spite of the strenuous efforts of the Ainus to perpetuate the "religious beliefs and

[9] "The Hairy Men of Yesso," *Transactions of the Ethnological Society of London*, N.S., Vol. IV (1866).

[10] Among Batchelor's works the following should be mentioned: "On the Ainu Term 'Kamui,'" *Transactions of Asiatic Society of Japan*, XVI (1888), 17–32; "Specimens of Ainu Folklore," *ibid.*, XVI (1888), 111–50; *The Ainu of Japan* (New York, 1895); *The Ainu and Their Folk-Lore* (London, 1901); *An Ainu-English-Japanese Dictionary* (2d ed.; Tokyo, 1903); *Ainu Fireside Stories* (Tokyo, 1924); "The Ainu Bear Festival," *Transactions of the Asiatic Society of Japan*, 2d Ser., IX (1932), 37–44; and "Ainus," in *Encyclopaedia of Religion and Ethics*, ed. James Hastings, I (1928), 239–52.

[11] (Listed also under "Kindaiti") *Kita-Ezo Koyo-ihen* ("Ancient Folklore of Northern Ezo") (Tokyo, 1914); *Ainu Seiten* ("Sacred Stories of the Ainu") (Tokyo, 1923); *Ainu Shinwa* ("The Ainu Mythology") (Tokyo, 1924); *Ainu no Kenkyu* ("Studies of the Ainu") (Tokyo, 1925); "Ainu no Kami to Kuma no Setsuwa" ("Ainu Lore Regarding *Kamui* and the Bear"), *Shukyo Kenkyu*, III, No. 6 (1926), 35-52; *Yukara no Kenkyu* ("Studies of *Yukar*") (Tokyo, 1931); *Ainu Bungaku* ("Ainu Literature") (Tokyo, 1933); *Ainu Life and Legend* (in English; Tokyo, 1941); *Yukara Gaisersu* ("Interpretation of *Yukar*") (Tokyo, 1943); *Ainu* (Tokyo, 1944); "Ainu Bunka to Nihon Bunka tono Kosho" ("The Fusion of Ainu and Japanese Cultures"), *Nihonbunka-Kenkyujo-Kiyo*, No. 2 (March, 1958), 16–39; *Yukara-shu*, Vol. I: *Pon Oina* (transcribed by Matsu Kinnari, trans. and annotated by Kindaichi) (Tokyo, 1959); *Ainu Minzoku-shi* ("Historical Study of Ainu Folklore") (Tokyo, 1960); and *Ainu Gogaku* ("Studies of Ainu Language") (Tokyo, 1960).

[12] *Ainu Goho Kaisetsu* ("Interpretation of Ainu Grammar"), with Kindaichi (Tokyo, 1936); *Ainu Minzoku Shiryo* ("Basic Data for the Study of Ainu Folk-Lore"), Vols. I (1936), II (1937); *Ainu Mintan-shu* ("Folk Tales of the Ainus") (1937); *Bunrui Ainu-go Jiten* ("Ainu Dictionary"— referred to as *Ainu Dictionary* in this article), Vols. I ("Vegetation") (1953), III ("Human") (1954); Chimei Ainu-go Sho-jiten ("Concise Ainu Dictionary of Place Names") (1956); *Ainu Bungaku* ("Ainu Literature") (1956); *Ainu-go Nyumon* ("Introduction to the Ainu Language") (1956); *Yukara Kansho* ("A Study of *Yukar*") (1957); etc.

practices of their ancestors" (*Ekashi uruoka hoppa itak*) from generation to generation.

When and how the Ainus came to settle where they are today will be discussed later. It is sufficient to say at this point that in prehistoric times the Ainus lived somewhere in central or northern Siberia where they were exposed to the cultural influences of neighboring peoples. Ever since their migration to their present habitat more than two thousand years ago, they have maintained some degree of cultural contact with the peoples in the eastern part of the Asian continent and with those in the Japanese Archipelago. It will be a mistake, therefore, to regard the Ainus as the bearers of an original archaic culture uncontaminated by the historic civilizations. In fact, we can detect many kinds of external influences in Ainu culture and society. Nevertheless, the Ainus have preserved a remarkable degree of continuity in their religious beliefs and traditions as exemplified in the epics (*yukar*) and in the observance of *Iyomante*. In a real sense, *Iyomante* is the supreme religious act of the Ainu community in that it embodies all the essential features of symbol, ritual, and myth through which and by which Ainus have found the cosmic significance of their existence throughout the ages.

Since the turn of this century, the Ainus have come under the strong impact of modern Japanese civilizations to the extent that the latter tends to undercut the foundations of traditional Ainu life and culture. An increasing number of Ainus have adopted the Japanese language, culture, and way of life, discarding their ancestral traditions. It has been pointed out that the number of Ainus who are well versed in their epics (*yukar*) and religious practices is rapidly decreasing, and even the observance of *Iyomante* might soon become a thing of the past.

In this crucial and also lamentable situation, the present writer considers it an unusual privilege to have participated in the *Iyomante* of the Hidaka tribe of the Ainus, held in Piratori, Hokkaido, on August 3, 1958. On this occasion, the presiding elder was the eighty-year-old *kotan korokuru* (the titular chief of the tribe) whose name is Hiranuma Kocha-shino.[13] (As the Ainu religious cult has never developed professional priests, all the liturgies are performed either by the chief of a tribe, the chief of a village, or the head of a family.) The *kotan korokuru* was assisted by two other chiefs and also by nearly eighty Ainus, mostly older people, who together performed the entire ceremony. There were hundreds of spectators, including a considerable number of young Ainus, many of whom were watching *Iyomante* for the

---

[13] His name is very significant. *Kocha* is the name of an ancient deity, and *shino* literally means "great." He also has a Japanese name, Hiranuma Kosaku. Many Ainus who were born in Piratori or Hiratori adopted the Japanese family name of Hiranuma, which simply signifies "the village of Hiratori or Piratori."

first time in their lives, since a full-scale celebration had not been held since 1935.[14]

Parenthetically, it might be added that the Japanese press in the summer of 1958 engaged in a heated controversy regarding the justification for killing a bear even in a sacred religious rite.[15] If one observer's impression has any relevance on this score, the ceremonial killing did not seem to imply wanton cruelty on the part of the officiants: rather there was an intensely reverent participation in an action in which man and animal alike played their special and inevitable roles. The *Iyomante* was a long ritual, and as it slowly moved from one stage to the next, there was a gradual heightening of religious feeling among those who watched and those who took part. As the ritual approached its climax, one could not help being drawn into a drama, re-capitulating a religious experience from the most remote past. The ecstatic expressions of those who participated in the singing, dancing, and praying gave one every reason to believe that for the Ainus, at any rate, the memorable experiences of their ancestors had become real again in the performance of *Iyomante*.

In this connection we may find it helpful, before considering the contemporary rituals in greater detail, to attempt to display for our study those aspects of Ainu life which modern scientific analysis of ethnological and archeological data, together with the records of the Japanese people, have contributed toward our understanding of the historical religious phenomena of this distinctive cultural group.

*The Ainus in prehistory.*—Agreement has never been reached among linguists, ethnologists, prehistorians, archeologists, and historians of religions as to who the Ainus are. Some Japanese scholars, basing their opinion on anatomical research, hold that the Ainu race bears no resemblance to any other ethnic group in the world. W. Donitz asserted in 1874 that the Ainus are Mongoloid, while Scheube claimed in 1882 that the Ainus are not Mongoloid. Erwin Baelz, Max Schmidt, and A. C. Hadden were inclined to hold that the Ainus are Caucasoid, and A. L. Kroeber, while agreeing that the Ainus are Caucasoid, felt that they had been tainted by Mongoloid elements. This controversy will undoubtedly remain unsolved for many years.[16] In physical characteristics the present-day Ainus are of medium height and stocky, with medium heads and wavy or straight dark-brownish hair. Although some of these features are closer to a Mongoloid type, their large sunken eyes of gray or greenish color and their hairiness find affinities with features of the Caucasoid groups.[17] For the moment, as far as their

---

[14] A very small *Iyomante* was reported to have been held in 1949, but only a few people participated in it.

[15] Cf. *Asahi Shinbun*, Hokkaido ed., July 30, 1958.

[16] Kindaichi, *Ainu Life and Legend*, pp. 13–16.

[17] Concerning the volume of hair on the Ainu see Hitchcock, *op. cit.*, pp. 444–50.

ethnic affiliation is concerned, we may safely agree with Linton that the Ainus are "one of those border-line groups who show relationship with two stocks in about equal measure, but they have been tentatively classed with the Caucasians."[18]

In stating that the Ainus are a borderline group between the Caucasoid and the Mongoloid, we are not making much headway regarding the question of their origin and when and how they migrated to Sakhalin, Hokkaido, and the Kurils. These questions have taxed the imagination of philologists as well. Since the pioneering work of A. Pfizmaier, of Vienna, who wrote *Untersuchungen über den Bau der Aino-Sprache* in 1851, many philologists have attempted to study the structure of the Ainu language, and in the course of time various theories have arisen concerning the possible connections between Ainu and other languages. For example, some resemblance in the use of numerals between Ainu and Eskimo, or between Ainu and the Fino-Ugric language, has caught the attention of students of linguistics. Batchelor was intrigued by the possible relationship between the Ainu and Basque languages. "It would not be at all surprising," he said, "to find that the two are connected, seeing that, as has already been intimated, the original Ainu in all probability came through Tartary to Japan. A very curious thing about them is that the ancient Basque and Ainu customs of Couvade, ridiculous as they were, resembled each other to a great degree."[19] Helpful though these speculations are, philological research alone will not clarify the prehistoric background of the Ainus.

Relating to this, the recent views of three Japanese scholars—Professors Masao Oka (ethnology), Ichiro Yahata (archeology), and Namio Egami (Oriental history and archeology)—regarding the Ainus may be of some interest. In all fairness to them, it must be pointed out that they discuss the prehistoric background of the Ainus in connection with the question of the origin of the Japanese people, even though their interest in the Ainus is far from being casual.[20] All three of them hold the view that the Ainus were one of the Paleo-Asiatic groups which lived in prehistoric times somewhere in central or northern Siberia and that they had cultural intercourse with Uralic-speaking peoples, such as the Samoyed, the Ostyak, and the Vogul, as well as with Altaic-speaking peoples, such as the Tungusic and the Turkic. Their opinions vary, however, regarding the date and process of the Ainu migration and the way in which other groups influenced them culturally.

Egami, who traces the migration of northern Eurasian peoples back to the Paleolithic age, holds that it was not a single movment in one sweep but was gradual, taking place over a long period of time, and that the eastward migration of northern Eurasian peoples covered a wide territory, from the

---

[18] Ralph Linton, *The Study of Man* (New York: D. Appleton-Century Co., 1936), p. 46.

[19] Batchelor, *An Ainu-English-Japanese Dictionary*, p. 72.

[20] Masao Oka, *et al.*, *Nihon-Minzoku no Kigen* ("Origin of the Japanese Race") (Tokyo: Heibon-sha, 1958).

coast of the Baltic Sea to the Lake Baikal area, during the Neolithic age. He
is not certain as to how early and how far east the northern Eurasian
influence reached but is inclined to believe that the Ainu followed this
general movement and reached the Pacific Coast somewhere between 300
B.C. and the end of the pre-Christian era. He arrived at this approximate
date, among other reasons, on the ground of the significant similarities
between the ancient Ainu fortress, known as *chashi*,[21] believed to be the
remains of Fino-Ugric peoples, discovered in Siberia. A few of these Siberian
caves are estimated to be as old as 800 B.C., but most of them are dated
roughly around 400–300 B.C. What interests Egami is not only the similarities in physical structure of the caves in Siberia and the *chashi* in
Hokkaido but also the fact that among the items dug from the Siberian caves
are bronze symbols—some with human faces—of the eagle, the owl, the
Siberian black kite, and the bear. These symbols are believed to represent
deities in the disguise of birds or bear. The Ainus, too, hold that the
mountain deity appears in the form of a bear and that the village diety
(*kotan-kor kamui*) visits the human world in the form of an owl. From this
evidence Egami concludes that the Ainu must have lived in close proximity
to the Fino-Ugric peoples and that they probably influenced each other.
And, judging from the approximate date of the Siberian caves, he thinks that
the Ainu must have crossed the Tatarski Strait sometime between 300 B.C.
and the end of the pre-Christian era.[22] Also, Egami thinks that it is possible
that, after the Ainus had settled in Hokkaido, they might also have been
influenced by another tribe that represented what might be termed the
"Okhotsk culture."[23]

Yahata is not certain whether the Ainus were instrumental in bringing
Stone-Age culture with them to Hokkaido when they migrated there or
whether they found it established previously by other groups, but he is
convinced that the Ainus experienced the Neolithic age in Hokkaido. He is
also of the opinion that the Neolithic culture in Hokkaido had some connection with the *Jōmon* ("rope-pattern") culture of the main island of Japan.
What concerns Yahata is the discrepancy between the prehistoric aspects and
the modern features of Ainu culture. In his view, the culture of the Ainus has
undergone many changes resulting from the influences of other groups that
came in contact with them and thus has to be seen as a composite of diverse
cultural traits. He cautions against the assumption that all the central or
nothern Siberian elements found in Ainu culture were brought by the Ainus
at the time of their migration to Sakhalin and Hokkaido from the Asiatic

[21] Cf. Masami Abe, "Hokkaido no Chashi," *Jinruigaku Zasshi*, No. 33. The *chashi* is either a
triangular cave surrounded by two hillsides that converge or a semicircular cave built along a
cliff, facing a river. There are remains of similar fortresses in the northeastern part of the Honshu
island of Japan.
[22] Oka *et al.*, *op. cit.*, pp. 205–9.
[23] *Ibid.*, p. 285.

continent. For example, Yahata, in agreement with Egami, postulates the existence of an "Okhotsk culture," coming from the north just at the time that the Neolithic culture was coming to an end in Hokkaido. This highly mobile culture of the Okhotsk had embodied some elements of Asian continental culture, and the Ainus were no doubt influenced by it. There is also the likelihood that the Ainus abandoned some of their earlier cultural ingredients. For instance, while modern Ainus do not make pottery themselves,[24] recent archeological research in Hokkaido convinces Yahata that their ancestors must have known the art of pottery-making. There may be other instances in which the earlier habits and customs of the Ainus were discarded under the impact of non-Ainu cultural influences.

The crucial question posed by Yahata is how to untangle Siberian, Japanese, and other elements so that we can reconstruct, as it were, the indigenous culture of the Ainus. There are a number of difficulties involved in such an endeavor. For example, the common designs in Ainu wood-carving, especially the symmetrical tassel, resemble closely the artistic motifs of the Gold tribe along the Amur River, which raises the question as to which group influenced the other. And, if we assume that the Ainus were influenced by northeast Asian art, the question still remains as to when this influence was exerted upon them? The fact that the Ainus in Sakhalin maintained contacts with various tribes in northern Manchuria and eastern Siberia for many centuries precludes the simple assertion that the Ainus were influenced by northeast Asian art before they migrated to Sakhalin and Hokkaido.

Another complicated problem centers on the ceremonial arrowhead, known as the *chirosh* (blunt arrow), which is used in the Ainu bear festival. Arrowheads of similar types have been discovered in Siberia and North and South America as well as in Japan; in fact, such arrowheads have been preserved to this day in the imperial treasure house, called *Shōsō-in*, in Nara. Was this type of arrowhead brought by the Ainus from the Asiatic continent, or was it later introduced into Hokkaido? Assuming that the latter was the case, the question may again be asked concerning its origin: Did it come from one of the Siberian tribes or from the Japanese? To complicate the matter further, the type of arrowhead used by the Japanese can also be traced to northern Asia. Unfortunately, according to Yahata, these baffling questions regarding the culture of the Ainus cannot be settled until further archeological research in Sakhalin, and also in eastern Siberia, is able to clarify a number of problems.[25]

Oka, who is well known in the West for his monumental work, *Kulturschichten in Alt-Japan* (1933), is primarily concerned with the ques-

[24] Romyn Hitchcock, "The Ancient Pit-Dwellers of Yezo," in *Report of the U.S. National Museum*, p. 419.
[25] Oka *et al.*, *op. cit.*, pp. 212–17.

tions of when and how the migration of the Ainu and the migration of the Yamato (or the "Tenno" clan—the dominant group that constitutes the Japanese people) took place and how these movements encountered each other in the Japanese Archipelago. He agrees with Egami and Yahata that the Ainus in prehistoric times must have lived near the Samoyed (one of the Uralic-speaking tribes) and the Eskimo (one of the Paleo-Asiatic tribes) somewhere in northern Asia. He holds that the great movement of tribes from Siberia to North America started as early as fifteen thousand years ago and that the Eskimo was the very last group that migrated to North America. Oka feels that it is highly plausible that the Eskimos, who had had cultural contacts with the Samoyeds, were instrumental in introducing some of the Uralic cultural traits into northern Siberia before moving on toward North America. One of the by-products of the great migration of tribes from the west to the east was the movement of the Ainu, who were driven onward by the Uralic and Altaic peoples until they reached the northeastern part of Siberia. There, they felt the pressure of the eastward movement of the Paleo-Asiatic tribes. The result was that the Ainus were forced to move to Sakhalin and Hokkaido and eventually reached the island of Honshu in Japan.[26]

Oka is inclined to believe that the great migration of tribes from Siberia to North America also resulted in the sporadic infiltration of other tribes, in addition to the Ainus, into the Japanese Archipelago from the north, and that this might account for the introduction of hunting weapons that are traceable to the Neolithic age. On the other hand, Oka holds that southeast Asian influences must also have penetrated the Japanese Archipelago.[27] In other words, according to Oka, there were two types of cultural penetration of Japan, one from the north and one from the south during the Neolithic age, known as the period of the *Jōmon* ("rope-pattern") culture. It is his thesis, however, that a newer and stronger culture appeared in Japan sometime after the middle of the Neolithic age. His assumption is that this cultural force came from some place either in Southeast Asia or southern China, from which it moved in two directions, one toward the regions of the South Seas and another toward the Japanese islands.

Concerning the so-called "Yayoi" culture (so named because of certain characteristic pottery found in a Neolithic site at a place called Yayoi), Oka regards it as an amalgam of several cultural forms. To start with, sometime toward the latter part of the Neolithic period a cultural system characterized by matriarchy and upland-rice cultivation was introduced into Japan from southern China by an Austro-Asian language group.[28] Shortly after this

[26] *Ibid.*, pp. 198–204.

[27] Cf. J. Maringer, "Einige faustkeilartige Geräte von Gongenyama [Japan] und die Frage des japanischen Paläolithikums," *Anthropos*, Vol. LI (1956).

[28] Professor Oka thinks that this Austro-Asian language group brought to Japan the myths regarding the three *kamis*, namely Amaterasu (the sun-goddess), Tsukiyomi (the moon-god), and Susano-o (the storm-god). This group also introduced the stone ax ("Vierkantbeil") to Japan.

immigration another group, probably speaking a Tungusic language, penetrated western Japan from Korea. Oka holds that the culture of this second group was originally characterized by patriarchical practices, millet cultivation, and hunting but was influenced by the culture of southern Korea and western Japan, marked by upland-rice cultivation. This second group contributed the "northern element" of the "Yayoi" culture. Meanwhile, a third group entered the picture around the fifth or the fourth century B.C. Its culture was characterized by wet-rice agriculture as well as fishing. Oka feels that this group originated in the Chinese coastal area south of the Yangtze River. Part of this group migrated to Japan by way of the Korean Peninsula, while another segment went directly to Japan. At any rate, this third group contributed the "southern" element of the "Yayoi" culture. In short, the so-called "Yayoi" culture is to be understood as a culture complex, consisting of northern and southern elements, under the influence of an Austro-Asian language group from Southeast Asia. Toward the end of the Neolithic period, the Japanese islands were inhabited by various ethnic and cultural groups. They intermarried and in time were influenced by Altaic linguistic forms. Wet-rice agriculture became widely accepted, and this encouraged the rise of provincial magnates.

Into this already complex situation came the so-called "Tenno clan," originally one of the Altaic tribes. Horseback-riding typified the culture of this group, and the unit of its social organization was known as the "uji" (clan). The "Tenno clan" encountered and subjugated the semihunting and semifarming Tungusic tribes in southern Manchuria and moved southward to the Korean Peninsula shortly after the beginning of the Christian era. After conquering various tribes in the Korean Peninsula, the "Tenno clan" migrated to the western part of Japan around the third century A.D. Under the leadership of this group, the so-called Yamato kingdom was established in which various tribes already in Japan began to lose their cultural and ethnic identities and to consider themselves as one "Yamato race" or "Nihon Minzoku." This in brief is the view of Oka regarding the prehistoric situation in the Japanese Archipelago.[29]

There is no question in Oka's mind that some of the Ainu living on Honshu island became assimilated into the Yamato kingdom and culture, while those Ainus who were not consolidated were pushed northward, not only back to Hokkaido and Sakhalin, but also to the Kuril Islands. In this connection, Oka rejects the view that the Ainus had come by way of the Kuril Islands when they originally migrated to Hokkaido from the Asiatic continent. Rather, only when they retreated northward under the pressure of the Yamato group did they reach the Kurils. He has been led to this view on the ground that the prehistoric remains discovered underneath the Ainu

[29] Oka *et al.*, *op. cit.*, pp. 293–97.

strata show marked affinity with the remains of the Eskimo found along the Bering Strait.[30]

As far as the Ainu language is concerned, Oka accepts the view that it is structurally similar to the Samoyed language, as advocated by W. Thablitzer and C. C. Uhlbeck, although he also acknowledges Kindaichi's theory that there is some kinship between the Ainu and the Eskimo languages. As to the bear ceremonials practiced widely by many tribes of the arctic and subarctic areas, Oka feels that the Ainu *Iyomante* resembles most closely the bear festivals of the Uralic-speaking peoples, especially the Vogul (Mansi) and Ostyak (Khanty).[31]

The problem of the *chashi* (cave fortress or dwelling place) of the Ainu presents serious difficulties. Oka agrees with the recent thesis of Ōbayashi that the prototype of the Ainu house shares certain characteristics with that of the prehistoric dwelling place of the Fino-Ugric peoples and that this form can be traced to the time before the Fino-Ugric tribes started domesticating reindeer.[32] There is not enough evidence, however, to show a positive relationship between the Ainu and the proto-Uralic peoples. For this reason, Oka has reservations regarding the theory that the Ainu brought the form of the *chashi* when they first migrated from the Asiatic continent to Hokkaido. He thinks that it is quite possible for the Ainus to have been influenced later by other groups that introduced the idea of *chashi* construction.[33] We know, for instance, that the Smelenkur, a Mongolian tribe living in Sakhalin, lived in semi-underground dwelling places, and it is quite plausible that other groups that migrated later to this region from Siberia could have influenced the Ainu.[34]

Helpful though these scholars' views are, we are more or less back where we started from. All scholars agree that the present-day Ainus are the descendants of an archaic ethnic group that originated somewhere in central or northern Siberia, from whence they migrated to Sakhalin, Hokkaido, and the Kuril Islands, but beyond that we are still left pretty much in darkness regarding, for example, the original characteristics of their culture and religion. Part of the difficulty is that the Ainus have been influenced by a number of other peoples throughout the ages. While the Ainus have never experienced anything like a religious and cultural transformation comparable to the Christianization of European peoples, their culture and society have undergone some changes during the historic period. Thus, it may be worthwhile for us to examine the references to the Ainus in the Japanese sources.

[30] *Ibid.*, p. 200.
[31] *Ibid.*, p. 298.
[32] Taryo Ōbayashi, "Die kulturhistorische Stellung des Ainu-Hauses," *Wiener völkundliche Mitteilungen*, Vol. IV, No. 2 (1956).
[33] Oka *et al.*, *op. cit.*, pp. 299–300.
[34] Hitchcock, "The Ainos of Yezo, Japan," *op. cit.*, p. 435.

*The Ainu in Japanese history.*—Of all the peoples that came in contact with the Ainus during the historical period, the Japanese naturally have had the closest cultural connection. One therefore would imagine that the Japanese sources might provide us with answers to many of the unsolved questions concerning the Ainus. Although Japanese sources certainly make frequent references to the Ainus, Japanese historical writings themselves are full of ambiguities.

Japanese records take for granted that the Japanese Archipelago was inhabited by other tribes before the "Tenno clan" or the Yamato people established their kingdom, but the records are vague about the identity of these predecesors of the Yamato. According to one account, the first legendary emperor Jimmu came across a great cave in which eighty dwarfs, called *tsuchi-gumo*, were residing. Some thought that the term *tsuchi-gumo* was a corruption of *tsuchi-gomori* ("those who hibernate under the ground") and jumped to the conclusion that this term referred to a group whom the Ainus called the *Koporok-guru* ("pit-dwellers").[35] In this respect, Chamberlain was convinced that the predecessors of the Japanese were the Ainus: "The dawn of history shows them to us living far to the South and West of their present haunts; and ever since then, century by century, we see them retreating eastwards and northwards, as steadily as the American Indian has retreated westwards under the pressure of the colonists from Europe."[36] This view has been largely discredited now, but there is no doubt that the Ainus formerly did live in parts of the Honshu isand of Japan.

In the historical records of Japan, the most frequent designation for the Ainus was the term *Ezo*, rendered also as *Emishi* or *Ebisu*. As far as we can tell, the land of the *Ezo* included not only Hokkaido but also the northeastern part of Honshu island (roughly north of a line stretching from Tokyo Bay to the present Niigata on the coast of the Sea of Japan) and probably the Sakhalin and the Kuril Islands as well. We are told that the land of the *Ezo* was inhabited by "Eastern barbarians," a term that referred to the *Ezo* and also to other ethnic groups living there. Japanese sources also make reference to *Koshi* and *Kebito*; there have been some disagreements concerning the identity of these tribes, although they are generally accepted as the Ainus. Harrison points out that the territory of the *Koshi no Emishi* ("fighting Koshi") included all of Honshu island north of the Tokyo area. He continues, "Now in time *Koshi* changed to *Kushi* and even in contemporary times the natives of the Kuriles were called *Kushi*."[37] The term *Kebito* literally means "hairy" (*ke*) "man" (*hito* or *bito*) and was most likely a descriptive term for the

[35] On this question, see Batchelor, *An Ainu-English-Japanese Dictionary*, pp. 24–32; Hitchcock, "The Ancient Pit-Dwellers of Yezo," *op. cit.*, p. 417.

[36] Chamberlain, "The Language, Mythology, and Geographical Nomenclature of Japan . . ." *op. cit.*, p. 74.

[37] Takakura, *op. cit.*, pp. 7–8, translator's n. *a.*

Ainu. For example, during the reign of the Emperor Bidatsu, an *Ezo* chief was referred to as the "great hairy man," in Chinese characters, but these characters were pronounced as "O-Emishi" or "great Ezo."[38] Judging from these examples, it is safe to assume that the terms *Koshi* and *Kebito* were used interchangeably with *Ezo*, *Ebisu*, or *Emishi*. The term *Emishi*, according to Kindaichi, came from the Ainu term *Enchiu* or *Emchiu*, a word for the first-person plural, which originally signified simply "man."[39]

According to the *Nihonshoki* or *Nihongi* ("Chronicle of Japan"), compiled in 720 A.D., the twelfth legendary emperor Keiko sent his minister, Takeshi-uchi no Sukune, to the northeastern regions for inspection. Upon his return, the minister reported on the existence of a state called Hidaka, the land of the *Emishi*. According to his report, both men and women of that state wore long hair, were tattooed, and had fierce natures. But the soil was rich in that state, and the minister recommended accordingly that the throne take over Hidaka.[40] Thereupon, Prince Yamato-takeru was dispatched to subjugate the *Emishi*. The accounts of this legendary hero are not altogether reliable—in fact, are full of romantic fancies—but they tell us something about the Ainus as viewed by the Japanese during the early period of Japanese history. Before leaving the capital, the prince was warned about the lawlessness of the northwestern regions, where no recognized chiefs maintained order and evil *kamis* dwelt in the mountains and malevolent spirits in the fields, causing the people to suffer. Men and women of the *Emishi* lived together, and there was no sense of courtesy between fathers and sons. In the winter they dwelt in caves, and in the summer they slept under trees. They wore animal skins and drank blood, and their nature was to be suspicious, even among brothers. They climbed mountains like flying birds, and they ran through the fields like animals. The *Emishi* were quick to forget a favor received but never forgot to seek revenge if a wrong was done to them. They stuck arrows in their hair and a sword inside their garment. They often threatened the border areas and took the Japanese as prisoners. If attacked, they hid in the grass; if one tried to capture them, they disappeared into the mountains. Thus, they had never been subjugated by the imperial power of Japan.

The campaign of Prince Yamato-takeru, according to the *Nihonshoki*, was eminently successful. Not only did he pacify the northeast region (*Michi no oku no kuni*), but he even captured some of the *Emishi* who became his devoted servants. After the death of Prince Yamato-takeru, his *Emishi* servants were presented to the court. But, "as they cut the trees of the sacred mountains indiscriminately and also threatened the life of the villages," so

---

[38] *The Nihonshoki*, chap. x, section on the tenth year of the emperor Bidatsu's reign.
[39] Kindaichi, "Ainu Bunka to Nihon Bunka tono Kosho," *op. cit.*, pp. 22–23.
[40] This name has no relation to the present Hidaka area of Hokkaido.

we are told, they were scattered to the five outlying provinces—Harima, Sanuki, Iyo, Aki, and Awa—for resettlement.[41]

The glowing account of Prince Yamato-takeru notwithstanding, the *Emi-shi* evidently continued to resist the power of the Yamato kingdom. During the reign of the Emperor Nintoku, they were reported to have rebelled against the throne, and the famous Japanese general, Tamichi, a veteran of the Korean campaign, was killed by the *Emishi*.[42] They again rose in arms during the reign of the Emperor Jomei in the first half of the seventh century.[43]

However, the policy of the Yamato regime of subjugating the Ainus changed to one of assimilating them by fraternization in the latter half of the seventh century. During the reign of Saimei (the second accession of the Empress Kōgyoku, who in her second reign occupied the throne 629–42), it is true that the government had to send an armada of 180 vessels, led by Abe no Omi, to the *Ezo* territory, and it is reported that after the campaign two hundred *Emishi* came to the capital to offer tribute. But the attitude of the Yamato regime toward the Ainus became extremely conciliatory. In fact, the government even offered court ranks to fifteen important *Emishi*, thus making them *de facto* minor aristocrats. Also it is interesting to note that when the Empress Saimei sent Sakabe no Muraji Iwashiki as the Japanese ambassador to the court of the T'ang, two Ainus (a man and a woman) were included in the diplomatic mission. The compiler of the *Nihonshoki* makes a special point of saying that the T'ang emperor was most curious about the Ainus and asked a number of questions about them. The Japanese envoy explained to the Chinese emperor that the Ainus lived in the northeast regions of Japan and that they were of three kinds: "Those who live in the furthest section are called *Tsugaru*. Next are *Ara-Emishi*, and the closest [to the capital of Yamato] are *Nigi-Emishi*. The *Nigi-Emishi* offer tribute to the throne of our country." He further stated that the Ainus did not grow the "five grains," but ate meat as a regular diet and that they lived in the mountains and not in houses.[44]

Many scholars have speculated as to why the Japanese government suddenly changed its Ainu policy in the latter half of the seventh century.

---

[41] *The Nihonshoki*, chap. vii.

[42] *Ibid.*, chap. xi.

[43] *Ibid.*, chap. xxiii.

[44] *Ibid.*, chap. xxvi. The Chinese record, *Hsin T'ang Shu* ("New History of the T'ang Dynasty") gives an equally descriptive account of the Ainus: "The beards of the Ainus were four feet long. They carried arrows at their neck, and without ever missing would shoot a gourd held on the head of a person standing several tens of steps away." Cf. Ryusaku Tsunoda, and L. Carrington Goodrich, *Japan in the Chinese Dynastic Histories* ("Perkins Asiatic Monograph" No. 2 [South Pasadena, Calif., 1951]), p. 39.

One plausible answer may be found in the threatened invasion of the northern borders of Japan by a tribe known as *Mishihase* or *Sukushin*. The identity of the *Mishihase* is not clear. Harrison thinks that they were the Tungusic Ju-chen living in the Sungari River area.[45] Egami is of the opinion that the *Mishihase* lived still farther north of the Ainu territory and suggests that they might have been the bearers of the "Okhotsk culture."[46] Be that as it may, the *Mishihase* are reported to have invaded the island of Sado during the reign of the Emperor Kimmei in the sixth century A.D.[47] During Saimei's reign (655–62), the governor of *Koshi-no-kuni* (the *Ezo* territory) fought the tribe of the *Mishihase*, and after the campaign, he presented to the Yamato court two living bears and seventy bear skins, presumably as loot from the enemies. Shortly after this, Abe no Omi was sent to fight against the *Mishihase* and commanded two hundred boats manned by the *Emishi* of the northeast (Mutsu) district. The *Nihonshoki* mentions that at this time about a thousand *Emishi* of *Watarijima* (Hokkaido) sent a plea to Abe no Omi to rescue them from the *Mishihase*. From all indications we can surmise that the threat of the *Mishihase* tribe brought the Japanese and the Ainu close together during the latter half of the seventh century in the face of a common enemy.[48]

How successful the policy of cultural assimilation of the Japanese government was in regard to the Ainus during the seventh century is not at all clear. It is safe to assume that the Ainus living in Hokkaido were hardly touched by the influence of the Japanese government and that the Ainus living in the northeastern region of Honshu island were barely kept under control by the military forces of the Japanese. Although two Ainus from the Mutsu district, Shiriko no Omaro and Kanaori by name, asked for and received court permission to enter the Buddhist priesthood during the reign of the Empress Jitō (reigned 687–97), it is difficult to judge how extensive Buddhist influence was among the Ainus at that time.[49]

During the eighth century, control of the northeastern frontiers was poorly managed. Some of the military commanders and civil officials appointed by the Japanese government cheated the government financially, and some of them even employed the soldiers on their own farms. Further-

---

[45] Takakura, *op. cit.*, p. 10, n. *a*. "The people dominated the continental shore of the Japan Sea in antiquity and frequently raided the northwest Japanese seacoast and the islands thereof from Tsushima to Sado."

[46] Oka *et al.*, *op. cit.*, p. 285. Sakuzaemon Kodama, M.D., of Hokkaido University, discovered in the Abashiri district of Hokkaido human bones buried with stone arrowheads, stone axes, and axes made of bones. Kodama thinks that these were left by people who were neither Japanese, Ainu, nor Tungu and that they show some kinship with the Eskimo. Egami thinks that these remains are possibly those of the *Mishihase*.

[47] *The Nihonshoki*, chap. xix.

[48] *Ibid.*, chap. xxvi.

[49] Ichiro Hori, *Waga-kuni Minkan-Shinko-shi no Kenkyu* (Tokyo: Sogen-sha, 1955), I, 189–91.

more, those aristocrats who held the lofty title of the "General for Subduing the East" (*Seitō Shōgun*) were, in the words of Sir George B. Sansom, "men of the pen rather than the sword." The breakdown of the Japanese dominance in the northern frontiers alarmed the government, which then was situated in Kyoto. The new post of "Barbarian-Subduing-Generalissimo" (*Sei-i-Tai-Shōgun*) was created in 794, and Ōtomo Otomaro was the first appointee. The real military authority was, however, in the hands of Ōtomo's subordinate, Sakanouye no Tamura-maro. Under the able leadership of Tamura-maro, a series of military expeditions against the Ainus was dispatched, fortresses were constructed in strategic centers, and Japanese settlers were encouraged to migrate to the areas where the Ainus were subjugated or pacified. By 812, the Japanese government was convinced that the Ainus in the northeastern frontiers were no longer a menace to the Japanese nation, even though Ainu revolts continued to take place from time to time.[50] In the tenth century, a priest of Mount Hiei, Kūya Shōnin (d. 972), known for his dancing devotion while invoking the holy name of Amida, is reported to have traveled in the *Ezo* territory and carried on a successful missionary campaign.

Japanese historical works after the middle of the eighth century make surprisingly few references to the Ainus in the northeastern frontiers. Does this mean that the Ainus were so completely assimilated to the cultural life of Japan that they had lost their identity? In asking this question, we leave aside the Ainus in Hokkaido and Sakhalin for the moment, because they did not come in contact with the Japanese until much later. Assuming that the Ainus under Japanese hegemony were assimilated, what role, if any, did they play in the cultural life of Japan? To deal with this question, we are compelled to examine two ambiguous terms, *fushū* and *ifu*. Harrison holds that these terms refer to two different kinds of peoples. In his words: "Ezo who were either captured or who voluntarily accepted Japanese rule were called *ifu* while Japanese who married Ezo or who left the Japanese limits to accept Ezo life and rule, and there was a surprising number of these, were called *fushū*,."[51] Harrison seems to be on safe ground in interpreting the etymological origins of these words in this manner. For instance, we know that during the reign of the Empress Shōtoku (reigned 765–70) about three thousand *fushū* in the Mutsu district petitioned the Japanese government to re-establish their status as Japanese subjects on the ground that they had been forced to accept Ainu rule. In time, however, many Ainus who accepted Japanese rule were also included in this category. In fact, both the *Shoku Nihongi* ("The Further Chronicle of Japan") and the *Sandai Jitsuroku* ("The Authentic Records of the Reigns of Three Emperors") use the terms

---

[50] Sir George B. Sansom, *Japan: A Short Cultural History* (rev. ed.; New York: D. Appleton-Century Co., 1943), pp. 196–293.
[51] Takakura, *op. cit.*, p. 11, Harrison's n. *a.*

*fushū* and *ifu* interchangeably to refer to persons of Ainu descent who had become assimilated into Japanese society.[52]

If we accept the view that *fushū* and *ifu* included the Ainus who had been naturalized and their descendants, we will be led to the conclusion that some of them had played prominent roles in Japanese history. For example, a powerful family, called the Abe, and their kinfolk, the Fujiwara (not related to the Fujiwara in Kyoto) in the Hiraizumi area of the northeastern part of Japan, proudly claimed to be *fushū* chieftains. Tragically, the Abe family was defeated by the rising Minamoto clan in a bloody war that lasted from 1051 to 1060. We are told that when Minamoto Yoshiiye surrounded the Abe's "Fort of Robes," he sent Abe Sadatō the following verse:

> Ah, your Fort of Robes
> Is at last reduced to tatters!

To which Abe Sadatō replied also in verse:

> What a pity!
> Long usage has caused
> The threads to wear out.[53]

While the historicity of this legend is not altogether established, it at least suggests that the Abe and other prominent *fushū* families were held in high esteem in Japanese society during the medieval period. We agree with Kindaichi that the culture established by the *fushū* families in the Hiraizumi area was a happy synthesis of Ainu and Japanese elements.[54] After the defeat of the Abe, the Fujiwara in Hiraizumi continued to hold sway over northeastern Japan, and when Minamoto Yoshitsune, the popular military hero in Japanese history, was persecuted by his brother, Minamoto Yoritomo, the founder of the feudal regime in Kamakura, Yoshitsune was given refuge by the Fujiwara. Although Japanese history tells us that Yoshitsune took his own life at Hiraizumi, there are numerous legends, both Japanese and Ainu, that he escaped to Hokkaido and became an important chief among the Ainus.[55] At any rate, the colorful history of the *fushū* in the Hiraizumi area came to an end when the Fujiwara were defeated in 1189 by Minamoto Yoritomo who, it is reported, commanded three great forces numbering over 280,000 men.[56] After this, it looks as though the Ainus and their descendants on Honshu island lost their identity, leaving behind them, however, many Ainu place names in various parts of Japan.[57]

[52] Kindaichi, "Ainu Bunka to Nihon Bunka tono Kosho," *op. cit.*, pp. 29–30.

[53] D. T. Suzuki, *Zen and Japanese Culture* ("Bollingen Series," LXIV [New York: Pantheon Books, 1959]), p. 389.

[54] Kindaichi, "Ainu Bunka to Nihon Bunka tono Kosho," *op. cit.*, pp. 31–32.

[55] Batchleor, *The Ainu and Their Folk-Lore*, p. 81.

[56] Sansom, *op. cit.*, p. 296.

[57] Cf. Chamberlain, "The Language, Mythology, and Geographical Nomenclature of Japan . . ." *op. cit.*, pp. 64–75; Kindaichi, "Ainu Bunka to Nihon Bunka tono Kosho," *op. cit.*, pp. 28–29.

For the most part, Japanese history ignores the existence of the Ainus in Hokkaido, Sakhalin, and the Kurils for many centuries until the middle of the fifteenth century, A.D., when they are reported to be trading with the small number of Japanese settlers living mostly on the southern tip of Hokkaido. The name of an Ainu chieftain, Koshamain (Kosham-ainu), plays a prominent role in a series of conflicts between the Ainus and the Japanese, in which the Japanese settlements were nearly wiped out. During the sixteenth century, the Japanese colonies barely held their own. From the middle of the sixteenth century onward, however, the picture changed somewhat. The Japanese interest in Hokkaido was in the hands of the Matsumaye family which, as one of the *daimyo* of the Tokugawa feudal regime (*Bakufu*), regarded the whole island as its fief until the mid-nineteenth century, except for brief periods when the *Bakufu* in Yedo (Tokyo) ruled the island directly.

At first, the Matsumaye regarded only a narrow coastal strip in the southern tip of Hokkaido as their territory and discouraged the Japanese settlers from moving into the Ainu areas. Gradually, however, the Matsumaye consolidated their power and began to expand their sphere of influence. In the middle of the seventeenth century, the discovery of gold on the island resulted in an influx of ambitious new settlers from Honshu island.[58] After the Ainu revolt in 1669, caused by a dispute regarding fish and game grounds, the Matsumaye assumed the prerogative of conferring the title of chief on those prominent Ainus who had pledged their allegiance to the Matsumaye. These chiefs were expected to keep their fellow Ainus in line. Takakura succinctly describes the change that took place in the relationship between the Ainu chieftain and the lord of Matsumaye: "Originally there was no difference in social position for at the end of the seventeenth century the chief was allowed to sit next to the lord. In later years the chief had to sit on a straw mat in the courtyard."[59] With the expansion of Japanese dominance over the Ainus, Japanese contractors began to operate fishing grounds exploiting Ainu labor. Partly due to the mismanagement of the Matsumaye and the oppression of the Japanese settlers, and partly due to the spread of contagious diseases, such as smallpox and measles, the number of Ainus began to decrease. For instance, "in 1550 the chief of the eastern *Ezo* lived in Shiriuchi but by 1704 there were no *Ezo* in this area."[60]

The excessive exploitation of the Ainus by the Japanese settlers resulted in the Ainu revolt of 1789 in eastern Hokkaido (in the areas of Kunashiri and Menashi). Although this was a minor local uprising, Takakura correctly points to the international political implications of this incident, since the Russians, known to the Japanese as "aka-Ebisu" ("Red Ainus"), were by then penetrat-

---

[58] Takakura quotes Minoru Matsuzaki's statement to the effect that a Roman Catholic priest, Carvalho, was able to enter Matsumaye territory and engage in missionary work because he had received a permit as a gold-miner. Takakura, *op. cit.*, p. 28, n. 26.

[59] *Ibid.*, p. 35.

[60] *Ibid.*, p. 37.

ing the Kurils. The arrival of the Russian envoy Laxman in 1792 and 1793 alarmed the Matsumaye as well as the Tokugawa feudal regime in Yedo. As a consequence, eastern Hokkaido was brought under Tokugawa rule in 1799, and eight years later the whole island came under the direct control of the Tokugawa; this lasted until 1821.[61]

On the whole, the Tokugawa's attitude toward the Ainus was more enlightened than that of the Matsumaye. At least, the architects of Tokugawa policy in Yedo attempted to formulate a series of measures that would enable the Ainus to raise their living standard, by encouraging them to grow crops and live on cereals in addition to fish and game. Under the Tokugawa there was also an attempt to introduce Japanese customs, Japanese language, and a Japanese type of village organization. These measures, however, were not carried out efficiently on the local level, and the reform policy was abandoned in Hokkaido early in the nineteenth century. The Tokugawa regime achieved a greater degree of success in its attempts at reform in the Kurils.[62]

The Tokugawa had to deal with the problems of Sakhalin island. For many years, the Ainus of Sakhalin maintained cultural contacts with tribes on the Asiatic continent, such as the Oroke or Oroches (possibly one of the Tungusic tribes), the Ju-chen-Manchus, and the Santan.[63] At times, the Sakhalin Ainus paid tribute to the Manchus. Takakura points out that the Ainu officials in Sakhalin who traded with the *Santan* "were presented with sealed appointments and had orders issued them as if they were a Manchurian colony while, on the other hand, the Santan entered Karafuto [Sakhalin] when they pleased and traveled about freely hunting in the mountains. In other words, Karafuto came under Manchurian hegemony."[64] Meanwhile, the gradual decline of Manchu power in eastern Siberia coincided with the eastward expansion of the Russian colonists, who in 1806 finally landed on Sakhalin and took Ainus as captives. Only after much

[61] *Ibid.*, pp. 49–50. Takakura notes that in 1697, V. Atlasov conquered Kamchatka, and in 1711 the Russian advance reached the Kurils. Russian missionaries reached Shimizu Island in 1747, Uruppu Island in 1785, and Etorofu Island in 1785. After the native uprising in 1771, Russians in the Kurils attempted to assimilate the natives to Russian culture, converting them to Christianity, changing their names and customs, teaching them Russian, etc. In 1779, Russians requested trade at Akkeshi, Hokkaido. In 1771, B. M. A. A. Beniowsky, a Hungarian, who had escaped from the Russians and reached Japan, warned the Japanese authorities regarding the Russian penetration from the north. Actually, the Matsumaye sent their representatives to meet the Russians at Akkeshi in 1779, but both the Matsumaye and the Tokugawa authorities kept this a secret. See also Hitchcock, "The Ancient Pit-Dwellers of Yezo," *op. cit.*, pp. 423–24 and Pl. LXXVI.

[62] *Takakura, op. cit.*, p. 63.

[63] *Ibid.*, p. 14, Harrison's n. *a*. The term *Santan* "comes from *Janta* or 'nomads,' a Gilyak name for the nomadic tribes who lived between the Amur River and the sea. The Ainu corrupted *Janta* into Santan." It is to be noted that today the term *Santa-guru* means a Manchurian.

[64] *Ibid.*, p. 66.

maneuvering, did the Tokugawa regime barely manage to keep Sakhalin within the Japanese sphere of influence.

In order to prevent Hokkaido, Sakhalin, and the Kurils from becoming enemy territories, the Tokugawa regime began to indoctrinate Ainus in these areas with Japanese culture and religion, for they had learned that some of the Kuril Ainus had become quite Russianized. As late as 1878, John Milne found people on Peroi Island in the Kurils calling themselves "Kurilsky" and following Russian customs.[65] Understandably, the Tokugawa regime, which had earlier stamped out Roman Catholicism in Japan, was horrified to find icons, crosses, and other symbols of Russian Orthodox Christianity on Japanese territory. So Buddhist priests were sent, and Buddhist temples were constructed and maintained at government expense, and Shinto shrines were established in various Ainu colonies. Kondō Juzō, a Tokugawa official who was instrumental in establishing a shrine for Minamoto Yoshitsune, gave the following directive: "To worship this god is to worship the god of Edo [Yedo or Tokyo] and it is as holy a god as the god of the sun and the moon. This god bestows good luck on the virtuous and bad luck on the evil. . . . This god protects Ezo and its surrounding sea so it is desired that this god be worshipped at all times without fail."[66] Indeed, Tokugawa officials worked hard to transform the Ainus so that they might become an asset to the cause of the national defense of Japan on her northern borders. For this reason, the Ainus were encouraged to give up such old practices as tattooing and the observance of the bear festival, as well as the alien customs and religion introduced by the Russians. The Tokugawas even encouraged intermarriage between the Ainus and the Japanese, but they could hardly overcome the fears on the part of the Ainus that accepting Japanese customs might bring about divine punishment. "Therefore," says Takakura, "when the policy of induced change was abandoned after the Russian invasion of 1808, the Ezo immediately went back to their old life."[67] Although the Tokugawa regime turned over the control of Hokkaido to the Matsumaye in 1821, the Tokugawa feudal government, frightened by the Opium War that started in China in 1840, tightened control over the border areas. Thus a commissioner was appointed from Yedo to be stationed at Hakodate for the purpose of overseeing the northern borders. However, with the fall of the Tokugawa from power in 1867, the control of Hokkaido and its neighboring islands was taken over by the Meiji regime.

One of the earliest steps taken by the new government of the Meiji was the appointment of the *Kaitaku-shi*, a governor for the development of the island, in 1869. The policy of the new regime was to consolidate Hokkaido as an integral part of the nation. Partly for the purpose of strengthening national

[65] Hitchcock, "The Ancient Pit-Dwellers of Yezo," *op. cit.*, p. 422.

[66] Quoted in Takakura, *op. cit.*, p. 76, n. 48.

[67] *Ibid.*, p. 80.

defense, and partly to provide livelihood for the former samurais who had lost their income through the dissolution of the feudal system, the Meiji government initiated the militia system in 1874 in Hokkaido and promoted a large-scale migration of people from Honshu island. In 1886, Hokkaido was recognized as an administrative entity with Sapporo as its capital. With the encouragement of the new government policy, the population of the Japanese in Hokkaido increased rapidly at the expense of the wellbeing of the Ainus. While the government in 1899 instituted the Hokkaido Aboriginal Protection Act to provide subsidies and protection to the Ainus, the impact of industrialized civilization inevitably disrupted the very foundations of traditional Ainu culture and society.

Today, in visiting Ainu villages, one notices changes in the traditional mode of Ainu life. Most Ainus live in semi-Japanese style houses complete with the Japanese form of straw mat (*tatami*), and Buddhist altars may be observed in many Ainu homes. Intermarriage with the Japanese is quite common, and all Ainu children are given Japanese education. And yet nearly a century of the intensive assimilation policy of the Japanese government has not erased from the mental life of the Ainus those sacred memories of the ancestors who can be traced a hundred generations back to the prehistoric period. Even the most urbane Ainus with a modern education will not forget the fascinating and tragic ancestral epics (*Yukar*) told and retold to them by their mothers in their childhood. And on great occasions such as *Iyomante*, when the whole Ainu community re-enacts the age-old ritual, they are once again absorbed into their sacred past, singing, dancing, and praying as all Ainus in every generation have done before them.

## THE TRADITION OF THE AINUS ("EKASHI URUOKA HOPPA ITAK")

Even such a brief survey of the Ainus' cultural contacts with neighboring peoples, as attempted here, makes it clear that it is exceedingly difficult to describe in detail the historical development of the traditional culture and religion of the Ainus. The beginnings of the Ainu race, like those of many other ethnic groups, are lost beyond the horizon. We are far from certain about those parts of the arctic or subarctic areas in which the ancestors of the Ainus lived originally, and we have only fragmentary evidence with which to reconstruct their manner of life: how they hunted, fished, married, buried the dead, built houses, and worshipped. We are not altogether certain concerning those elements in traditional Ainu culture which have been borrowed from outside and those which are truly of Ainu origin. Nevertheless, thanks to the untiring efforts of scholars, we are in a better position than ever before to probe into the nature of the religious and cultural traditions of the Ainus.

Ethnologists have used various terms such as "primitive," "preliterate," "precivilized," and "folk" to describe Ainu society. Although these terms are unsatisfactory and misleading, they do have the suggestive connotation that such a society is "small, isolated, non-literate, and homogeneous, with a strong sense of group solidarity."[68] On the other hand, Evans-Pritchard rightly reminds us that so-called primitive societies are neither earlier in time nor inferior to other kinds of societies. "As far as we know, primitive societies have just as long a history as our own, and while they are less developed than our society in some respects they are often more developed in others."[69] In other words, primitive societies are not "primitive" in quality but are different kinds of societies from our own in the modes of social structure, human relations, and underlying world views.

In many parts of the world, the gradual processes of the food-producing revolution and the urban revolution transformed the preagricultural, preliterate folk society into civilization.[70] Moreover, the impact of a great civilization altered the nature and texture of less advanced societies that came in contact with it. For example, Langdon Warner described vividly how Japanese society experienced a social and cultural revolution during the period between the sixth and the eighth centuries under the influence exerted by Sino-Korean civilization. The organization of Japanese social relationships was regulated and rationalized by Confucianism, while lofty metaphysics and the fine arts were supplied by Buddhism and Taoism, and superior techniques and skills of all sorts—from agriculture to astronomy—were transplanted from China. Perhaps the most important of all was the introduction of the art of writing that changed the cultural orientation of the Japanese from sole dependence on oral transmission to written documents. Thus the *Kojiki* ("The Records of Ancient Matters") was compiled in 712 A.D. from the memory of Hieda no Are, a professional transmitter and reciter of ancient myths, legends, and historical events. In the metaphor used by Warner: "the T'ang dynasty of China was hanging like a brilliant brocaded background, against which we must look at Japan and its capital city of Nara to watch the eighth century, while the Japanese were at work weaving their own brocade on *patterns similar but not the same*."[71]

In sharp contrast to this development in Japan, Ainu society, despite the fact that it maintained cultural contacts with more complex and literate civilizations on the Asiatic continent and in the Japanese Archipelago for over fifteen hundred years, preserved much of folk or preliterate society until the latter part of the nineteenth century. That the Ainus have borrowed certain goods and cultural habits from their neighbors over the years is taken for granted. However, their basic attitude toward life and the world and their

[68] Robert Redfield, "The Folk Society," *American Journal of Sociology*, LII (January, 1947), 297.

[69] E. E. Evans-Pritchard, *Social Anthropology* (Glencoe, Ill.: Free Press, 1952), p. 7.

[70] Robert Redfield, *The Primitive World and Its Transformations* (Ithaca, N.Y.: Cornell University Press, 1953), p. 26.

[71] Langdon Warner, *The Enduring Art of Japan* (Cambridge, Mass.: Harvard University Press, 1952), p. 6. (Italics are mine.)

way of preserving the integrity of their society and culture have remained unchanged fundamentally from the time of their remotest ancestors. Even today the Ainus, having no written language of their own, have a remarkable capacity for retaining legend and lore in memory, and as in the case of other non-literate peoples, the Ainus tend to think and speak in colorful, glowing pictures, full of actions and symbols. It is thus readily understandable why oral traditions, especially the *yukar* (epics), have played such an important role in the life of the Ainus. Kindaichi goes so far as to say that the *yukar* "are a history, a literature, a philosophy, a science, a scripture, a code. In other words, folk-tales are a learning, a religion, a law—culture itself. In order to live as an independent Ainu, it is necessary to know an outline of the legends and traditions of his community; and especially is it so for those who command others."[72]

The term *yukar* (*i-ukar*) stems from the combination of *i* (the first person singular objective case of the personal pronoun) and *ukar* (a transitive verb meaning "to imitate"), and connotes "self-expression" or "tales about my experiences as told by my own words." There are two kinds of *yukar*. The epics of heroes, known simply as *yukar*, are based on stories of a series of battles that took place roughly from 800 to 1300 A.D. between the Ainus and other tribes that invaded Hokkaido from the northeastern parts of Asia and from the Okhotsk region. Chiri holds that these epics took their present form about five or six hundred years ago, and that the form of the *yukar* (the epics of heroes) was modeled after the general form of the *kamuy-yukar* or *kamui-yukar* ("the sacred traditions" or "the stories about the *kamui* or gods told by themselves") which had been handed down from a much earlier period.[73] On the whole, the epics of heroes tend to be very long. For instance, the *Ainu yukar*, the story of a legendary hero, Poiyaumbe, runs from three thousand to ten thousand lines, depending on the version. The *kamui-yukar* incline to be shorter, except for the sacred traditions of Okikurumi, the founder of the human race. It is to be noted that Okikurumi is also called *Ainu-rak-kur* ("man like an Ainu") or *Aeoina Kamui* ("our hereditary *kamui*"), and his teachings are known as the *Oina* ("inheritance").[74] These epics have been handed down by the *Oina-kur* ("the reciter of the *Oina*") and *yukar-kur* ("the reciter of the *yukar*"), who belong to hereditary families of oral transmitters. They chant these epics with traditional melodies that are melancholy sometimes and then again quite animated. It is significant that the local dialects of the Hokkaido Ainus are so different from those of the Sakhalin Ainus that they can hardly communicate with each other but "they can equally understand a *yukar* if it is recited."[75]

[72] Kindaichi, *Ainu Life and Legend*, p. 60.
[73] Chiri, *The Ainu Dictionary*, III, 457.
[74] Kindaichi, *Ainu Life and Legend*, pp. 57–58.
[75] *Ibid.*, p. 61.

It is not at all certain how far we can trace the development of the *kamui-yukar*. It is generally accepted, however, that they were derived from the divine oracles uttered by the shamanic women in their state of ecstasy (*tomochi*).[76] This is probably why the *kamui-yukar* are narrated in the first person. In the traditional Ainu society, it was the man's duty to worship the *kamui* (gods), while it was the woman's prerogative to engage in shamanistic divination and witchery (*tusu* or *mupur*). Kindaichi cites the examples of male shamans, especially among the Sakhalin Ainus, but more generally shamanic diviners among the Ainus are female. In fact, the formal attire of the Ainu women was taken completely from that of the shamanic diviner.[77] Usually, the Ainu women's power to perform shamanic diviniation is attributed to the fact that in their childhood they were possessed by the serpent.[78] At the mention of a serpent, those who are believed to have been possessed by it will manifest emotional disturbance. "This habit is called *imu* and is caused by a slight mental disease. It is after experiencing this propensity that a woman is thought to be able to practice witchcraft. . . . Of these women, those who can bring themselves into an extraordinary state of mind by self-induction can be excellent witches."[79] When the chief of a village has to make important decisions, he usually consults the will of the *kamui* through the shamanic divination performed by his wife or sister. According to Kindaichi:

> Previous to this, he offers *sake* to the god and worships him. He drinks half the *sake* he offered to the god, and then gives the remaining half to the witch. She drains the wine-cup and begins to sing a witch-song. While singing, the woman becomes possessed with a spirit. The tone of the voice changes into an extraordinary one. At last it becomes the voice of the god and sings something suggestive. The chieftain guesses the meaning of the song, and thereby judges or decides the event of the village.[80]

[76] The term *tomochi* was originally the same word as *topochi*, which is now the designation of lower female *kamui*. This term is used more frequently as a verb, *etomochine*, that is, "e" (in connection with) "tomochi" (the state of unconsciousness) "ne" (to become).

[77] Kindaichi, *Ainu Life and Legend* p. 27. "The jewels they wear when in full dress are called *tama-sai*; this custom is derived from Shamanism. A ring-shaped cap, which is two or three inches high, is an imitation of the crown-like cap worn by a Shaman when performing oracles." In addition, a shamanic diviner puts on leather belts on ceremonial occasions. "Each belt has many dangling round pieces of metal, which are as large as coins and serve as ornaments. When the wearer moves, these pieces of metal make a clinging sound."

[78] For many accounts of the serpent legends, see Batchelor, *The Ainu and Their Folk-Lore*, pp. 355–74.

[79] Kindaichi, *Ainu Life and Legend*, pp. 67–68.

[80] *Ibid.*, pp. 68–69. In this connection, it is interesting to note that, in the northeastern part of the Honshu island of Japan, where historically Ainu influence was most strongly felt, we find even today many types of shamanic diviners (*miko*) that are not too different from the Ainu

Moreover, not every Ainu woman has equal ability in performing shamanic divination. Some well-known shamanic diviners seem to possess special charismatic qualities. At any rate, the songs chanted by these women in a state of ecstasy are believed to be the words of the *kamui* (gods), and there is every reason to believe that the *kamui-yukar* that have been orally transmitted to our day can be traced to these shamanic songs of ancient times.

Moreover, the *kamui-yukar* contain many important clues for our understanding of the ancient Ainus' beliefs and modes of life. However, interpretation of these ancient traditions that have been transmitted orally is an extremely hazardous task. There are many reasons for this difficulty. For one thing, different tribes have developed various versions of the same theme, and inevitably they have modified minor details, to a large extent because of local conditions under which they lived. At times external influences corrupted the original motifs. The extreme example of this is seen in the fusion of the Okikurumi legend and that of the Japanese hero, Minamoto no Yoshitsune. According to one tradition, Yoshitsune arrived in the land of the Ainus some time after Okikurumi had begun to teach the Ainus the art of living. Yoshitsune, here portrayed as a cunning fellow, ingratiated himself with Okikurumi, so that the latter gave his daughter to Yoshitsune in marriage. Yoshitsune persuaded his bride to steal the treasures and books and then ran away leaving his wife behind. Since that time, so the legend tells us, the Ainus have lost the arts of writing and pottery.[81] In addition to these difficulties we must also bear in mind that the Ainu language has undergone many degrees of subtle change. For instance, Chiri reminds us that ancient Ainus, contrary to the thinking of present-day Ainus, regarded rivers as living beings that sleep at night and lose weight in the summer. Two rivers that meet were viewed as having sexual intercourse (*u-tuman-pet* or *oukot-nay*) that results in the birth of a child-river (*pon-pet*, *po-pet* or *mo-pet*). In general, however, rivers were thought of in female terms. So, the mouth of a river was called "o" (the term for the female sexual organ), from which fish enter the body of the river. Accordingly, Chiri analyzes and translates a passage from the *kamui-yukar*, "*pet-e-riki-kur / puni kane / pet-o-raw-takur / rori kane*," as follows:

pet     (river)
e       (of its head)
riki    (high place)

shamanic diviners. Cf. Shojun Sato, "Hachinohe-shi-shuhen no Miko no Gyotai," *Shukyo Kenkyu*, No. 146 (December, 1955), pp. 38–39, and Shojun Sato, "Iwete-ken-ka no Oshira no Ruikei," *ibid.*, III, No. 33 (March, 1960), 86–87.

[81] On this question, see Chamberlain, "The Language, Mythology, and Geographical Nomenclature of Japan . . ." *op. cit.*, pp. 17, 37; Batchelor, *The Ainu and Their Folk-Lore*, p. 81.

kur      (*adverbial suffix)
puni     (to hold up)
kane     (*this word is sometimes suffixed to verbs to change them into
         adverbs or the adverbial phrase, "whilst . . .")
pet      (river)
o        (tail, end)
raw      (low place)
takur    (*taw-ta-kur implies "to low down to low place")
rori     (to sink, to low down)
kane     (*see above)[82]

Some of these experiences are no longer precisely understood by present-day Ainus, so that the interpretation of the original meaning of the *kamui-yukar* presents serious problems. Nevertheless, the careful work of many scholars, especially that of Kindaichi and Chiri, have made it possible for us to have a glimpse of the religious perspective of the Ainus.

"*Kamui.*"—the Ainu term *kamui*, usually translated as "god" or "gods," bears a close resemblance to the Japanese term, *kami*, and the possible interrelation of these two terms has been discussed by a number of writers.[83] According to Batchelor, *kamui* refers to a god or a bear; it is "a title applied to anything great, good, important, honourable, bad, fierce or awful; hence used of animals and men, gods and devils." As a prefix, *kamui* serves as an adjective, as in the case of *kamui nishpa* ("a great master"), and as a suffix, it may be regarded as a noun, for example: *ape-kamui* or *abe-kamui* ("fire god"), *rera kamui* ("wind god"), *rep un kamui* ("sea gods"), and *nitne kamui* ("devils").[84] The use of the term *kamui* is by no means confined to the above categories. For instance, the female organ was believed to have some connection with *kamui*. Women who have white pubic hair were believed to share the same quality with sea gods or "dolphins" (*rep-un-kamui-ko-upsor-kor-pe*), while those with black pubic hair were believed to have the blessing of the mountain *kamui* or "bear" (*kimun-kamui-ko-upsor-kor-pe*). Also, women's breasts (*toho* or *totto*) that are long are known as "dolphin's breasts"

[82] Chiri, *The Ainu Dictionary*, III, 22–23, 457–60. In fairness to Chiri, it should be pointed out that he translated this passage from the Ainu into Japanese, from which the present writer translated it into English. Thus, he is not responsible for any errors in the English translation.

[83] Cf. Batchelor, "On the Ainu Term 'Kamui,'" *op. cit.*; and Chamberlain, "Reply to Mr. Batchelor on the Words 'Kamui' and 'Aino,'" *op. cit.*

[84] Batchelor, *An Ainu-English-Japanese Dictionary*, p. 205. Also see Batchelor, "Ainus," *op. cit.*, I, 239–40. Chamberlain was convinced that the Japanese term, *kami*, is the original of the Ainu term, *kamui*: "The Aino *kamui* is a substantive, and nothing more. The Japanese *kami* still lives, as of old, as a pliable word, which may be a noun, an adjective, or a particle, according to circumstances. It is more organic." Chamberlain, "The Language, Mythology, and Geographical Nomenclature of Japan . . ." *op. cit.*, p. 40.

*(rep-un-kami totto)*, while those that project are known as *"bear's breasts"*
*(kimun-kamui toho)*.[85] Death is often described as *kamui ne okere* ("to
become a *kamui*") or *kamui-kotan orun oman* ("to go to the world of the
*kamui*"); a deceased person's soul is called *rai* ("dead") *kamui*, and the soul of
the dead, evil spirit is called *wenkuru kamui*.[86]

The almost indiscriminate use of the term *kamui* indicates the Ainu
belief in the *kamui* nature permeating the universe. Not only do all men have
*epunkine* ("guardian") *kamui*, who protect them from evil spirits, but they
can always depend on *rupa-us* ("road-side") *kamui* to provide them with
additional protection. Men and women are, of course, expected to pay due
respect to the *kamui* wherever they may happen to be. For example, if
people go to hot springs, they must make offerings not only to *nu-kor-kamui*
("the *kamui* of the hot spring"), who is regarded as a female *kamui*, but to her
consort as well.[87] When someone suffers from certain kinds of ailments, such
as toothache or stomach-ache, each of which is believed to have been caused
by a particular *kamui*, the healer or "those whose palms have healing power"
*(tek-nimaw-kor)* are called in. The healer places his palms on the ailing part
of the patient's body. In the course of time, the healer begins to shake
*(tususatki)* or to shake and dance *(tusu-ko-tapkar)*. In the state of ecstasy of
the healer, the ailment is either healed or diagnosed *(kamui-itakte)* by the
healer's *kamui*.[88]

Among all the *kamui* that cause sicknesses, the most powerful, and thus
feared greatly by the Ainus, is the *kamui* of smallpox *(pa-koro-kamui)*.
Numerous legends are told about the birth of this *kamui*, and according to
some traditions he is even regarded as the father of the founder of Ainu
culture, *Aeoina-kamui* (also known as Ainu-rak-kur and Okikurumi).[89] The
*kamui* of smallpox are also known significantly as *apkas-kamui* ("wandering
*kamui*") and *utar-kor-kamui* ("the *kamui* who have many relatives"). They
and their relatives are believed to live very much like human beings, falling
in love, holding drinking parties, and enjoying singing and dancing. In their
own world, they form villages like Ainu villages; the villages of the *kamui* of
smallpox are divided into *hure* ("red"), *siwnin* ("green"), and *kunne* ("black")
*kotan* (villages), and those living in these villages wear clothes of corresponding colors. Various traditions of the *kamui-yukar* identify the world of the
*kamui* of smallpox somewhat differently. The Ainus hold that the *kamui* of
smallpox "visit" the human world as regularly as seasonal birds come around,
and when they come they appear in the form of birds, commonly called

[85] Chiri, *The Ainu Dictionary*, III, 57–58, 252.
[86] *Ibid.*, pp. 199, 243.
[87] *Ibid.*, pp. 591–92.
[88] *Ibid.*, pp. 273–74.
[89] See Chiri's comparative research on the three different traditions about the birth and the lineage of the *pa-koro-kamui*, *ibid.*, pp. 368–73.

*pakoro-chikap-po* ("little bird demons of disease"). Batchelor mentions the following legend about them:

> During the early spring, little birds of a greyish-coloured body, but with a small patch of red on the top of their heads, come and settle upon the seashore. They come in large flights. If a person should kill one of them, many evil diseases would at once attack the villages. One must therefore not even pretend to throw a stone at them, call them names, or even say so much as one word to them. He should turn away from them, and pretend not to see them.[90]

While records of smallpox epidemics that raged in Ainu villages are limited to the last four centuries only, they are enough to enable us to imagine the fear that must have possessed the minds of the Ainus in ancient times. It is understandable, therefore, to find numerous magical formulas and rituals for avoiding the "visit" of the *kamui* of smallpox.[91]

Confronted by all these diverse and contradictory accounts of the *kamui-yukar*, we are not altogether certain about the ancient Ainus' "theological" understanding, if you will, of the nature of the *kamui*. Various theories have been advanced by scholars. For example, Batchelor, while acknowledging the polytheistic character of the present-day Ainu religion, asserted that originally the religion of the Ainus was monotheistic. Only after the original monotheism had given way to polytheism, so he argued, did the Ainus develop various kinds of pantheons. He attempted to make a clear distinction between the two terms, *pase kamui* ("the God of God," or "Creator and Protector of heaven," according to his own translation), and *yaiyan kamui* ("common deities," also "near" and "distant deities").

> *Pase* is an adjective, and points to rank and authority, its first meaning being "weighty," "true," and "superior in rank." And so *Pase Kamui* may well be translated by the word "chief" or "true God." . . . Thus far, then, we have reached a real basis for two articles of Ainu belief, viz. (*a*) "I believe in one supreme God, the Creator of all worlds and places, who is the Possessor of heaven, whom we call *Pase Kamui,* "The true God," and whom we speak of as *Kotan kara Kamui, Moshiri kara Kamui, Kando koro Kamui*; (*b*) "I believe also in the existence of a multitude of inferior deities (*Kamui*), all subject to this one Creator, who are His servants, who receive their life and power from Him, and who act and govern the world under Him."[92]

---

[90] Batchelor, *The Ainu and Their Folk-Lore*, p. 296.
[91] Chiri, *The Ainu Dictionary*, III, 377–85.
[92] Batchelor, "Ainus," *op. cit.*, I, 240.

Suggestive though this view is, we are inclined to believe that Batchelor had unconsciously, if not consciously, imposed his own understanding of religion on the religion of the Ainus. Others in rejecting Batchelor's view also tended to impose their own theories of religion on the ancient Ainu. Here we face a methodological problem famliar to all students of *Religionswissenschaft*.[93]

One difficulty we face in regard to the Ainu religion is that the Ainus, like many other preliterate peoples, have never developed conceptual ways of thinking, abstract systems of doctrines and theologies. If one asked the Ainu the meaning of a word, he would not give a synonym, "but he would 'paint' in words, quickly and unfailingly, a picture that illustrated the exact meaning. In describing a person [or a *kamui*] the illiterate would not talk about his character but rather tell significant stories about him."[94] And the task of the historian of religions is to try to enter the world of these myths and stories, as well as of the symbols, rituals, and other aspects of the life of the Ainus, to find the invisible, but nevertheless real, structure of their religion without resorting to the usual clichés, such as monotheism, polytheism, or pantheism. Of course, this is much easier said than done. The frustrating thing is that we cannot apply our usual religious categories, such as "ultimate reality," "nature," and "man," to Ainu religion. Try as we may, the distinction between the *kamui* and man, or between the *kamui* and animals, birds, fishes, and plants, cannot be drawn sharply. To be sure, the notion of interchangeability among different beings has been held by other peoples too. But the Ainus have their own way of apprehending and expressing the interchangeability and indivisibility of nature and man, or of *kamui* and nature. We may, at the risk of being somewhat arbitrary, choose the ideas of "correspondence" and "*maratto-ne*" (literally translated, "to become a guest") to characterize the religious perspective of the Ainus.

*Correspondence of the "Kamui" and man.*—As far as we can reconstruct, the Ainus' view of the universe is based on the interpenetration and fusion of numerous kinds of *moshiri* ("the world" or "a country"; more literally, it connotes "floating earth"). According to one legend:

> The place in which we dwell is called by two names, first, *kanna moshiri*, i.e. "the upper world," and then *Usekari uotereke moshiri*, i.e. "the world in which the multitudes trample one another's feet." It is also called *Uare moshiri*, i.e. "the place in which to multiply one another." It

[93]Cf. Mircea Eliade, and J. M. Kitagawa, eds., *The History of Religions: Essays in Methodology* (Chicago: University of Chicago Press, 1959), chapters on "The Supreme Being: Phenomenological Structure and Historical Development," by Raffaele Pettazzoni, pp. 59–66, and "Methodological Remarks on the Study of Religious Symbolism," by Mircea Eliade, pp. 86–107.

[94]H. R. Weber, *The Communication of the Gospel of Illiterates* (London: S.C.M. Press, 1957), p. 26.

is the upper world, because there is another world under foot. That world [*Nitne Kamui moshiri* ("the world of the devils") or *Teine-pokna-moshiri* ("the wet underground world")] is very damp and wet, and when wicked people die they go there and are punished. But by the side of this place there is another locality, which is called *Kamui moshiri*, i.e. "the country of the gods" or "heaven." It is to this place that the good people go after death. They live there with the deities and walk about upside down, after the manner of flies, so that their feet meet ours.

When it is day upon this earth it is night in heaven, and when it is daylight there, it is dark here. Now, when it is dark in this world, men should neither do any work, nor trim one another's hair, nor cut the beard, for at that time the deities and ghosts of men are busy in their own spheres. If, therefore, the inhabitants of this world work during the hours of darkness, they will be punished with sickness and meet with an early death.[95]

The Ainus also have poetic expressions to describe the several layers of heavens, such as *urara kando* ("fog skies"), *range kando* ("hanging skies"), *Nochiuo kando* ("star-bearing skies"), *shinish kando* ("the high skies of the clouds"), and *shirik un kando* ("the skies in the most high").[96] Each one of these *moshiri* is again subdivided into smaller units, as has been indicated in connection with the *kamui* of smallpox (*pa-koro-kamui*). Each unit of such a *moshiri* is ruled by its head, who in some ways is subject to the head of a larger unit, just as in Ainu society the *chise-korokuru* ("the head of the family") is subservient to the *utarapa* or *utarapake* ("chief of a clan") and *kotan korokuru* ("the chief of the village"). Most prominent "chiefs" of the larger *moshiri*, in the eyes of the Ainus, are *ape huchi* or *abe huchi* (the female *kamui* of fire, also known as *kamui-huchi*) who rule the household of the Ainu; *kotan-kor-kamui* (the owl, the *kamui* of the village, also known as *kamui-a-yupi*) who protects the Ainu village; *pa-koro kamui* (the *kamui* of smallpox) who is the chief of all *kamui* who cause diseases; *kimun-kamui* (the bear) who is the chief of the mountain; the *rep-un-kamui* (the dolphin) who is the chief of the sea.

The traditional Ainu view took for granted that the pattern of life in all the *moshiri* was pretty much the same, and not too different from life in the Ainu *kotan* (village). It is significant to note that the Ainu village was a permanent social unit but was not tied permanently to any particular locality until recently, although a village remained more or less in the same geographical region. More often than not, the Ainus settled by rivers not far from the seashore. Not having an exact spot that could be equated with their village, the Ainus identified their whereabouts by means of the river. And

[95] Quoted in Batchelor, *The Ainu and Their Folk-Lore*, p. 58.
[96] *Ibid.*, p. 60.

since, according to the Ainu view the river is a living being, each river was given a name, including the smallest stream.[97] According to Kindaichi, the Ainu divided the year into two seasons—summer and winter. While in summer they lived chiefly on fish, in winter they hunted wild game, which was added to the smoked fish that had been preserved from summer. In July and August trout came up the rivers from the sea, followed by salmon in September and October; the Ainus called these fish *kamui-chep* (divine fish). They also went out to sea to catch or harpoon sunfish and swordfish.[98] Generally fishing and hunting grounds were common properties of members of a certain village or of a group of villages, and outsiders were not privileged to enter. In some areas, bear dens were also regarded as common properties of a group of hunters from specific villages. The Ainu villages were thus economic and social units. Members of a village shared a common ancestry and common ancestral *kamui*, and understandably took special pride in their family lineage. At festivals heads of families gathered in the house of the chief of the village to venerate the ancestral *kamui*. As such, the Ainu village had the earmarks of a religious community as well.[99]

The Ainus hold that the *kamui* in their own *moshiri* form a *kotan* (village) similar to the Ainu village. They are believed to live with their own families in a house with a fireplace and all other household utensils. They quarrel, fight, fall in love, marry, and bear children. The *kamui* visit among themselves, entertain and are entertained, dance, sing, eat, and enjoy drinking. For example, in the *Pon Oina* ("A Small Tradition of *Oina*"),[100] transmitted in the Horobetsu district of Hokkaido, we are told of a colorful and eventful love affair between Oina-Kamui (also known as Ainu-rak-kur, Aeoina-Kamui, or Pon Okikurumi) and a lovely female *kamui* of Horobetsu. As in all other *kamui-yukar*, the story is told by the female *kamui* in the first person singular. According to this story, she had an elder sister and an elder brother. When she became old enough to wear *mo-ur* ("the dress of a grown woman") and be tattooed,[101] her brother instructed her to move into a new house. This exemplified the old Ainu custom which allows suitors to visit the

---

[97] Chamberlain points this out as an important cultural habit of the Ainus: "The Japanese, on the other hand, frequently leave a river without any proper appellation, simply designating it, at various points of its course, as 'the river of such and such a village.' In Aino a similar custom prevails with regard to mountains, which are commonly known as 'the mountain from which such and such a river flows,' whereas the Japanese custom is to give each mountain a name" (Chamberlain, "The Language, Mythology, and Geographical Nomenclature of Japan . . ." *op. cit.*, p. 60). Kindaichi also discusses the remains of the Ainu river names, now regarded as place names, in the northeastern part of the Honshu island of Japan (cf. Kindaichi, "Ainu Bunka to Nihon Bunka tono Kosho," *op. cit.*, pp. 27–29).

[98] Kindaichi, *Ainu Life and Legend*, pp. 31–32.

[99] Takakura, *op. cit.*, p. 17.

[100] *Pon Oina*, trans. Kindaichi, *op. cit.*

[101] On tattoo, see Sakuzaemon Kodama, M.D., and Shoichi Ito, "Ainu no Irezumi no Kenkyu" ("Studies in the Tattooing of the Ainus"), *Hoppo Bunka Kenkyu Hokoku*, monograph, Hokkaido

prospective bride in her own dwelling. There she serves a bowl of food of her own cooking to each young man. "The young visitor, after eating half of the food, was to return the bowl to the young hostess. If she accepted it and ate the remaining food, it signified that she complied. If not, it was a sign of disapproval."[102] Returning to the story of the *Pon Oina*, one day, an unknown *kamui* from the western coast called at her brother's house, and there he met her and fell in love. He was poorly dressed, but there was something noble, strong, and attractive about him and she returned his love. A local *kamui*, who had always wanted her, nearly murdered her from jealousy on this account, but she was rescued by the unknown western *kamui*. The latter, who eventually revealed himself as Ainu-rak-kur (Aeoina-Kamui), meanwhile had to go out fighting in a series of battles and barely escaped being killed, but was miraculously saved from the tragedy. In the end, he recovered and returned to Horobetsu to claim the beautiful *kamui*, whom he married.

This story examined more in detail shows clearly that the *kamui* follow all the customs and ceremonials known to the Ainus. There are a number of other such sacred traditions, equally attributed to the *kamui*, that disclose everything known to the Ainus—from the creation of the world to the art of making wine. In the words of Kindaichi: "the substance of the *Oina Yukar* is not merely to be heard with pleasure, but to be believed in. It is a history, a scripture, or a statute, which makes a standard in everyday life, settles disputes, or warns against various swervings of human conduct."[103] To be sure, the Ainus do not engage in conceptual formulation or debate in the philosophical manner. But they have a rich body of knowledge about the life and behavior of the *kamui*, who provide models for everything and every conceivable problem that confronts the Ainu individually and collectively. To them, the life in this *moshiri* (world) is nothing but a counterpart of the *moshiri* of the *kamui*, and these parallel realms have a great deal in common to the extent that they are *de facto* interchangeable. As a collorary of the notion of interchangeability between the world of man and that of *kamui* the idea exists that man is not merely human, just as the *kamui* has many human qualities. In a real sense, the Ainu's life is not confined to this world; from the cradle to the grave, he lives ever so close to the *kamui*, both benevolent and malevolent. He is protected by the former and threatened by the latter. Ainus believe that a state of madness (*kosimpu-kinkara-kar*) is caused by the possession of evil spirits (*kosimpu*), either the evil spirit of the mountain (*iwa-kosimpu*) or that of the sea (*rur-kosimpu*). According to the Ainu, all evil spirits are white in color, and often manifest themselves in white foam or bubbles. The male *kosimpu* frequently falls in love with an Ainu woman and

---

University (October, 1939). When an Ainu girl becomes thirteen, her upper lip is tattooed; and when she becomes fifteen, the lower lip is also tattooed.

[102] Kindaichi, *Ainu Life and Legend*, p. 39.

[103] *Ibid.*, p. 72.

the female *kosimpu* with an Ainu man. Thus, when a man, upon seeing white foam, goes mad and dies, the Ainu interprets it to be the result of the love of a female *kosimpu* who took his soul away so that they could get married in her world. As a compensation for this act, the widow of the dead man is believed to receive magical power or to accumulate wealth.[104]

Sometimes one feels intensely that evil spirits are chasing him; in that case, he should move around a walking stick and chant words of incantation. Or, one feels as though someone has called him, and yet there is no other person in sight. Such experiences of hallucination (*oha-inkar, oha-inu* or *owa-inu*) are taken very seriously by the Ainus.[105] When one hears his name called, say in the mountain or on the sea where no one else is in sight, the Ainus believe that there is a *kamui* who happens to have the same name and that he is in conversation (*uko-hotuypa*) in the other *moshiri*. In such a situation, the Ainu is careful not to reply, for doing so means involvement in the affairs of the other world and this might cause his early death. Should one reply by mistake, he has to "change his name" (*oya-re-kore*) immediately.[106] The significance of pronouncing the name, either of the *kamui* or of man, should be mentioned. For instance, a married woman, being a potential shamanic diviner, should never mention her husband's name even when she talks to him. She simply calls him *anokay* ("you"). If she dares to call his name, this action implies "giving a dried or dead name" (*sat-re-kore*) which is to invite a great misfortune and endanger her husband's life.[107]

The Ainus feel that they are in some sense participating in the life of the other *moshiri* during sleep. It is widely held that when one sleeps, his soul (*ramat*) leaves the body either through the nose or the mouth and flies around in the form of a bee, a fly, a butterfly, or a small bird. Thus, when an insect is hovering about a sleeping man, the Ainus are careful not to kill it. Also, a man in his deep sleep should not be awakened abruptly, for the soul (*ramat*) may not have time to re-enter the body and therefore might fly away (*ramat oman*). At any rate, what one dreams in his dream, no matter how unrealistic and extraordinary it may be, is to be understood as a thing that has actually been observed by the soul (*ramat*) during its flight away from the body.[108]

Such an intimate relationship between the world of man and other *moshiri*, in the traditional view of the Ainus, underlies the notion of *maratto-ne*.

"*Maratto-ne*" (*visitor*).—The term *maratto*, or *marapto*, or more commonly *maratto-sapa*, refers to a bear's head at the time of the bear festival

[104] Cf. Chiri, *The Ainu Dictionary*, III, 143–45.
[105] *Ibid.*, pp. 391–92.
[106] *Ibid.*, pp. 601–2.
[107] *Ibid.*, pp. 521–22.
[108] *Ibid.*, p. 686.

(*Iyomante*), while the bear's head with the skin of the body attached is known as *oruskor-marapto*. The feast that is a part of *Iyomante* is often called *kamui-maratto*. The origin of this term is not clear, but we are inclined to accept Kindaichi's thesis that the term *maratto*, or *marapto*, was either a corruption of, or at least related to, the Japanese term *marebito, marahito, marabito*, or marōdo, signifying the "visitor."[109] Whether or not this Japanese idea of the "visitor" had some connection with the Melanesian and Polynesian notions of the "foreigner" and of "hospitality," as suggested by Masao Oka, is another intriguing question, but beyond the scope of this paper.[110] The more immediate problem is the relation of the Ainu view of *maratto* to the Japanese concept of *marebito*. Regarding the latter, we share the view of Shinobu Origuchi and Ichiro Hori that the *marebito* was not just another human visitor, but that he was a *kami* who came to visit the world of man from *Tokoyo* ("the other world," that is, "the world of the *kami*") at certain appointed times and seasons. Hori has traced the residue of this belief in the rites preserved in the imperial palace and also among peasant communities in various sections of Japan and Okinawa. Generally, the *marebito* were believed to come on the eve of harvest season. But they were not the *kami* of the land. Rather, they were the *kami* from the distant world, and they "descended" to the world of man in order to assure certain benefits and blessings for the coming year. The *marebito* were invariably dressed in a straw hat and coat that signified the status of the *kami*, and either the mistress or the maiden of each household was to attend them all night.[111]

The Ainu view of *maratto-ne* ("to become a visitor or a guest"; *ne* means "to be" or "to become") used in connection with the bear shows singificant similarities with the ancient Japanese notion of the descent of *marebito*. However, the bear is not the only visitor from *moshiri* of the *kamui;* all animals, birds, insects, fish, plants, trees, and even inanimate things are believed to be *kamui* who are "visiting" the world of man in their respective "disguises," because the world of man is more beautiful than the world of the *kamui*. According to Kindaichi, the Ainus believe that the *kamui* call the world of man the "cradle of the *kamui*," and the female *kamui* often come down here to give birth to children.[112]

Once the *kamui* visit (*maratto-ne*) the world of man wearing some "dress" or disguise, be it the form of owl, hare, or what not, they cannot return to their own *moshiri* unless man robs them of their "dress" or disguise. In this process, the *kamui* give their flesh, and/or furs, to men as

---

[109] Kindaichi, "Ainu no Kami to Kuma no Setsuwa," *op. cit.*, p. 51.

[110] Masao Oka, "Ijin sono Ta," *Minzoku*, III, No. 6, 79–119.

[111] Cf. Shinobu Origuchi, " 'Tokoyo' oyobi 'Marebito,' " *Minzoku*, IV, No. 2, 1-62; Hori, *Waga-kuni Minkan-shinko-shi no Kenkyu*, I, 336–40. Cf. also Alexander Slawik, "Zur Etymologie des japanischen Terminus marebito 'Sakraler Besucher,' " *Weiner Völkerkundliche Mitteilungen*, 2 Jahrgang, Nr. 1 (Wien, 1954), pp. 44–58.

[112] Kindaichi, *Ainu Life and Legend*, p. 50.

souvenirs, and they can return to the *moshiri* of the *kamui*, with all kinds of offerings from men. The *kamui* thus emancipated from their disguise, however, do not disappear altogether from the world of men. Their *seremak* ("soul" or "spirit"; *sere* means "back" or "rear" and *mak* means "behind") "remain" (*a-e-horai,* which literally means "I remain or sit upon") in or around the person who did the favor of "releasing" the *kamui* from the bondage of this world and watch over him and protect him in his daily life. From the standpoint of the man, one may accumulate as many *seremak* of the *kamui* as possible so that his own *seremak* will be strengthened and protected by the potency of the *seremak* of the *kamui.*[113]

The *seremak* of the *kamui* are also present in some sense in the man-made *inau* or *inao,* that is, whittled wooden wands. A group of such *inau* are collectively called *chipa* or *nusa.* They are usually made of wood or willow, with the long curled shavings pendent. "Some have short spirals directed upward and covered with bark at the lower end."[114] While the exact nature of *inau* cannot be defined, according to Batchelor, *inau* "must for the most part, and taken together with a variety of other subjects, be looked upon as fetishes, some of which are invested with life of a higher or lower degree and nature as the case may be, while others are to be considered as having no life at all apparent in any particular, though . . . the essence of life will be found to be latent in all."[115] However *inau* is defined, it is clearly the most significant religious symbol of the Ainus. In every Ainu house, at least two *inau* are set up in honor or as the symbol of the *abe-kamui* (the *kamui* of fire). There are also a number of whittled wands for outdoor use which are sometimes several yards long. And, "to every Ainu family such a row of *nusa* was a household altar and regarded as the most sacred place."[116]

Needless to say, the Ainu men consider the making of *inau* as a sacred task. Older Ainu men often devoted their remaining years to making *inau.*[117] Not only the finished *inau* but even the shavings are believed to possess some spiritual potency, so that healers and shamanic diviners often wipe the patient's body with *inau-rochi* ("shavings from the *inau*") for the purpose of healing the ailment.[118] It is almost as if the *inau* itself is a "visitor" from the *moshiri* of the *kamui.* At any rate, the Ainu offer *inau* to all kinds of *kamui* on every conceivable occasion. In a way, the *inau* is simultaneously both the man's highest offering to the *kamui* and the embodiment of the *seremak* ("soul" or "spirit") of the *kamui* who has come to their abode.

There is every reason to believe that the Ainus regard human beings likewise as temporary visitors on this earth. After they are emancipated from

[113] Kindaichi, "Ainu no Kami to Kuma no Setsuwa," *op. cit.,* p. 47.
[114] Hitchcock, "The Ainos of Yezo, Japan," *op. cit.,* p. 473.
[115] Batchelor, *The Ainu and Their Folk-Lore,* p. 92.
[116] Kindaichi, *Ainu Life and Legend,* p. 24.
[117] Cf. Greey, *The Bear-Worshippers of Yezo,* p. 77.
[118] Chiri, *The Ainu Dictionary,* III, 461.

the bondage of human disguise, the *seremak* of the deceased become *seremax* or *seremaka* ("ancestors"). This belief is well expressed in the funeral rites of the Ainus. The Ainu custom of keeping the wake is characterized by the sorrow of parting, on the one hand, and the effort to console the deceased by telling amusing tales or singing songs or narrative poems, on the other. When death occurs, the deceased is carefully clad and laid out, and food and drink are placed beside the body. Then, having no professional priest, the head of the family prays to the *abe-kamui* ("the *kamui* of fire") to take charge of the soul of the deceased and guide it to the heavenly abode. The presiding elder solemnly addresses the dead man by saying: "While you were alive you were an Ainu just like one of us, but you have become like unto the gods [*kamui*], and can see and hear everything. We now, therefore, offer this food and drink for your acceptance. . . . Please partake thereof, for this is our 'good-bye' feast made especially for you."[119] Then a pair of leggings is placed on the legs of the body and a pair of mittens on its hands. The departed soul of the deceased is urged not to lose its way and to depend on the *abe-kamui* for guidance. According to Kindaichi, a rich dinner is served on the day of burial both for the deceased and also for the mourners. As the coffin is about to leave the house, the officiant again addresses the dead person as follows:

> In accordance with the hereditary custom, we have made a splendid staff to see you off. Take fast hold of the top of the staff and go your way straight, minding your feet, lifting them as you raise the staff, lowering them as you lower it, and looking neither to the right or to the left. You have plenty of food and *sake* as souvenirs. Go quickly and delight your old ancestors with your presents. Don't think you have had brothers and sisters and relatives in this world. Go your way without hankering after them. They are safe and sound under the care of the old Goddess of Fire [*abe-kamui*]. People will laugh at you if you yearn after them. This you must know well. Never behave in such a foolish manner.[120]

The Ainus bury the dead with their earthly possessions, such as swords, bows, and quivers for the man, and jewelry, kitchen utensils, and weaving looms for the woman.

The Ainus are under the impression that they have to do a favor for the dead by destroying their earthly memories and sentimental ties. Thus a part of the house is broken to carry out the coffin, and the broken part is repaired immediately so that the spirit of the dead cannot find the way to come home.[121] Also, the mourners walk backward from the graveyard until they

---

[119] Batchelor, *The Ainu and Their Folk-Lore*, p. 556.

[120] *Ainu Life and Legend*, pp. 43–44. The "staff" mentioned in this exhortation refers to the gravepost.

[121] *Ibid.*, p. 44. "When the mistress of the house is dead, her body is carried out of the house

come to a turning-point. The widow is not supposed to mention her dead husband's name, because pronouncing his name will bring his soul back to this earth. It is the custom of the Ainus to hold *shinnurappa* ("the great festival") three times a year, commemorating all the ancestors, by inviting friends and relatives. On such occasions, "a small *inau* is specially set up before one of the large *chipa* [or *nusa*]; and there some offerings are made and very consolatory prayers duly said to the spirits of the dead."[122] In all of this, the Ainus follow minutely the sacred tradition transmitted by the ancestors *(Ekashi uruoka hoppa itak)*, which are ultimately attributed to the heavenly model of the *moshiri* of the *kamui* revealed, as it were, by the *kamui* themselves.

The traditional beliefs of the Ainus in the *kamui* and in the correspondence of the world of *kamui* and that of man, however, are not formulated in doctrinal systems. Rather, they are practically "lived" and "acted out" in their daily attitudes toward all animate and inanimate beings which the Ainus consider as temporary "visitors." Of all the *kamui* who become "visitors" *(maratto-ne)*, the heavenly visitor par excellence is the bear.

## THE BEAR FESTIVAL ("IYOMANTE")

The prominent role that the bear plays in the traditional life of the Ainus can hardly be exaggerated. Like other fishing and hunting people who originated in the arctic and subarctic zones of northern Asia, the Ainus practiced many ceremonials related to the bear,[123] the most important among them being the bear festival *(Iyomante, Iyonmande, or Kamui Omante*, signifying "to see off" or "to send off" the *kamui*). While some scholars hold that *Iyomante* was not an indigenous feature of Ainu custom and that it was borrowed from some neighboring tribe, such as the Gilyak,[124] many others believe that *Iyomante* is as old as the oldest traditions of the Ainu race. Even if they had borrowed it from some other group, the Ainus most probably considered it their own by the time they migrated to Sakhalin and Hokkaido many centuries ago, judging from the numerous myths concerning the bear that dominate the very structure of Ainu culture and society.

*The bear.*—The bear *(kimun kamui)* enjoys an exalted status both as the *kamui* of the mountain and the chief of the animal world. In this dual

---

under the pretense of moving her into another house. And the old house is burned down soon after."

[122] *Ibid.*, p. 48.

[123] Cf. A. Irving Hallowell, *Bear Ceremonialism in the Northern Hemisphere.* (Philadelphia: University of Pennsylvania, 1926) (published Ph.D. dissertation).

[124] This view was expressed in many writings of the late Ryuzo Torii, a prominent Japanese anthropologist. Cf. R. Torii, "Études archéologiques et ethnologiques des Ainu des Iles Kouriles," *Journal of the College of Science* (Imperial University, Tokyo), XLII (1919).

capacity, the bear becomes the "visitor" *(maratto-ne)* in the world of man. As such, the bear is simultaneously venerated, feared, and welcomed by the Ainus. As an animal, it gives flesh and furs to men, but the bear is stronger, fiercer, and mightier than other animals. Its kidney and bile (gall) are believed to possess a special potency and are used for medicinal purposes. Its virility is admired and envied by man.

When a young bear is caught, it is nursed by an Ainu woman as if it were a human baby. The Ainus know where the bears' dens are, when they hibernate, and how they eat, what they do, and why they behave the way they do. It is almost as if the Ainus project themselves into the world of the bear and also project the life of the bear into the world of the *kamui*, so that these three realms become interpenetrating and interfused. The Ainus' taboos regarding the bear, their contradictory attitudes toward it, and the myths that portray the bear at one time as the *kamui* and at other times as if it were human, reflect this three-dimensional view of the Ainus. For example, when an Ainu woman encounters a bear in the mountain, she assumes that the bear, having semihuman instincts, has come to "visit" her in order to have a glimpse of the hidden part of her body. Thus, she performs a magical act known as *hoparata* (*ho* refers to "the hidden part," *para* means "to spread," and *ta* means "to strike"), chanting the following incantation:

| | |
|---|---|
| *e-nukan rusui-pe* | (that which you want to see) |
| *e-nukan rusui kusu* | (in order to see) |
| *e-iki-p ne nankor* | (you must have come) |
| *pirika-no nukar* | (take a look at it to your satisfaction) |
| *pirika-no nukar* | (repeats last line) |

She would also utter, "hus! hus!" (that is, a husky breathing sound) toward the bear, and then, they believe, the bear would not harm her.[125] And yet, the same Ainu woman would have no difficulty in regarding the bear as an exalted visitor from the world of the *kamui*, and venerate it.

Inevitably, the numerous Ainu myths about the *kamui*, the bear, and man have similar and interchangeable motifs. The usual accounts regarding the beginnings of the world and of man are summarized by Kindaichi as follows:

According to Ainu mythology, heaven was governed by two brother gods. The elder had six daughters. . . . When by order of the elder god of heaven the god of land-creation descended and created the world of men, it was a desolate world without trees and grasses. After considering who should be the first deity to govern this world, he at last chose

[125] Chiri, *The Ainu Dictionary*, III, 47, 67.

Princess Chikisani (literally means "wood with which we strike fire," or a kind of elm-tree) to be goddess of it. . . .

Now the younger god of heaven had been in love with Princess Chikisani for some time. Evening after evening he secretly descended from heaven and called on her. Thanks to this, fire was brought down to this lower world. But as the light was seen twinkling every night in this world, the secret was revealed. The two were envied so much that war at last broke out. All the gods in heaven and earth made incessant attacks upon them, and they had little time to take their rest and meals. Wherever the younger god in love went, there fire burned. When the enemies came, he was gone, and only the charred earth and grass were found. So he was nicknamed "Land-burner" or "village-burner." Chikisani was with child by him, and in due time she was delivered of a boy, who was named Pon Okikurumi (Younger or Smaller Okikurumi). He was the founder of the human world and established Ainu civilization. Professing himself to be an Ainu or a man, this god lived the same life as the Ainu do to-day. The people called him, therefore, *Ainu-rak-kur* ("man smelling of the Ainu" or "man like an Ainu"). . . . He is also called *Aeoina Kamui* [or Oina Kamui, meaning "our hereditary god"].[126]

A similar motif runs through the myth of the bear as recorded by Batchelor, although in this case the bear is the central figure. According to this account, there was a man and a wife in the remote past. The husband died, but the wife later gave birth to a boy. When others asked her who the father of the child was, the widow gave the following answer:

> One evening there was a sudden appearance in the hut in which I was sitting. He who came to me had the external form of a man, and was dressed in black clothing. On turning in my direction he said—"O, woman, I have a word to say to you, so please pay attention. I am the god who possesses the mountains (i.e., a bear), and not a human being at all, though I have now appeared to you in the bodily form of a man. The reason of my coming is this. Your husband is dead, and you are left in a very lonesome condition. I have seen this, and am come to inform you that you will bear a child. He will be my gift to you. . . ." After saying this he left me.[127]

And, according to this account, the boy thus born became the father of the Ainus. There are many other similar accounts that also suggest that the *kamui* descend to the world of the animals and to the world of man, that basically all animate and inanimate parts of this world share the same *kamui* nature. This basic affirmation of the Sacred that underlies the realm of

---

[126] Kindaichi, *Ainu Life and Legend*, pp. 56–57.
[127] Batchelor, *The Ainu and Their Folk-Lore*, pp. 9–10.

existence gives a sense of dignity to everything and every being that exists. And this affirmation of the source of life enables the Ainus to say either that they are the descendants of Okikurumi (*Ainu-rak-kur* or *Oina-kamui*) or that they are the descendants of the bear who was really the *kamui* of the mountain in human disguise.

In this connection, Kindaichi calls our attention to a myth that relates Okikurumi to the bear. According to this account, they did not see each other at first when they both descended to this world. Thus, when Okikurumi made *sake* and invited other *kamui*, the bear *(kimun-kamui)* was not invited. Nevertheless, the bear invited himself to Okikurumi's feast and sat near the entrance to the hut. When the bear left, Okikurumi, wondering who this impressive looking *kamui* was, followed his footsteps and, after climbing the mountain, finally reached a golden house on the top. The master of the house, who was none other than the strange *kamui* himself, pricked Okikurumi's knee with a reed, and the latter felt a terrible pain. Thereupon, the strange *kamui* told Okikurumi as follows: "You and I were sent by the great god to govern the world as a pair of rulers. But you have thus far ignored me and invited other *kamui* whose status is far below mine. This is why I am punishing you now. If you desire to remain alive, you must promise me that you will instruct men to offer the *inau*, food, and drinks to us, the *kamui* of the mountian, when we become 'visitors' *(maratto-ne)* in the world of man." This Okikurumi promised, and the *kimun-kamui* immediately cured his pain, and, needless to say, Okikurumi taught men to treat the bear courteously when it visits the world by offering the *inau*, food, and drinks and performing an elaborate feast of sending off the *kamui (Iyomante)*.[128]

This account is interesting because it elevates the *kimun-kamui* (the *kamui* of the mountain, i.e., the bear) to a position at least equal to that of Okikurumi. Thus, in the eyes of the Ainus, the bear deserves to receive courtesy and respect. When a bear is killed, its meat is carried into the house through a special window.[129] This window, known as *kamui kush puraya* ("the window through which the *kamui* pass"), is located in the east end, opposite the entrance, and behind the window stands the outside *nusa* (Fig. 1). According to a legend told to Greey, in ancient times there was a *kamui* named Kocha who was skilled in fishing and hunting. He used to put bear meat and fish at the window of the Ainus' huts. Undoubtedly, the ignorance of the Ainus offended Kocha, who decided to quit the Ainus and return to heaven. Since then, the Ainus believed that only the *kamui* should look through the window of the hut. But when an Ainu "is going to fish for seals,

---

[128] Kindaichi, "Ainu no Kami to Kuma no Setsuwa," *op. cit.*, pp. 48–51.

[129] Hallowell, *op. cit.*, p. 134. "Correspondences to this practice are, curiously enough, characteristic of such remote peoples as the Lapps on the one hand and the Micmac Indians of eastern America on the other." Regarding the "holy door" of the Scandinavian Lapps see Carl-Martin Edsman, "Bear Rites among the Scandinavian Lapps," *Proceedings of the IXth International Congress for the History of Religions* (Tokyo: Maruzen, 1960), p. 30.

or hunt a bear, his harpoon or his spear and bows and arrows are passed through the window; and on his return every thing he captures is taken into the house through the same aperture."[130]

The religious significance of the Ainu hut as an earthly center or meeting place of the *kamui*, modeled after the house in the *kamui moshiri*, should be mentioned. Many present-day Ainus build their houses in semi-Japanese style, but their parents and grandparents invariably lived in traditional dwellings. Those who have firsthand knowledge of the old Ainu huts complain that household comfort was not of paramount importance. What was important to the Ainus was that the original hut had descended from the *kamui moshiri* with the *kamui* of fire, and no matter how humble the hut was, it was regarded as *kamui kat tumbu* ("the room which the *kamui* built") or *chirange tumbe* ("the room which descended"). These huts were built according to the tradition of the ancestors, with simple log posts and beams covered with thatch. Also, following an ancient belief, the Ainus painted boat-shaped marks on the beams with dog's blood; this practice, called *chise-senitex-konte*, was believed to protect the house from evil spirits.[131] In the center of the unfloored room the hearth was built. When the hut was

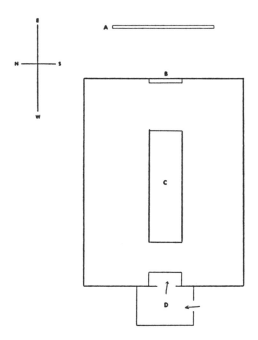

FIG. 1.—Floor plan of an Ainu hut. *A*, outdoor *nusa* (whittled wands); *B*, the *kamui* window; *C*, hearth; *D*, entrance.

130 Greey, *op. cit.*, p. 131.
131 Chri, *The Ainu Dictionary*, III, 250.

destroyed, it too was believed to return to the *kamui moshiri*. Unfortunately, the most important part of the hut was the window of the *kamui* on the east end. According to Batchelor, the prayers to the *kamui* and the ancestors ought to be addressed through this window. "Also, when *inao* [*inau*] are to be placed among the *nusa* outside, they should be made and consecrated by the hearth and then passed through the window. So, too, when a bear or deer or bird has been killed, it ought always to be taken into the house through the east window."[132] That is to say, the "visitor" from the *kamui moshiri* is courteously "invited" into the earthly temple where it is warmly welcomed by the *abe-kamui* ("the kamui of fire"), and the "visitor" and the "hostess" are believed to spend all night visiting. Men and women gather around the hearth and entertain the *kamui* by singing and dancing, and the following day the flesh of the "visitor" is eaten in the feast. Offerings are placed before the *maratto* ("the head of the bear"), and the *kamui* is "sent off" with prayers and souvenirs from this world.

Whether such general rituals connected with the hunt preceded the more elaborate and less frequent *Iyomante*, as Hallowell is inclined to conclude, is a difficult question that cannot be discussed here.[133] We may with interest note that the simple hunting rites and *Iyomante* have exactly the same motif. An old myth recorded by Kindaichi describes the motif in the words of a female bear:

> I used to live with my parents and two brothers. They often "visited" the world of man, and "returned" home with drinks, food, and *inau*. I envied them and wanted to become a "visitor" (*maratto-ne*) myself, but my family urged me not to do so, because of my excitable temperament that might scare the Ainus.
>
> One day, I wanted to eat the *shikerebe-ni* ("Phellodendron amurense") berries and "descended" from the mountain. While I was eating the berries, two arrows stuck on my neck. Although I wanted to run, I was held back by *un-kotuk kamui* ("the *kamui* of *un-kotuk* or the resin of the Pecea ajanensis," meaning the poison of the arrow) and fell on the ground. Two young men came to worship me.
>
> In the morning, many men came to me, and took my meat from my body. They carried me to a big hut in the village. The *abe-kamui* ("the kamui of fire") of that house, well dressed and leaning on a golden stick, warmly welcomed me, and I became the "visitor" (*maratto-ne*) in that house. While I was enjoying my visit with the *abe-kamui*, men and women gathered in the house and "kept a feast" (*marapto-an*).[134]

---

[132] Batchelor, *The Ainu and Their Folk-Lore*, p. 123.

[133] Hallowell, p. 135.

[134] This is a very brief outline of the account given in Kindaichi, "Ainu no Kami to Kuma no Setsuwa," *op. cit.*, pp. 41–43.

Kindaichi also records another *kamui-yukar* that is an autobiography of a young and beautiful female bear. According to her own account:

> I was instructed by the chief *kamui* to watch over my lazy husband. One day my younger sister brought me some millet which was brought back by my brother who had returned from the world of man. Although my sister gave it to me personally, my lazy husband got up suddenly and ate it all, and made me very sad.
>
> When my sister came again with food for me next time, she brought me the message from my brother to the effect that I should not let my lazy husband touch the gift. This angered my husband, and he not only killed my dear sister but also my brother as well. Whereupon I became furious and fought my husband with all the strength left in me. But he was so strong that I was severely wounded.
>
> When I came to myself, I found my body was hanging from a tree, and not far from my body was lying the body of a wild bear (meaning "my husband"). Suddenly, Okikurumi appeared and cursed my husband and kicked him to the world of darkness.
>
> Then Okikurumi carefully took the meat from my skin and performed an elaborate feast of "sending off the bear" for me as well as for my brother and sister. As a token of my gratitude, my *seremak* ("spirit" or "potency") has been remaining *(a-e-horari)* with the soul of Okikurumi ever since.[135]

The sacred traditions phrased and rephrased in numerous ways enable us to understand something of the Ainus' attitude toward the bear—an attitude which, to outsiders, appears very complicated and contradictory. To the Ainus, no less than to the Scandinavian Lapps, the bear is an honored "visitor" from the world of the *kamui* and as such deserves all the gifts and prayers offered by man. At the same time, the bear is the host, inviting men and women to a great festival. The bear that comes from the mountains is believed to "return" to his world and thereafter to return to be hunted again and again to receive the same honors.[136] Furthermore, according to the traditional belief of the Ainus, the *kamui* needs man's assistance in order for him to return to the *kamui moshiri;* in this sacred work man earns the spiritual potency *(seremak)* of the *kamui* to protect and strengthen him.

These motifs are intricately woven into, and dramatically "acted out," in the bear festival *(Iyomante)* which is the supreme religious act of the traditional Ainu community. The entire ritual moves slowly like a kaleidoscope from the scene in which the bear is affectionately spoken to as though it were a dear friend to the scene in which the bear is saluted as a

---

[135] *Ibid.,* pp. 44–47. My translatiion has simplified Kindaichi's version.
[136] Edsman, *op. cit.,* p. 31.

*kamui*. The prayers, dancing, and singing reflect various moods and motifs that are sorrowful, joyful, or melancholy. And when the whole thing is over, the bear has become none other than the *chinukara-kuru* ("the guardian") who is distant and yet very near and dear!

*The rites of Iyomante.*—There are a number of eyewitness descriptions of the bear festival *(Iyomante)* of the Hokkaido Ainus. Among them, Greey's does not mention the exact date on which he participated, but we know that he first toured Hokkaido and Sakhalin in 1853 and that he witnessed *Iyomante* at a small Ainu village called Hokuyak-bets.[137] Scheube saw *Iyomante* at Kunnai near Oshamambe around 1880.[138] Batchelor, who lived for over fifty years among the Hokkaido Ainus, has contributed perhaps the most factual account (even though somewhat colored by his views) and the one with the most comprehensive type of information on the subject.[139] Other versions by Japanese travelers and scholars are also important to fill us in on details. As stated earlier, the present writer participated in *Iyomante* on August 3, 1958, at Piratori.

To begin our description, then, we may note that a bear's cub is caught alive—usually toward the end of the winter—and is well cared for until September or October when *Iyomante* is held; however, the timing of the festival is actually flexible. While most small-scale *Iyomante* take place around an Ainu-type dwelling, the one at Piratori was held in the village playground with a temporary hut and *nusa* set up for the occasion. The whole series of rites usually lasts for three days.

Little needs to be said about the long period of preparation that precedes the festival itself. During this time, the bear cub is put in a cage that is placed behind the sacred window of the *kamui* (*kamui kush puraya* or simply *kamui puraya*). The bear cub *(hepere)* is given the utmost courtesy and affection. It is fed dried fish, millet, and, according to Scheube and Batchelor, it is even given human milk. Batchelor witnessed a group of women sitting in a circle, giving their breasts to the *hepere* by turns.[140] The *hepere*'s cage is usually about 10 feet high and 7 feet square, and each of the four corner poles has on its top an *inau* that is to watch over the "visitor" inside the cage. On one side, there is a hole through which food is given to the *hepere*. When the time approaches, whoever holds the *Iyomante* sends the following invitation to friends and relatives: "I, so and so, am about to sacrifice the little divine thing who resides among the mountains. My friends

[137] Greey, *op. cit.*, pp. 133–54.

[138] Scheube, "Die Bärencultus und die Bärenfeste des Ainos . . . ," *op. cit.*

[139] Important among the writings of Batchelor on the subject are his *Ainu and Their Folk-Lore*, chap. xlii, pp. 479–96, and "The Ainu Bear Festival," *op. cit.*

[140] Batchelor, *Ainu and Their Folk-Lore*, p. 484.

and masters, come ye to the feast; we will then unite in the great pleasure of sending the god [*kamui*] away. Come."[141]

Meanwhile, millet is pounded and made into cakes with a simple mortar and pestle. This is done to the accompaniment of a kind of community singing. The millet cakes and dumplings are not only offered to the *hepere* to be taken in remembrance to his home in the mountains but also are eaten by the guests. Much millet (*piyapa*) wine is brewed for the occasion. The Ainus are careful that the intoxicant should not attract evil spirits, and for this purpose the *inau* of *kotankor kamui* ("the *kamui* of the village," that is, the owl) is placed on top of the barrel. The millet wine (*kamui-ashkoro* or "ferment for the *kamui*") is also offered both to the *kamui* and to the guests.[142] In addition to the millet cakes and wine, new *inau* and ceremonial arrows have to be made. The latter, known as *hepere-ai* ("arrows for the bear cub"), are not meant to inflict injury when they are thrown at the *hepere*, but rather they are considered as gifts which are to be taken back to heaven by the "visitor." Usually, the male *hepere* receives fifty and the female sixty. At the time that they make new *inau* and *hepere-ai*, they also make a rope with which the *hepere* is to be tied, a ceremonial robe for the animal, and earrings (*kamui ninkari*).

The guests, both men and women, old and young, put on ceremonial dresses and earrings. As was mentioned earlier, the Ainu women's formal attire recalls that of the ancient shamanic diviner. The women are elegant in their jewels, caps, and colored clothes. As the guests arrive, a series of elaborate greetings and salutations are exchanged within the group made by the host and his guests. The men rub their hands together, drawing back first on the right and then on the left, and also rub their own knees gently, again first on the right side and then on the left, etc. The women rub one another's head above the ears. While they go through these motions, they inquire after one another's health. A number of *inau* are stuck in the hearth as offerings to various *kamui*. Later the *inau* are carried outside and placed at the *inau-san* ("the wand-domain"). The host offers millet wine (*kamui-ashkoro*) to the *abe-kamui* ("the *kamui* of fire") and other *kamui*, followed by the guests who murmur prayers as they do so. First they exculpate themselves before the *kamui* for what they are about to do the following day and ask the *abe-kamui* to notify the other *kamui* that the *hepere* will return to the home of its parents. Having finished their prayer inside the hut, they go out and pay respects to the *hepere*, offering it some millet wine. Then follows the dance of the women and maidens before the cage.

[141] Quoted in *ibid.*, p. 486.
[142] Kindaichi, *Ainu Life and Legend*, pp. 36–37. "The Ainu in the island of Karahuto [Sakhalin] do not always offer *Sake* when they worship their gods. If they happen to have any, they offer it to them. If they have not, they offer a kind of leek or garlics instead, eat some of them and pray to the gods. It seems to us that this was an older way of praying to the gods."

This part of the proceedings was minutely recorded by Greey. According to his account, women brought food to the cage, and the foster-mother softly spoke to the *hepere*, saying, "I beg of you to be patient, and not to bite, my son." Then, men and women danced around the cage, singing: "To-day we worship you as a god, therefore eat what we offer, and enjoy yourself."[143] According to the ancient custom, only *upopo* ("to sing lustily together") is allowed for consoling the *kamui*. This is a type of dancing and singing by women beating on, say, wooden boxes with the palms of their hands. Usually, the first part of the song is sung in unison, followed by two groups singing antiphonally. The songs sung at Piratori included such simple themes as "The *kamui* has descended from heaven to the branch of the tree," and "The *kamui* has descended from the eastern sky to the hill-side, for we hear a clinking sound of gold there." These phrases are repeated again and again. As the number of participants grows and enthusiasm mounts, people get up and dance, changing their hand gestures depending on the themes of the singing.[144] Then men and women enjoy a feast that lasts until early in the morning. There is a strict taboo that forbids *uko-pirkap-kor* ("sexual intercourse") that night. If anyone has violated the taboo, it is believed that the *hepere* will not run the following day during the festival; when this happens, the ritual is temporarily terminated, and the violaters are sought out so that they may atone before the *kamui*, and only then might the ritual be resumed.[145]

The main part of the *Iyomante* takes place on the second day. In the festival at Piratori, this occasion fell on August 3, 1958. From the temporary hut we could see the outdoor *nusa* with six *inau* and *takusa* ("a stick with the tuft made of Arundinaria," which is used to brush down the bear when it refuses to move). Between the six *inau* was a stick with a V-shaped top on which the head of the bear was to be placed later. In addition, swords, bows, arrows, and ornaments for the bear were suspended there (Fig. 2). Behind the *kamui* window of the hut was the cage, and not far from it stood *tush-op-ni* ("the tree for tying up"—a stake ornamented with *inau* and leaves of Arundinaria to which the bear was tied in order to rest in the midst of the ritual). Inside the hut, we could see men and women sitting around the hearth. The chiefs wore crownlike *shaba umpe* ("a ceremonial bark headdress, plaited of the bark of a wild vine and adorned with spiral shavings, bear's claws, etc.") and carried heavily ornamented swords. In addition to the three presiding elders, the functionaries for the occasion included (1) a young man who was to put the rope around the *hepere* in his cage, (2) a middle-aged man whose duty was to wave *inau* over the *hepere* during the

[143] Greey, *op. cit.*, p. 135.

[144] Japanese National Commission for UNESCO, *Japan—Its Land, People and Culture* (Tokyo: Japanese Government Printing Bureau, 1958), p. 781.

[145] Chiri, *The Ainu Dictionary*, III, 162.

ritual to keep evil spirits away, (3) an elderly man to clothe the *hepere* in a festive robe, (4) a young man to hold ceremonial arrows that were to be distributed among the guests later on, (5) a young man who was to put earrings and other ornaments on the *hepere*, and (6 and 7) two husky men who were assigned to do the ceremonial dressing of the bear's carcass after its death.

The highlights of the ritual may be described briefly in the following order:

1. *Uweshopki* ("to sit facing one another") in the hut. As the guests sit around the hearth, one of the elders prays to the *kamui*, asking for their assistance in carrying on this important festival without mishap. Then, the host, who is the owner of the bear, goes to the cage and murmurs a long

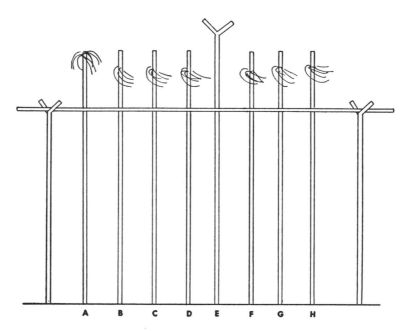

FIG. 2.—*Nusa* at Piratori. *A, takusa; B, inau* for the *hepere's* parents; *C, inau* for the chief of the world of bear; *D, inau* for the owl; *E*, pole to put the bear's head on; *F* and *G, inau* for the *hepere; H, inau* for the *kaumi* of the village (eagle-owl).

prayer addressed to the *hepere*. One such prayer, recorded by Batchelor, runs as follows:

O thou divine one, thou wast sent into the world for us to hunt. O thou precious little divinity, we worship thee; pray hear our prayer. We have nourished thee and brought thee up with a deal of pain and trouble, all because we love thee so. Now, as thou hast grown big, we are about to send thee to thy father and mother. When thou comest to them, please speak well of us, and tell them how kind we have been; please come to us again and we will sacrifice thee.[146]

Kindaichi records a similar, but more direct, version of such a prayer, which runs: "You are now grown up; it is time for you to go back to your father and mother, who are now deities in the world of gods. You shall have a lot of souvenirs, with which your parents will be greatly delighted. Go straight to your parents without hanging about on your way, or some devils will snatch the souvenirs. Go back straight and quick!"[147]

2. Dancing around the cage. This is the kind of *upopo*, sung "lustily" together, which was explained earlier. This is to be the last human dance the *hepere* can enjoy on this earth, and the *upopo* is meant to assure the *hepere* that it ought to accept the role willingly and quietly because it is the only way that the "visitor" can return to heaven. The theme of the *upopo* is a simple one: "As we are getting ready to send the *hepere* to the *kamui moshiri* ("the world of the *kamui*"), let us all get up and join in, and sing and dance for this festive occasion." The phrase is repeated a number of times.

3. The roping. About noon that day, the young man appointed for the task climbed to the top of the cage with a rope and, after several unsuccessful attempts, managed to put the rope around the *hepere*. The logs on the top of the cage were removed, and with the help of two other men, the man in charge of the roping pulled the *hepere* out of the cage.

4. Farewell walk of the *hepere*. Now the *hepere* is led around the sacred ground several times, ostensibly to bid farewell to the participants. The rope is tied to the cub in such a way that two men can hold the two ends of the cord at a distance from the "visitor." They try to make the *hepere* "play around." If it does not move, the man with the *takusa* ("the stick with a tuft made of Arundinaria") tickles the *hepere* with it. From time to time, the *hepere* is tied to the *tush-op-ni* ("the tree for tying up") so that it can rest a while. As the *hepere* passes in front of the guests, people shoot *hepere-ai* ("arrows for the cub") at the "visitor." These are also called the "flower arrows" because they have, instead of barbed points, blunt wooden ends decorated with a piece of red cloth. Although the *hepere-ai* are offered to the departing "visitor" as a souvenir, people can take them home as good-luck charms.[148] We were told that only the owner of the *hepere* uses a special arrow without the red color. Describing this part of the ceremony, Batchelor writes: "The shouting now becomes deafening, and the bear sometimes

---

[146] Quoted in Batchelor, *The Ainu and Their Folk-Lore*, p. 487.

[147] Quoted in Kindaichi, *Ainu Life and Legend*, p. 53.

[148] On that occasion, the writer and his wife, as well as Kingdom Werner Swayne, then American Consul at Sapporo, were also invited to shoot the *hepere-ai*.

furious. But the wilder the bear becomes the more delighted do the people get."[149]

5. Shooting the final arrow. This part of the ceremony seems to have varied, according to different eyewitness accounts. Batchelor reported that the *hepere* was dragged along to the place of throttling.

> While being so dragged two young men rushed forward and seize him by the face and ears and others catch hold of his fore and hind legs. He is thus taken to two poles lying on the ground, having had an *inau*-wand thrust in his mouth at which he bits hard. In some places an arrow is shot into his heart and all the blood carefully caught in a vessel and drunk warm by the elders. . . . In some places, however, the creature is not given the *coup de grâce* by the arrow till after the throttling has commenced.[150]

At Piratori, arrows were used to dispatch the *hepere*, not once but two or three times. The blood was caught carefully and drunk. Those who drink fresh bear's blood at *Iyomante* have to stay away from women until the coming of the new moon. If they do not do so, it is believed that they will die. For this reason, only the elders are urged to drink the bear's blood warm.[151]

6. *Rekuchi numba* ("squeezing the bear's throat"). This part of the rite is conducted near the outside *nusa*. Two long poles (*ok numba ni* or "poles for strangling") were used to clamp the neck of the *hepere*.[152] Many Ainus tried to take part in this throttling of the animal while women chanted in a mournful way. (The blood from the bear is sometimes sprinkled on paper and sent to sick people.[153])

7. *Iri* ("skinning the bear"). This is also called the *kamui memanke* ("the cooling of the *kamui*"). After the animal died, it was skinned, except for the ears, the paws, and some three inches of the snout. It was then carried into the hut through the *kamui* window and placed on a mat. Prayers of all kinds were offered to the *kamui* while women sang and danced two kinds of *upopo* and one *shinotcha* ("song") outside the hut. The *upopo* sung at this time were the same ones which had been sung previously. The *shinotocha* was a tender love song, which is said to attract benevolent *kamui*. In some instances, as reported by Greey and Scheube, the skinning does not take place until the following day.

8. Post mortem. Batchelor provides us with the most detailed account of

[149] Batchelor, *Ainu and Their Folk-Lore*, p. 488.

[150] Batchelor, "The Ainu Bear Festival," *op. cit.*, pp. 40–41.

[151] Chriri, *The Ainu Dictionary*, III, 250.

[152] See the picture in Kindaichi, *Ainu Life and Legend*, p. 54, and the drawing in Greey, *op. cit.*, p. 139.

[153] Cf. Batchelor, "Ainu," *op. cit.*, p. 250.

the post mortem rites following the skinning. Greey reported that the foster-mother's husband "advanced with a sword, with which he touched the bear's eyes, nose, and ears, all the male Ainos following his example."[154] This may be a local custom. The rite at Piratori followed in the main the account of Batchelor, although the time was greatly shortened. According to Batchelor, following the skinning, food, drink, and *inau* were placed before the carcass. Then the inside of the stomach was taken out, and a portion of it was cooked in the hearth. A small segment of the cooked meat was placed under the snout of the bear. Also presented to the dead "visitor" was the *marapto itangi* ("the cup of the feast"), which was a bowl of soup with bear's meat in it. Batchelor records two sets of prayers to be said by the elder after the post mortem ceremonies:

> O divine cub, we present thee with these sacred wands, dried fish, dumplings and precious liquor. We offer them to thee. Take them with you to your forebears and say to them: I have been right well cared for for a long time by an Ainu father and mother. I have been preserved by them from harm, and have grown up. Now I come to thee. I bring with me many various good viands for a feast. Pray let us eat and rejoice! If you say this they will all be pleased and happy.
>
> My beloved cub, pray listen to me. I have cared for thee for a long time and now present thee with wands, dumplings. . . . Ride thou upon these wands and carry with thee the good things presented to thee. Go to thy father and mother. Be happy. Cause them to rejoice. Upon arrival, call together multitudes of divine guests and make a great feast. Come again unto us that we may once more rear thee and enjoy another feast with thee. I salute thee thou dead cub: Depart thou in peace.[155]

9. Decoration of *maratto* ("bear's head"). After the post mortem, the head of the *hepere* was removed from the skin, and the contents of the skull were taken out. Just as morticians decorate the face of the deceased, the Ainus decorated the *maratto* with various kinds of *inau*, such as the *inau* of the ears, the *inau* of the head, the *inau* of the nose, etc. All this was a preparation for the long journey which the "visitor" was to undertake to return home. The Ainus' sense of propriety in this matter, following the sacred tradition of their ancestors, is well expressed in the speech given by the chief, quoted by Greey. In his words:

> To-day we have built that god-fence, in order to honor the deity who lies there. You see it is formed of nice new mats, and that we have adorned it with the skulls of the god-bears who have gone before this one

[154] Greey, *op. cit.*, p. 138.
[155] Batchelor, "The Ainu Bear Festival," *op. cit.*, p. 42.

. . . with old swords, bows, and arrows. . . . The *arukitsufu* (god-bear) reclines with dignity upon a new mat, with his nose sniffing at cups of wine and oil. On either side of him are beautiful articles. . . . The bear has rings in his ears, and a sword on his left side; and those boxes contain the clothes he is going to wear, now he is a deity.[156]

While this elaborate preparation was going on, a number of dances take place. One of them, the *tapukaru*, is performed by long-haired old men, weaving back and forth while lifting their arms in the guise of praying. From time to time, they emit strange calls, and women clap their hands, shouting "au'cho!" "au'cho!" Women perform several kinds of *harara-shinot*, a sort of pantomime dance, imitating at one time wild geese and swallows flapping their wings, or at other times snipes. As they danced in a circle *(rimuse)*, they sang: "I am a bird, and I can fly / over the river and mountain / I am a *kamui*." Women also sang tender love songs *(shinotcha)*. Toward the end, men and women joined in a very rhythmical dance, called the *horippa*, which is a name given by the Hidaka tribe of the Ainus for a special kind of *upopo*. The *horippa* is believed to be especially effective in driving evil spirits away.[157]

10. *Keyomante* ("sending away" of the *kamui*). Now the head of the bear is taken to the *nusa* and placed on the V-shaped top of the pole, known as *keyomante-ni* ("the pole of sending away"). This pole is decorated with the *inau* and bamboo leaves, and a sword and quiver are suspended under the head of the bear. The *hepere* is now called *chinukara-kuru* ("the seer" or "guardian"), and the *maratto-sapa* ("bear's skull") is also called *kamui-sapa* ("the *kamui*'s head"). After a proper offering of *kamui-ashkoro* ("ferment for the *kamui*"), the elder bids farewell: "My god, to-day, I, the chief, send you forth as a god [*kamui*]. If you come again—as a little bear—next year, I will take care of you. Now you kindly leave."[158] Then the head of the "departing *kamui*" is turned toward the east, and the *keyomante-ai* ("the arrow of sending away") is shot toward the eastern sky, signifying the safe departure of the *kamui*. Immediately after the shooting of the *keyomante-ai*, the skull is turned around to face the west, and the main part of *Iyomante* comes to an end.

We were told by an elderly Ainu at Piratori that in former times the main part of *Iyomante* lasted all day and all night so that *keyomante* coincided with the first sign of the dawn of the following day. We were also told that *Iyomante* was not over until all the meat of the bear was consumed by the guests. According to Greey, he was presented with "a large iron pot con-

[156] Quoted in Greey, *op. cit.*, p. 143.
[157] For a more detailed explanation of these Ainu dances, see *Japan—Its Land, People and Culture*, pp. 781.
[158] Quoted in Greey, *op. cit.*, p. 144.

taining a stew made of bear's flesh, ground millet, *haa*-roots, and fish-oil."[159]
The skull of the bear, as well as the skulls of other animals, are hung on an
outside fence and are venerated as *akohsiratki kamui* ("divine preservers")[160]

*Postscript.*—The experience of participating in *Iyomante* is something
that cannot easily be forgotten. How to make sense out of it, however, is
quite a different problem. One approach would be to compare the Ainu bear
festival with similar rites of other peoples, especially those who also practice
various kinds of bear ceremonials. Such a study would help us to understand
not only man's general attitude toward these animals but also man's understanding of his relation to this mysterious cosmos, his destiny, and his view of
the ground of existence. Animal figures, like those preserved in cave art from
the Paleolithic age, clearly demonstrate that our ancestors felt a sense of
kinship with animals in that they, also, had an important place in the
universe. Prehistoric man undoubtedly had a quite different conception of
life from that of ours. In the words of Hallowell:

> To him the animal world often represents creatures with magical or
> superhuman potencies, and the problem of securing them for their hide,
> meat or fur involves the satisfaction of powers or beings of supernatural
> order. Consequently, strategy and mechanical skill are only part of the
> problem. Success or failure in the hunt is more likely to be interpreted
> in magico-religious terms than in those of a mechanical order.[161]

This line of inquiry, though important beyond doubt, is not what has
been attempted in the present paper. Our goal was much more modest in
scope and aim. We tried to show the Ainus as a tribe that can trace their
heritage to the prehistoric period; we tried to "understand" the racial
memories of a hundred generations of these people, preserved in sacred
traditions, in myths, symbols, and rituals. What struck us is the fact that the
oral traditions of the Ainus—hero epics, the *kamui yukar*, and others—and
their rituals complement each other to a remarkable degree. To be sure, the
Ainu understanding of the *kamui*, man, other beings, and nature, has never
been articulated in any system of doctrines or dogmas, but it has been acted
out in rituals.

Anyone's understanding of another people, especially so-called primitive
man, is colored by his own perspective and assumptions.

There seems to have been a pendulum swing from extreme to
extreme in speculations about primitive man. First he was a little more
than an animal who lived in poverty, violence, and fear; then he was a

[159] *Ibid.*, p. 146.
[160] Batchelor, "The Ainu Bear Festival," *op. cit.*, p. 44.
[161] Hallowell, *op. cit.*, p. 10.

gentle person who lived in plenty, peace, and security. First he was lawless; then he was a slave to law and custom. First he was devoid of any religious feelings or belief; then he was entirely dominated by the sacred and immersed in ritual. First he was an individualist who preyed on the weaker and held what he could; then he was a communist who held lands and goods in common. First he was sexually promiscuous; then he was a model of domestic virtue. . . .[162]

Obviously, the truth must be somewhere in between these extreme views. As far as we can tell, the Ainus certainly cannot be characterized in any simple category. They seem to have their share of all kinds of human virtues as well as weaknesses. Moreover, it is extremely dangerous to judge the Ainus on the basis of what we can know about them under present-day circumstances—on account of the constant influence of other cultural and ethnic groups throughout the ages. Some references were made in this paper to changes that took place in various aspects of their social and cultural life. We are, of course, fully aware of the fact that a great deal more research has to be done in order to delineate the indigenous tradition of the Ainus, apart from those elements that have been taken over from other peoples.

Nevertheless, Ainu study has advanced considerably during the present century. For example, even John Batchelor, who dedicated his whole life to the cause of the Ainus, failed to understand the nature of *Iyomante*. To him, it was first and foremost a sacrifice—"not a sacrifice to the gods, but an offering to the victim himself and his worshippers in common."[163] Today among scholars this notion of "sacrifice" in reference to *Iyomante* is no longer considered appropriate.[164] Also, as late as 1932, Batchelor wondered why, at the conclusion of the main part of *Iyomante*, the *keyomante-ai* ("the arrow of sending away") was shot "to the north-east part of the skies, as a parting salute." He said, "this is one of the great mysteries of Ainu religion which I have never yet heard them explain," and so he sets forth his own theory based on a description of the position of the north star *(chinukara-kuru)*.[165] But a more plausible explanation regarding the "eastern sky" may be found in Ainu belief, in regard to the soul of the deceased person, that the soul that ascends to the eastern sky is believed to be "pushed back by the *kamui*" *(kamui tasare)* to this earth again to enjoy life; whereas, the soul that ascends to the western sky will have no chance of returning *(ear-oman-no)*.[166] Thus, the Ainus, believing that the bear would return again to the world of man as a "visitor," would naturally send off the soul of the bear to the "eastern sky."

---

[162] Evans-Pritchard, *op. cit.,* p. 65.
[163] Batchelor, *The Ainu and Their Folk-Lore,* p. 482.
[164] Cf. Kindaichi, "Ainu no Kami to Kuma no Setsuwa," *op. cit.,* p. 52.
[165] Batchelor, "The Ainu Bear Festival," *op. cit.,* p. 44.
[166] Chiri, *The Ainu Dictionary,* III, 244.

These examples are cited to indicate that recent scholarship in Ainu studies has helped us to develop a greater and better understanding of Ainu life and religion.

We concentrated here on the rite of *Iyomante* among all the important festivities and ceremonials because *Iyomante* is the supreme act of the Ainu community transmitted from the remote past to the present time. It is the most significant communal ritual that solidifies the organic unity of the Ainu people since in this rite the people are made to realize that they are not simply men confined to the bondage of this earthly existence. Rather, they are made to feel the organic unity between this world of man and all other worlds of the *kamui*, so that "the participants recover the sacred dimension of existence, by learning again how the gods [*kamui*] or the mythical ancestors [Okikurumi, Ainu-rak-kur, or Aeoina kamui] created man and taught him the various kinds of social behavior and of practical work."[167]

[167] Mircea Eliade, *The Sacred and the Profane*, trans. Willard R. Trask (New York: Harcourt, Brace & Co., 1959), p. 90.

# 4

# THE MAKING OF A HISTORIAN OF RELIGIONS

Any attempt to reflect on the state of the history of religions *(Religions-wissenschaft)* in America might profitably begin with a candid recognition of its strange popularity in our time. Colleges and universities are offering an increasing number of courses to meet the growing enrollment in this field, and publishers are frantic in their search for new authors and new textbooks to capitalize on the current trends. As far as I can remember, the situation was vastly different twenty years ago when a handful of us studied the history of religions under the late Joachim Wach at the University of Chicago. We struggled then without the benefit of handsome fellowships or opportunities to study abroad, and our professional future did not look promising at all. Understandably, in those days the field did not attract many students. Today, we receive more applicants than we can responsibly handle in the discipline, even though our resources are much greater now than two decades ago.

It is significant to note, however, that many of those who wish to study the history of religions today are rebelling against their own religious traditions in one way or another, and not a few are looking for what amounts to a kind of new religion. Some are motivated by misguided enthusiasm for a subject matter that appears to be exotic and alluring. Only a small number of applicants seem to have even a vague notion of what the history of religions is all about. All in all, there seems to be a rather widespread ambiguity about the nature of the discipline in spite of, or because of, its popularity. The ambiguity is no less apparent among those who are teaching the subject today. We can cite many reasons for this, of course. For instance, in the days when the current professors were doing their graduate work, opportunities to study the history of religions were rather limited. In fact, a number of the presentday teachers had their academic training in some other field, and while many of them have acquired competence in this area more or less by their own initiative, some have not moved beyond the level of interested amateurs. Besides, the fact that many professors are expected to teach courses in two or three different areas does not allow them to devote an adequate amount of time and energy to scholarly pursuit in the field. Although the picture has improved greatly in this respect during the past few years, some college administrators who write to us nowadays asking for new instructors in the area still show an amazing lack of understanding of the nature of the discipline itself. It is not surprising, therefore, that the recent survey conducted by the History of Religions Committee of the American Council of Learned Societies regarding the proposed program of the scholar-in-residence revealed once again the ambiguity that haunts the subject.

It is a matter of utmost irony that practically every institution is in favor of teaching some phases of the history of religions, but many do not know exactly what it is or what to do with it in practice. In many cases, courses in the field are administered in departments of religion while others are taught in conjunction with studies of Asian cultures, philosophies, societies, and civilizations. In a number of situations, professors in religion departments and those in Asian studies collaborate in designing and teaching courses in the history of religions. I do not question the academic or practical rationale, necessity, and even advantage, of each of these arrangements. Nor do I deny the fact that the history of religions derives much of its data from the religions of Asia and Africa as well as from the so-called primitive religions. Indeed, many leading historians of religions have made notable contributions to the study of Hinduism, Buddhism, Islam, and primitive religions. I am, however, somewhat uneasy about the tacit assumption prevalent today that the history of religions is nothing but an inquiry into non-Western and non-Judeo-Christian faiths. This assumption becomes all the more ironic when it is pointed out that the checkered background of our discipline in the United States before World War II, as well as the current enthusiasm in many segments of the academic community and the dormant suspicion in some circles toward it, might have arisen from an oversimplified identification of the discipline solely with the subject matter of non-Western and non-Judeo-Christian religions.

## IN RETROSPECT

1. Since this is not the occasion to recount the well-known history of the religious and cultural heritage of America, it is probably sufficient to mention that the Protestant tradition, which for so long dominated the mainstream of American religious life, inherited a large amount of pietism from Europe. This accounts for the strong evangelistic temper and enduring biblicism, couched in moralistic tones, of American Protestantism. While it may be too simple to explain away the tension between the social gospel and fundamentalism, or between liberalism and neo-orthodoxy, in terms of the persistent pietist strand and the reaction against it, it is nevertheless true that American Protestantism, true to its fideist principle, has never questioned the superiority of the Christian revelation to other religions, the gospel (kerygma) to ecclesiastical tradition, and faith to understanding. In the course of time, the religious character of America came to be modified by the coming of large numbers of Catholics and Jews. However, both Roman Catholicism and

Judaism, as much as Protestantism, were primarily concerned with their own internal affairs, and did not exert significant scholarly influence on institutions of higher learning except in denominational institutions.

This does not imply, of course, that the religious groups in America were deprived of scholarship. Earlier, Jewish, Catholic, and Protestant seminaries either sent men to Europe for training or imported scholars from abroad. In most recent decades the divinity schools of the major private universities and the interdenominational theological seminaries have developed high-level scholarship, and have in turn helped to raise the scholarly standards of denominational seminaries. However, in all of them, serious study of other religions was not stressed. In the main, American religious groups sharply divided religions into two levels or categories: "their own" versus all others. From time to time they showed a great deal of interest in the teachings and practices of other religions of the world, motivated either by humanitarian or apologetic interests as reflected in a number of introductory courses on comparative religion in the seminaries and sectarian colleges. These latter courses, with some notable exceptions to be sure, either sentimentalized the differences among diverse religions or indulged in a superficial cataloguing of the main tenets of various religious systems, often with an implicit or explicit attempt to demonstrate the superiority of the Judeo-Christian tradition. Hence, even when critical insights were applied to the study of other religions, the sanctity of their own was carefully safeguarded. In short, American religious scholarship, which took seriously the European tradition of hermeneutics, especially in biblical studies, achieved practically no resonance with the heremeneutical tradition developed in the area of *Religionswissenschaft*.[1]

2. In sharp contrast with the mainstream of American religious tradition, the humanistic intellectual tradition in America has always shown keen interest in, or rather curiosity about, the religions and cultures of Asia. The impetus for such interest in Oriental subjects, coupled with either mild or strong antipathy toward the traditional Western religious systems, no doubt came originally from Europe. We might recall that the vogue of Chinese philosophy and Indian religions, which had captured the imagination of many European intellectuals from the time of the Enlightenment, had direct influence upon elite circles on the New Continent, so that a number of talented writers and artists, e.g., Emerson, Thoreau, La Farge, and Henry Adams, idealized and romanticized the "spiritual East." The fact that Edwin Arnold's *Light of Asia*, published in 1879 in England, soon went into eight editions in America indicates the widespread influence, however superficial, of Indian religion and Buddhism on the American reading public in the latter

[1] For a fuller discussion of this problem, see Philip H. Ashby, "The History of Religions," in Paul Ramsey, ed., *Religion*, Englewood Cliffs, N.J.: Prentice-Hall, 1965, pp. 3–49.

half of the last century.[2] In such an atmosphere, the World's Parliament of Religions, held in Chicago in 1893, much to the delight of humanistic intellectuals and some liberal Christians and Jews, generated enthusiasm for Eastern religions and philosophies. It is said that the establishment of many chairs of Oriental philosophy and comparative religion in the United States was occasioned by the Parliament. Probably the statement of purpose for the initiating of the Harvard Oriental Series indicates the mood of the time. It says, in part:

> The central point of interest in the history of India is the long development of the religious thought and life of the Hindus,—a race akin, by ties of blood and language, to the Anglo-Saxon stock. The value of the study of non-Christian religions is coming to be recognized by the best friends of Christianity more and more every day. The study tends to broaden and strengthen and universalize the base of religion,—a result of practical and immediate benefit. Works which promote this study stand first in the plans of the Oriental Series; and they are essentially timely now, when so much of the widespread interest in Buddhism and other Oriental systems is misdirected by half-knowledge, or by downright error concerning them.[3]

Notwithstanding the optimism of the above statement, the serious humanistic study of religions did not take root in American soil until recent years, except to a limited extent in the philosophy of religion and the study of languages. Significantly, many humanists also took it for granted that the religions of the world were to be divided into two levels or categories, only with the order reversed from that held by the pietist tradition. In this connection, the late D. T. Suzuki once spoke of how the free-lance philosopher Paul Carus and his father-in-law E. C. Hegeler, who invited him to come to America in 1897, regarded religions, especially Christianity and Buddhism. In Suzuki's words, "they believed that religion must stand on scientific foundations, and they thought that Christianity was based too much on mythology. . . . What impressed Dr. Carus and Mr. Hegeler about Buddhism was the fact that Buddhism was singularly free from such mythological elements. For example, in contrast with Christianity, which accepts Christ as God-man, Buddhism regards Buddha as a human being. In a sense, Buddhism may be regarded as rationalistic and positivistic. . . ."[4] Such an

[2] See Arthur E. Christy, "The Sense of the Past," in Christy, ed., *The Asian Legacy and American Life*, New York: The John Day Co., 1942, pp. 1–55.

[3] Quoted in Henry Clarke Warren, *Buddhism in Translation*, Harvard Oriental Series, Vol. III, Cambridge: Harvard University Press, 1896, p. 388.

[4] Daisetz Teitaro Suzuki, "Introduction: A Glimpse of Paul Carus," in J. M. Kitagawa, ed., *Modern Trends in World Religions*, La Salle, Illinois: The Open Court Publishing Co., 1959, p. x.

assumption, or I should say affirmation, about the nature of religion, however congenial it may have been to a certain philosophical temperament, was not conducive to the development of a well-balanced inquiry into the full range of Eastern religions, to say nothing of the study of the Judeo-Christian tradition and Islam. And yet, an amazing number of self-styled experts on Oriental religions have never questioned the validity of such an assumption or its variations, which are as one-sided and biased as is the Christian or Jewish apologist's approach to the study of religions. It is also to be noted that the American humanists' incurable romanticism vis-à-vis the religions of far-off lands had neither the benefit of edifying support nor such scholarly correctives as might have come from the disciplines of Indology, Buddhology, Sinology, and Islamics. These were hardly known in America—partly because the United States, unlike European colonial nations, had no political incentive to encourage serious Asian and African studies until World War II. Meanwhile, many Americans, under the spell of residual isolationism, religious prejudice, and racial bigotry, came to view Oriental religions and cultures as esoteric subjects that concerned only a tiny group of ivory-tower Orientalists, missionaries to the "heathen" lands, or talented crackpots. All this, however, changed markedly after the War.

## RECENT DEVELOPMENTS

Much has been written about the new mood that has penetrated the religious and intellectual outlook in America since the end of World War II. While we need not labor over the many internal and external factors that have together brought about significant changes in our time, we should refer to two matters of direct bearing upon the discipline of the history of religions: the expansion of non-Western studies, and the proliferation of departments of religion, especially in state universities.

1. It goes without saying that World War II marked a decisive turning point in the development of Asian studies in the United States. Before the War, American education, which was almost completely devoted to the study of the Western tradition, produced educated citizens who knew practically nothing about the non-Western world. As Meribeth E. Cameron once quipped, "few Americans could name any Asiatics except Confucius, Gandhi, and Chiang Kai-shek." But with the outbreak of hostilities, the national emergency required training programs in Asian subjects, and there appeared an amazing array of books and articles on Asia, from the very scholarly to the ridiculous. "Overnight the few experts on the Far East who had been clinging to the fringes of American academic life became national assets. Audiences were eager to hear about Asia, conferences of specialists and laymen multiplied, and the academic world was edified by the spectacle of college administrators eager to inaugurate courses on the Far East at the very moment at which many of those best qualified to give them were being called

into the armed forces or into government employment."[5] Further, the newly-aroused American interest in Asia did not diminish when the War ended. It grew even more in the post-war period, as testified by the steady increase in Asian and other non-Western studies at various universities, and the phenomenal growth of the Association of Asian Studies.[6]

Many educators and intellectuals—heirs of the humanistic tradition in America—remain critical, and with some justification, of hastily improvised courses on Asian subjects or lament the practice of devoting a large part of college education to the study of non-Western civilizations. As late as 1951, the former chancellor of the University of Chicago, in his preface to the Great Books Series, went so far as to say: "The pretense that we are now prepared within the educational system to include understanding the East as one main pivot in a liberal curriculum will obstruct, not assist, the solution of the central problem of producing a liberally educated generation." While acknowledging the eventual necessity of learning about non-Western traditions, he went on to say: "at the moment we have all we can do to understand ourselves in order to be prepared for the forthcoming meeting between East and West. . . . The time for that will come when we have understood our own tradition well enough to understand another."[7] In a sense, the vogue in Asian subjects sweeping the country today may be seen as a form of rebellion among present-day intellectuals against the hitherto accepted notion that the business of the American university is to teach primarily, if not completely, the intellectual and cultural tradition of the West, with the assumption that only when Americans have understood the Western tradition well enough, can they begin to understand another tradition. It is equally significant that current non-Western studies in America are no longer the monopoly of a few Orientalists or scholars of the humanities. An increasing number of disciplines in the social sciences are involved in non-Western subjects.[8] And in the name of interdisciplinary cooperation, the scholar of the history of religions is often welcomed or wooed to serve as the expert on religion in the program of non-Western studies.

2. Little needs to be said concerning the proliferation of departments of religion in various institutions. From all indications it seems clear that such questions as whether or not it is possible or desirable to provide courses in religion, and whether or not religion study is an essential ingredient of humanistic education, have been settled affirmatively in the minds of many

[5] Meribeth E. Cameron, "Far Eastern Studies in the U.S.," *The Far Eastern Quarterly*, VII, 2 (February, 1948), 119–20.

[6] In this article I discuss Asian studies primarily, although similar observations might be made of other non-Western studies.

[7] Robert Maynard Hutchins, *The Great Conversation*, in *Great Books of the Western World*, Vol. I, Chicago: Encyclopaedia Britannica, 1951, pp. 72–3 (my italics).

[8] See Felix M. Keesing, "Problems of Integrating Humanities and Social Science Approaches in Far Eastern Studies," *The Far Eastern Quarterly*, XIV, 2 (February, 1955), 161–8.

educators. However, we have a long way to go before coming to terms with equally difficult questions respecting the nature of the curriculum, the relation of religion studies to other disciplines of the university, and the quality and qualifications of the faculty.

However, some serious efforts are being made to grapple with these problems. Already, many departments of religion have formulated and experimented with curricula in very creative ways, with the result that their students receive better training than did their own teachers. Many present teachers are fully aware that their own training, either in interdenominational theological seminaries or in divinity schools affiliated with private universities, was strongly colored by a predominantly Protestant theological ethos. The efforts of these teachers to provide better balanced instruction in religion in a university setting have resulted in two main types of approach, with differing variations and combinations. The first is the interfaith approach, which takes into consideration the religious pluralism of American society. The second is the humanistic approach, which is primarily concerned with religion(s) as academic subject matter. I will not discuss the relative merits of these approaches. I want only to point out that both are attempts to provide in a university setting meaningful study in religion different in aim and character from that in seminaries and divinity schools. Nevertheless, I incline to agree with Clyde A. Holbrook's observation concerning the curricular offerings, in general, of departments of religion: "Courses in Western religions are more widely offered than those in Eastern religions; biblical courses make up more of the curriculum than do courses in religious phenomenology as such; Protestant orientations are more common in religious courses than are other forms of American religious traditions."[9] As one means of rectifying this situation, departments of religion in various universities are giving serious consideration to appointing more teachers in the history of religions.

## ACADEMIC MYOPIA

From a different perspective, it may be asserted that the strange popularity of the history of religions in our time is largely due to the academic myopia of American colleges and universities. I am not altogether unhappy that many programs of non-Western studies now include some aspects of religion studies, and that teachers of the history of religions are often asked to cooperate in such programs. Something is to be said in favor of such a trend. In addition to such mundane benefits as the availability of more research funds and more students with better linguistic preparation, the historian of religions is bound to broaden his horizons and to be stimulated by close contact with scholars of other disciplines. On the other hand, as Wilfred

[9]Clyde A. Holbrook, *Religion, A Humanistic Field*, Englewood Cliffs, N.J.: Prentice-Hall, 1963, p. 153.

Cantwell Smith has forcefully pointed out, the historian of religions might easily become merely one more "expert" on non-Western studies, who is expected to expound the role of Hinduism, Islam, or Buddhism merely as one factor, alongside economic, political, and other factors, in the cultures and civilizations of the non-Western world.[10] Furthermore, when many of our colleagues in non-Western studies invite a historian of religions, they actually think of him primarily as an expert on one religion of whatever cultural area concerns them. Ironically, well-trained Islamicists, Buddhologists, and specialists in other religions are not too plentiful. Also, even for them it is not easy within the framework of current non-Western studies to present the totality of human life in Islamic, Buddhist, or any other religious terms. In this situation, while the historian of religions, to the extent that he has done specialized research in one religious tradition, may contribute something to the study of non-Western religions, he will be greatly frustrated if he wishes to bring to bear the basic thrust of the methodology and outlook of the history of religions.

It seems to me that another kind of academic myopia is operating in the minds of many who are engaged in programs of religion studies in a university setting. It is probably a logical necessity for those who advocate the interfaith approach in religion studies to take seriously what adherents of other religious traditions believe. It may be granted that ultimately this is the central question in our attempt to understand various religions. But it is neither feasible nor desirable, even with the best of intentions, to compromise this lofty goal by attempting to have a perpetual interfaith conference in the classroom. Thus, visits to the class by a local swami or travelling Zen master become "highlights" of the course, with the result that the teacher of the history of religions tends, in effect, to be relegated to the status of a poor substitute for "Mr. Hindu" or "Mr. Buddhist." Here again there seems to be a great discrepancy between what the historian of religions is expected to teach and what his scholarly objectives demand. On the other hand, those who are concerned with the study of religions as a humanistic discipline often take the easy way out by polarizing the religious subjects into Western and Eastern, motivated by practical necessity or some other consideration. Accordingly, the historian of religions is expected to stay in the corner of the Eastern religions exclusively.

I am not primarily criticizing the fact that the historian of religions must carry the impossible burden of posing one day as an expert on the doctrines, history, ethics; and cults of Hinduism, and the next day as an expert on all aspects of Islam and so on, while his colleagues have more manageable responsibilities, such as the biblical literature, the development of the

[10] Wilfred Cantwell Smith, "Non-Western Studies: The Religious Approach," *Report on an Invitational Conference on the Study of Religion in the State University*, New Haven: The Society for Religion in Higher Education, 1964, pp. 50–65.

American religious heritage, or contemporary religious thought. What I am lamenting is the fact that the discipline of the history of religions is, by practical necessity, interpreted solely as the teaching of non-Western religions. In the main, very little effort has been made to reassess the total endeavor in religion studies, taking seriously the insights and concerns of the history of religions. For the most part, it is business as usual as far as the department of religion is concerned, with a heavy dose of Judeo-Christian studies, even though there are now added a few glamorous courses with pretentious titles such as World Religions, Asian Religions, Eastern Mysticism, and Zen, to satisfy the curiosity of the intellectual hippies. Only in rare cases is the program of religion studies designed to relate, even superficially, all religions, Western as well as Eastern, to the total historical and religious experience of the human race.

## THE MAKING OF A HISTORIAN OF RELIGIONS

Unfortunately, there is no alchemy that can quickly overcome the academic myopia. Even the magic of curriculum change, which many administrators invoke as the cure of all evils, cannot solve overnight the basic problems of the history of religions. In reality, the problem is not a shortage of courses in the field or even of teachers able or willing to teach them. There are courses, but they are often misconceived and inadequately taught. Douglas Horton once remarked that "in general, a community is not better than its churches; in general, a church is not better than its minister; and in general, a minister is not better than his training." A similar observation may be applied to the historian of religions. In short, those in the field are keenly aware that well-trained historians of religions are not many, and good training programs in the field are few.

In this respect, I am happy to note that our first cousins—Islamicists, Indologists, Buddhologists, or specialists on Chinese, Japanese, and primitive religions—have fared better in recent years. While I have no direct knowledge of the inner workings of such programs as the Institute of Islamic Studies at McGill University, graduate programs in Buddhist studies at the Universities of Wisconsin and Washington, and similar study centers on Hinduism and other religions in various universities, all these seem to have well-structured programs in terms of research, training, teaching, and publications, thanks to generous subsidies from foundations, the government, their own institutions, and private individuals. I certainly hope that those who aspire to go into the history of religions will take full advantage of the resources now available for linguistic training and in the historical, sociological, and cultural studies that are pertinent to the understanding of various religions.

We must, however, be crystal clear concerning the basic distinction between the study of specific religions and the history of religions. We are all aware, of course, that in the popular mind the history of religions is often thought of as a convenient semantic umbrella that covers all the independent studies of specific religions. But the objective of the history of religions (*Religionswissenschaft*), in the technical sense in which we use this term, must be nothing short of scholarly inquiry into the nature and structure of the religious experience of the human race and its diverse manifestations in history. This means, for example, that unlike the Islamicist and Buddhologist, who study Islam and Buddhism, respectively, as their main objectives, the historian of religions concerns himself with the study of these and other religions because they are integral parts of the religious history of mankind. While the objectives of both approaches are legitimate and closely interrelated, their differences should not be overlooked.

Obviously, it is humanly impossible for the historian of religions to study all the religions of the world, past and present, with equal intensity. In practice, he has to depend on the researches of experts in various specific religions. At the same time, it is necessary for him to be technically competent in scholarly research in at least one or two religions, because this enables him to understand in depth, as much as scholarly inquiry can make possible, the nature, structure, and history of these particular religious traditions in concrete form, and also because without such specific competence he cannot even begin to appreciate the scholarly researches of all other religions. Of equal importance are the genuine cooperative inquiry and mutual checking that benefit alike the historian of religions and experts in specific religions regarding researches in areas of common concern.

There is another dimension of the task, a dimension that constitutes the unique contribution of the history of religions to other disciplines concerned with religion studies. I refer to the articulation of the nature, structure, and meaning of man's religious experience, an articulation based on historical and systematic inquiry into concrete religious configurations—past and present, primitive and historic, and Eastern and Western. Granted that the hermeneutical task of the history of religions has been greatly influenced and enriched by the contributions of normative and empirical studies of religions, in the final analysis it is only the historian of religions who must carry the awesome burden of articulating what Joachim Wach termed the "integral understanding" of religious phenomena, as required by the discipline of the history of religions. This is probably the most controversial aspect of our discipline in the sense that "integral understanding" involves selectivity of data and a telescoping of the long and complex historical development of man's religions. The lack of data is not at all our problem. Our real problem, to use a phrase of G. van der Leeuw, is that the manner in which the data are "significantly organized" inevitably varies according to the personal sensitivity, religious outlook, and scholarly training of the individual historian of religions. This is one reason why I for one hesitate to use the English translation of the term, *Religionswissenschaft*, since the very nature of "integral understanding" defies precise "scientific" verification in the sense that the English word "science" implies (although I am not altogether happy with the expression, the "history of religions," either).

This does not imply that the history of religions possesses no coherence as a discipline or that there is no systematic way of training people in the field. Indeed, it is possible for us to provide a fairly solid body of knowledge and important categories as well as viable methodological principles, so that upon completing their doctoral programs our graduates can offer relevant courses effectively either on an elementary level or on a more advanced level, and either within the context of a department of religion or in a program of non-Western studies. However, while graduate training in this field can train competent teachers, it cannot necessarily and automatically make creative historians of religions out of them. The bitter truth is that creative scholars, like great artists, are not easily found. It is fairly certain that not too many of the large number of today's applicants will remain as creative scholars. Of course, some truly great potential historians of religions may be tucked away, hidden from all of us at the moment, and there are no doubt men who can rightly be classified as geniuses. But more often than not creativity in scholarship comes not from a sudden flash of insight but from many years of disciplined and dedicated work, permeated by an awareness of the significance of what one is wrestling with and stimulated by the serious researches of other historians of religions and scholars in related disciplines—provided of course that one has had the benefit of a fairly good academic training.[11]

I am not suggesting that the path of the historian of religions is more difficult than that of scholars in other disciplines. I am, however, keenly aware of the peculiar temptations that confront the historian of religions today because of the popularity of the discipline coupled with the ambiguity that envelops it. It takes a considerable amount of determination for a historian of religions in-the making to work toward creative scholarship without succumbing to the temptation to produce instant relevance either as a pseudo-Orientalist or a quasi-theologian—especially now that the history of religions has become a "favorite" addition either to programs of non-Western studies or departments of religion. Also, people in various quarters—with the best of intentions, to be sure—try to lure us into becoming spokesmen for the brotherhood of man, world peace, and intercultural and interfaith understanding. These are all important objectives. They must concern all of us. And it may be true that historians of religions with their particular knowledge might be sensitive to these worthy causes as by-products of their

[11] The creativity that comes as a result of long and hard work is seen in the fact that it took Felix Mendelssohn three years to complete his Symphony No. 4, A Major, Italian. When he finished it, he wrote: "My work, about which I had recently many doubts, is finished; and now when I look it over . . . I feel that it shows progress, and that is the main point. . . ." Likewise, progress in scholarship is probably not possible without some agonizing experiences along the road.

scholarly work. However, in the spirit of John Henry Newman, who held that the object of a university is intellectual and not moral, we must be clear in our own minds that the primary object of the history of religions is the scholarly task of "integral understanding" of the structure and meaning of man's religious history, in elucidation of the fact that in order to be really human in every culture and every phase of history, man has always seen the total aspect of existence in relation to sacral reality.

In that perceptive and satirical poem, "A Ballad of Artistic Integrity," E. B. White recounts an imagined conversation between one of the Rockefellers and Diego Rivera, who was commissioned to paint the mural for the lobby of the RCA Building. The poem starts with a series of questions addressed to Rivera, such as, "What do you paint?," "Will there be any doves, or a tree in fall? Or a hunting scene, like an English hall?" The artist simply replies, "I paint what I see." To another series of further queries, he says: "I paint what I paint." After a third round of questions concerning the significance of the mural's theme, Rivera answers, "I paint what I think."

> "I paint what I paint, I paint what I see,
>   I paint what I think," said Rivera,
> "And the thing that is dearest in life to me
>     . . . is Integrity."[12]

In this day of religious confusion and academic myopia, we need more historians of religions who can honestly and courageously say:

> I write what I write, I write what I see
>   I write what I think.
> And the thing that is dearest in life to me is
>   scholarly integrity.

[12] Quoted in *The New York Times Magazine*, April, 1967, p. 30.

# 5

## HUMANISTIC AND THEOLOGICAL HISTORY OF RELIGIONS WITH SPECIAL REFERENCE TO THE NORTH AMERICAN SCENE

### INTRODUCTION

Any attempt to assess the development of the History of Religions during the past 100 years, especially in North America, cannot ignore the impact of two of the major international assemblies on the discipline, namely, the World's Parliament of Religions, held in Chicago in 1893, and the first Congress of the History of Religions, held in Paris in 1900. Both were sponsored and promoted not only by religious or scholarly interests but also by strong business interests as well.

The World's Parliament of Religions was held as a part of the Columbian Exposition, which marked the 400th anniversary of Columbus' discovery of America. Civic leaders of Chicago were determined to outdo two previous affairs—the Centennial Exposition of Philadelphia in 1876 which displayed Alexander Graham Bell's telephone, Thomas Edison's telegraph machine, the typewriter and the sewing machine, and the Paris Exhibition of 1889 which lured the curious multitudes to the newly built Eiffel Tower. Thus, side by side with the first gigantic Ferris wheel and other novelties, the Chicago Exposition sponsored an ambitious assembly of representatives of major religions of the world. It is interesting to note that the planners of the 1900 Paris exhibition, knowing the success of the Chicago Parliament seven years earlier, gave full support to the first Congress of the History of Religions although, as one participant observed wryly, other events—especially a feminist congress and one on postage stamps—aroused more interest than did the scholarly gathering of the historians of religions.

### THE WORLD'S PARLIAMENT OF RELIGIONS

In a sense, the World's Parliament of Religions reflected the growing interest of Americans in exotic non-Western religions, an interest which may be illustrated by the fact that Edwin Arnold's *Light of Asia*, first published in England in 1879, immediately went into 80 editions in America.[1] In 1890 the American Society of Comparative Religion was organized by Frank Field

---

[1] See Arthur E. Christy (ed.), *The Asian Legacy and American Life* (New York: John Day Co., 1942), p. 43.

Ellingwood, author of *Oriental Religions and Christianity*. In 1891 Harvard University appointed George Foot Moore to the chair of History of Religions, while in 1892 the newly created University of Chicago established the Department of Comparative Religion and appointed George Stephen Goodspeed. Also in 1892 "The American Lectures on the History of Religions" was established jointly by Columbia, Cornell, Johns Hopkins, Pennsylvania, Yale and other universities. Significantly, many professors from leading universities were involved in the Parliament as representatives of their respective denominations. To be sure, many of them were scholars of Comparative Religion or History of Religions, but they were inclined—theologically and religiously—to share the motto of the Parliament: "To unite all Religion against all irreligion; to make the Golden Rule the basis of this union; to present to the world . . . the substantial unity of many religions in the good deeds of the Religious Life . . . and [to demonstrate] the marvelous Religious progress of the nineteenth century. . ."[2]

As might be expected, the presence of Muslim, Hindu, and Buddhist representatives in exotic attires, coupled with eloquent discourse of their religious tenets—exemplified by the activities of Swāmī Vivekānanda—impressed many participants. Moreover, in the minds of many Americans the cause of the Parliament (which was rhapsodically endorsed by Max Müller among others as a unique and unprecedented event) became inseparably related to the aim of Comparative Religion or History of Religions. What interested the supporters of the Parliament was not the critical, scholarly inquiry concerning religions, but rather the religious or philosophical basis for the unity of all religions. This motivation has brought about some salutary practical consequences. For example, in 1894 Mrs. Caroline E. Haskell, "recognizing the great interest aroused by the Parliament of Religions," established the Haskell Lectureship on Comparative Religion at the University of Chicago. She also established another endowment for lectures to be given primarily in India in which "the great questions of the truths of Christianity, its harmonies with the truths of other religions . . . should be presented" and which were to be given in honor of John Henry Barrows, the guiding light of the Parliament. The impact of the Parliament was such that in 1897 the American Oriental Society formed a section for the historical study of religions. The Parliament also stimulated the churches: in 1899 Union Theological Seminary in New York instituted a chair for the philosophy and history of religions, and in 1904 the conference of the Foreign Mission Boards of the Christian Churches in the United States and Canada recommended that theological schools of all denominations provide for missionary candidates courses of instruction in Comparative Religion and the History of Religions.[3]

[2] The World's Religious Congress, *General Programme* (preliminary ed., 1893), p. 19.

[3] Louis Henry Jordan, *Comparative Religion: Its Genesis and Growth* (Edinburgh: T. & T. Clark, 1905), p. 375.

Elsewhere I have touched upon the checkered career of the comparative and historical study of religions in North America, its popularity throughout the 1910's and 1920's, its uneasy alliance with theological liberalism and certain types of philosophy of religion, and its sudden decline in the 1930's accelerated by the impact of neo-orthodox theology, the Depression, and the impending war.[4] Through it all, a serious "humanistic" study of religions, especially the History of Religions, did not take root in North America until after World War II. Exceptions to this were the archeological and linguistic studies of ancient and classical religions and simplistic studies of the so-called "Oriental philosophies." Moreover, such disciplined studies as Indology, Buddhology, Islamics and Sinology, which might have informed and nurtured the "humanistic" History of Religions, were not well established before the war. On the other hand, the ghost of the Parliament of Religions—with its liberal and relativistic temper—continued to survive among the remnants of those who were theologically or religiously motivated in their study of non-Western religions: Hendrick Kraemer, for example, articulated a certain "theological" History of Religions. However, he did not find many followers, most likely due to his exclusivistic Christian stance. After the war the Parliament was forgotten by many except as an insignificant dot in recent history. However, its spirit is not altogether lost among those who are engaged in Comparative Theologies, Theology of Religions, or the "theological" History of Religions. These studies now depend on a wide variety of theological, philosophical, psychological and anthropological resources. Ironically, today there seems to be a kind of confusion in certain quarters: the fundamental distinction between the two genuine enterprises, i.e. "humanistic" and "theological" approaches to the History of Religions, is not adequately appreciated. This confusion impoverishes both approaches, as I will discuss presently.

## THE EXHIBITION AND THE CONGRESS

As we turn our attention to the first Congress of the History of Religions, which was held in connection with the Paris exhibition of 1900, I am reminded of Mr. Irving Kristol's statement that "the 19th century came to its end a little later than the calendar prescribed. It was not the organized festivities of 1900 but rather the organized hostilities of 1914 that decisively concluded a chapter in human history,"[5] which was followed by the period of "interregnum" that lasted until World War II. But the exhibition, often characterized as the "cathedral of commerce," and the discipline of the

---

[4]Cf. "The History of Religions in America," in *The History of Religions: Essays in Methodology*, ed. by Mircea Eliade and J. M. Kitagawa (Chicago: The University of Chicago Press, 1959), pp. 1–30.

[5]Irving Kristol, "The 20th Century Began in 1945," *The New York Times Magazine* (May 2, 1965), p. 88.

History of Religions were the products of the 19th century. Whether we like it or not, the 19th century was a time when the West dominated the entire world politically, economically, and even culturally. A series of large-scale exhibits and fairs were held in various parts of Europe. These fairs, starting with the 1851 exhibition at the Crystal Palace in Hyde Park, London, which was spearheaded by the prince consort of mighty Queen Victoria, symbolized the technological, industrial, artistic and commercial achievements of the West-European nations. In hindsight we can see that in spite of the disastrous Franco-German War there yet remained some semblance of the unity of European community during the 19th century.

I do not have to say much to this learned audience about the intellectual development in 19th century Europe. Even in my college days in Japan, I was awed by the achievements of Hegel, Nietzsche, Comte, Darwin, Schelling, Dilthey, Schleiermacher, Bergson, and the Grimm brothers. The enormous intellectual vitality, born of the Renaissance and the Enlightenment, resulted in the development of a series of academic disciplines, both natural and humanistic, during the 19th century. Also, Europeans came to know a great deal about the languages, customs, and religions of non-Western peoples through the accounts of travellers, businessmen, Christian missionaries and colonial officials. Even the hitherto unfamiliar sacred scriptures of Eastern religions began to be translated into European languages. The enormous data thus collected were devoured by scholars of languages, ethnology, arts, history, philosophy, and religions, all of whom were then eager to broaden their intellectual horizons as well as to solidify their disciplines. It is not surprising, therefore, that É. Burnouf predicted in 1870: "This present century will not come to an end without having seen the establishment of a unified science whose elements are still dispersed, a science which the preceding centuries did not have, which is not even yet defined, and which, perhaps for the first time, will be named science of religions."[6] And, as if to follow his prediction, some European historians of religions had a conference in 1897 in Stockholm,[7] although it was in Paris in 1900 that the first full-scale Congress for the History of Religions, so recognized, was convened.

## THE 1900 CONGRESS FOR THE HISTORY OF RELIGIONS

Undoubtedly the 1900 Paris Congress set the tone in various ways for subsequent Congresses, and, indirectly, the later development of four aspects of the discipline of the History of Religions. First, unlike the 1893 World's Parliament of Religions, the Paris Congress was a scholarly, and not a religious, conference. Its roster included prominent scholars of various areas and disciplines that were relevant to the inquiry into diverse religious

[6] É. Burnouf, *La Science des religions*, 3rd ed., 1970, p. 1.
[7] See *ACTES of the 5th International Congress for the History of Religions* (Lund: C. W. K. Gleerup, 1930), p. 29.

phenomena. Notable among these schoalrs were Bertholet, Durkheim, Foucher, Maspero, Oldenburg, C. P. Tiele, E. B. Tylor, and van Gennep. There also were some clerics in attendance, for example, Nathan Söderblom, who was then a pastor in Paris, but they participated in the Congress as scholars. The name of Swāmī Vivekānanda, one of the leading stars of the 1893 Parliament, is listed in the minutes, but there is no record that he took any active part in the Congress. A curious question, however, was why did Mrs. Mary Baker Eddy of Christian Science fame appear at the Congress? She was not typical of the general academic tone of the meeting. Second, there were a variety of scholarly approaches and competencies represented at the Paris Congress. Indeed, there were many scholars who were not "Historians of Religions" in terms of academic and disciplinary affiliations. Most of them, however, were engaged in critical, humanistic or social scientific investigation and research into the rich phenomena of religions, including those of precivilized and civilized, ancient and modern, peoples. Their primary purpose was the search for an "understanding" of the nature of religions. It was this "unified concern" which brought together biblical scholars, ethnologists, linguists, historians, philosophers, classisists, and "Orientalists" including Arabists, Indologists, and Buddhologists. In short, the Paris Congress was not simply an umbrella for these different scholars and disciplines; it assumed—rightly or wrongly—that these scholars representing different competencies and approaches were indeed engaged in the common broadly conceived enterprise of the "History of Religions."

Third, in spite of the "unified concern" with a strong historical bent, the format of the Paris Congress was more "horizontal" in nature. By this I mean that it divided its program into eight sessions—(1) Religions of non-civilized peoples and of the pre-Columbian Americans, (2) Religions of the Far East, (3) Ancient Egyptian Religion, (4) Assyrian, Babylonian, Judaic and Islamic—that is, Semitic—religions, (5) Indo-Iranian religions, (6) Greco-Roman religions, (7) Nordic, Teutonic, Celtic and Slavonic religions, and (8) Christianity. Inevitably, the historical concern was dealt with primarily within each designated area; only incidental and occasional references to cross-area historical phenomena were forthcoming. Even with its "horizontal" concern, the program conceivably could have been devised with a slightly different format. For example, it might have addressed such fascinating topics as the historical interactions among Iranian, Jewish, Hellenistic, and Christian religious traditions shortly before and after the beginning of the Common Era, or the interactions of Jewish, Christian, and Islamic traditions around the Mediterranean world during the middle ages, or perhaps the religious convergence along the Indian Ocean. But, ironically, the format of the Paris Congress was followed without much deviation by the subsequent Congresses for the History of Religions. Only in the seventh Congress, held in Amsterdam, was there added a section on the Phenomenology of Religion, and in the eighth Congress, held in Rome, another section on Psychology of

Religion was recognized. Also, it must be mentioned that since Amsterdam in 1950, where the IAHR was officially formed, general topics, such as the "Mythical-Ritual Pattern" (Amsterdam), the "Sacred Kingship" (Rome) and "Origins and Eschatology" (Marburg), have been chosen by each Congress. These topics still were pursued by horizontally divided sessions.

Fourth, the Paris Congress did little, if anything, to move from the "unified concern" of the History of Religions to a "unified discipline," as envisioned by Burnouf and others. Nor was any serious effort attempted to articulate the nature of the discipline of the History of Religions until the 1950 Amsterdam Congress.

## DISCUSSIONS ON THE NATURE OF THE HISTORY OF RELIGIONS

Significantly, at every Congress since 1950 the leaders of the IAHR have urged historians of religions to be self-conscious about the nature, objective, and methods of the discipline. For example, in Amsterdam Professor van der Leeuw stressed on one hand the independence of the History of Religions from theology, and on the other hand the necessity of the History of Religions to maintain rapport with philosophy, archaeology, anthropology, ethnology, psychology and sociology in order to attain a "synthetic view." In this connection, it is interesting to note that as late as 1955 at the Congress in Rome, Professor E. O. James candidly acknowledged that the History of Religions has not as yet been firmly established as an independent discipline in Britain, even though there were a number of scholars who were interested in, and specialized in, adjacent fields. By 1955 the members of the IAHR were concerned with the relationship between the phenomenological study of religions, which were ably championed by Professor C. J. Bleeker, and historical studies of religions, advocated by Professor Raffaele Pettazzoni and others. Pettazzoni criticized the phenomenological study of religions for not being attentive to the historical development of religious events. At Rome, Professor Herbert Schneider also stressed that *"religious* phenomena are essentially historical, and that the historical study of religion is central to all humanistic studies."[8]

Serious discussions on the nature of the discipline of the History of Religions have continued. In the 1960 Congress at Marburg a proposal to change the nomenclature of the organization from "International Association for the History of Religions" to "International Association for the Science of Religion" was rejected in favor of retaining the former, chiefly on the ground that the "science of religion" includes Philosophy of Religion, which is not a part of the History of Religions.[9] Also at Marburg a number of participants signed a statement that stressed the following four points: (1) Although the

[8]*ATTI of the 8th International Congress for the History of Religions* (Florence: C. G. Sansoni, 1956), p. 44.

[9]*X. International Congress for the History of Religions* (Marburg: N. G. Elwert Verlag, 1961), pp. 21–22.

*religionswissenschaftliche* method undoubtedly is a Western creation, it would be misleading to juxtapose "occidental" and "oriental" methods in the History of Religions, whose aim is "a better understanding of the variety and historic individuality of religions, whilst remaining constantly alert to the possibility of scientifically legitimate generalizations concerning the nature and function of religion." (2) *Religionswissenschaft* "understands itself as a branch of the Humanities." It studies the religious phenomenon as a creation of human culture. As such the awareness of the numinous or the experience of transcendence are understood to be empirical facts of human existence and history—to be studied, as are all human facts, by the appropriate methods. Thus, while the value systems of various religions present empirical phenomena and, therefore, are legitimate objects of our studies, "the discussion of the absolute value of religion is excluded by definition, although it may have its legitimate place in . . . completely independent disciplines such as theology and philosophy of religion." (3) Likewise, the notion that "the value of religious phenomena can be understood only if we keep in mind that religion is ultimately a realization of a transcendent truth" is not a legitimate foundation of *Religionswissenschaft.* (4) "The study of religions need not seek for justification outside itself," for every quest of historical truth is "its own *raison d'être.*"[10]

Then, in 1965, when the Congress met for the first time in North America (that is, at Claremont, California), there were two presentations that touched on the relation of our discipline to the nature of religion or religions. First, in the opening address Professor Bleeker stressed the two elements of our discipline, namely, "history" and "religion." "We are historians," he said: "This means that whether we study the dead religions of the past or the living religions . . . the approach will be the same, i.e., the historical one." On the other hand, our subject matter, namely, religious phenomena, refer to the "supernatural, the transcendental, the Holy." Quoting his teacher W. B. Kristensen, Bleeker suggested that the task of the historian of religions must be "to understand the faith of the believers." Obviously, the "faith of the believers" might be approached from various perspectives and with different objectives. Professor Bleeker himself is of the opinion that, unlike scholars of theology or the philosophy of religion, the historian of religions must deal with religion as a human phenomenon. Accordingly, he asks a central question: "where the core and kernal of religion is to be situated."[11]

[10] Statement drafted by Professor R. J. Zwi Werblowsky, and signed by Professors Abel (Brussells), Brandon (Manchester), Brelich and Brezzi (Rome), Duchesne-Guillemin (Liege), Eliade, Kitagawa and Long (Chicago), Goodenough (Yale), Hidding (Leiden), Hoffman (München), Kishimoto (Tokyo), Lanternari and Pincherle (Rome), Simon (Strasbourg), and Zaehner (Oxford). This statement was presented in response to the statement circulated by Professor C. J. Bleeker.

[11] *Proceedings of the XIth International Congress of the International Association for the History of Religions* (Leiden: E. J. Brill, 1968), Vol. I, pp. 7–9.

The second presentation I refer to was made by Professor Wilfred Cantwell Smith, who began his address with a critique of his assigned topic, "Traditional Religions and Modern Culture." While Professor Smith does not need anyone to interpret his well known views on the nature of Comparative Religion, let me recount—almost arbitrarily—a few of his points which are relevant to our present discussion. (i) Smith shifted the focus from "a religion and its plural" to "religion" as such, which he understood in terms of "faith." And, because "faith" is by nature "timeless" and "present," religion has "linked each succeeding present moment to eternity."[12] He insisted, therefore, that the subject matter of our study "is not merely tradition but faith, not merely the overt manifestations of man's religious life, but that life itself."[13] (ii) According to his scholarly agenda, the historical study of religion should serve primarily to illumine "what is happening in our day to the quality of life that those traditions used to represent and foster."[14] He wrote that his task, therefore, was "to discover and report how far and wherein these inherited symbols are today performing their earlier functions as one part of one side of the complex dialectic between man's spirit and his material environment."[15] (iii) With his preoccupation with contemporary forms, Smith pointed to various types of religiousness of contemporary man. One such type is the religiousness "without phenomena" reminiscent of Dag Hammarskjold's view. Another is a phenomenon-less religion, or the "religionless faith" of Bonhöffer. Both of these positions have their counterparts in other parts of the world. (iv) In order to do justice to the religiousness of contemporary man, Smith rejected the type of scholarship that "would give priority to discipline over subject matter, and would exclude from consideration all facets of a problem that do not neatly fit one's extant techniques." Instead, he called for a "new venture" in religious scholarship. For him this endeavor includes, for instance, "phenomenology of religion but will pass well beyond it," because "man's religiousness always transcends phenomena." Moreover, Smith was persuaded that such a "new venture" in Comparative Religion, which aims at the study of man in his religious diversity "is coming into being, perhaps especially on this continent," (meaning North America) even though he acknowledged that its accomplishments are as yet incipient and its methods groping.[16]

I hope my admittedly spotty summary of Professor Smith's presentation has not unduly distorted his main thesis, which has relevance to my own assessment of what is happening in our discipline in North America. Before going into that subject, however, let me refer briefly to the opening address

[12] *Ibid.*, p. 62.
[13] *Ibid.*, p. 68.
[14] *Ibid.*, p. 69.
[15] *Ibid.*, p. 70.
[16] *Ibid.*, p. 71.

given by Professor Geo Widengren at the 1970 Congress in Stockholm. In sharp contrast to Smith's view presented at Claremont, Widengren reiterrated the importance of the historical character of the History of Religions that has been the hallmark of all the Congresses from 1900 onwards. While he acknowledged the importance of the Phenomenology of Religion and published a learned volume on the subject, he viewed the overwhelming domination of phenomenology with some misgivings. He worried about its implication for methodology, especially on two grounds. First, the Phenomenology of Religion takes its material from the History of Religions. Thus, he asked, "is it possible to understand the phenomenology of religion, and especially the phenomena of a given religion, without knowing its history?" Second, it is history that informs our understanding of contemporary religious phenomena. In his own words: "although we may think we could base our research exclusively on the *modern* history of the great religions, how would it be possible to understand the problems of modern times without the historical perspective? And on the other hand what would a phenomenological study . . . be like, if the ancient religions were left out of consideration."[17] Thus, Widengren lamented the anti-historical ethos of our time with its growing hostility against all historical research and historical interpretation of facts. In his opinion, the anti-historical trait may also account for the loss of prestige of the disciplines of the History of Religions. Again, in his words: "It is as though the subject itself had lost its good name, its reputation, in some quarters—especially in Germany."[18]

Widengren also was alarmed by the excessive "compartmentalization of scholarship" and its implication for the common enterprise of the History of Religions. He readily understood why specialists in Classics, philology, and specific religious traditions are involved in their own respective learned societies; but he was distressed by the fact that even the historian of religions, working in the field of  let us say—Islamics, "feels more interested in what is going on in this field than in the vast domains of the History of Religions in general, where one is more or less lost, and is often exposed to the accusation of dilettantism if one should try to keep in touch with what is going on outside one's own field."[19] Widengren was unhappy about the myopia of specialists who think they can study specific religions without any reference to the general history of religions. In fact, he felt, it is the general history of religions, which requires the cooperation of all specialists, which in turn provides proper perspective to the study of specific religions. Thus, while "voices have been heard claiming that Islam [for instance] is singularly ill-suited to be associated with studies in our field," he states, "there should

[17] *Proceedings of the XIIth International Congress of the International Association for the History of Religions* (Leiden: E. J. Brill, 1975), p. 20.

[18] *Ibid.*, p. 18.

[19] *Ibid.*, pp. 17–18.

be more Islamic studies oriented from the viewpoint of the History of Religions in general. . . ."[20]

Even such brief accounts of the discussions at various Congresses on the nature of the History of Religions may serve as a reminder that this is by no means a closed issue and that wherever we may be situated, and whatever our competencies may be, all of us must make every effort to clarify the nature of our discipline for the sake of our common task. With this in mind, let me present my own assessment of the state of the History of Religions in North America, and my own understanding of the nature of our discipline. I am particularly concerned with the ambiguous relationship between the "humanistic" and the "theological" approaches to the History of Religions.

## THE HISTORY OF RELIGIONS IN NORTH AMERICA

Earlier I mentioned that Comparative Religions and the History of Religions became popular subjects in North America following the Parliament of Religions and during the first three decades of our century. They suddenly declined due to such factors, among others, as the impact of theological neo-Orthodoxy, the Depression and the impending war. The mood of the 1930's and early 40's was such that a serious quest for the unity of religions, which was the main theme of the Parliament and which was pursued, for example, by the Harvard Philosopher, William Ernest Hocking,[21] did not attract many followers. Similarly, erudite lectures on the History of Religions sponsored by American Council of Learned Societies did not arouse much public interest.

The impetus for the renewed interest in the History of Religions—or at least certain aspects of it—after the end of World War II came from several quarters: (i) a sudden interest in things Eastern, including historic Asian religions and modern Eastern cults; (ii) the proliferation of Religion Departments in colleges and universities, that pursue the non-theological nature of the History of Religions as well as general studies of non-Western religions; (iii) the growing fascination among some social scientists in non-Western myths, symbols, cults, social structures and cultural patterns; and (iv) a new interest among influential theologians in dialogue not only with Judaism but also with Eastern religions.

(i) Much has been written regarding the penetration of Oriental art, literature, cuisine, martial arts, meditation, and Eastern religions into Europe and North America. As far as Canada and the United States are concerned, the newly aroused interest in Asia resulted in the establishment of many programs in Asian Studies in academic institutions. This is reflected by the phenomenal growth of the Association of Asian Studies. Such programs on Asian Studies, which until recently enjoyed foundation and govern-

[20] *Ibid.*, p. 16.
[21] See his *Living Religions and A World Faith* (New York: Macmillan, 1940).

ment subsidies, often appointed historians of religious to their faculties. While there are some obvious benefits in such appointments, I share Professor W. C. Smith's anxiety that the historian of religions in this situation might easily become just one more Asian expert, whose contribution will be confined to the explication of the role of religions only as one factor (alongside economic, political and other factors) in Asian societies and cultures.[22]

(ii) Undoubtedly, the establishment of Religion—or Religious Studies—Departments in universities and colleges potentially is one of the most salutary developments in the history of education in North America. However, partly because this has been such a recent venture, there is not sufficient clarity as to what is meant by religious studies. In some cases, religious studies programs seem to be little more than watered down theological studies minus a faith commitment and staffed by those who have received traditional theological training but have been disenchanted by institutional religion. Or, in a few cases, the program is staffed by ministers, priests, and rabbis who have academic credentials but have little understanding about the academic study of religion(s). There are also some programs which are based on an assortment of unrelated courses, such as psychology of religion courses from the psychology department, medieval history courses from the history department, sociology of religion from the sociology department, etc. Therefore it is very difficult to make any general statements about religious studies programs at the moment.

At present, many institutions offer courses on "Western religious traditions," "American religious studies," or their variations such as "Catholicism, Protestantism, and Judaism," "Black religious traditions," and "the role of the feminine in religion." Many of them also offer courses on psychology of religion, Bible, philosophy of religion, sociology of religion and primitive and/or non-Western religions. It has become a common practice for Religion Departments to offer a course in the History of Religions, partly because the non-theological character of the discipline is readily acceptable to the faculty of arts and sciences. But, almost invariably, a historian of religions is chosen not on the ground of his or her training in general history of religions but on the ground of his or her knowledge of a specific non-Western religion. The most amusing and extreme example is a case of a two-person department in which one person is expected to cover all "western" subjects, while the second person is responsbile for everything "eastern." Also, while many programs of religious studies are now looking for various organizing principles—such as "conceptual" (philosophy of religion, comparative doctrines or ethics, etc.), "historical" (history of ideas, history of doctrines, etc.), and

[22] Wilfred Cantwell Smith, "Non-Western Studies: The Religious Approach," *Report on an Invitational Conference on the Study of Religion in the State University* (New Haven: The Society for Religion in Higher Education, 1964), pp. 50–65.

"dialogical" (religion and psychology, religion and law, religion and literature)—they have not seriously looked at the History of Religions as one of the viable options.

(iii) The establishment of Religion Departments in colleges and universities has brought religion scholars, including historians of religions, close not only to scholars of the humanities but also to social scientists. The latter now show growing interests in religious data; but to be sure, their interest arises from the perspectives of social sciences. It might be worth recalling that throughout its development the History of Religions has had close rapport with psychology (especially depth psychology), sociology, and anthropology, as well as with theology and philosophy of religion. One noticeable trend in North America today is that many historians of religions have lost meaningful contacts with theologians and philosophers of religion, and are turning to social scientists as their primary "conversation partners." Ironically, some of them have been so heavily influenced by the works of a Lévi-Strauss, a Turner, a Douglas, or a Geertz, that they pay little attention to historical research, which is, after all, the cornerstone of the History of Religions.

(iv) It is interesting to note that while many main-line churches in North America have lost much of their incentive for overseas missionary enterprise, they show increasing interest in "dialogues" with other religions. Numerous seminars, workshops, and conferences that have been held for this purpose, and to which a number of historians of religions have been invited, exhibit a wide range of qualities and perspectives. These range from simplistic exchanges of main tenets of various faiths, reminiscent of the 1893 Parliament, to some sophisticated searches for a common language or common frame of reference as a basis for a meaningful dialogue with other religions. In addition, some theologians here are now trying to develop the viable disciplines of "Theology of Religions," "Comparative Theologies," and "Theological History of Religions." One of the most serious attempts in setting forth the principles of a "Theological History of Religions" was made by Paul Tillich. These theological efforts are beginning to create confusion in the minds of some people, including some scholars, concerning the proper distinction and/or relation between the "humanistic" and "theological" approach to the History of Religions, as I will discuss presently.

## History of Religions—"Theological" and "Humanistic"

I realize that to make a distinction between the "humanistic" and "theological" approaches to the History of Religions is easier in theory than in practice. After all, a historian of religions, like other human beings, has many facets. The same is true with a theologian. By "Theological History of Religion," however, I do not mean theological reflections of a scholar whose academic commitment is toward the humanistic enterprise in dealing with the history of religions. Admittedly, this distinction is more difficult to make when a person has a double commitment—one to theological and the other to humanistic enterprises. This, indeed, was the case for a number of the forerunners of our discipline, Nathan Söderblom and Friedlich Heiler, for example. When one has such a double commitment, one has to train himself or herself to be a "disciplined schizophrenic," as it were, so that one has to make clear whether one is making a theological or humanistic statement. Equally difficult to establish is the difference between theological and philosophical perspectives. This is true especially in Asia, whose scholars—such as Dr. S. Radhakrishnan and many others—have not made a sharp distinction between the two. Nevertheless, in Asia the distinction between philosophical/theological on one hand and humanistic/scientific approaches on the other is clearly recognized. When, in the early 1930's, D. T. Suzuki said, "Formerly Buddhists were glad to welcome a scientific approach to their religion. But nowadays . . . instead of relying on scientific arguments for the rationalization of the Buddhist experience they are . . . trying to resort to its own dialectics,"[23] he was saying that Buddhists were now self-consciously committed to a philosophical, not a humanistic/scientific, enterprise in dealing with their religion. Such a stance is analogous to the Western "Theological History of Religions." What is confusing in North America today is that some scholars mix theological and humanistic assumptions, procedures of study, and conclusions.

Paul Tillich made it clear that he was engaged in a theological enterprise, even though he wanted to use data provided by the History of Religions. In his own words:

A theological history of religion should interpret theologically the material produced by the investigation and analysis of the pre-religious and religious life of mankind. It should elaborate the motives and types of religious expression, showing how they follow from the nature of the religious concern and therefore necessarily appear in all religions, including Christianity in so far as it is a religion. A theological history of religion also should point out demonic distortions and new tendencies in the religions of the world pointing to the Christian solution . . . that the New Being in Jesus as the Christ is the answer to the question asked implicitly by the religions of mankind.[24]

Tillich was convinced of the importance of applying the phenomenological approach to basic concepts in theology, thus "forcing its critics first of all to

[23]Quoted in A. Eustace Haydon (ed.), *Modern Trends in World-Religions* (Chicago: The University of Chicago Press, 1934), p. 38.

[24]Paul Tillich, *Systematic Theology* (Chicago: The University of Chicago Press, 1951), vol. 1, p. 39.

see what the criticized concepts mean and also forcing itself to make careful description of its concepts and to use them with logical consistency. . . ."[25] Furthermore, realizing that the phenomenological method is only partially competent in dealing with spiritual realities like religion, he advocated a "critical phenomenology"—the method which supplies a normative description of spiritual meaning—in theological enterprises.[26] He found this method used implicitly by Rudolf Otto, whom he knew well while teaching at Marburg.

> The phenomenological description of the holy in Rudolf Otto's classical book *The Idea of the Holy* demonstrates the interdependence of the meaning of the holy and the meaning of the divine, and it demonstrates their common dependence on the nature of ultimate concern. When Otto calls the experience of the holy "numinous," he interprets the holy as the presence of the divine. When he points to the mysterious character of holiness, he indicates that the holy transcends the subject-object structure of reality. When he describes the mystery of the holy as *tremendum* and *fascinosum*, he expresses the experience of "the ultimate" in the double sense of that which is abyss and that which is the ground of man's being.[27]

Tillich's methodological procedure in his proposed "Theological History of Religion(s)" rested on what he called a "dynamic typology," which he claimed to be more adequate than a one-directed dialectics *à la* Hegel.[28] Using the means of a dynamic typology, he wanted to characterize the typical structures within the unique forms of various historical religions and to compare them with the typical structures appearing in Christianity as a historic religion. Only when both Christian and other religions were "subjected to the criterion of final revelation"[29] was the final task of the Theological History of Religions possible. For example, "in the dialogue between Christianity and Buddhism two telos-formulae can be used: in Christianity the telos of every*one* and everything united in the Kingdom of God; in Buddhism the telos of every*thing* and everyone fulfilled in the Nirvana." He further added that "these, of course, are abbreviations for an almost infinite number of presuppositions and consequences; but just for this reason they are useful for the beginning as well as for the end of a dialogue."[30]

My reference to Tillich does not imply that he was the only advocate of a

---

[25] *Ibid.*, p. 106.

[26] *Ibid.*, p. 108.

[27] *Ibid.*, pp. 215–16.

[28] Paul Tillich, *Christianity and the Encounter of the World Religions* (New York: Columbia University Press, 1963), p. 56.

[29] Tillich, *Systematic Theology, op. cit.*, pp. 220–21.

[30] Tillich, *Christianity and the Encounter . . . , op. cit.*, p. 64.

Theological History of Religion(s). There are many other serious attempts being made today along this line of inquiry. Although he has dealt with concrete data only in his small work, *Christianity and the Encounter of the World Religions*, I refer to Tillich because to me personally his assumption and methodological principles are clearer than others. Since dialogues among Catholic, Protestant, and Jewish groups have been going on in North America, and since various religious groups are beginning to engage in dialogues with non-Western religious groups, a variety of theological approaches to the history of religions—regardless of different nomenclatures—will continue to be devised. Some North American historians of religions have already been involved in such dialogues. The present danger is that the line of demarcation between theological and humanistic approaches to the history of religions is not safeguarded—much to the disservice of both enterprises.

Inasmuch as my assessment of the North American scene is made from my limited perspective, I should state briefly what I understand the History of Religions to be, acknowledging of course that my own understanding is not the only, or perhaps the best, one. I have a sneaking suspicion that today in North America, and probably in other places too, the designation the History of Religions refers to so many different enterprises that share no "unified concern" that this term is losing its own integrity. I do not want to restrict the term "History of Religions" to mean only the historical aspect of our study, leaving out the phenomenological and other legitimate dimensions of our discipline. I realize that there are different emphases and approaches within our discipline. This is why I have been encouraged by discussions on the nature of the discipline that have been carried on at previous Congresses, and I certainly hope we compare notes and learn from each other on this subject at this Congress. My concern arises from my observation that today any study that touches on historical dimensions of any religion, usually non-Western religion, from any perspective and utilizing any methodological principle, is accepted as the History of Religions. I already have cited the "theological" History of Religions as a legitimate theological enterprise, but not to be confused with the "humanistic" History of Religions. I also have indicated that the popular equation of the History of Religions with the study of "World Religions" goes back to the Chicago Parliament of 1893. Regarding the use of the category of "World Religions" as such, which is used widely in academic circles in North America, I refer you to the insightful critique of my colleague, Jonathan Z. Smith, in his recent book entitled *Map is Not Territory*.[31] Another broad category, "Asian Religions," which has been made an acceptable term by programs of Asian Studies, has now crept into the

---

[31] Jonathan Z. Smith, *Map is Not Territory: Studies in the History of Religions* (Leiden: E. J. Brill, 1978), pp. 295–97.

vocabulary of Religion Departments and of the American Academy of Religion. The popularity of this subject, however loosely interpreted, is illustrated by the recent survey that lists 1,653 professors who teach Asian religious traditions in colleges and universities in Canada and the United States.[32] This list, however, does not indicate the disciplinary training and/or affiliation of these professors; we are not told who among all of these scholars are theologians, comparative ethicists, social scientists, philosophers of religions, or historians of religions.

I do not wish to suggest that the History of Religions is the most important discipline in the study of religions. However, I am persuaded that the History of Religions is a legitimate scholarly enterprise in spite of many problems involved, and that it is not merely a collective title for a number of related studies, such as the historical studies of Islam, Christianity, Buddhism, Hinduism, and primitive religions, for example, or the comparative studies of doctrines, practices, and ecclesiastical institutions of various religions. I interpret the History of Religions, following my mentor Joachim Wach, as an approximate—and not altogether satisfactory—English term for *Allgemeine Religionswissenschaft*, which is an autonomous discipline situated between the normative studies, such as philosophy of religion and theology, on one hand, and descriptive studies such as sociology, anthropology, psychology, on the other. *Religionswissenschaft* is composed of two complementary aspects—the "historical" and the "systematic" procedures of study. The historical task requires a mutual interaction between the historical studies of specific religions and the study of general history of religion, while the systematic task aims at disciplined generalizations and structuring of data and depends on a collaboration of phenomenological, comparative, sociological, psychological, and other studies of religions.

Like other historians of religions, I affirm that the point of departure of *Religionswissenschaft* is the study of the historical forms of religions as humankind's response to the sacred dimension of life and the world, recognizing that each religion is an individual totality, incomparable in its uniqueness. The goal of a historical study in *Religionswissenschaft* is to gain understanding into the various facets of each religion, facets that have together come to form the totality of the various religions, but which do not remain the same from one historical stage to the next, without losing their *Lebensgefühl*. In this endeavor, we must study a specific religion in its environment. Following Raffaele Pettazzoni's advice, we also study "its relation to other cultural values belonging to the same environment, such as poetry, art, speculative thought, social structure and so on."[33] It must also be mentioned that in this historical study of specific religions, a "humanistic"

---

[32] See *Professors in the United States and Canada Who Teach the Religious Traditions of Asia*. . . (Hamilton, N.Y.: Fund for the Study of Great Religions-Colgate University, June 1980).
[33] Raffaele Pettazzoni, *Essays on the History of Religions* (Leiden: E. J. Brill, 1954), p. 216.

historian of religions—unlike a "theological" historian of religion or a philosopher of religion—does not have a speculative purpose, nor does he resort to an *a priori* deductive method. At the same time, while the historical task of *Religionswissenschaft* has to abide by descriptive principles, its inquiry must be directed to the "meaning"—which links, in a sense, the descriptive and normative concerns—of the religious data which constitute its subject-matter. In this respect, my learned colleague Professor Mircea Eliade reminds us that the meaning of a religious phenomenon can be understood only if it is understood to be something religious. "To try to grasp the essence of such a phenomenon by means of physiology, psychology, sociology, economics, linguistics, art or any other study is false; it misses the one unique and irreducible element in it—the element of the sacred."[34] It might also be mentioned that the comparative method is a necessary tool for the understanding of the nature and meaning of specific religions.

Of course, the historical study of specific religions within the framework of *Religionswissenschaft* has much in common with, say, histories of Hinduism, Buddhism, and other religious traditions. But historical study within *Religionswissenschaft* must view specific religions not only as entities in themselves but also as parts of the total history of the religions of mankind. This is why at Stockholm in 1970 Professor Widengren suggested that we need more scholars who are oriented to the viewpoint of the History of Religions in general to study Islam and other religions. We realize, of course, that our audacious aim to gain an "integral understanding" of the general history of religions requires that we view the total religious history of mankind from our limited horizon. Such a task—here the historical task borders the systematic task—requires a selectivity of data and a telescoping of the long and complex historical tapestry of various religions. In this respect, the task of the historian of religions is something analogous to that of the historian of cultures and civilizations; it involves "thinking about a civilization," to use the phrase of Robert Redfield. According to Redfield, "thinking about" is "something different from getting information and acquaintance, though this third activity requires and is guided by the first two. It is to develop formed and namable thoughts about the civilization. It is to conceive it, and make it a mental artifact, a shaped work of the intellect."[35] If such "thinking about" civilization involves some risks, then thinking about the religious history of the human race involves far greater risks and difficulties. And yet this is precisely what the historian of religions is expected to contribute to the humanistic study of religions.

I must humbly confess at this point that the longer I study the History of

[34] Mircea Eliade, *Patterns in Comparative Religion* (New York: Sheed & Ward, 1958), p. xi.
[35] Robert Redfield, "Thinking about a Civilization," in Milton Singer (ed.), *Introducing India in Liberal Education* (Chicago: University of Chicago Press, 1957), p. 3.

Religions the more difficulties I encounter in relating the historical and the systematic dimensions of *Religionswissenschaft*. I have almost come to a simple conclusion that some people are born to be more historically oriented, while others are systematically oriented. I also recognize the rarity of the kind of encyclopedic mind that can develop adequate systematic works. And yet, I also am inclined to believe that in the long run *Religionswissenschaft* will stand or fall with the systematic structuring of the data on its own ground. Certainly, the task of *Religionswissenschaft* is not the gathering of data for the benefit of other academic enterprises. To be sure, philosophers and theologians are at liberty to utilize our research, but their interpretations must remain within the philosophical or theological discipline. Conversely, the exclusive utilization of philosophical or theological data by *Religionswissenschaft* turns ours into a philosophical or theological discipline. The common danger I find in our discipline is to fall into the temptation of systematizing our data on the basis of a framework borrowed from philosophical, sociological, anthropological or psychological models.

Our discipline is haunted by the difficulties in deriving systematic categories to focus and study. The forebears of our discipline seemed to have borrowed not only data but also categories from various other disciplines, especially from philosophy. Even C. P. Tiele, who rejected a metaphysically or religiously colored philosophy, resorted to philosophical categories because, in his view, *Religionswissenschaft* was essentially a philosophical inquiry into the universal human phenomena called religion.[36] According to Wach, it was Max Scheler who first envisioned an independent, religio-scientific mode of inquiry called the "concrete phenomenology of religious objects and acts," whose aim was to study religious phenomena by means of religio-scientific categories.[37] Nevertheless, the systematic or phenomenological inquiry of *Religionswissenschaft*, in spite of its use of religio-scientific categories, often has been mistaken by others as a philosophical or pseudo-theological endeavor. More recently, due to the strong influence of the social sciences on *Religionswissenschaft*, our discipline's systematic study appears to look, at least to some people, more like anthropology or psychology. These and other kinds of misunderstandings notwithstanding, the primary task of the systematic dimension of *Religionswissenschaft* is not so much to unfold novel generalizations as much as to articulate its research procedures and methods.

Rightly or wrongly, I feel that it is crucially important for historians of religions to begin their work with "classical" religions. Our scholarly categories, inadequate though they may be, are derived primarily from the classical forms of religions in which religious manifestations are more clearly discerna-

---

[36] Joachim Wach, *Religionswissenschaft—Prolegomena zu ihrer wissenschaft-theoretischen Grundlegung* (Leipzig: J. C. Hinrichs, 1924), pp. 117–19.
[37] *Ibid.*, pp. 126–28.

ble than in the ambiguities of modern or less-known precivilized situations. Thus, unlike social scientific disciplines which have refined research procedures to deal with modern as well as primitive religious phenomena, the "humanistic" History of Religions must first develop sufficient understanding of classical forms and types of religious phenomena. These forms may then provide a means with which to deal with other religious modalities. In this connection, I would also add a word of caution against the uncritical use of the "traditional versus modern" formula, which often appears to our anti-historical contemporaries to offer simple resolutions for the complex problems presented by the discipline of the History of Religions. Such a stereotyped dichotomy, however, fails to do justice to the rich historical heritage or the tradition *(traditio)* which has remained alive and resourceful to the present. I am keenly aware of a series of difficult problems that confronts the History of Religions, methodological or otherwise. But, I believe, our problems will find their solutions—to the extent that any scholarly problems are ever solved—by our asking important religio-scientific questions and by our refining our research procedures and categories.

As you may recall, in the 1870's Burnouf predicted the impending emergence of a unified science of religion. Again in the 1950's Pettazzoni added an optimistic note to the effect that the division of *Religionswissenschaft* into historical and systematic (or phenomenological) dimensions represents "merely a stage on the road towards the foundation of a single science of religion on its essential bases and in its undivided form."[38] Those of us who are wrestling with the task of bridging the two dimensions of our discipline, without too much success, may feel Burnouf and Pettazzoni were visionaries or dreamers. Even then, we can ill afford to lose such a lofty dream and vision—here in North America and elsewhere!

[38] Pettazzoni, *op. cit.*, p. 128.

# 6

## THE HISTORY OF RELIGIONS AT CHICAGO

Shortly after I came to Chicago in 1946, by chance I ran into Joachim Wach, who had come to the University of Chicago as Professor of the History of Religions *(Religionswissenschaft)* from Brown University. I thought at first that he must be the son of the Joachim Wach who had written many important books and articles in the Twenties and whose name had been well known to me before the war, while I was still in Japan. Needless to say, I was delighted to find that he was Joachim Wach himself. In 1947, I enrolled as a student of the history of religions with Noah Fehl (who died in Hong Kong while teaching at Chung Chi College), Philip H. Ashby (who is now retired from Princeton University), Harmon H. Bro (now a pastor in Park Ridge), and Richard Bush (currently Dean of Oklahoma City University). Wach's classes were open to students in other "fields" (which is what they were then called) of the Divinity School and from other segments of the university. Thus I often saw the faces of such currently well-known figures as Jerald C. Brauer (then a student of the history of Christianity in the Divinity School), Morris Philipson (then a philosophy student, now Director of the University of Chicago Press), Maurice Friedman (then in the Committee on Social Thought, who later wrote many books on Martin Buber), Arthur Cohen (a student in the college, to become later an active participant in the Jewish-Christian dialogue), Yoshio Fukuyama (now Dean of the Chicago Theological Seminary), Yoshiaki Fujitani (then an M.A. student, now Bishop of the Honpa Honganji Buddhist Mission in Hawaii). I discovered that Wach was deeply concerned with both the past and the present of *Religionswissenschaft* at the University of Chicago; thus it seems to me important to put down my recollections of those days as a historical record of the history of religions for the future.

### THE PAST

In 1947, the University of Chicago was barely fifty-five years old, but it had already experienced three phases of orientation as far as *Religionswissenschaft* was concerned. The founding president of the young university, William Rainey Harper, was motivated to lead a second reformation of Christianity through scholarship. According to him, the center of the university was the life of the Divinity School, even though he had designed the curriculum with Old Testament, New Testament, and Comparative Religion as part of the Liberal Arts (now called the Humanities), outside of the Divinity School. Convinced that the liberal spirit was the highest achievement of civilization, he regarded the liberal traditions of Judaism and Christianity as one unified religious tradition; and although trained in Hebraica but not in other branches of *Religionswissenschaft*, he had the strong feeling that what he called "Comparative Religion" was more inclusive and in keeping with the critical methods and scientific spirit needed for a university discipline than was the "history of religions," which other institutions, including Harvard, continued to require in their divinity schools.

Harper and his close personal friend, confidant, and colleague, Rabbi Emile Hirsch, agreed with the goal of, and fully supported, the 1893 World's Parliament of Religions, held in Chicago. A child of his time, Harper never questioned that Western civilization would eventually dominate the world, and he was convinced that the Judeo-Christian conciliatory approach to other religions, as exemplified by the Parliament of Religions, would be the best—and the most humane—solution for tensions and conflicts among religions of the world.

Thus it is understandable that the first phase of Comparative Religion at the University of Chicago closely echoed the spirit of the World's Parliament of Religions. Initially important was George Stephen Goodspeed (d. 1905), author of *A History of the Babylonians and Assyrians*, who in the early days of the university was appointed Professor of Comparative Religion and Ancient History. Indications exist that Goodspeed was not happy with the term "Comparative Religion," although he fully supported the World's Parliament of Religions. It is well known that Mrs. Caroline Haskell, a wealthy supporter of both the Parliament and the University of Chicago, donated the Haskell Lectureship on Comparative Religion and the Barrows Lectureship that sends Western Christian scholars to India and other parts of Asia, as well as the Haskell Oriental Museum, behind Swift Hall and the home of the Department of Anthropology in recent years. Goodspeed was assisted by Edmund Buckley (author of *Phallicism in Japan* [1895]), then docent; and when the Parliament was over, John Henry Barrows, permanent chairman of the Parliament, joined the Department of Comparative Religion as special professorial lecturer.

As far as we can tell, Goodspeed was a well-trained historian of ancient Near Eastern and Mediterranean religions. He was also a theological liberal, convinced that Christianity was the most liberal of all religions and capable of fulfilling the religious needs of all mankind. Thus he was entirely sincere when he expressed on behalf of Mrs. Haskell at the opening of the Haskell Oriental Museum the hope that "there will go forth from these halls enlightenment, inspiration, and guidance in that learning which has come from the East and West, culminating in the Book of Books and in the teachings of the Son of Man, [which] will ever abide as our most precious possession" (quoted in *A History of the University of Chicago,* by Thomas W. Goodspeed [Chicago, 1916], pp. 299–300). He believed that the Department of Comparative Religion, and not the Divinity School, which he felt was not free from sectarian dogmatism, should serve as the central focus of the university's intellectual inquiry into religion. Unfortunately, however, the Department of Comparative Religion at this time did not attract many advanced degree candidates; its courses interested primarily students from the Divinity School and returned missionaries.

In 1902, Louis Henry Jordan, a Canadian scholar trained in Scotland, was appointed special lecturer in Comparative Religion, since Barrows had left Chicago to become the President of Oberlin College; Jordan stayed only one year, leaving to survey and write on the state of the discipline. His work includes *Comparative Religion: It's Genesis and Growth* (1905), *Comparative Religion: A Survey of Its Recent Literature* (1910), and *Comparative Religion: Its Adjuncts and Allies* (1915). With Goodspeed's death in 1905 and Harper's a year later, the first phase of *Religionswissenschaft*, which had welcomed critical methods but had been dominated by theological liberalism, passed.

The second phase of the discipline, best described as a period of interregnum, lasted until the end of World War I. During these years, the Divinity School, in sharp contrast to the Department of Comparative Religion, which had not produced a single doctoral candidate, was emerging as a national powerhouse and a center of liberalism, modernism, the social gospel, and the socio-historical method. Shailer Mathews (1963–1941), tireless Dean of the Divinity School from 1908 to 1933 and author, lecturer, and champion of the social gospel, assembled a group of able scholars including Gerald B. Smith, J. M. P. Smith, Galusha Anderson, Charles R. Henderson, Shirley Jackson Case, James Breasted, Ira M. Price, and Edgar J. Goodspeed. Slowly, public attention shifted from the concerns of Comparative Religion to the controversies between fundamentalism and the social gospel, between conservatives and liberals; with this shift, the focus on the study of religion moved from the colleges and universities to the theological seminaries.

The discipline of *Religionswissenschaft* began to disappear from seminary curricula, except perhaps as a poor appendage to courses on world missions; however, the rigorous, disciplined study of *Missionswissenschaft* never took root in American seminaries. Even in those institutions where some form of *Religionswissenschaft* continued to exist—Boston, Cornell, and New York Universities; the Universities of Pennsylvania and Chicago; and Harvard Divinity School—it depended heavily on the expertise of individual professors rather than on the scholarly concern for religious phenomena as objectifications of the religious experience of mankind. It had come to be regarded as a kind of three-storied house. The first storey comprised a narrow historical study of specific religious traditions, conceived as the

simple study of "raw" religious data often colored by an evolutionary ideology; the second storey, "Comparative Religion," aimed to classify religious
data in order to provide the basis for the third storey, a "philosophy of
religion" or a "theology" which would provide a meaning for the enterprise
of Comparative Religion as a whole. This three-level scheme met with
relatively wide acceptance among students of Comparative Religion and
*Missionswissenschaft* in Europe, and was advocated in North America by
Morris Jastrow (1861–1921), Professor of Semitic Languages at the University
of Pennsylvania; Louis Henry Jordan (1855–1923) of the University of Chicago; and George Burman Foster (d. 1918), also of Chicago and a specialist in
the philosophy of religion. This domestication of the three-level European
scheme lent a peculiar slant to the American approach to *Religionswissenschaft* in the sense of viewing all religious phenomena through
the window of one religious and cultural tradition—usually one's own—
which made for a unique blending—conscious or unconscious—of the insights of *Religionswissenschaft* and *Missionswissenschaft*.

Spearheaded by A. Eustace Haydon (d. 1975), sole member of the
Department of Comparative Religion and an erudite scholar and eloquent
speaker, the third and final phase of *Religionswissenschaft* at Chicago was a
critique of and a reaction to the two preceding phases. Haydon had outgrown
the fundamentalist faith of his childhood by the time he graduated from the
Divinity School, and he realized that this loss of orthodoxy held three
important implications. First, religious reality gave way to considerations of
the ethical and the aesthetic, to use Kierkegaardian shorthand, and he
increasingly stressed "ethical" rather than "religious" aspects, to the degree
that there was little difference in his own mind between Comparative Religion and Comparative Ethics. (He later became a spokesman for the Ethical
Culture movement.) Second, he became an ardent advocate of religious
relativism as the only intellectual framework for the enterprise of Comparative Religion; and third, he supported Comparative Religion, which he
understood as an umbrella term for a series of objective studies of specific
religious traditions undertaken by specialists with little concern for the intra-
religious or universal factors involved.

In Haydon's view, human needs originally created various forms of
religion. Throughout history, all religions had to wrestle with the problem of
change, which he called the perennial problem of "modernism." The historic
religions in the twentieth century had been compelled to come to terms with
hitherto unknown revolutionary forces, namely, the "new scientific thinking"
and "applied science." The former force held profound implications for all
aspects of human life, and especially for traditional religions and their
ancient cosmologies, theologies, and supernaturalisms. Applied science,
especially modern machinery, communications, and systems of transportation, had already reshaped the face of the world.

In response to the new foci, as a comparative religionist Haydon organized in 1933 the World Fellowship of Faiths. This conference was concerned with six faiths that he felt shared common problems—Islam, Judaism, Christianity, Buddhism, Confucianism, and Hinduism. It addressed four major topics: World Religions and Modern Scientific Thinking; World Religions and Modern Social-Economic Problems; World Religions and Inter-Cultural Contacts; and the Task of Modern Religion.

By far the most salient feature of the 1933 conference—and, by implication, of the third Chicago orientation—was the manner in which it equated religion and morality and Comparative Religion and science. To quote K. Natarajan of Bombay: "The task of religion in all ages has been to assert the supremacy of the moral law over the lives of individuals and nations" (in *Modern Trends in World-Religions*, ed. A. Eustace Haydon [Chicago, 1934], p. 221). Further, Haydon's close friend, Rabbi Solomon Goldman, stated, "The ancient techniques of prayer and ritual need be retained only insofar as they are aesthetically appealing. Modern religions must become the friend and not the enemy of science" (ibid., p. 220). Haydon agreed that the task of Comparative Religion was to help people to overcome the anti-scientific bias and to show them the synthesis of science and idealism that would become the religion of tomorrow. "The whole world," he said, "wrestles with the same problems, aspires toward the same ideas, and strives to adjust inherited thought-patterns to the same scientific ideas. In such times, the prophetic fire of religious aspiration flames anew and religions move into new embodiments . . . the religions of tomorrow are emerging surrounded by a multitude of modernization of the old" (ibid., p. ix).

It is interesting to note that the 1893 World's Parliament of Religions, whose spirit dominated the first phase of Comparative Religion in Chicago, and the 1933 World Fellowship of Faiths, the brainchild of the third phase, both recognized religion only in organized forms such as Hinduism, Buddhism, Christianity, and Judaism. These conferences were "tone-deaf" to those religious experiences of the human race expressed in myths, symbols, and rituals; hence their complete indifference to "primitive" religions and to the religions of native and Meso-Americans. In treating historic religions, they divorced religious realities from human communities, so that participants spoke, for example, of Buddhism apart from Buddhist community life. The 1893 conference did at least indicate concern for the past of the various religions; the 1933 conference concerned itself solely with the modern phases and movements of "living" world religions.

Notwithstanding his personal convictions about the nature of Comparative Religion and the fact that he was a serious scholar, Haydon was an unhappy man, shouldering the responsibility of running the Department of Comparative Religion alone for two-and-a-half decades, with his office in the Divinity School (Swift 403) surrounded by philosophers, philosophers of religion, historians, theologians, and biblical scholars. Most of the students who took his courses were Divinity School students, and, by necessity, he became an expert on non-Christian and non-Western religions, subjects which became identified as the scope or area of Comparative Religion. During his long tenure, he trained only a few degree candidates, and they were encouraged to become primarily experts on specific non-Western religions rather than students of a broader *Religionswissenschaft*. Comparative Religion finally ceased to exist as a department in the Division of the Humanities, and it was Haydon, fundamentalist-turned-skeptic, who brought the program into the Divinity School shortly before his retirement in 1945.

## THE ISSUES

The newly arrived Joachim Wach had to consider both how to adjust himself to and what to do in the situation as he found it at the University of Chicago and how to sort out the "past" of *Religionswissenschaft* here. In the mid-Forties, the University of Chicago was an intellectually alive and stimulating place. Robert Maynard Hutchins reigned over the campus as chancellor. Under him was President Ernest Cadmon "Pomp" Colewell, formerly Dean of the Divinity School. During World War II, the university had welcomed many refugee scholars from Germany and Italy who greatly enriched the scholarly atmosphere. At this time the Divinity School was in the midst of negotiations to form the Federated Theological Faculty (hereafter the FTF) from its staff and the faculties of Chicago Theological Seminary, Meadville Theological School, and the Disciples Divinity House. The FTF curriculum offered Constructive Theology (Bernard M. Loomer, Charles Hartshorne, Bernard E. Meland, Daniel Day Williams); Historical Theology (Wilhelm Pauck); Ethics and Society (James Luther Adams, Samuel Kinchloe, Victor Obenhaus); Bible (J. Coert Rylaarsdam, Amos Wilder, Ernest C. Colewell, Alan P. Wikgren, Paul Schubert); Church History (Sidney E. Meade, James H. Nichols); to these were added within a few years the fields of Religion and Personality and Religion and Arts. Wach proposed to use the designation of "history of religions" instead of "comparative religion" as a more appropriate translation of *Allgemeine Religionswissenschaft*, and his proposal was accepted. His great headache then became the development of the history of religions within the framework of the Divinity School curriculum.

This is not the place to trace the development of the discipline of the history of religions (see my *History of Religions: Retrospect and Prospect*, [Macmillan, 1985]). There is some truth to the statement that the history of religions has been particularly stimulated by three kinds of conversation partners: the philosophy of religion and theology, especially in Germany; the social sciences, especially in Germany and France; and *Missionswissenschaft*, especially in Scandinavia, The Netherlands, and the British Isles.

Wach for a long time thought of religion in primarily humanistic terms.

Although raised a Christian, he was proud of his ancestor, Moses Mendelssohn and of his own dual Jewish and Christian heritage. As a scholar, he spoke of the importance of faith, piety, and devotion to religion, but he did not feel that he was personally and existentially involved in religion. Thus, although he had studied thoroughly the philosophy of religion and theological hermeneutics (see his three-volume *Das Verstehen*), he pursued *Religionswissenschaft* by following the humanistic model of philology and the social scientific model of sociology successively. Indeed, his first book in English and the fruit of his research during his tenure at Brown, was a very sociological work entitled *Sociology of Religion* (University of Chicago Press, 1944).

Wach's flirtation with theology occurred much later, and in a strange manner. Although not politically minded, he soon realized that the action of the government of Saxony of dismissing him in 1935 from the faculty at Leipzig purely on the grounds of ethnicity was both an example of the terrifying phenomenon of Nazism in Germany and a colossal embodiment of human evil. The League of Nations and the enlightened cultural tradition and autonomy of the German universities were powerless before Hitler, but the church managed to maintain a stubborn resistance to the Nazification of Europe. To Wach, whose mother and sister were interned, this was an illuminating experience; and once awakened to the reality of the church as a living religious community, his interest in theology deepened. Yet even so, it took him ten years—his entire tenure at the University of Chicago—to sort out the relationship between *Religionswissenschaft* and theology; he was in a sense, pulled in opposing directions between the two. Unfortunately, his reflections on this issue were only partially recorded in his posthumous publication, *The Comparative Study of Religions* (New York, 1958).

In order to understand *Religionswissenschaft* at the University of Chicago in the mid-Forties, we must keep three things in mind. First, it was clear that Wach wanted to teach the history of religions or *Allgemeine Religionswissenschaft*, an autonomous discipline located between the normative studies of the philosophy of religion and theology and the descriptive studies of sociology, anthropology, and psychology. He was also clear that *Religionswissenschaft* consisted of two complementary dimensions, the "historical" and the "systematic" procedures of study. The "historical" task required a mutual interaction between the "general history" of religion and the "historical studies" of various *specific* religions; the "systematic" task aimed at disciplined generalizations and the structuring of data, and depended upon an application of phenomenological, comparative, sociological, and psychological studies of religions. That historical and systematic inquiries were two interdependent dimensions of one and the same discipline called the history of religions cannot be too heavily stressed.

Wach believed that the history of religions should ideally be taught as a part of human studies, but he also understood why in America it was taught as a part of the divinity curriculum, as had been done at Harvard Divinity School and later at the University of Chicago. He liked to think that the example of Marburg, which had one chair in the philosophy faculty and another in the theological faculty, might be repeated at Chicago. Thus, he joyfully accepted the assignment of teaching the history of religions as a part of the FTF curriculum, but he also spent much energy in making it an important element in the university's Committee of the History of Culture.

The second thing we might remember is that, irenic in temper, Wach wanted to relate his new enterprise to each orientation of the three phases of comparative religion at Chicago. Accordingly, he paid special attention to (1) the special place of Judaism and Christianity in Western civilization, which the *Religionswissenschaft's* first phase in Chicago stressed, reflecting as it did the 1893 World's Parliament of Religions; (2) the relationship between the *Religionswissenschaft* and the philosophy of religion (or theology), stressed during the second phase, by George Burman Foster especially; and (3) the concern for specific religious traditions—Hinduism, Buddhism, and Islam—as exemplified in the orientation of the third phase. He always lamented, however, the lack of interest in the so-called "primitive religions" in North America or, rather, the fact that "primitive religions" was regarded as the private preserve of anthropologists and not the concern of students of religion in North America. He was particularly sensitive to the fact that the usual variety of comparative religion in North America, which in effect was a peculiar halfway house between the *Religionswissenschaft* and *Missionswissenschaft*, tended to regard, for example, Hinduism and Buddhism as the expressions of solely Hindu or Buddhist religious experiences. He was persuaded that behind Hindusim or Buddhism lay the underlying religious experience of humankind, described as the experience of the "holy" by Rudolf Otto and as the experience of "power" by G. van der Leeuw. He was also sympathetic to the desire to find a special place for Judaism and Christianity in the study of religion, a hope which the 1893 Parliament had stressed. But unlike those who viewed all religions through the window of the Judeo-Christian tradition, Wach insisted that Judaism and Christianity, like all other religions, must be seen as parts of the "whole" religious experience of the human race. It is interesting that in the last ten years of his life Wach was often mistakenly thought to be in the camp of the second Chicago orientation, a situation which necessitated his stating repeatedly that while the philosophy of religion often applies an abstract philosophical idea of what religion is to the data of empirical, historical studies, the history of religions must begin with the investigation of religious phenomena, from which, it is hoped, a pattern of "meaning" might emerge. We should keep in mind, however, that the history of religion's inquiry into the "meaning" of religious phenomena *leads* one to questions of a philosophical and metaphysical nature, but the history of religions as such cannot deal with those questions philosophically.

The third thing to be kept in mind is that the situation of the history of religions at Chicago in the mid-Forties was further complicated both by Wach's new interest in theology and by the emergence of a strong theological ethos based on Whiteheadian process philosophy in the FTF. (Incidentally, Wach dedicated his volume, *Types of Religious Experience: Christian and Non-Christian*, to his colleagues of "The Federated Theological Faculty of the University of Chicago." Chapter 1 of this volume is significantly entitled, "The Place of the History of Religions in the Study of Theology," the subject which most occupied his thoughts during the last ten years of his life.) Wach, who had many questions about the neo-Kantianism that had influenced him earlier, read Whitehead seriously in hopes—or wishful thinking—that process thought might give new insight into the raw stuff of human experience unconditioned by separate cultural and religious traditions. He was persuaded that underneath religious and cultural divisions was the truth and life, which somehow must be united. Thus, in his words, "interpretation of expressions of religious experience means an integral understanding, that is, full linguistic, historical, psychological, technological, and sociological enquiry, in which full justice is done to the intention of the expression and to the context in which it occurs, and in which this expression is related to the experience of which it testifies" (*Types of Religious Experience*, pp. 28–29). He wanted to go beyond just an "integral understanding," however: he aspired to become an "integrated person" for whom all branches of knowledge, especially the history of religions and theology, could become parts of the larger unity. He was not trying to find a new coherence following his earlier work, *Religionswissenschaft: Prolegomena zu ihrer wissenschaft-theoretischen Grundlegung* (1924). He was not trying to formulate one more "Theological History of Religions" after the manner of Paul Tillich, one more "Missionswissenschaft" after the manner of Hendrick Kraemer, or another social scientific approach to religion as a cultural, social, or psychological system. He simply wanted to explore the possible linkage between two legitimate studies of religious reality, namely the history of religions and theology. He must have known that there was no miraculous resolution for such inquiries, but he sensed that the mere fact that we wrestle with these quests makes them worthwhile.

## PROGRAMS

Joachim Wach was not asked by the University of Chicago to teach a well-established discipline such as sociology or philosophy. He was aware that the state of *Religionswissenschaft* in the Division of the Humanities at Chicago had not been lively, to say the least, for a long time. While it was in one sense good to start with a clean slate, including the new nomenclature of the "history of religions," Wach could not count on either the faculty or the students to understand what his discipline entailed. Actually, many people assumed that the history of religions was a historical discipline dealing largely with non-Christian and non-Western religions, whereas those who remembered the old comparative religion thought of it as either a branch of philosophy of religion or some form of apologetics.

Wach attracted a variety of students who constituted the so-called "Sangha." He regarded his early students as the pioneers, interpreters, and builders of the intellectual resources of the history of religions in North America. With this in mind, he almost arbitrarily assigned as topics for Ph.D. theses those subjects which would be necessary to the young discipline in the coming years. For instance, if my memory serves me correctly, he assigned to Noah E. Fehl the subject of Greek and Christian approaches to the study of religion during the Patristic period; to Philip H. Ashby, the topic of the relationship between *Missionswissenschaft* and *Religionswissenschaft;* to Charles J. Adams, the method of Nathan Soederblom; to Jay Fussel, the primitive religions; and to F. Stanley Lusby, the development of *Religionswissenschaft* in North America. His fame was soon such that students came from other continents—two at least from Europe, two or three from India, and two from Japan.

In post-war America, Wach found both an enormous openness to humanistic and social scientific studies of religion and the temptation to look for an easy way out, or to trivialize, the complex subject of religion. On both accounts he was right. Few people then predicted the mushrooming of departments of religion or of religious studies, usually as part of the arts and sciences curriculum of American colleges and universities, which became a new fashion in the post-war period. The popularity of religious studies, however, unfortunately was accompanied by intellectual sloppiness in some quarters. Wach was particularly sensitive to the mental attitudes of historians of religions—to their emotional stability, maturity, and empathy—and not just to their intellectual preparation in the knowledge of languages, cultural background, and history. He was also clear about the distinction between two often confused legitimate studies, namely, the studies of individual religions such as Islam, Hinduism, or any of the primitive native religions, and the study of the history of religions; and he urged those interested in Islam to go to the Institute of Islamic Studies at McGill and those interested in Buddhism to enroll in the University of Wisconsin at Madison's program in Buddhist Studies. Yet realizing that other institutions would undertake much more easily understood approaches to individual religions, Wach wanted to reserve a program at Chicago for those interested in the more demanding discipline of the history of religions. It was his aim that Chicago graduates combine *Religionswissenschaft* with the study of individual religions. I still remember the words of exhortation I received from him shortly after I joined the faculty in 1951:

If one wants to study a specific religion, one has to make certain that one's views of that religion are acceptable to those who are inside that tradition; if one is an historian of religions, one has to make sure that one's views make sense to his peers or the fellow historians of religions beyond the level of information in which one's knowledge of religions can be checked by those inside those communities.

## FROM WACH TO ELIADE

During the first half of Wach's tenure at Chicago during the Forties, the FTF provided scholarly stimulation to both Wach and his students. He also was active in the degree-granting Committee of the History of Culture and in various seminars, including that on the "birth of civilizations" organized by Robert Redfield, and in numerous lecture series; he was always "on the go." In spring, he and his students had their annual outing at the beach house of Professor and Mrs. Robert Platt at the Indiana Dunes. Every summer he visited his mother and sister in Orselina, Switzerland. His less than robust health was threatened in 1950 by a heart ailment, but he was well enough to go to India in 1952 as the Barrows Lecturer.

Wach received many visitors, including Martin Buber, Gershom G. Scholem (Wach's fellow student at Munich), D. T. Suzuki, Gerardus van der Leeuw, Jacques Duchesne-Guillemin, A. A. Fyzee, and H. Kishimoto, all of whom delighted Wach's students by appearing in his classes. He was vitally interested in strengthening the program of the history of religions through inviting great scholars as Haskell Lecturers, notably his own teacher, Friedrich Heiler, who came after Wach's death; Louis Massignon, who came during Wach's visit to India; and Mircea Eliade, whom Wach considered the most astute historian of religions in his time.

During the second half of Wach's tenure at Chicago in the Fifties, the seams of the once solid FTF began to ravel. The departure of some of his close colleagues and friends from Chicago, especially Wilhelm Pauck to New York, was hard on the emotionally sensitive Wach. He was invited to assume the coveted chair of his mentor, Rudolf Otto, at Marburg, but after much deliberation, he declined this honor. He participated in the Seventh Congress of the International Association for the History of Religions held in Rome in the spring of 1955. He died in Switzerland in the summer of 1955 while visiting his mother and sister.

In the autumn of 1955, Friedrich Heiler taught at the University of Chicago; in 1956, Mircea Eliade agreed to deliver the Haskell Lectures and to teach at the Univesity of Chicago, and he remained for thirty years as a professor in both the Divinity School and the degree-granting Committee on Social Thought. It was fortuitous that Eliade came to Chicago during the years of the expanding religious studies movement in North America. Many of his books were translated into English and were widely read by people in all walks of life. His name attracted a large number of students from various continents, and many Chicago graduates assumed positions of leadership in educational institutions, on committees, and in associations of local, national, and international reputation. In 1961, Eliade was instrumental in inaugurating *History of Religions: An International Journal for Comparative Historical Studies*. Although he and Wach were very different in personality, approach, and academic orientation, the fact that they agreed wholeheartedly on the nature of the history of religions made for a smooth transition after Wach's death. The following statement, penned by Eliade in History of Religions 1, no. 1, could have been made without qualification by Wach; it eloquently addresses the problems and challenges of the history of religions which we in Chicago are destined to nurture for the sake of North America and the whole world:

> Despite the manuals, periodicals, and bibliographies today available to scholars, it is progressively more difficult to keep up with the advances being made in all departments of the History of Religions [*Religionswissenschaft*]. Hence it is progressively more difficult to become a historian of religions. A scholar regretfully finds himself becoming a specialist in *one* religion or even in a particular period or a single aspect of that religion.
>
> This situation has induced us to bring out a new periodical. . . . (*History of Religions* 1, no. 1 [Summer 1961]:1)

In retrospect, the program of the history of religions at Chicago in recent decades has been fortunate in attracting successively Professors Charles H. Long, Gösta Ahlström, Frank E. Reynolds, Jonathan Z. Smith, Wendy D. O'Flaherty, and Lawrence Sullivan. Granted there will always be unavoidable differences of opinion among both faculty and students in the coming years; still, I consider it a great privilege to have been associated with this program for four decades, first as a student and then as a faculty member. As I close my eyes, I am overwhelmed by the memories of so many wonderful and talented men and women who have gone through our program. Many of them have cooperated with Eliade in recent years on his monumental enterprise, the sixteen-volume *Encyclopedia of Religion* New York: Macmillan, 1987), which will remain for many years to come a minor classic in the history of religions and in the humanistic and social scientific study of religion.

# 7

## RELIGIOUS STUDIES AND THE HISTORY OF RELIGIONS

### INTRODUCTION

In the autumn of 1981, I went to China as a member of the University of Chicago delegation invited by the Chinese Academy of Science. Much to my personal embarrassment, many of our Chinese colleagues were intensely curious about the fact that the Chicago delegation included a person like myself, born and raised in Japan. They kept asking me, as a "fellow Oriental," what I thought of American universities in comparison with their Chinese and Japanese counterparts. And realizing that I was teaching the history of religions, they pressed me as to why and how religion is taught as an academic subject in American educational institutions. In fact, they raised many questions which I had not thought through before, and since then I have been trying to sort out some of the issues in my own mind.

When I studied the history of religions in the mid-1940s under Joachim Wach at the University of Chicago, the history of religions and religious studies were hardly established in North America. Since then I have witnessed the growing popularity of the History of religions and the sudden mushrooming of religious studies in various colleges and universities, both public and private. There is no question in my mind that the establishment of the academic study of religion in recent decades is one of the most salutary innovations in American institutions of higher learning. However, the all-too-sudden flowering of religious studies has left many of the ambiguities involved in the enterprise unresolved. Thus, before we undertake the task of "revisioning" the study of religion, we might profitably reflect on some of the unresolved issues.

I am reminded of Heidegger's criticism of Marx's statement: "The philosophers have interpreted the world, but it is up to us to change it." Heidegger commented that to change the world, one needs another—a new or a different—philosophical interpretation of the world.[1] Similarly, "revisioning the study of religion" requires more than simply adjusting to changing factors in our society such as economic retrenchment or anti-

---

[1] See R. J. Z. Werblowsky, "Crisis Consciousness and the Future," *Diogenes* 113–114 (Spring-Summer 1981): 69.

intellectualism on the part of Jewish and Christian religious groups. Rather, it requires that we hammer out a scholarly rationale that will enable us to present the study of religion as an essential ingredient of the humanistic inquiry of the college or the university. With this in mind, I would like to reflect on the muddled relationship between religious and theological studies as *one* of the unresolved issues for those concerned with the task of revisioning the study of religion in our time.

## RELIGIOUS STUDIES

I fully realize that today many people see no reason to be concerned anymore with the relationship between religious and theological studies. In fact, some people go so far as to define Religious Studies simply as what theological study is not. Even those who recognize the existence of some kind of relationship—antagonistic or congenial—between the two are not altogether certain as to how these two types of inquiry should be interrelated in practice. You may be interested to know that as early as the 1890s William Rainey Harper, the first president of the University of Chicago, himself a Biblical scholar and an enthusiastic advocate of both types of inquiry, assigned to the Divinity School the theological study of the New Testament as the basic resource for the faith of the Christian community; but he expected the Department of New Testament and Early Christian Literature in the Division of the Humanities to be engaged in religious-humanistic inquiry into the New Testament as an important text that has exerted a significant influence upon Western civilization. In principle, Harper's resolution of the two ways to study the New Testament was neat; but in practice, it has not been easy to maintain such a clearcut division of labor. After all, both approaches deal with the same texts. Inevitably there are areas in which both concerns converge, even if no two scholars from either side have agreed on how and where the convergence should occur.

Similar tensions exist between the history of Christianity and church history. William Clebsch reminds us that "Christianity belongs in a sense to the church and in a different sense to Western culture." Accordingly, says he, "church history is the history of institutional Christians *by* institutional Christians *for* institutional Christians."[2] "Although church history may flirt with critical history by day, by night she goes to bed with theology, her true husband."[3] Yet, "what Christianity has been and what it is to become—of, by, and for Western culture—is the proper concern of historians of Christianity and is properly the task of historical studies in universities, in allegiance to the humanities."[4] In spite of Clebsch's admirably clear distinction

[2] William A. Clebsch, "History and Salvation: An Essay in Distinctions," in *The Study of Religion in Colleges and Universities*, Paul Ramsay and John F. Wilson, eds. (Princeton, 1970), p. 71.

[3] Ibid., p. 66.

[4] Ibid., p. 71.

between the history of Christianity and church history, these two approaches also converge on some level.

It has been argued—cogently by some—that the basic difference between religious and theological studies can be defined primarily in institutional terms. That is to say, religious studies belong to the university and theological studies belong to theological schools. There is no question that the establishment of religious studies during the last three decades has signalled the institutional separation of religious and theological studies. The separation has yielded benefits, but it has also had an impoverishing effect on both sides. On the side of theological schools, the institutional separation gave implicit credence to shifting the main focus to "professional education" at the expense of *theologia,* that is, "a dialectical reflection which presides over faith's self-consciousness and critical responses to the world."[5] Although theological schools have been influenced by various features of religious studies, such as its all-too-elastic notion of "religion," more than they are willing to admit—mostly through learned societies and publications—they have lost direct channels through which they might receive critical input and necessary correctives from religious-humanistic studies of religion.

The situation of religious studies on the undergraduate, M.A., and doctoral levels defies any simple characterization. Very different types of programs share this nomenclature. In some institutions, religious studies programs seem to be little more than watered-down theological studies devoid of faith commitment, programs in some instances staffed by those who have received traditional theological training but who have been disenchanted by institutional aspects of religion. In a few cases, the program depends heavily upon ministers, priests, and rabbis who may have academic credentials but who have little understanding of the academic study of religion in the college or university setting. In still other cases, often designated "programs" rather than "departments," religious studies consist of an assortment of unrelated courses—courses from the psychology department on the psychology of religion, courses from the history department on medieval history, courses from the sociology department on the sociology of religion, and so forth—to which a smattering of language and introductory courses has been attached. Fortunately, some of the idiosyncratic differences have been eliminated to a great extent over the years, thanks largely to the influence of various learned societies.

Nevertheless, there is not as yet anything like uniformity among various programs of religious studies. At present, many institutions still operate with programs on the "Western religious tradition," "American religious studies," or variations of either one, such as "Catholicism, Protestantism, and Judaism." Many also add some courses on the philosophy of religion, the psychol-

[5] Edward Farley, *Theologia: The Fragmentation and Unity of Theological Education* (Fortress, 1983), p. 196.

ogy of religion, the sociology of religion, religion and literature, the Black religious tradition, women and religion, and primitive and/or non-Western religions. Many programs also offer joint courses with Near Eastern and other civilizational programs, art, English, philosophy, psychology, history, sociology, anthropology, and others. For the most part, religious studies programs appoint specialists who in turn guard their sacred precincts by means of implicit or explicit non-aggression pacts with their colleagues.

The model of religious studies as a group of specialists has its effect. It is easier for individual scholars to find congenial conversation partners in cognate areas in their college or university and/or fellow specialists in other institutions than among their own colleagues in the same religious studies department. To be sure, religious studies faculty members spend enormous amounts of time discussing the nature of religious studies as such, but very few agree on direction, standards, or even criteria for evaluation of their colleagues. That religious studies lack coherence is seen most conspicuously when it is time to promote colleagues. Is a colleague to be promoted primarily because he/she is a competent specialist, or is he/she to be promoted because of his/her expertise in interpreting the nature of religious studies? Or both? And, if so, what are the norms of religious studies as a whole?

In many cases, those who depend primarily upon the specialists' model are inclined to feel that they can muddle through in the future as they have done in the past, rather than raising knotty issues about the "coherence" of religious studies, even though many of them are concerned with the "balance" of course offerings. Yet, because of internal as well as external reasons, religious studies will have to come to terms sooner or later with the issues of norms, paradigms, standards, and criteria. In this process, they will have to deal with such an old skeleton as the relation between religious and theological studies.

There is much truth in David Tracy's characterization of today's religious studies, with which many insiders seem to agree:

> Religious studies is a study of religion in keeping with the standards, methods and criteria of all scholarly study of any phenomenon. It cannot and should not allow for the use of special criteria (for example, a demand for personal faith in a particular religion in order to understand that religion). Theology, conventionally understood, demands just such a special criteria. As a discipline, theology belongs, therefore, to the churches and its seminaries. . . . It does not belong in a secular university in a pluralistic culture.[6]

It is to be noted that this statement does not represent Tracy's own view of what religious studies ought to be, but rather his assessment of how

---

[6] David Tracy, *The Analogical Imagination* (Crossroad, 1981), p. 16.

religious studies often understands itself—especially its negative attitude toward theological inquiry. At the same time, there are those who are not satisfied to define religious studies simply as the non-theological, humanistic, and "scientific" study of religion. They raise serious questions as to whether the subject matter of religious studies is confined to religions as such or also includes determinate cultural and religious traditions. They also raise questions about methodological principles appropriate to the subject matter, however it is determined. Futhermore, they raise questions about the levels of meaning to be aimed at by religious studies. All these questions must be faced squarely by those who are concerned with "revisioning the study of religion" in our time. To put it more concretely, how do we respond, for example, to the following statement by Edward Farley:

> To teach Buddhism is not simply to communicate information about Buddhist history or present practices but so to stage and evoke participation in its texts and their claims that the insightfulness of Buddhist meditation is insightfully grasped by the student. The same holds for Romantic poetry, French existentialism, and studies in Marx and Freud. The representation of determinate historical and cultural experience, even if it is religious in character, does not disqualify a subject matter, movement, or literature from university studies. . . . What disqualifies a subject matter is an approach to it which eschews critical method for mere authority, special pleading, or ideology.[7]

Side by side with the questions raised thus far, religious studies in the 1980s must also deal with a series of issues on another level: How adequately can we or should we try to deal with various aspects or areas of religious studies? What kinds of interdisciplinary cooperation will be needed? For example, as Jacob Neusner rightly points out, to study the Jewish religious tradition requires the cooperation of experts on Jewish history (ancient, medieval, and modern); Hebrew language, scriptures, and literatures; Jewish law, philosophy, art, and community.[8] Similarly, the study of Roman Catholicism, Buddhism, and the psychology or sociology of religion also requires the collaboration of many scholars and disciplines. Confronted with the necessity for both interdisciplinary cooperation and selectivity governed by carefully established priorities, programs of religious studies have chosen various organizing principles: "conceptual" (philosophy of religion, comparative theologies, ethics), "historical" (history of ideas, doctrines, and institutions), "dialogical" (religion and law, religion and politics, religion and literature, religion and art), and so on. In this situation, some institutions are

---

[7] Farley, p. 198.

[8] Jacob Neusner, "Juadaism in the History of Religions," *History and Theory: Studies in the Philosophy of History*, Beiheft 8 (Middlebury: Wesleyan University Press, 1968), p. 37.

seriously wondering whether the history of religions might serve as a cornerstone, if not a unifying impulse, for religious studies in the future.

Let me turn now to my reflection on the history of religions.

## THE HISTORY OF RELIGIONS

Throughout my academic career, I have attempted—and, I might add, without much success—to dispel the popular misconception that the history of religions is nothing but a convenient semantic umbrella that covers all of the independent studies of specific religions, such as primitive religions, Hinduism, Islam, Buddhism, Chinese and Japanese religions. This misconception is shared widely, from aspiring students to college and university administrators. No doubt it arises partly from the fact that many historians of religions are also engaged in research on some of these religions, even though their perspectives are different from those of, say, Islamicists or Buddhologists. Oddly enough, many of those who equate the history of religions with studies of specific religions tend to exclude Judaism and Christianity from the orbit of the history of religions—another misconception I have been trying to dispel.

The ambiguity that surrounds the nature of the history of religions derives in part from terminological confusion. It might be helpful to identify different approaches to the study of religion with which the history of religions is often confused. The first approach consists of independent studies of specific religions, historical and contemporary. All of these are legitimate scholarly inquiries, but they are not to be confused with the history of religions. Pedagogical reasons may lead us to group certain non-Western religions together for teaching purposes, but this does not imply that the history of religions is the study of non-Western religions, as is often thought in colleges and universities where courses on religion are included in programs of non-Western civilizations.

The second approach involves comparative religion, a term generally used in Great Britain, where historical and philosophical studies of religion are not sharply differentiated. For the most part, comparative religionists acknowledge the importance of historical study, but only as a preliminary phase in which they collect raw religious data. To them, the objective of their study is comparative religion which, according to Louis Henry Jordan, "compares the origin, structure, and characteristics of the various Religions of the world, with the view of determining their genuine agreements and differences, the measure of relation in which they stand one to another, and their relative superiority and inferiority when regarded as types."[9] I have a feeling, rightly or wrongly, that comparative religionists have another implicit agenda—philosophy of religion in many cases but theology in others—which they call upon to adjudicate the results of comparative religion in

[9] Louis Henry Jordan, *Comparative Religion: Its Genesis and Growth* (New York, 1905), p. 63.

order to delineate religion's overall meaning. As a result, the comparative religion approach to the study of religions has been favored by some philosophers, theologians, and missiologists, and by psychologists and other social scientists as well. It should be noted that there are variations of comparative religion. For example, some comparative religionists approach religion primarily as phenomena to be studied, while others take the truth claims of each religion seriously. Still others stress "dialogue" between religions as their goal. Personally, I have great admiration for comparative religion, especially its emphasis on thorough familiarity with some particular religious traditions; but I do not consider comparative religion to be simply another designation for the history of religions as I understand the latter.

A third approach with which the history of religions is often confused is a variety of the so-called "scientific" study of religions, which attracts many students today. We might recall in this connection that Friedrich Max Müller (1823–1900), one of the pioneers of the history of religions, used the term "science of religion" as the equivalent of *Religionswissenschaft*. His rhetoric was alluring, if misleading, when he stated:

> A Science of Religion, based on an impartial and truly scientific comparison of all, or at all events, of the most important, religions of mankind, is now only a question of time. . . . Its title, though implying as yet a promise rather than a fulfillment, has become more or less familiar in Germany, France and America . . .[10]

It was not clear what this German-English scholar had in mind when he used the term "science of religion"—whether he had in mind the German sense of Wissenschaft or the English usage of "science," which has more affinity with a model of natural science characterized by predictive connotation. The ambiguity of this question has remained to this day, and in some quarters, scholars are seriously debating whether or not a "science of religion" in the English sense of "science" is possible.[11]

Another significant development today is the growing fascination among some social scientists with myths, symbols, cults, social structure, cultural patterns, and religious institutions. Many scholars in religious studies who had earlier carried on meaningful discourse with philosophers and theologians have turned to these social scientists for insights and methodological models. It goes without saying that religion is not only a religious phenomenon but also historical, social, anthropological, psychological, and cultural, and we should be edified by social scientists' studies of religious phenomena.

[10] F. Max Müller, *Introduction to the Science of Religion* (1882; reprint ed., Varanasi, India, 1972), p. 26.
[11] See, for example, Donald Wiebe, "Is a Science of Religions Possible?" *Sciences Religieuses/ Studies in Religion* 7, 1 (1978): 5–17.

We should also recognize, however, that their aim is to delineate the historical, social, anthropological, psychological, and cultural meanings of religion, none of which is identical with religious meaning. Thus, while acknowledging the legitimacy of the so-called "scientific" study of religions, we should not view it as an equivalent to or a substitute for the history of religions.

\*     \*     \*

What, then, is the history of religions? I use this designation in the way in which it is used by the International Association for the History of Religions (IAHR), that is, as a not-so-satisfactory English counterpart to the German *Religionswissenschaft*, or *Allgemeine Religionswissenschaft*, to be more exact. Its aim is to study the nature and structure of the religious experience of the human race and its diverse manifestations in history, such as the manner in which humankind has perceived and developed various models of the religious universe. In other words, the task of the history of religions is to delineate the religious meaning of humankind's religious experience and its expressions through the integration and "significant organization" of diverse forms of religious data.

The point of departure of the discipline is the historical study of particular religious data; but for the historian of religions, all particular religious traditions are "parts" of the "whole" of humankind's religious experience, and should be studied from the perspective of the whole. The principle of the "priority of the whole" differentiates the history of religions from independent studies of specific religions as well as from comparative religions. Side by side with historical studies of religious data, the history of religions must be engaged in its systematic task of developing generalized statements about the meaning of religious experience and its diverse manifestations unfolded in human history. But the systematic task of the history of religions does not depend on the philosophy of religion or on theology, nor does it resort to an *a priori* deductive method. Whereas the historical task of the discipline abides by the descriptive principles, its systematic task must be directed to the "meaning" of religion, which, it should be noted, does not imply the "truth" in religion. Of course, there have been theologians, such as Paul Tillich and some contemporary Roman Catholic and Protestant thinkers, who advocate theological inquiry based on the historical studies of the history of religions. Such a "theological history of religions" is a legitimate theological enterprise, but it is not a part of the history of religions in our sense.[12]

Clearly, the history of religions has inherited from the tradition of the *Geisteswissenschaften* the notion that the task of *Wissenschaft*—in this case, *Religionswissenschaft*—is to bring into view the whole of all knowable par-

---

[12]On this subject, see J. M. Kitagawa, "Humanistic and Theological History of Religions . . ." *Numen* 27, 2 (1980): 198–221.

ticulars. Such a task involves the act of recognition, that is, the "re-cognizing" of that which has been previously cognized as religious meaning by human beings in other times and places, and the reconstruction in its totality, in principle at least, of that which does not appear as a whole. The history of religions also inherited Dilthey's concern with the relationship between "experience, expression, and understanding (Erlebnis, Ausdruck, and Verstehen); the interdependence of self-knowledge and knowledge of other persons; and . . . the understanding of social groups and historical processes."[13] All these concerns must be woven into the hermeneutical framework of the history of religions. I might reiterate, too, that the objective of the history of religions *(Religionswissenschaft)* is distinct from that of other human and social sciences, with which it otherwise shares many features. Its objective, to be precise, is the commitment to explore the religious meaning, and not the cultural or the social meanings, of religious phenomena. In this respect, my learned colleague, Mircea Eliade, rightly reminds us that the meaning of a religious phenomenon can be understood only if it is understood to be something religious: "To try to grasp the essence of a phenomenon by means of physiology, psychology, sociology, economics, linguistics, art, or any other study is false; it misses the one unique and irreducible element in it—the element of the sacred."[14]

## THE HISTORY OF RELIGIONS AND RELIGIOUS STUDIES

It has never been argued, and I have no intention of suggesting, that the history of religions is the only legitimate inquiry into the subject of religion. The future development of the history of religions as a self-conscious discipline depends to a certain extent upon the way it relates to other modes of inquiry into religions and upon the manner in which it is informed by them. Thus the academic location of the history of religions is a matter of some significance.

As far as can be ascertained, some of the difficulties that the history of religions has had in establishing itself as an academic discipline are due in part to its being placed, from the late nineteenth century until recently, as a guest, as it were, in the theological faculties of many European universities, with the notable exception of French academic institutions. Sometimes it has even been placed in both the theological and the philosophical faculties simultaneously, as in some German and Scandinavian universities, again as an appendage to their respective curricula. Occasionally the relationship of the history of religions with theological studies was congenial, even though history of religions never held a central position in theological faculties. This

[13] See H. A. Hodges, "Dilthey, Wilhelm," *Encyclopaedia Britannica*, 1971 ed., vol. 7, p. 439; and Rudolf A. Makkreel, *Dilthey: Philosopher of the Human Sciences* (Princeton, 1975), pp. 270–71.

[14] Mircea Eliade, *Patterns in Comparative Religion* (New York, 1958), p. xi.

was especially the case where the *wissenschaftliche* character of theology was stressed or when historians of religions, for example, Nathan Söderblom and Gerardus van der Leeuw, were also engaged in theological inquiries. Inevitably, however, the history of religions came to be affected by theology's search for its own identity and for disciplinary status within the university. Some theologians wanted to appropriate aspects of the history of religions for theological, apologetic, or missiological purposes, while others resented the non-theological character and the then-fashionable evolutionary orientation of the history of religions. For the most part, theological colleagues denied historians of religions the right to deal with Christianity, while in other instances the history of religions became involved in theological controversies such as that regarding the claim of the *Religionsgeschichtliche Schule*.

In North America, too, where the history of religions has been attached to the theological faculty of the university, its own disciplinary development has been greatly affected by the rise and fall of the disciplinary status of theological studies. Moreover, the history of religions has usually been assigned the modest role of teaching "non-Christian religions" or merely of providing data for systematic theologians. Joachim Wach, who taught the history of religions in a philosophical faculty in Germany for ten years, in an American liberal arts college for ten years, and in the theological faculty of the University of Chicago for ten years, sensed the real need for mutual understanding and assistance between the history of religions and theology, two modes of study which were even then struggling for the clarification of their respective disciplinary identities and status in the university.[15] Wach was also the close personal friend of the late George Thomas of Princeton, and he was keenly interested in the development of the Religion Department in that university and its potential implications for the disciplinary development of the history of religions in North America.

\* \* \*

Although Wach died in 1955 without personally witnessing the phenomenal growth of religious studies in North America, his own students have been actively involved in this development. Understandably, the relation between the history of religions and religious studies will be determined to a great extent by the self-definition of each side. I, for one, as a historian of religions, have many questions about the nature of religious studies, just as I am sure that many in religious studies have questions about the history of religions. I am reminded that at the turn of the century, Morris Jastrow included in the study of religion such subjects as religion and ethics, religion and philosophy, religion and mythology, religion and psychology, religion and history, religion and culture, and so forth.[16] Since then, many other

---

[15] On Wach's scholarly rationale for the co-existence of the history of religions and theology, see J. Wach, *Types of Religious Experience: Christian and Non-Christian* (Chicago, 1951), pp. 27–29.

[16] See Morris J. Jastrow, Jr., *The Study of Religion* (New York, 1902).

subject matters have been added to the orbit of religious studies, especially because of the growing social scientific interest in religious phenomena.

I would like to know which way the wind is blowing currently in religious studies: (1) Is it aspiring to become an academic discipline and, if so, a "compact" or a "diffuse" discipline, to use Stephen Toulmin's terms?[17] Either way, will it aspire to absorb the history of religions, or will it consider the history of religions a partner to be kept at arm's length? (2) Is religious studies going to develop into an interdisciplinary scheme in reference to the study of religion? If so, what will it expect the history of religions to contribute to such a scheme? (3) Or, will religious studies continue to remain a sort of academic condominium in which several studies of religion will be housed with varying degrees of cooperation?

\* \* \*

I am also intrigued by John Wilson's suggestion that the history of religions might play a more central role in religious studies in the future. In his own words,

> It is commonly assumed that a unifying impulse during the coming years will be provided by systematic and comparative studies of various classes of religious phenomena across diverse traditions and cultures, Western as well as Eastern. This field—about which some ambiguity exists—already forms a significant part of the study of religion, and probably its most immediate limitation (at the moment) is in the small number of trained personnel available for academic appointments. . . . [A] common feature of most reflection about future study of religion is the candid presumption that history of religions may provide an overall coherence and orientation possibly absent at present in the field of religious study.[18]

Whether the history of religions will play such a role depends, no doubt, largely on the future shape of religious studies itself. Meanwhile, I agree with Wilson's observation that there is still a lack of trained historians of religions and that the history of religions has some ambiguities as a discipline. These two factors are involved in somewhat of a vicious circle.

There is a sufficient number of college students interested in some aspects of the history of religions, but in many cases they do not seem to receive adequate training or proper guidance. Many of them knock on the door of graduate school not only with poor preparation but also with misguided notions of the subject matter itself. Then students soon discover that it is more feasible financially and more rewarding psychologically to spend

---

[17] On the nature of "discipline," I follow Stephen Toulmin, *Human Understanding*, vol. 1 (Princeton, 1972).

[18] Paul Ramsay and John F. Wilson, eds., pp. 20–21.

their limited time, money, and energy focussing on the study of one or two religious traditions and the specific languages needed for such a study, rather than to invest the greater amounts of time, money, and energy in the more comprehensive historical and systematic studies of religious phenomena needed for the task of the history of religions. They may be interested in the larger vocation of becoming competent generalists, that is, historians of religions; but the current academic situation encourages them to become narrow specialists in particular religious traditions rather than to prepare themselves for the general, and more taxing, training in the history of religions.

Moreover, when a precious few manage to complete a hazardous graduate program in the history of religions, they become discouraged not only by the very limited opportunities for teaching, but also, when appointed, by the misguided expectations on the part of their (usually senior) colleagues as to what historians of religions are called upon to teach. This usually amounts to introductory courses on "non-Western religions" and, if they are lucky, courses on a specific religion, most likely one of the non-Christian religions. It is sad but true that their initial experience in a teaching career is not an encouraging one: they are surrounded by senior colleagues who expect their new colleagues to accept without question an established curriculum which has no significant place for the history of religions; they are faced with inadequate library resources; and they find no fellow historians of religions in their immediate area. Thus, with time, a once-promising young historian of religions often turns into another "specialist," largely due to the reward system of today's academy.

Meanwhile, in the course of their own scholarly growth, a number of budding scholars who manage to stay within the sphere of the history of religions have to wrestle with the ambiguities involved in the discipline. It is not an easy task for young scholar-teachers to blend successfully the historical and systematic dimensions, or to deal with the specific-general dichotomy of the discipline. Not only do they have to become familiar with various methodological emphases within the discipline, e.g., historical (Pettazzoni), phenomenological (van der Leeuw), morphological (Eliade), sociological (Wach). They also have to become informed about other humanistic, social scientific, philosophical, and theological approaches to religion at the same time that they develop for themselves a notion of the "classical" which will provide the most substantial methodological foundation for their own scholarship.

Nevertheless, despite all the ambiguities which exist within the discipline and in its relation to other forms of studies, I am persuaded that the history of religions can make important contributions to the study of religion by offering an important perspective, namely, the "priority of the whole": a comprehensive methodological framework based on the interpenetration between historical and systematic dimensions and a commitment to develop general statements about the "meaning" of religious phenomena. As I once stated elsewhere, such an "integral understanding" of the religious experi- ence of the human race and its expressions unfolded in human history involves a selection of data and a telescoping of the long and complex religious history of humankind. In this respect, the task of the historian of religions is somewhat analogous to the task of historians of cultures and civilizations, a task which requires, to use the phrase of Robert Redfield, "thinking about a civilization." "Thinking about," he says, is "something different from getting information and acquaintance, though this third ac- tivity requires and is guided by the first two. It is to develop formed and nameable thoughts about the civilization. It is to conceive it, and make it a mental artifact, a shaped work of the intellect."[19]

If such a "thinking about civilization" involves some risks, thinking about the religious experience of the human race involves equally serious risks and difficulties. Yet, with all the ambiguities and risks involved, the history of religions can greatly enrich the scholarly study of religion, a study which is needed more than ever to prepare future generations for the realization of what it means to be human in this otherwise bewildering world of our time.

[19] Robert Redfield, "Thinking about a Civilization," in Milton Singer, ed., *Introducing India in Liberal Education* (Chicago, 1957), p. 3.

PART II: APPLIED RELIGIONSWISSENSCHAFT

# 1

## THE WORLD HAS MANY CENTERS

This indeed is a memorable and happy day, not only for the graduates and their families, but for the entire university community as well. The Convocation provides an occasion to remind all of us that a university is an expression of the human spirit, and that particular sort of expression which is never fully realized. That is to say, the educational institution is in large part the life of human beings, and if the university is to be alive, the students, the faculty and the alumni must together continue to discover and rediscover the unique genius of the institution and to unfold and actualize its potentialities. Thus, on this occasion, this university community not only salutes the academic achievements of the graduates and welcomes them simultaneously to the rank of alumni, but in so doing reaffirms and reexamines its commitment to the original vision which brought about the birth of the University and the development of that vision on the part of those who have sustained it through its history.

Speaking more personally, exactly two decades ago, I, too, sat where the graduates sit today. But much to my embarrassment I recall only dimly the eloquent address delivered by a learned gentleman on that occasion. Then I was somewhat bewildered by the mystery of the graduation exercise, which marks a turning point in one's life. And, in a state of half daydreaming during the ceremony I recalled my early childhood in the peaceful countryside of Japan, the college life in the great metropolis of Tokyo, and my graduate student days here at Chicago. My recollection was mingled with memories of teachers and friends who had played significant roles in my personal growth and education both in my native land and here in this country.

Since my graduation, I have had opportunities to visit other parts of the world. Wherever I travel, I am struck by a simple fact: every individual, every people, every culture lives not only in a geographical or physical world but also in what might be termed a "world of meaning." Some are more conscious than others of the mental and psychic processes involved in the ordering of diverse experiences and meanings that comprise the mystery of life. But what is true for virtually all individuals, communities, or nations is that each thinks its "world of meaning" is most important or most central.

In Helen Keller's charming little book, *Teacher*, we are told how Annie Sullivan attempted to teach the deaf and blind child by spelling in Helen's hand, suiting the word to the action and the action to the word. Although it took some time before Annie Sullivan could reach the mind of the child, she patiently repeated this method of instruction until the child made contact with reality. One day, according to the book, "while Annie Sulllivan pumped water over her hand it came to the child in a flash that water, wherever it was found, was water, and that the finger motions she had felt on her palm meant water and nothing else. In that thrilling moment she found the key to her kingdom. Everything had a name and she had a way to learn the names." This, to be sure, is an extreme example, but like a slow-motion film it shows how each one of us learns to grow out of that phase of life which Helen Keller calls "a phantom living in a world that is no-world." To be fully human means to be able to shape one's own structure of meaning, through association and imagination, through education and effort, regarding things we observe and experience.

Unlike Helen Keller, most of us acquire our "world of meaning" in a more normal manner—at home, in playgrounds and schools, and through our association with a wide variety of people and events. For the most part we inherit what has been handed down to us—not only the language with its "magical circle of words" and ideas as well as values, but also the small intimate habits of daily life, the way of greeting friends, putting on clothes, or hushing a child to sleep. Thus, consciously and unconsciously, our own "world of meaning" approximates the "world of meaning" implicit in our culture and religious traditions, which in turn exert decisive influence in patterning our behavior, beliefs and goals in life. In this respect, university education, too, however unsettling it may appear to be at times, nurtures men and women to become educated and useful citizens who relate to the mores and values of the society to which they belong.

The task of the university, however, cannot be exhausted only by preparing students for respective professions in their own society. As the first President of The University of Chicago, William Rainey Harper, made abundantly clear, the primary purpose of the university is to make men and women sensitive to the fundamental issues and problems of civilizations. The realization of such a vocation for the university is exceedingly difficult, and yet all the more important in our own time, when the very foundation of human civilization seems to be shaken by a tremor of social and cultural change which is felt on every continent. Whatever the setting, however, it is the peculiar task of the university, here as elsewhere, to try to understand the basic issues that confront civilization today.

Coming as I did from Asia, I may be more conscious of the fact that part of the dilemma of our time is due to the fact that the nineteenth century, in which the "world of meaning" of the Westerners dominated the main stage of the whole world, lasted a little longer than simply the year 1899. Actually, to the majority of the human race, which lives outside Europe and the Americas, it was not the year 1900 but the year 1945 which marked a significant line of demacartion between two worlds of experience. Thus, according to the "world of meaning" of modern Asians and Africans, to repeat Irving Kristol's way of putting it, the twentieth century began only in 1945. In a real sense, the basic problem of our time is not the emergence of many new and quarrelsome nations in Asia and Africa in the post-1945 era, but rather what both caused and resulted from their political independence, namely, the momentous redefinition of man's conception of the dignity, value, and freedom of humankind. Conversely, people in Asia and Africa are now destined to experience, as much as Westerners do, the anguish and agony of life in the twentieth century, for the world in which all of us live today, shaped by science, technology, industry, and business, tends to repudiate the sacred pieties, morals, and rituals of former times. Thus, modern people everywhere, having lost much of the old sense of the absolute, are now looking for a new "world of meaning," which will take full account of common, basic problems of human existence without, however, obliterating the particularities of diverse ethnic, national, and cultural experiences. This is one of the great issues which confronts human civilization in our century.

It is no accident that people everywhere, especially the educated ones, are disturbed by the brokenness of human community. Yet many of them, including some with university educations, are driven toward premature resolution either by resorting to oversimplified formulae which promise instant relevance or by resorting to a pre-modern, parochial "world of meaning," which still has an aesthetic appeal to those who view life in terms of their own ethnic, national or cultural framework. It may well be that modern man, in order to comprehend the new coherence, is destined to realize, as Thomas Mann's Joseph realized in Egypt, that "the world has many centers."

This is to recognize that individuals and communities, nations and cultures, do indeed have a "world of meaning" which orders their experience. It is even to recognize that these "worlds of meaning" will be held and defended passionately, as some will hold that their own "world of meaning" is most important and central. But to know that the world has many centers means that it is ever more important to cherish the life of the university, where these "worlds of meaning" can be explored, examined, and understood. As institutions in particular societies universities will always be enticed to defend their particular "worlds of meaning." At the same time some will claim that the university can only be true to itself when no world or worlds of meaning are expressed. The University, however, like the world, has many centers: and that is why, fragile though it be, it has such importance to the well-being, and even survival, of civilizations.

# 2

## RELIGION AS A PRINCIPLE OF INTEGRATION AND CO-OPERATION FOR A GLOBAL COMMUNITY

> We are dealing with a topic, complex and many-sided. It comprises the deliverances of the understanding as it harmonises our deepest intuitions. It comprises emotional responses to formulations of thought and to modes of behaviour. It comprises the direction of purposes and the modifications of behaviour. It cuts into every aspect of human existence. So far as concerns religious problems, simple solutions are bogus solutions.
>
> ALFRED NORTH WHITEHEAD

### INTRODUCTION

My assignment is to discuss "religion as a principle of integration and co-operation for a global community." I must readily admit that being a historian of religions, concerned primarily with the historical, phenomenological and comparative study of religions, I have no magical formula to deal with the shaping of the future of humankind. Rather, my hope is to make a modest contribution by raising and clarifying some of the important issues involved in this discussion.

I hope that by now we have become sensitive to the common error of assuming that a high ideal can be actualized automatically by passing resolutions and making pious pronouncements without regard for the practical difficulties that lie in the way of realizing any lofty objective. In fact, I would not assume at the outset that religion is, or religion provides, a principle of integration and co-operation for a global community in light of the abundant historical evidence to the contrary. I would rather ask a question: *does* religion provide a viable principle of integration or co-operation for a global community? Or, more narrowly: what difference, if any, do religious faith and tradition make in the manner in which men and women of diverse ethnic, linguistic, national, cultural, and religious backgrounds lead a harmonious corporate life on a global level? Or, what insight can we derive from religious belief and practice that enhances our perception, understanding, and critical judgment concerning the nature of a global community as well as the manner in which we should strive toward such an objective?

Here I am not trying to resolve the seemingly impossible task of defining religion in such a way that everyone can agree. I only wish to recall that religion is a generic term referring to a realm of reality derived from various historic religions. In this sense, the relation of *religion* to *religions* is somewhat analogous to the relation of *language* to *languages*. Understandably, opinions vary widely as to what religion or the essence of religion is or ought to be. My concern at this point is not to pursue this intricate exercise in trying to define religion, but rather to caution us against uncritically using the term religion as though it were self-evident. Ironically, religion to many people is what they and their society and culture accept religion to be by custom or otherwise. This leads to inevitable misunderstanding and confusion in inter-religious and inter-cultural gatherings where people from different backgrounds try to find either superficial similarities or lowest common denominators among various religions in order to discuss what "religion" can do for the cause of peace, justice, or what have you.

And then there is the complexity of all religions. I do not have to belabor this obvious point except to point out that each religion, be it any of the so-called primitive religions or a historic religion such as Hinduism, Buddhism, Shinto, Judaism, Christianity, and Islam, is a multi-dimensional phenomenon, consisting of beliefs, doctrines, codes of ethics, cults, and a variety of forms of organization. Moreover, each historic religion has shaped and nurtured culture, which is the domain of values, ideology, science, arts and imagination. Also, each religion has been integrally related to socio-political structure, modes of social change and levels of economic development.[1] One of the salient features of all religions is their "imperialistic temper," not necessarily because each religion attempts to dominate other peoples, though this too has happened all too often in history, but more basically because each religion *defines* the nature and levels of reality, including ultimate reality, which is the source of cosmic, social, and human order. Accordingly, even the most universalistic religious vision is usually anchored in the particularistic perspective of the religion in question which defines the nature of reality, the world, and human destiny.

Let us now take a cursory look at how some of the so-called world religions have viewed historically the tension between the unity and division of humanity.

## UNITY AND DIVISION OF HUMANITY

Throughout the history of mankind, even the most ethnocentric and nationalistic minds have never seriously questioned that humanity is basically one despite all the external differences. Archeologists, anthropologists, and pre-historians may not agree about the specific time of the appearance of the first *Homo sapiens* or his predecessor, *Homo nean-*

[1] "Culture," according to Clifford Geertz, "is the fabric of meaning in terms of which human beings interpret their experience and guide their action; social structure is the form that action takes, the actually existing network of social relations." See "Ritual and Social Change: A Javanese Example," in William A. Lessa and Evon Z. Vogt, eds., *Reader in Comparative Religion: An Anthropological Approach* (Evanston: Row, Peterson & Co., 1958), p. 501.

*derthalensis*, upon earth, but they agree that all branches of the human race, including the Pygmies of the Congo, the Bushmen of South Africa, and the Negritos of the Andaman Islands, are to be regarded as one organic species.

How, then, can one explain the division of humanity into various ethnic, cultural, and linguistic groups? This is one of the most baffling questions that has been asked by men and women throughout the ages, and since the dawn of history various religions and philosophies have attempted to find some answer to it. For example, Zoroastrianism, with its belief in Ahura Mazda's eschatological war against the forces of evil, tried to overcome the chaos and division of humankind; human beings were called upon to co-operate with God "in the great effort to establish on earth an order of truth, righteousness and peace, the Kingdom of God."[2] Ancient Hinduism taught the appearance of "a universal, world-wide empire of enduring tranquility under a just and virtuous world-monarch, cakravartin . . . who should put an end to the perpetual struggle of the contending states."[3] As might be expected, this ancient Hindu notion of "the superman turning the wheel" influenced Jainism and Buddhism. Thus, "like the Cakravartin," says Heinrich Zimmer, "the Buddha is the master, not of a national or otherwise limited communion, but of the world. His wheel, the Buddhist dharma, is not reserved for the privileged castes, like the dharma of the Brahmans, but is for the whole universe. . . ."[4] The ancient Chinese too had the vision of the grand commonwealth as expressed in *The Great Learning*. And, according to Fung Yu-lan, "from the age of Confucius onward, the Chinese people in general and their political thinkers in particular began to think about political matters in terms of the world."[5]

It was the ancient Greeks who envisaged the unification of peoples in the "oikoumene" or the "inhabited quarter" of the world by means of Hellenistic civilization and Greek language (*koine*). While the audacious dream of Alexander (356–323 B.C.) to establish a vast cultural, political, and economic empire was doomed to failure, Oriental-Hellenistic culture remained for centuries the framework for cultural development in the Mediterranean world. Meanwhile, in the Middle East the once-tribal religion of the Hebrew community developed ethical universalism under the influence of the prophetic movement, whereby the God of Israel came to be conceived of as the divine head of all humankind.[6] And, since the meaning of history was understood by the Hebrews in an eschatological sense, their "covenanted community" came to be seen as the norm and the bearer of salvation for all

[2] C. J. Bleeker, ed., *Anthropologie Religieuse* (Leiden: E. J. Brill, 1955), p. 182.

[3] Heinrich Zimmer, *Philosophies of India*, ed. by Joseph Campbell (New York: Pantheon Books Inc., 1951), p. 128.

[4] *Ibid.*, pp. 129–30.

[5] Fung Yu-lan, *A Short History of Chinese Philosophy*, ed. by Derek Bodde (New York: Macmillan, 1950), p. 181.

[6] See R. G. Collingwood, *The Idea of History* (Oxford: Clarendon Press, 1946), p. 17.

humanity. It is interesting to note that although Christianity and Islam developed within the orbit of Oriental-Hellenistic culture, both of them inherited much of their religious ethos, especially beliefs in the unity of the human race, from the Hebrew religious tradition. Accordingly, the early Christian community considered itself the new Israel, coming into existence at Pentecost, an event which signified the reversal of the Tower of Babel in that the human race, scattered and divided according to language, race, and nationality, was now reunited, potentially at least, as one. In a similar vein, Islam, which accepts the disunity of humankind as the work of God's inscrutable decree, nevertheless affirms that all those who surrender to Allah and His prophet are to be included in Ummah or the congregation of Allah.[7]

Historically, in the Eastern world neither the Hindus with their cosmic orientation nor the Chinese with their universal outlook propagated their religions and philosophies outside their respective spheres of influence. Significantly, it was the Buddhist king Asoka (r. 274–233 B.C.) who initiated and supported an energetic missionary expansion beyond his vast empire. Buddhism thus shouldered the responsibility of guiding not only seekers and believers but a complex society, nation, and civilization. Accordingly, the Buddhist community came to be understood as potentially a world-wide community, embracing peoples and nations outside India. Although Asoka's empire was short-lived and Buddhism eventually lost ground in India, subsequent Buddhist expansion in other parts of Asia owed its original impetus to Asoka's vision of a humanity united by means of Buddhist dharma.

In the Western world the emergence of Islam in the 7th century A.D. successfully confined Christianity to Europe. Thereafter, the *corpus Christianum* and the *corpus Islamicum* were destined to exist side by side, sometimes as antagonistic and other times as fraternal enemies.

## WESTERN CIVILIZATION—A PSEUDO RELIGION

It was taken for granted by medieval Christendom that "the full freedom and independence of the Church was only reached when the temporal powers were subordinate to the Church . . . and directed by her in all matters pertaining to salvation."[8] And since everything is ultimately related to salvation according to the Christian view, soteriology became equated with ecclesiology. The foundation of the Corpus Christianum, however, was undermined by the Renaissance, which now affirmed the new conception of "civilization" as a pseudo religion of secularized salvation. Rejecting the medieval notion of the state as subservient to the church, the secular idea of human personality accepted the political community as the framework of

[7] "Umma or Ummah," *Shorter Encyclopaedia of Islam* (Leiden: E. J. Brill, 1953), pp. 603–04.
[8] Ernst Troeltsch, *The Social Teachings of the Christian Churches*, tr. by Olive Wyon, Vol. I (Second impression) (Glencoe: The Free Press, 1949), pp. 229–30.

civilized life. In this situation, much as the ancient Hebrews considered themselves the chosen people proclaiming the true religion, modern Europeans came to regard themselves as the bearers of true civilization. This conviction was the motivating force behind the colonial expansion of the modern West. While modern Europeans did not question the unity of humankind, they came to believe that the West was the inventor and transmitter of true civilization, which must be propagated for the edification of the "backward" people in the non-Western world. "This is the philosophy of the white man's burden, as Kipling called it—a strange compound of genuine idealistic responsibility, blindness and hyprocisy, with a strong dose of will-to-power as the basic component."[9]

It was this secularized view of the human being as the creator of cultural values that the so-called Pietists rejected in the 18th century. Thus the initial ethos of the Christian foreign missions, inaugurated by the Continental Pietists and English evangelicals, ran counter to the spirit of secular European civilization. During the 19th century, however, the Christian missions in Asia and Africa co-operated unwittingly or otherwise with European colonialism, whereby Christianity was propagated as one—albeit an important one—of the constituents of Western civilization. The combined forces of Western civilization, Christian missionary enterprise, and colonial expansion brought about social, political, economic, cultural and religious changes in much of the non-Western world by the end of the 19th century. Therefore, many Westerners, who subconsciously assumed that they could determine the destiny of the world, felt that "the absorption of the Eastern by the Western world appeared to come inevitably."[10]

The period covering the two world wars was a turbulent era for the entire world. The first world war effectively destroyed the European community's facade of unity, which development set the stage for Western civilization—a pseudoreligion of secular salvation—to be challenged by its heretical offshoot, communism, which may be characterized as a pseudoreligion of atheism. "It is this Bolshevist message of inevitable universal salvation," says Hans Morgenthau, "of which the Soviet government makes itself not only the spokesman, but also the executioner. . . ."[11] But the Russian revolution that Lenin inspired did not usher in utopia for the oppressed any more than the League of Nations which Woodrow Wilson inspired succeeded in ending Western colonialism. The disunity of the West was further aggravated by the rise of Fascism and Nazism, which defied the Western democratic tradition as much as communism did.

[9] William S. Haas, *The Destiny of the Mind—East and West* (London: Faber & Faber, 1956), p. 303.

[10] Hendrik Kraemer, *The Christian Message in a Non-Christian World* (London: The Edinburgh House, 1938), p. 36.

[11] Hans J. Morgenthau, *In Defense of the National Interest* (New York: Alfred A. Knopf, 1951), p. 63.

Meanwhile, in the non-Western world, there emerged political independence movements which aimed at rectifying the political injustice imposed by Western colonial powers. The independence movements were accompanied by a self-conscious re-awakening of the Eastern peoples about the value of their ancestral cultures and religions. The anti-Westernism thus developed was therefore not only a political slogan; it had the element of a new gospel of salvation, which provided meaning and purpose for many people in the Middle East and Asia. There, people began to understand themselves not simply as victims of greedy Western imperialists, mistreated and misunderstood, but, potentially at least, as the bearers of a new gospel for the future, not only for their children and grandchildren, but also for the materialistic, spiritually-barren peoples of the West. This sense of mission accelerated the so-called resurgence of indigenous religions and cultures in the non-Western world during and after the second world war.

## VISION OF A GLOBAL COMMUNITY

Let us turn our attention to the contemporary situation. I share Irving Kristol's thesis that "the 20th century began in 1945." The 19th century, he says, "came to its end a little later than the calendar prescribed. It was not the organized festivities of 1900 but rather the organized hostilities of 1914 that decisively concluded a chapter in human history," which was followed by the period of an "interregnum" that lasted until World War II.[12] This way of reckoning history is more meaningful to people in the non-Western world, to whom the year 1945 marked a significant line of demarcation between two worlds of experience. The emergence of the series of independent nations in Asia and Africa that followed signified not only the end of the period of modern Western colonial imperialism but also a momentous redefinition of our conceptions of the dignity, value and freedom of humanity. The fact that two-thirds of the human race, whose destiny had been controlled by a minority, has now attained full citizenship, as it were, gives additional impetus to the contemporary "revolution of rising expectations," to use Adlai Stevenson's famous phrase. Underlying the revolution of rising expectations is a persistent hope and vision of a unified, global human community, however it is understood.

It is an irony of history that the new nations of Asia and Africa attained independence after the era of the nation-state was over. To be sure, nationalism played a decisive role in liberating non-Western peoples from the yoke of colonialism, but nationalism as such is no longer adequate today to guide the explosive energy of the peoples of Asia and Africa. As Harold Isaacs pointed out nearly three decades ago:

[12] Irving Kristol, "The 20th Century Began in 1945," *The New York Times* Magazine (May 2, 1965), 25.

The revolutionary pressures go far beyond the matter of national independence to the issues of the whole structure, relations on the land and between classes, the terms and methods of economic development. . . . They are soluble no longer within the confines of separate national economies: *a new world community is wanted.*[13]

Thus, while no nation wishes to give up its national sovereignty, many nations—new as well as old—now feel the need for some sort of regional and global cooperation and collective security.

In retrospect, it becomes evident that the influence of Western civilization has left lasting imprints on economic, political, and technological developments in every corner of the earth. Thus, in one sense it is true that today tribal, racial, geographical and national limits have been undercut and overcome by global transportation and communication systems. However, in spite of the shrinkage of physical distance and the breaking down of historic barriers which had kept peoples and nations apart, the world is still divided along cultural and religious lines. Toynbee goes so far as to say that "while the economic and political maps have been Westernized, the cultural map remains substantially what it was before our Western society started on its career of economic and political conquest."[14] In so stating, Toynbee of course does not imply that non-Western cultures and religions have not changed. Indeed, the spirit of "modernity," which had earlier shaken the foundations of Western culture and society, has been inhaled consciously or unconsciously by religions and cultures in Asia and Africa. Moreover, many religious leaders in the non-Western world are now keenly aware of important issues which concern not only the welfare of their own peoples but also the well-being of humanity as a whole, such as the issues of human dignity, justice, poverty, disarmament, peace, and the relations among different religious and cultural traditions.

## RELIGIONS AND A GLOBAL COMMUNITY

In today's world, where there is more than one religious tradition that claims the Truth as its own, the choice of attitudes is limited. One may hold that different religions are fundamentally the same, as advocated by what might be termed the "liberal wings" of various religions. Or one can stress, as indeed many adherents of different religions do, the exclusive value and unique meaning of a particular religious system. To the former the

[13] Harold R. Isaacs, "The Dimension of Crisis: Asia's Multiple Revolution," *Saturday Review of Literature*, XXXIV (August 4, 1951), 14. (My italics.)

[14] Arnold J. Toynbee, *A Study of History*, abridgment of vols. I–VI by D. C. Somervell (New York: Oxford University Press, 1947), p. 36.

uniqueness of each religion is its disgrace, while to the latter universality implies the surrender of truth. Yet, all of us know that we are caught between our basic affirmation of the unity of human community and the fact of religious pluralism.

It must be readily admitted that in our divided world a commonsense appeal for a global community cannot be dismissed as sheer sentimentality. The liberal wings of various religious traditions have made great contributions to our thinking in this respect by emphasizing the common bond of humanity, which crosses religious and cultural lines; this is a necessary emphasis which we dare not ignore or forget. However, in their eagerness to stress the universal aspect of religions, enthusiasts tend to soft-pedal the tenacity and importance of differences that exist among different religions. Thus, in their adherence to a one-dimensional truth about the universal features of religions, naive liberals often become "exclusivists in a concealed way" by claiming that interfaith discussions are possible only when all religions drop at the outset their uniqueness and accept simply "the tenet of the one, universal religion, hidden in all religions" as the normative concept. [15] On the other hand, advocates of the absoluteness of one religion face difficult problems in an interfaith conversation, because to them all other religions are "counterfeits" of the true religion and thus should be eliminated or displaced. Thus, by interpreting the meaning of the unity of the human community only on their terms, they refuse to acknowledge a profound "religious" meaning in the very fact of the co-existence of diverse religious traditions.

I began my reflections by asking questions, such as: "Does religion, however it is understood, provide a viable principle of integration or co-operation for a global community?"; "What difference, if any, do religious faith and tradition make in the manner in which men and women of diverse backgrounds lead a harmonious corporate life on a global level?"; and, "What insights can we derive from religious belief and practice that enhance our perception, understanding, and critical judgment concerning the nature of a global community as well as the manner in which we should strive toward such an objective?" I am still struggling with these questions without coming to any easy resolutions. If pushed, my answers to these questions must be "yes" and "no" with many "if's."

Some of the difficulties we face stem from the fact that we don't always know how to deal with religions "religiously." Certainly, it is much easier to discuss ethical, philosophical, psychological, sociological or political aspects of religions *vis-à-vis* an issue such as that of a global community. In so doing, however, we run into a semantic trap whereby we set aside a domain of life called "religious" apart from other areas and activities such as commerce,

---

[15] Hendrik Kraemer, *World Cultures and World Religions* (Philadelphia: The Westminster Press, 1960), p. 364, footnote 1.

politics, culture and art. In fact, it has become quite common in our time to depict more obviously identifiable items, namely, doctrines, ritual practices, and ecclesiastical institutions as components of the "religious" dimension, differentiated from the so-called "non-religious" or "secular" dimension of life. But, we have come to realize how misleading it is to deal with religions in this way. "It would be," as Eliade reminds us, "like the description of a man founded only upon his public behavior and leaving out of account his secret passions, his nostalgias, his existential contradictions and the whole universe of his imagination, which are more essential to him than the ready-made opinions that he utters."[16]

As we reflect "religiously" on the relations of religions to a global community, we are compelled to face the contradictory features of religions, especially the manner in which "universal" and "particular" dimensions are intricately interwoven. Basically, all religions address themselves to human existence, and as such they share a concern with universal humanity. And yet, religions must address themselves not to human existence *in abstracto* but to man-in-a-particular-society-and-culture, with the firm conviction that one humanity has within it infinite possibilities which can be actualized in various historic forms of societies and cultures, all of which must be taken seriously. Moreover, all religions, however universalistic their orientations may be, have their own social bases, i.e., religious communities, each with its own particularities.

As far as I can ascertain, I personally do not foresee the emergence of a super-religion, which will surpass or include all religions. Like it or not, various religions will continue to develop according to their own dynamics, crisscrossing the face of the earth. Each religion will continue to seek the meaning of a global community, not only in terms of the human community but also relating the human community to ultimate reality, however it is understood. In the course of time, there will be temptations for all religions to distort their own religious character, because religions have built-in demonic tendencies. Nevertheless, one of the hopeful signs of our time is that many scholars and leaders of various religions are now willing to engage in open exchanges of witness and experience as well as in joint inquiries. I do not expect any one religion to have the monopoly of wisdom to guide a divided humanity toward the goal of a united global community. But I hope and pray that all religions will have sufficient religious resources which will give men and women faith, courage, and hope to live in ambiguity without resorting to what Whitehead called simple and bogus solutions.

[16] Mircea Eliade, *Myths, Dreams and Mysteries*, trans. by Philip Mairet (New York: Harper & Brothers, 1960), p. 107.

# 3

## WESTERN UNDERSTANDING OF THE EAST

On January 1, 1968, the president of Nationalist China, Chiang Kai-shek, issued his customary New Year's message, reiterating his now-familiar theme of delivering his 700 million compatriots on the mainland from the "Communist Hell." On this occasion President Chiang indulged in a bitter personal attack on Mao Tse-tung as an archcriminal, a notorious liar, an egocentric, a devil-tyrant, and a self-centered bandit-chief. He went so far as to say that the seventy-four-year-old Mao was "crazed and struggling in his death throes."[1] Of course, given the political situation of Formosa and mainland China, no one expected Chiang to send a get-well greeting to Mao in Peking. But many people felt that Chiang, himself not in robust health and no longer young at the age of eighty-one, was hardly in a position to comment about Mao's declining age. Meanwhile, we are all aware that the future of the world will be greatly affected by the passing of both these men.

What may happen in China after Mao and Chiang, important though it may be, is only one dimension of the monstrous global puzzle confronting us. We must be reasonably prepared for various eventualities, yet perhaps the best we can hope to do is reflect on the main thrusts of our historic experiences and assess the dynamics of the present situation, recognizing that new factors can radically alter the course of history. The most precarious aspect of such a reflection is the ambiguity of our own perspectives. This is particularly true in analyzing the encounter of the East and the West.

### FOUR ANCIENT CULTURAL TRADITIONS

The so-called meeting of the East and West—that is, the encounter of the cultural traditions of Europe and Asia[2]—is a relatively modern phenomenon. All the civilizations of the ancient world—those of Mesopotamia, Egypt, Crete, India, China, Mexico, Peru, and Palestine—considered themselves as exclusive and self-sufficient ways of life. It was taken for granted in the ancient period that the migration of an ethnic group into certain areas, such as the penetration of the Aryans into India, Persia, and Europe, or the

---

[1] Quoted in *Chicago Sun-times*, January 2, 1968.

[2] See my article "East and West: A Dialogue," *Perspectives*, VI, no. 1 (January–February 1961), 19–38.

settlement of the Scandinavians in Iceland, implied the wholesale transplantation of the civilization of the invading group over the entire region. In the course of time there developed several great empires, some of which competed with rival powers in expanding their political and cultural influences over wider territories. For instance, the ancient Babylonian empire was conquered by the rising Persian empire, which extended its hegemony to Asia Minor, Egypt, and the border of India around the fifth century B.C. It was the obscure Macedonian king, Alexander (356–323 B.C.), a one-time disciple of Aristotle, who during his short life established a vast cultural, political, and economic network stretching from western Macedonia to the Punjab region of India in the East, which was administered by a series of Greek territorial monarchies.

Alexander's audacious dream to unify the whole world was doomed to failure. Shortly after his death even his own empire lost its political unity. In the East, half a century after Alexander's departure from Indian soil, King Asoka (r., 274–232 B.C.) unified the Indian subcontinent and ushered in a glorious age of Buddhist expansion, not only within his own realm but also into India's neighboring countries as well. In the Far East the third century B.C. witnessed the unification of China for the first time under the "First Emperor" (Shih Huang Ti) of the Ch'in dynasty, which was followed shortly afterward by a more stable Han rule. (During the Han empire, which lasted over four centuries, Confucianism established itself as the dominant ideological system in China.) In the West the Roman empire began to expand during the first century B.C. and reigned over the Mediterranean world for centuries to come. It was to provide the medieval foundations of Western civilization, blending within it Judeo-Christian religious tradition, Greek philosophy, and Roman jurisprudence. Thus by the beginning of the Christian era there emerged at least four major cultural spheres in the world, namely, China, which considered itself the Middle Kingdom with its Confucian universalism; India, with its cosmic vision as expressed in Hinduism as well as in Buddhism and Jainism; the Middle East, which was the cradle of great world religions (Zoroastrianism, Judaism, Christianity, and, later, Islam); and Rome, which inherited and amplified Hellenistic cosmopolitanism.

Unfortunately, our knowledge of the relationships among these four great ancient cultural spheres is quite fragmentary. We do know that there was active trade between Rome and China via the overland caravan route; as well as between India, Iran, and the Mediterranean world by means of ocean routes, whereby gold from Siberia, amber from Northern Europe, pepper from India, and silk from China, for example, found their ways into all corners·of the known world. The commercial traffic between Europe and Asia was such that as early as the first century B.C. Cicero warned his fellow Romans that if the Chinese government were to pursue an adverse trade policy, it could easily result in a financial panic in Rome. But the interrelationship between Europe and Asia was not confined to trade. Frederick Teggart, who studied the relationship between Rome and China during the period from 58 B.C. to 107 A.D., reminds us that "of the forty occasions on which outbreaks [of war] took place in Europe, twenty-seven were traceable to the policy, or rather changes of policy, of the Han [Chinese] government."[3] While active commercial trade across the steppes and desert began to wane after the third century A.D. because of the internal decay of China and of Rome, religious and cultural intercourse continued for some time. Among the consequences were the penetration of the Middle Eastern mystery cults and Christianity into the Roman empire, establishment of Syrian Christian communities in South India and northwestern China, spread of Manicheanism throughout Central Asia, and expansion of Buddhism into various corners of Asia.

## ISLAMIC EXPANSION

The historic East-West relationship was greatly affected by the rise of Islam in the Middle East in the seventh century. Within ten years after the death of Muhammad, Syria, Iraq, and Egypt were claimed by the Muslim empire. In less than a century Islam conquered the Christian belt of North Africa, the home of St. Augustine and many other eminent Christian saints and patriarchs, and reached the Iberian peninsula. In the eighth century Muslim forces crossed the Pyrenees into France. The Muslim traders were soon found in Canton as well as in northern China, and they began to settle in the islands of the East Indies, now known as Indonesia, shortly afterward. Nor did Islam leave India untouched. As early as 712 the Sind region was conquered by Muslim invaders. It took three more centuries before the Punjab was added to Muslim rule, but after 1526 the whole of India came under the control of the Muslim Mughal dynasty. Understandably, such a rapid and widespread expansion of Islam sharply disrupted the historic intercourse between Europe and Asia.

The vitality of Islam was not confined only to its military and political domains during the first four centuries after its inception. The world of Islam, under the Abbasid rulers in Baghdad (in the present Iraq), the Umayyad rulers in Cordova, Spain, and the Fatimad rulers in Egypt, made extraordinary progress in commerce, industry, and culture. For instance, thanks largely to enlightened Muslim rule, Spain became one of the richest European nations during the Middle Ages. The intellectual life of the Muslims was greatly enriched by the translation of Greek philosophical works and Persian and Indian scientific books into Arabic. Muslim universities in Cordova and Granada, as well as other schools and libraries in Spain, attracted Muslim, Jewish, and Christian students from other parts of Europe

[3] Frederick J. Teggart, *Rome and China: A Study of Correlations in Historical Events* (Berkeley, 1939), p. vii.

and Africa. Significantly, Christian Europe first became acquainted with the major works of Plato and Aristotle through the writings of Muslim scholars.

The balance of power between the world of Islam and Christian Europe began to shift around the eleventh century, when Christian forces regained control of Sicily, Sardinia, and later the Iberian peninsula. Meanwhile, the Seljuq Turks, a nomadic group from the Turkestan steppes, migrated westward and defeated the Byzantine forces. The Turks' mistreatment of Christian pilgrims to Jerusalem provided a ready excuse for European Christendom to undertake a series of bloody Crusades between 1096 and 1291. Actually, the Crusades, in which saints and scoundrels fought side by side with a mixture of spiritual and mundane motives, failed to dislodge Muslim power, although they left unpleasant memories of European Christendom in the minds of the Muslims. On the other hand, the two centuries of fanatic campaign propaganda, sanctioned by the papacy which was then consolidating its political power, greatly distorted the Europeans' image of non-Europeans, much to the detriment of East-West relations for centuries to come. Indeed, as Edwin Calverley points out, "The false reports brought back by those who returned from the wars filled the West with popular misinformation about Islam that Western mass education has not yet been able to remove."[4] Subsequent religious developments in Europe—the Reformation, the Counter-Reformation, and the rise of Pietism—only added more fuel to Europeans' prejudice against non-Western religions and cultures, and this in turn hardened the attitudes of the Muslims and other non-Western peoples toward "Christian" Europe. As Norman Daniel observes, once a normal and peaceful channel of communication is broken down,

> under the pressure of their sense of danger, whether real or imagined, a deformed image of their enemy's beliefs takes shape in men's minds. By misapprehension and misrepresentation an idea of the beliefs and practices of one society can pass into the accepted myths of another society in a form so distorted that its relation to the original facts is sometimes barely discernible.[5]

The East-West relationship, which deteriorated on account of the Crusades, was further strained by the dramatic appearance of the tribes from the Central Asian steppes onto the world scene beginning in the thirteenth century. The first to be mentioned are the Mongols, who not only conquered China but quickly overpowered Muslims from the Oxus frontier to the Euphrates, and subjugated all of Russia. Around 1241 the Mongol hordes devasted southern Poland and Hungary. Only the death of the son of Jenghiz

[4] Edwin E. Calverley, "Islamic Religion," in T. Cuyler Young, ed., *Near Eastern Culture and Society* (Princeton, 1951), p. 103.
[5] Norman Daniel, *Islam and the West: The Making of an Image* (Edinburgh, 1960), p. 2.

Khan saved Western Europe from their onslaught. After the Mongols, the Mamluks, originally a Turkish slave family, established a dynasty in Egypt and dominated international commerce during the fourteenth and fifteenth centuries. Not until 1498, when Vasco da Gama discovered the sea route to India by the Cape of Good Hope, could Europe challenge the commanding position of the Mamluks' Egypt in international commerce. The Ottomans, too, a tribe of the Ghuzz Turks which had earlier been driven from their homes in Central Asia by the Mongols, moved westward. In 1453 they defeated the forces of Byzantine Christendom and established the vast Ottoman empire, embracing within it a large portion of the Eastern Orthodox as well as Arab Muslim territories. The Ottoman's attempted siege of Vienna in the seventeenth century frightened European nations, especially Austria, Venice, Poland, Russia, and the papacy, which formed an alliance to check the advance of Turkish power.

## WESTERN DOMINANCE

Even this superficial account of the historic relationship between East and West enables us to appreciate the intensity of emotion that has been involved in the encounter since the sixteenth century. There is much truth in Toynbee's observation that "in the encounter between the [non-Western] world and the West that has been going on by now for four or five hundred years . . . it has not been the West that has been hit by the world; it is the [non-Western] world that has been hit—and hit hard—by the West."[6] A new page of history was turned when the Mongol rule of Russia came to an end in 1480, followed by the expulsion of the Moors from Granada, Spain, in 1492. In contrast to China, India, and the Middle East, which were then showing signs of stagnation, the enormous vitality of Europe was apparent in the emergence of modern nation states, economic nationalism and a new social structure as well as the Renaissance in the cultural domain, and the Reformation and Counter-Reformation in the religious domain. The self-confidence of the new Europe was also evidenced in the aspirations of new maritime powers of Europe, such as Portugal and Spain, which tried to control vast territories in the non-Western world. This colonial expansion brought two kinds of results. First, the new continents of North and South America, and later Australia, were completely colonized by Europeans and became for all intents and purposes an extension of Europe, culturally and religiously. Second, many parts of Asia and Africa were subjugated, politically and economically, by the European powers, but they were not heavily colonized, except in certain areas, and as such their cultural and religious traditions were not replaced by those of the Europeans.

The phenomenal colonial expansion of the West during the sixteenth century may be graphically seen in the Spanish conquest of Mexico (1520),

---

[6] Arnold Toynbee, *The World and the West* (New York, 1953), pp. 1–2.

Peru (1531), Argentina (1535), the Rio Grande territory (1540), Florida (1565), and Manila, Philippines (1571). Soon Portugal colonized Brazil and established settlements on the west coast of India and in the Spice Islands. In all these ventures the most blatant form of economic exploitation was mixed with fanatic religious motivation. "In fact," says William Sweet, "the early Spanish *conquistadores* considered themselves Christian crusaders and brought over to the New World the ideas which had grown up in the long wars which they had fought against the Moors in Spain, using the same battle cries and evoking the same saints in the New World that had served them in the old."[7] The Portuguese, with similar fanatic zeal, tried to root out "infidels" in their colonies. Thus, for example, "Hindu temples in Goa were destroyed and their property distributed to religious orders [like the Franciscans] in 1540, [and even] the Inquisition was established in 1560."[8]

In the meantime Great Britain, which defeated the "invincible Armada" of Spain in 1588, and France and the Netherlands began to compete with Spain and Portugal for the control of North America, the West Indies, Africa, and Asia. In the north, Russia expanded eastward along the Amur River and established a settlement in the port of Okhotsk in 1638. Belgium, Germany, and other European nations also pursued their own colonial policies. By the end of the nineteenth century much of the non-Western world was under the yoke of Western colonial imperialism, which sought new markets and new fields of profitable investment in an aggressive manner. It is reported that King Leopold II of Belgium and his associates "reaped a fortune in the Congo, but the cruelty of their methods of exploitation shocked the conscience of the entire civilized world."[9] Other nations were not much better in this respect. After the infamous Opium War (1840-1842), China was penetrated by British, French, Russian, and German as well as by Japanese interests. Before the turn of the twentieth century, Indo-China was taken by the French; the islands of Java, Sumatra, the Celebes, parts of Borneo and New Guinea were taken by the Dutch; the Bismarck Archipelago, the Ladrone Islands, and some islands of Samoa were occupied by the Germans; and the islands of Hawaii, the Philippines, Guam, and Wake came under American control. Much of the Middle East and the continent of Africa were also divided into spheres of interest by various colonial powers.

There is no intent here to discuss the pros and cons of colonialism, except to point out that under colonial rule the initiative was completely in the hands of the West. Those who came under the rule of the colonial powers had nothing to say about the handling of their own affairs. In such a situation it was impossible to achieve a genuine encounter between the East and the

---

[7] William W. Sweet, "Christianity in the Americas," in Archibald G. Baker, ed., *A Short History of Christianity* (Chicago, 1940), p. 227.

[8] K. M. Panikkar, *Asia and Western Dominance* (London, 1959 ed.), p. 280.

[9] Henry W. Littlefield, *New Outline History of Europe, 1815–1949* (New York, 1949), p. 137.

West. To be sure, a few European thinkers from the time of the Enlightenment voiced their admiration for the ancient wisdom of China and India, and some liberal churchmen and humanists in Europe criticized Western political and economic imperialism and crude forms of Christian missionary activities. But their voices were not listened to by men of practical affairs. Rather, the prosperity brought by colonial policies led many Westerners to feel that their culture, religion, technology, and socio-economic and political systems must be successful precisely because they were attributes of a superior race. Many Europeans took it for granted that "biology and sociology point to the superiority of the Caucasian or white races over the coloured races of the earth. Superiority in physical and mental constitution, together with superiority in civilization and organization entail responsibility as well as privilege."[10]

Thus many came to accept an oversimplified formula: European equals Christian equals superior race *versus* non-Westerner equals pagan equals inferior race. Otherwise it would have been difficult to comprehend how Bartolomé de las Casas, known as the "Apostle to the Indians" in Latin America, was instrumental in initiating slavery in the sixteenth century, and how modern European nations which advocated the importance of human dignity, welfare, and freedom at home did not even bother to conceal their contempt for the natives in their colonies. The so-called "pig trade," which kidnaped and illegally shipped Chinese laborers in the mid-nineteenth century, was no less cruel than the earlier slave trade of the African natives. It is reported that "to San Francisco alone 108,471 Chinese laborers had been taken before 1863."[11] Lord Elgin, who ordered the burning of the Summer Palace in Peking, undoubtedly acted with the mistaken notion, prevalent among the colonial rulers, that international morality was not applicable in the West's dealings with non-Western peoples.[12] In short, the East-West relationship, which historically had been understood as the confrontation on the same plane of two rival groups, each with its peculiar beliefs, cultural traditions, and ways of life, even during the bloodiest period of the Crusades, came to be seen by many Europeans as a vertical relationship, with the superior European race destined to conquer, rule, or enlighten the poor natives in the non-Western world. Conversely, there developed a strong suspicion among non-Westerners that Westerners were aggressors and exploiters without regard for human welfare, coupled with a conviction that the only effective means to deal with the Westerners was to adopt their ways—and especially their technical know-how—in order to

[10] A. J. Macdonald, *Trade Politics and Christianity in Africa and the East* (London, 1916), p. 270.

[11] Panikkar, *Asia and Western Dominance*, p. 141.

[12] *Ibid.*, p. 104. Panikkar writes: "The burning of the Summer Palace has not been forgotten and the present writer was told by a high official of the Central People's Government in 1951 that the account is still left open and awaits settlement."

resist their further encroachment and eventually to be emancipated from their yoke.

## SELF-FULFILLING PROPHECY

The development of seemingly irrational and tragic relations between East and West during the modern colonial period amply supports the well-known sociological theory of the self-fulfilling prophecy," which tells us that if people define situations as real, they often become real in their own minds regardless of the objective features of situations. According to Robert K. Merton: "The self-fulfilling prophecy is, in the beginning a *false* definition of the situation evoking a new behavior which makes the original false conception come true." This leads Merton to conclude that "social beliefs father social reality."[13] Often, those who fail to understand that they can hypnotize themselves by their own deep-seated racial prejudices or cultural prejudgments regard their distorted views as the only objective view of social realities. In difficult circumstances like colonial rule, both the Western colonial masters and their non-Western subjects became easy victims of self-fulfilling prophecies.

One of the common by-products of the self-fulfilling prophecy is the practice of "typing" and "categorizing" things and people, often in sharp dichotomy. Indeed, the diaries and letters of many nineteenth-century Western colonial officials, army personnel, missionaries, and business representatives who lived in the Eastern world betray how pervasive such easy categories were. In most cases Westerners portrayed themselves as civilized, honest, hard-working, fair, generous, kind, and reasonable, while the "natives," to use a word which acquired ugly connotations during the colonial period, were characterized as superstitious, dishonest, lazy, cunning, ungrateful, cruel and irrational, and so forth. Conversely, many Easterners who resented colonial rule and the penetration of Western ways indulged in similar oversimplifications—in reverse order. When the two sides "typed" each other, responding not to the reality of the situation but to the meaning this situation had for each side respectively, their "antagonistic cooperation" became a vicious circle.

The self-fulfilling prophecy was built into the very structure of colonial rule. In colonial administration there was, generally speaking, under the throne or the home government, something like a colonial office which functioned to supervise the viceroy or governor-general of a given colony. Usually the latter official ruled the colony not directly but through a kind of nominal legislative body that embraced a few "representatives" of the colonial subjects. By far the most complex colonial administrative machine was developed in India under British rule. According to Sir Reginald Coupland, the main strength of the British *raj* was the Indian Civil Service, which

---

[13] Robert K. Merton, *Social Theory and Social Structure* (Glencoe, Ill., 1949), pp. 182ff.

attracted the cream of English youth, usually those who were educated in Oxford and Cambridge. Next in importance to the Indian Civil Service (ICS) was the Indian Police Service (IP). There were other technical services, such as education, agriculture, and forestry, which were considered less important than the ICS and the IP, and these permitted a substantial number of native Indians to enter their ranks. Under these so-called All-India Services, there were also many Provincial Services which were staffed almost entirely by non-British personnel. It was reported that as early as 1900 the British *raj* employed over 500,000 Indian and 4,000 British personnel.[14] Britishers often cited this type of statistic to illustrate the magnanimity of enlightened British colonial policy, following Queen Victoria's proclamation "that, so far as may be, our subjects of whatever race or creed be freely and impartially admitted to offices in our service, the duties of which they may be qualified by their education, abililty, and integrity duly to discharge." Such an interpretation of statistics never impressed the Indians, because they knew too well that the best-paid jobs and decision-making posts were almost completely in the hands of British personnel, while their Indian counterparts were relegated to minor positions with meager pay.

Defenders of colonial policy can find many reasons for a certain amount of inevitable inequality in such arrangements, and they cite the recent examples of some European nations which under the Allied Occupation after World War II were also subjected to unequal treatment. But the real tragedy of the colonial period is that the inequality and lack of social contact between Westerners and Easterners were rationalized not on the grounds of political and military necessity or cultural differences but on racial grounds. On this ground, for example, Rabindranath Tagore, the Bengali poet who received various international honors including the Nobel Prize, or Dr. Sarvepalli Radhakrishnan, renowned professor of All Souls, Oxford, and later President of India, were not permitted to step into many of the social clubs in their own homeland, even as guests of the Britishers.

The ugly practice of discrimination based on color and race, which spread like a contagious disease in the modern period wherever the West was in political or economic control—in Africa, the Middle East, Asia, the Americas, and Australia—poisoned the wellspring of mutual understanding between Westerners and non-Westerners. After all, no gesture of good will toward the Chinese on the part of Westerners, for example, was effective when the Chinese were not even allowed to enter the exclusive parks in the foreign concessions on Chinese soil. Long before apartheid became the adopted policy in South Africa, the "white Australia" of the later decades of the nineteenth century excluded all "colored" immigrants; this policy was liberalized somewhat only in the early 1960's. The United States, too, during the first quarter of the twentieth century excluded immigrants from India,

Siam, Arabia, Indo-China, the Malay Peninsula, Afghanistan, New Guinea, Borneo, Java, Ceylon, Sumatra, the Celebes, China, and Japan on the grounds of race or color. As late as 1922 Mr. Justice Sutherland, speaking for a unanimous Supreme Court, interpreted the wording of the 1790 Naturalization Act—that "any free white alien was eligible to become a citizen of this republic"—to mean that only members of the white "race" were eligible, and insisted that the test was membership in the Caucasian "race," regardless of color. In that same year, in dealing with a high-caste Hindu, Justice Sutherland, again speaking for a unanimous Court, concluded that a person may be a member of the Caucasian "race" and yet not "white," on the grounds that "the words of the statute are to be interpreted in accordance with the understanding of the common man from whose vocabulary they were taken." This unusual legal logic was later extended to the extreme by Mr. Justice Cardozo, who stated: "Men are not white if the strain of colored blood in them is a half or a quarter, or, not improbably, even less. . . ."[15]

Apparently the encounter of the modern West and the Eastern world, coming as it did immediately after Europe's centuries-old struggle against the world of Islam, had an unfortunate beginning. The phenomenal expansion of the West, which came to control a vast portion of the non-Western world, convinced many Europeans of their superiority, not only militarily, politically, and economically but also "racially." Inevitably they looked at the non-Western world from this perspective, which in turn prompted non-Westerners to react against racism as the most intolerable component of modern Western colonial imperialism. To complicate the matter further, mutual suspicion and hostility were kept alive by the "self-fulfilling prophecies" of both sides, so that both Westerners and Easterners regarded each other not as living human beings but as complexes of virtues, vices, types, and categories.

As far as non-Westerners are concerned, their worst suspicion—that Westerners are imperialists and racists—is firmly confirmed by their experiences at home and by the behavior of Western nations in other parts of the world. Much of the thinking and behavior of the people in the East has been rooted in this reading of the modern world situation in which they find themselves. For their part, Westerners have their share of self-fulfilling prophecies. Their self-confidence as masters of the world is confirmed by their economic, political, technological, and military achievements; it is their manifest destiny to reshape the world according to their own image.

---

[15] See Milton R. Konvitz, *The Alien and the Asiatic in American Law* (Ithaca, 1946), pp. 81, 88, 89, 95. The racial aspect of the qualification for U.S. citizenship was modified by the McCarran-Walter Act, or the Immigration and Nationality Act, of 1952, which was passed over presidential veto.

Whether or not this view coincides with the reality of history is not questioned; they have defined it as real, and thus it has become real in their own minds.

## Unfinished Drama

While formal colonialism came to an end in many parts of the world by the middle of the twentieth century, the drama of the East-West encounter continues. It has so far seen three distinct phases in modern times. In the West these were (1) economic and political control of the East, (2) Westernization of the East, and (3) permanent tutelage over the East. In the East the corresponding phases were (1) passive resignation, (2) aspiration for modernization and equality with the West, and (3) an anti-Western campaign and the independence of the East.

Little need be said about the first phase of the drama, in which the West decisively took the initiative. Overwhelmed by the military, economic, and technological superiority of the West, the bewildered East could only accept the situation with passive resignation. In turn, the West took this as a sign of the political and cultural weakness of the East. There were, to be sure, different kinds of initiatives taken by different Western nations. For example, the earlier colonial empires, such as Spain and Portugal, which were motivated both by economic exploitation and religious enthusiasm, tried to superimpose their political, economic, and religious systems on the Eastern world. Nevertheless they were determined not to enlighten the Easterners too much. For example, when the Jesuits arranged a European tour (1582-1586) for a few Japanese Catholics, "they were not to learn anything of Christian divisions and especially nothing about Protestantism. Their tour was carefully chaperoned and of limited duration so that they would receive only the best possible impression of Catholic Europe."[16] The later colonial powers adopted a much more explicit policy, at least initially, of concentrating on economic gains, with no attempt to introduce Western culture and religion to their colonies. Thus when the Moravian mission began its work in the jungle of Dutch Guiana, "the Dutch government issued orders forbidding the Indians to join any Moravian settlement."[17] Similarly, the British East India Company took the position during the eighteenth century that "to hold India in subjection Christian missionaries must be excluded. It was not only that the arrival of Protestant emissaries of this faith might anger Hindu priests and Muhammadan mullahs, but *it would open the eyes of the Hindus and Hindis to the great facts of the world.*"[18]

This attitude began to change during the second phase of the colonial

---

[16] Donald F. Lach, *Asia in the Making of Europe*, I, Part II (Chicago, 1965), 691.

[17] Charles H. Robinson, *History of Christian Missions* (New York, 1915), p. 53.

[18] Macdonald, *Trade Politics*, pp. ix–x, italics added.

period. By that time the colonial powers, ostensibly to expedite the import-
ing of raw materials from and the exporting of merchandise to the colonies,
established harbors, roads, railroads, banks, and telecommunications. They
were compelled to train a corps of minor officials, for which they had to
provide a degree of Westernized education and streamline the administrative
structure. This development coincided with the growth of a messianic complex coupled with feelings of racial superiority among Europeans, which in
turn resulted in a policy of Westernization of their colonies and spheres of
interest in the non-Western world. Some of the colonial officials even boasted
with an air of self-righteousness of the tangible benefits of colonialism to the
East. This shift in the Western attitude toward the East was epitomized by
the famous British policy, advocated by Macaulay in 1834, to create "Indians
in blood and color, but English in taste, in opinion, in morals, and in
intellect." With this shift the colonial administrators, who had been hostile
earlier toward Christian missionary work, began to welcome missionary
activities—educational, medical, and other philanthropic as well as evangelistic programs. And Western missionary societies, unconsciously if not
consciously, began to cooperate with the aims and policies of the colonial
administrators.

Meanwhile, the East began to recover from the shock of the onslaught of
the West. Progressive elements in the Eastern world, especially the iconoclastic youth, were attracted by certain features of Western civilization.
They were instrumental in writing in the East the second phase of the
confrontation, advocating the modernization of social, economic, and political institutions as well as humanistic and scientific education. In so doing
they hoped that the East would be accepted as an equal by the West. To be
sure, they championed "modernization" and not "Westernization" of Eastern
society. Ironically, their dedicated effort to reform Eastern society by appropriating some Western ways appeared very much as though they were
advocating Westernization of the East—at least it appeared so to Westerners—and their enthusiasm, which the conservative majority by no means
shared, nevertheless encouraged the West to promote a wholesale Westernization of Eastern societies and cultures. The large number of Eastern students who flocked to Western universities in the nineteenth and twentieth
centuries convinced many Westerners that while the East had everything to
learn from the West, the West had nothing to learn from the East. Thus
many Westerners came to believe that ancient cultural traditions were
doomed to extinction, despite a small number of scholars and romanticists
who appreciated Eastern religions and cultures. The expectation of the
decline of the East also encouraged Christian missions, as illustrated by the
motto of the Student Volunteer Movement around the turn of the century:
"The evangelization of the whole world in this generation." As late as 1928 a
spokesman of Western Christendom went so far as to say, "These [Eastern
religions and cultures] are going to be smashed anyhow, perhaps not quickly,

but surely, and what is going to do it . . . is modern science, modern commerce, and modern political organization."[19]

During and immediately following World War I a marked change took place in the attitudes of East and West toward each other. Leaders in the Middle East and India, for example, who advocated cooperation with the West with the hope of gaining the West's respect for their causes, were disillusioned by the postwar settlement. On the other hand, the dreams of Westerners who crusaded for rapid Westernization of the East gave way to a series of disappointments because of the tenacity of the indigenous Eastern way of life, which stubbornly resisted the influence of the West. As a consequence, the new Eastern stance was formulated by those who espoused the cause of national independence. In the words of H. A. R. Gibb: "Western political and economic controls in the Near and Middle East, and the disregard of Western political leaders for human and social interests, forced the nationalist leaders to devote all their energies to the struggle against Western domination."[20] In India and many other parts of Asia developments followed the same pattern. Anti-Western sentiments in the East quickly united diverse social and religious reform movements which otherwise had little in common. Undoubtedly the most dramatic Asian figure to emerge in this period was Mahatma Gandhi, whose shrewd political strategy and profound dedication to religious ideals enabled him to lead India to political independence.

As for the West, World War I revealed the bankruptcy of the European state system which had existed since the sixteenth century. The façade of European cultural, religious, and moral unity was shattered, and two new powers, the United States and Soviet Russia, stepped into the forefront of world history, each claiming universal validity for democracy or communism. The fragile fraternity of the West could not prevent the emergence of Nazi Germany and fascist Italy, which together with Japanese militarists brought about World War II. The power vacuum thus created in the East after the war made it possible for non-Western nations to achieve political independence. Nevertheless, many Westerners still assume that the West will remain as the model and provide tutelage for generations to come in the less advanced nations of the non-Western world.

## DIMENSIONS OF UNDERSTANDING

The end of World War II ushered in a new phase of modern world history. The lofty dreams of "one world," four freedoms, and the rest, which

[19] The Jerusalem Conference of the I.M.C., *The Christian Life and Message in Relation to Non-Christian Systems of Thought and Life*, I (New York and London, 1928), 366.
[20] H. A. R. Gibb, "Near Eastern Perspective: The Present and the Future," in Young, ed., *Near Eastern Culture and Society*, p. 230.

had given hope to millions of people during the postwar period, were rudely shattered by a series of breathtaking events, including the Cold War and crises in the Middle East, Africa, South America, and Asia, which continue today. In each of the three generally accepted divisions of the world, namely, the "Free World," the "Communist World," and the "Uncommitted World" of Asia and Africa, life has become infinitely more complex than before. The West's expectation that it would remain the tutor of the non-Western world has eroded in the face of the independence of former colonies in Asia and Africa and the emergence of Communist China. The East is disillusioned because the end of colonial rule did not solve all its problems. Soviet Russia, a wayward cousin of the West, which has tried to identify itself with the causes of Asians and Africans with some measure of success, is no longer certain how long it can maintain even nominal alliance with Communist groups in Asia and Africa.

Nevertheless, all segments of the divided world of our time have something in common. Whether we like it or not, we must acknowledge that the four-centuries-old dominance of the West has left lasting imprints on economic, political, and technological developments in every corner of the earth. It is hard to deny that worldwide trade and transportation and communication systems have helped to break down historic barriers which had kept peoples and nations apart. Realizing this, many dreamy-eyed idealists chant the litany of "mutual understanding," which according to their oversimplified logic will follow automatically the shrinkage of physical distance. This theme has been enthusiastically espoused by Westerners recently because they find in the non-Western world many things familiar to them— airlines, automobiles, universities, hospitals, and modernized defense systems—except at less advanced levels of development. Ironically, these idealists fail to see that under a surface which appears similar, the world is divided culturallly. The basic issue, to quote Toynbee, is the fact that "while the economic and political maps have now been Westernized, the cultural map remains substantially what it was before our Western society started on its career of economic and political conquest. On the cultural plane, for those who have eyes to see, the lineaments of the four living non-Western civilizations are still clear."[21]

This does not imply that traditional cultures of the Middle East, India, and China, for example, have remained unchanged. Indeed, the spirit of modernity, which had earlier shaken the foundation of traditional Western culture, has greatly stimulated and rejuvenated Eastern cultures. But the effects of modernity have been different in the East and in the West. That is to say, the impact of modernity has compelled every one of the Eastern cultures, each in its own way, to come to terms with some of the significant

[21] Arnold J. Toynbee, *A Study of History*, abridgement of Vols. I–VI by D. C. Somervell (New York, 1947), p. 36.

features of the Western culture, whereas the West, which has developed global systems of economics, politics, and technology, has preserved its own "provincial" cultural outlook without being exposed to serious dimensions of non-Western cultures. This fact has deep implications for the present and future interplay of, and mutual understanding between, the East and the West. In this context, says Barbara Ward:

> . . . it may well be that we in the West may have more to learn at this stage because the patient assimilation of other peoples' ideas is not something that "comes naturally." Our brothers in Asia have undergone for centuries the immense battering impact of western ideas, and they have had time, as it were, to sit and sort them out, to consider them, to compare and weigh them, whereas we have not given ourselves comparable opportunity to live with eastern ideas or assimilate the great traditions of Asia.[22]

Cora DuBois makes the same point equally emphatically in terms of languages.

> To the extent that the Asians know our language but we do not know theirs, they are in a better position to understand us than we to understand them. To the extent that Asians know English and we are ignorant of their language and literature, they have the right-of-way in travelling what the State Department likes to call "that two way traffic."[23]

Happily there are more Westerners today than ever before who are concerned with the study of non-Western languages, ideas, religions, and cultures. Even so, the West's effort is very limited. Many Westerners, impressed as they are by the West's contribution to world economic, political, and technological development, still are tempted to think that what is required for mutual understanding between East and West is simply the propagation and extension of the "provincial" Western culture to the rest of the world. The Western perspective has been so shaped and conditioned by its last four centuries of experience that nations and peoples in the West think of the non-Western world primarily in terms of order and security; Easterners, who view the past four centuries from an opposite perspective, are passionately concerned with freedom and welfare, though they also recognize the importance of order and security as necessary prerequisites. This difference in perspective has been a major factor hindering the development of mutual respect and understanding between the East and West in our

[22] Barbara Ward, "A Summing Up," in Cora DuBois, et al., The East and West Must Meet: A Symposium (East Lansing, Mich., 1959), p. 130.
[23] Cora DuBois, "The Cultural Interplay Between East and West," in ibid., p. 10.

time. In the main, when crucial decisions are to be made, Western policy-makers, who advocate mutual respect and mutual understanding in their oratory, would rather settle for order and security even at the expense of the freedom and welfare of the peoples involved. Conversely, emotional and often irrational criticisms of Western policies by vocal minorities in the East, motivated as they are by a genuine concern for the freedom and welfare of the people, show little sympathy for the anguish of great powers who shoulder the main burden of international peace and security.

The events of our time do not encourage optimism about the future of the world. We sense that we are in a new era of world history, in which problems must be seen from a new perspective. Already we have some notions as to the new modes and styles of thinking and behavior, cultural, religious, and moral sensitivities, or lack of them, which will affect the course of the future as much as economic, political, technological, and military factors. For one thing, we are beginning to learn by bitter experience that in this post-imperialist era no great power, Western, Communist, or Eastern, can in the long run dictate the destiny of others, including "less developed" nations. Increasingly, military intervention, however necessary, will have to be regarded only as a temporary measure, for, as Walter Lippmann succinctly points out, "supreme military power and political mastery do not necessarily go together."[24] We have also come to accept the idea of regional or global economic cooperation and assistance, although existing programs may fall far short of our ideals.

More basically, we are beginning to realize that our common habit of polarizing the world into East and West, a habit which has been deeply ingrained in us, is based on a relatively modern phenomenon in the history of the world. We are also beginning to appreciate the tenacity of cultural and religious traditions which condition and color the perspectives of peoples, who in turn draw the meaning of a situation from their own perspectives and act according to the principle of the self-fulfilling prophecy. Our realization of these factors will help us develop a more adequate perspective for the West's understanding of the East and the East's understanding of the West, as much as for self-understanding on both sides.

[24] Walter Lippmann, "Superpowers Can't Govern World," *Chicago Sun-Times*, July 23, 1967.

# 4

## SEARCH FOR SELF-IDENTITY

### ASIAN PEOPLE TODAY

Travelers who visit Asia nowadays cannot help feeling that something significant is happening in the life of the people there. Those who knew Asia before World War II invariably comment that Asians have changed, not so much in the way they dress and live as in the way they feel and talk about themselves and about others. Call it the "spiritual revolution" or the "revolution of rising expectations," if you will; there is definitely something new in the air. Externally, Asia has not changed much, except for the conspicuous absence of Westerners in high places and a few other indications that colonialism is a thing of the past. On the surface, the new Asia has many old landmarks. The sight of teeming populations, for example, is nothing new, and the great metropolises—Bombay, Calcutta, Rangoon, Bangkok, Saigon, Hong Kong, Manila, and Toyko—were there long before the war. But the way people talk and the way they approach life are in marked contrast to their prewar attitudes. People are no longer as leisurely as they once were; they seem to be in a terrible hurry. One has the impression that they are excited about something, and they look hopeful. Even those who sit on the roadside do not appear idle. They chatter as though they had found a purpose in life.

These impressions become increasingly strong as you talk to people. Not only politicians, businessmen, journalists, labor leaders, and students but simple shopkeepers and farmers also talk as though they were on the main stage of world history. Once on a ferry between Hong Kong and Kowloon, I overheard a conversation between two middle-aged clerks about the significance of Nasser for the world scene. What struck me was the fact they were both well informed about world affairs. In Rangoon, I met an elderly, yellow-robed monk who, in the course of his exposition on the Buddhist approach to human relations, hotly denounced the segregation in Little Rock. He knew what was going on in North America, South Africa, and other parts of the world. I must confess I was a little surprised when a waiter in a Nepalese restaurant voiced his approval of the betrothal of a commoner to the crown prince of Japan. Little did I realize that people in this isolated country on the slopes of the Himalayas felt so strongly about events in other lands. In Colombo a taxicab driver volunteered his opinion as to why the late Mr.

Solomon Bandaranaike, then prime minister of Ceylon, had left Christianity and become a Buddhist. In Calcutta a barber was hopeful that a summit conference would be held in order to ease world tension, and a bearded man at a typewriter shop in New Delhi expounded to me what Sikhism could offer to the "materialistic" West. Such experiences, trivial though they may sound, at least awakened me to how people in Asia feel about what is happening in other parts of the world and in their own midst.

After listening to many people in all walks of life and in different Asian countries, I was suddenly struck by the fact that their words seemed to have a common theme. The settings are different, and the traditions are different, but they all have more or less the same message. At first I was irritated by such stereotyped expressions as the "materialistic West" and the "spiritual East," the "failure" of the West and the "sacred duty" of the East to save the world from a possible destruction by man-made weapons. But then it dawned on me that what they were driving at was not so much a denunciation and criticism of others as a sort of thinking aloud about themselves, about their own hopes and fears. When they talked about their proud heritage of the past, they really meant that their future must be grounded in their religious and cultural traditions. "To us Buddhists," said a monk in Japan, "history starts tomorrow." Certainly, Asians are proud of what they are doing, and they need little encouragement to formulate opinions, positive or negative, about themselves or about others. How can we account for such a mood, attitude, and ethos among present-day Asians? This was the question that intrigued me as I traveled through various parts of Asia last year.

There are undoubtedly many different explanations and interpretations of the present mood of the peoples in Asia. Many people attempt to interpret it in terms of the influence of the West upon the East. For example, according to Toynbee, the drama of modern world history has two main actors, the "West" and the "rest of the world." During the last four or five hundred years the West was the aggressor: "It is the world that has been hit—and hit hard—by the West." But in recent years the tables are being turned; the West is being attacked by Russia and China, who are becoming new aggressors. "The West's alarm and anger at recent acts of Russian and Chinese aggression at the West's expense are evidence that, for us Westerners, it is today still a strange experience to be suffering at the hands of the world what the world has been suffering at Western hands for a number of centuries past."[1] I am inclined to believe that such a "villain-and-good-guy" theory á la western movies, useful and suggestive though it may be, does not do justice to the depth and complexity of the spiritual struggle of the people in Asia.

There are many difficulties involved in our attempt to understand and interpret Asia and the Asians. For instance, we have many preconceived

[1] Arnold Toynbee, *The World and the West* (New York: Oxford University Press, 1953), p. 4.

notions about them, such as the oft-repeated and widely held "myth" of the
unity of oriental culture. Admittedly, there are some important similarities
between, say, the cultures of India and China, but, historically, with the
exception of the Buddhist expansion from India to China, these two great
cultures developed quite independently of each other. In the main, Asia
witnessed the development of several autonomous cultures existing in jux-
taposition, and there was little feeling on the part of each culture that it
belonged to a greater unified cultural tradition that might be termed "oriental culture." Even the satellite cultures of India or of China maintained
relative autonomy and insularity. While we have to resort to such general
terms as "Asian peoples," "oriental cultures," and "Eastern societies," we
must use them with the full realization that they are general terms, referring
to greatly diversified phenomena.

Second, we must bear in mind that each one of the cultures and peoples
in Asia has a long history. Although Asians do not share the Westerner's
understanding of the meaning of history, they can never forget their own
histories. Asians, whom Westerners tend to think of as "Völker von ewigen
Stillstandes," have had eventful careers. The history of Asia has its share of
war and peace, revolutions and counterrevolutions, the rise and fall of
empires, invasions and migrations, prosperity and poverty, religious awakening and spiritual bankruptcy. Asia defies simple characterizations; the "spiritual East," represented by Gautama, Confucius, and Gandhi, also produced
bloodthirsty warriors like Genghiz Khan and Timur Lane. Nevertheless, the
cultures and societies in Asia have managed to preserve their *Lebensgefühl*
despite numerous social, political, and cultural changes throughout the ages.
While the modern West has exerted a decisive influence on the East, this
does not imply that the contemporary situation in Asia is only a chapter of
the expansion of Western civilization. Unfortunately, many books available in
the West today suffer from this type of Europocentric obsession. We must
make a conscious effort to interpret what has taken place in Asia in the
modern period in relation to the historical development of Asian cultures and
peoples.

Third, we must remind ourselves that Western categories and Western
modes of thinking are not the best or most reliable tools for our attempt to
understand the religions and cultures of Asia. This does not mean that there
are no universal elements in human experience and cognition. All men
everywhere go through the same cycles of life, such as birth, naming,
initiation, marriage, sickness and recovery, war and peace, death and burial.
But the ways of structuring these experiences are not the same universally.
As Lily Abegg points out (*Ostasiens denkt anders*), Asians have their own
perspectives from which they interpret the events of life and the meaning of
history. Those who believe in the transmigration of souls feel the sorrow of
parting just as much as anyone else, but they certainly will never say, "O
death, where is thy sting?" In fact, "to be raised incorruptible from the dead"

is not good news to those who are trying to be delivered from the chain of birth and rebirth. Thus, in order to "understand" Asian peoples, their religions and cultures, one must enter as much as possible into the very structure of their thought and spiritual experience, and this takes more than a sheer intellectual endeavor. Unlike Westerners, who try to grasp the nature of an object "objectively," Easterners are preoccupied more with the act of knowing, or the state of consciousness and cognition, than with the object as such, because to them "knowing" is another form of "being." That is why our effort to "understand" Asians involves a total understanding, implying a sort of *metanoia*.

## HISTORICAL PERSPECTIVE

Today, we frequently hear about the "resurgence of Eastern religions" and the "march of nationalism" in Asia. To accept, as I do, these characterizations does not necessarily imply the acceptance of a simple cause-and-effect theory, for example, that Eastern religions were overpowered by Western culture during the colonial period, and now, as the weight of the West is being lifted, Eastern religions are reasserting themselves with the help of nationalism. Such an observation may partially explain the external factors involved, but it misses the deeper dimension of the agonizing spiritual struggle of the Asian peoples. I call this underlying spiritual struggle the "search for self-identity."

All of us have some sort of image of who we are and what we are. We are members of our family, community, and nation, and we are heirs of some cultural and religious traditions. We have names; we can identify ourselves, and we can be identified. We know how to act, how to greet others, and how to treat others. We have a sense of what to do and what not to do in various situations. We have pride, a sense of self-importance, and we respect others' sense of dignity. From time to time we have bad moments, disappointments and failures, but we cling to our own image of who we are and what we are; we know we belong! Also we have some basic affirmations about life and the world. Everyone has, wrote Carlyle, "the thing a man does practically believe and this is often enough without asserting it even to himself, much less to others, the thing a man does practically lay to his heart, and know for certain, concerning his vital relations to this mysterious universe, and his duty and destiny there."[2] Our own image of ourselves and our sense of self-identity are related to, and sustained by, our basic affirmations about life and the world.

Asian people have always had an image of what they were and who they were, although their sense of self-identity has not always been clearly articulated. For example, a man in traditional India may have wondered why he

[2] Joachim Wach, *Sociology of Religion* (Chicago: University of Chicago Press, 1944), p. 383.

was born into the priestly caste or the outcaste. He no doubt asked searching
questions about the mystery of life as he encountered personal crises. But his
self-identity was never a serious problem to him because he knew he had a
definite place in the world. His daily labor may have been boring, but he
knew it had to be done. Life to him was not a series of decisions. The fact that
he was born was not his own decision. The die had been cast by something
other than himself. What was needed was his decision to follow the prescribed course of life, fighting against boredom, monotony, and weariness.
He had little sense of being an individual; he was essentially an insignificant
part of a community in which he was needed and wanted. "From the very
first breath of life, the individual's energies are mastered, trained into
channels, and co-ordinated to the general work of the superindividual who is
the holy society itself."[3] His family, his caste, and his community embraced
three kinds of members—past members who are no more, present members
who are living, and future members who are to come into being. Man also,
according to Hindu orthodoxy, is not superior to nature; he is an integral part
of nature itself. Running through the mysterious universe and the world of
nature and man is the cosmic, eternal law (dharma), which dictates, sustains,
and guides every aspect of human life. Traditional Hinduism provided its
people with such a secure sense of self-identity.

The traditional Chinese also had their image of who and what they were.
Their sense of belonging was defined in terms of family relationships, because the family was the center of the society, nation, and universe. Men and
women, old and young, masters and servants, knew how to behave, talk, and
live in this cooperative commonwealth. The author of *Fousheng Liu Chi* ("Six
Chapters of a Floating Life") describes his wife:

> As a bride, Yün . . . was never sullen or displeased, and when
> people spoke to her, she merely smiled. She was respectful towards her
> superiors and kindly toward those under her. Whatever she did was
> done well, and it was difficult to find fault with her. When she saw the
> grey dawn shining through the window, she would get up and dress
> herself as if she had been commanded to do so.[4]

That she acted as though she had been commanded is significant, because
she had a clear image of who she was and what she was expected to do at all
times. Thus, when she met a lovely singsong girl, Yün secretly arranged to
have her own husband take this girl as his concubine and became literally
sick when someone else snatched the girl away. "Life is like a spring dream
which vanishes without a trace," so wrote an ancient Chinese poet. Yes,

[3] Heinrich Zimmer, *Philosophies of India*, ed. Joseph Campbell (New York: Pantheon Books,
Inc., 1951), p. 155.

[4] Lin Yutang (ed.), *The Wisdom of China and India* (New York: Random House, 1942), p. 971.

individual life vanishes like a spring dream, but what is important is the continuity of the greater life of the family, embracing both the living and the dead.

The fact that peoples in traditional Asian societies once had a secure sense of self-identity meant that their cultures were based on certain metaphysico-social principles. The values—religious, cultural, political, economic—were kept in balance in unified value systems, which were believed to be grounded in the cosmic laws, that is *Dharma* in India and *Tao* in China. In this collectivistic scheme each individual had a definite place, but his value as an individual was defined by the status he held, which was not to be questioned. For example, a man had to behave as a father to his son, as a husband to his wife, as a son to his own father, and as an employer to his employee. The status did not require efficiency or productivity so much as loyalty and conformity to the prescribed roles. An individual felt secure because he held statuses and he had roles to play, and except in emergency situations these roles and statuses were to be respected. Old age was respected not because an old man was necessarily wise or capable but because he held the status of father, of grandfather, or of great-grandfather and elder in the community. In this connection it must be remembered that the East understood social and political institutions to be rooted in the "natural," which in turn is identified with the "original." William Haas astutely observes: "The East admits no reason, no *logos*, in opposition and superior to the natural. The natural possesses, so to speak, its own reason. And it is the part of human wisdom to recognize and submit to it."[5] In this "immanental theocracy" the religious ideal is to "return" to the pristine past, to restore the original harmony of values, and to be united with the Real. Furthermore, the empirical societies are imperfect manifestations of the original community, and the only way to improve the societies is by restoring the original metaphysico-social principles.

Here lies the root of the Asian type of "interiorized messianism," which implied an ultimate self-salvation (*Selbster-lösung*). But the self did not mean self in the modern Western sense. Individuals did not matter. The importance was the accumulation of values and the transmission of these values from one generation to the next within the larger self, which was the holy society.

Each Asian society had its traditional priests, who were guardians of the social institutions and systems and transmitters of saving knowledge. A noteworthy example was the Brāhman caste in India, which was intrusted with the harmonious operation of the cosmos and all its component parts. While rituals and dogmas changed with time, the metaphysico-social principles were regarded as immutable by Hindu orthodoxy. In Buddhist countries the monks were bearers of the religiocultural and social values, and in the

---

[5] William S. Haas, *The Destiny of the Mind—East and West* (London: Faber & Faber, 1956), p. 69.

Shinto tradition of Japan the priests performed this function. In China the class of scholars (the *Ju*, commonly referred to as "Confucian scholars") shouldered this responsibility. It was the sacred duty of these "priests," regardless of whether or not they were so classified in the ecclesiastical institutions, to master the saving knowledge of the past, to transmit it to the present generation, to guard the social institutions, and to interpret contemporary experience in the light of accumulated wisdom. According to Confucius:

> A *Ju* lives with the moderns but studies with the ancients. What he does today will become an example for those in the generations to follow. When he lives in times of political chaos, he neither courts favors from those in authority, nor is boosted by those below. And when the petty politicians join hands to defame or injure him, his life may be threatened, but the course of his conduct may not be changed. Although he lives in danger, his soul remains his own, and even then he does not forget the sufferings of the people.[6]

So long as these "priests" maintained their rapport with the people by interpreting their contemporary experiences and problems in terms of the accumulated wisdom of their tradition, the people had a sense of mental security; they had their own image of who and what they were. The long history of Asia records many men and women of creative insights and noble visions who had lasting influences on the life of the people; it also records how these creative impulses were rigidified, institutionalized, and eventually lost. All religious and cultural traditions have experienced ups and downs, as well as periods of reform, revival, renaissance, and revolt. With the gradual stratification of societies, and the changes in social, political, cultural, religious, and economic values, the Asian peoples found it extremely difficult to maintain the traditional sense of self-identity. This became particularly apparent after the fifteenth century A.D.

The disintegration of Asian cultures was a complex phenomenon. Here we can only state that the slow process of internal stagnation in Asia was accelerated by the advance of the West during the eighteenth and nineteenth centuries. The traditional ideal of the East was the integration of all values and the balance and harmony of the diverse elements within the society, as illustrated by the reciprocal principles of Confucian ethics and the middle-way principle of Buddhism. Such an ideal presupposed the existence of a certain fluidity and flexibility within the ordered society. In the old days the people, whether they were agrarian or pastoral, lived close to nature. Despite floods, famines, wars, and pestilence, which plagued them from

---

[6] Lin Yutang (ed. and trans.), *The Wisdom of Confucius* (New York: Random House, 1938), p. 6.

time to time, people had a sense of security in their identification with the land and their membership in their communities. The order of society was maintained not so much by police or army but mostly by a strong sense of allegiance to traditional authority. In most cases the elders of the community guided and arbitrated but did not coerce. Even kings and emperors ruled mostly by customary powers, sanctioned primarily by religious authority.

The fluidity and flexibility of Asian cultures were lost with the stratification of society, the stagnation of cultural values, and the institutionalization of religious systems. Furthermore, the ruling classes superimposed political values upon all other values. This was the case with the Moghul rule in India, the Manchu rule in China, and the Tokugawa rule in Japan. The rulers did not reject traditional religions and cultures. On the contrary, they actually supported them in many ways. But at the same time religion had to bow to political authority. For example, the Manchu rulers in China saw in Confucianism "not only a practical philosophy for the masses, but a broad foundation upon which they might base their theocratic, paternal, and autocratic powers. . . . The happy and prosperous state, as pictured by the Manchus, was one built on the filial respect and blind obedience of the people."[7] These rulers, by confining religious leaders to the domain of "religion," denied the very function which the Brāhmans, monks, scholars, and priests traditionally fulfilled, namely, transmitting the spiritual and cultural values and interpreting the contemporary experiences of the people in the light of the accumulated wisdom. Instead, it was the rulers who claimed this "priestly" function of interpreting the nature and destiny of the people. Inevitably, the traditional pattern of culture was disrupted, and peoples' images of who they were and what they were became confused; they were no longer certain about their own self-identity.

## ASIANS IN THE MODERN PERIOD[8]

The encounter between the East and the West in the modern period must be seen in its historical context. We are not concerned here with the moral implications of Western colonialism but are only trying to understand the minds of Eastern peoples as they came in contact with Western civilization. In retrospect, it is evident the peoples, with their confused images of themselves, and the cultures and societies stagnating from within, could not halt the onslaught of Western civilization. The most significant outcome of the meeting of the East and the West was the development of three kinds of people in Asia—the new intelligentsia with Westernized education, the old

---

[7] Paul E. Eckel, *The Far East since 1500* (New York: Harcourt, Brace & Co., 1948), pp. 53–54.

[8] This section is a composite of my reading and interviews. I have freely used other people's categories, insights and views, especially those of my friends in Japan and Raimundo Panikkar of Benares.

or traditional intelligentsia, who resented anything new or Western, and the masses.

It must be noted that the influence of the West was felt differently in different parts of Asia. For example, in Japan and China, their own leaders (i.e., the Meiji reformers and the pioneers of the Kuomintang led by Dr. Sun Yat-sen) attempted to "utilize" Western learning and technology without losing their traditional cultural values. On the other hand, in India and other parts of Southeast Asia, Western colonial administrators attempted to "transform" the traditional cultures by means of Western education and institutions, as was explicitly stated in Macaulay's directive in India that education should produce citizens who were Indians in blood and color, but English in taste, in opinion, in morals, and in intellect. Nevertheless, in both cases the "new intelligentsia" with Westernized education claimed to be the new "priests," interpreting their people's contemporary experiences not with the accumulated values and wisdom of Asia but with cultural, social, economic, and political values of the West. Inevitably, there resulted what Ananda K. Coomaraswamy has called "the separation of literacy from culture," whereby those who were educated were uprooted from their ancestral ways of living and beliefs, while those who preserved traditional cultures could not adjust themselves to new situations.

The new intelligentsia in Asia were passionate converts of Western civilization, with its promise of a secularized salvation. Their theology was democracy, and their sacred scriptures were science. Consciously and unconsciously, they inhaled the messianism of modern Western civilization, which had a "strange compound of genuine idealistic responsibility, blindness and hypocrisy, with a strong dose of will-to-power as the basic component."[9] It must be noted, however, that these new Asian intelligentsia were not the vanguards of Western colonialism. That some of them were manipulated and used by colonial administrators cannot be denied. But in their own minds they were passionately Asians. Nevertheless, they were dedicated to the cause of reforming the disintegrating oriental cultures and societies with the new gospel of salvation—liberty, equality, fraternity, democracy, and modernity. With the passion of new converts they re-examined the traditional image of Orientals about themselves as reflected in the mirror of Western civilization. They were astonished at the discrepancy between what they potentially could be and what they then were. They were not naïve iconoclasts; they wanted to offer a new sense of identity to their people, who were burdened by the dead weight of hollow customs and traditions. Thus commented V. Sriniva Rao:

> Our present-day social practices are no doubt the natural outcome of certain religious beliefs. Unless such beliefs are shaken, the present social practices cannot be permanently shaken. If an attempt is made, as

[9] Haas, op. cit., p. 303.

has till now been made, to shake the present-day customs, without previously or simultaneously attempting to shake their foundations deep-rooted in religious beliefs, the result cannot be otherwise than what it is at present, viz. a creation of many halting and half-hearted "sympathizers" of social reform, who accept one reform and oppose another, evidently oblivious to the fact that the same root principles underlie all the reforms and are opposed to the principles that gave rise to the existing social customs.[10]

Similarly in China, Confucianism was mercilessly attacked by the new intelligentsia. Wu Yü went so far as to characterize Confucian filial piety as a "big factory for the manufacturing of obedient subjects." Dr. Hu Shih dares to state: "In the last two or three decades we have abolished three thousand years of the eunuch system, one thousand years of foot-binding, six hundred years of the eight-legged essay, four or five hundred years of male prostitution, and five thousand years of judicial torture. None of this revolution was aided by Confucianism."[11]

In this connection it is a matter of great interest that some of the new Asian intelligentsia embraced Christianity. While we do not intend to deal with the problem of Christianity in Asia, we may briefly note the inevitable conflict between the orientation of the Western missionary and that of Asian Christians. While the Western missionary worked toward the goal of Christianizing (and be it noted that this often implied Westernizing) Asians, some of the Asian Christians regarded Christianity as a means to reform and reconstruct their own sense of self-identity. These Asian Christians tried to be "liberated" from the meaningless religious and cultural values and practices which they had known, but they had no intention of allowing themselves to be "uprooted" from their own culture. The tragedy of modern Christian missionary work in Asia lies in the fact that the spiritual struggles of such Asian Christians as Kanzo Uchimura in Japan were not understood by the leaders of the missionary enterprise.[12] All too often, those who blindly conformed to the mores of the "mission compounds" were taken as genuine converts, while those who attempted to relate Christian faith to the indigenous culture and history were accused of not making a clean break with the pagan past. As late as 1928 a delegate at the International Missionary Council conference at Jerusalem went on record: "These [non-Christian] religions are

[10] Quoted in J. N. Farquhar, *The Crown of Hinduism* (Oxford: Humphrey Milford, Oxford University Press, 1913), p. 110.

[11] Quoted in Wing-tsit Chan, *Religious Trends in Modern China* (New York: Columbia University Press, 1953), pp. 17–18.

[12] Cf. Emil Brunner, "A Unique Christian Mission: The Mukyokai (Non-Church) Movement in Japan," in *Religion and Culture—Essays in Honor of Paul Tillich*, ed. W. Leibrecht (New York: Harper & Bros., 1959), pp. 287–90.

going to be smashed anyhow, perhaps not quickly, but surely, and what is going to do it . . . is modern science, modern commerce, and modern political organization."[13] The subsequent developments in Asia make it clear to us now that someone misread the timetable.

Under the impact of the West, and by the dedicated effort of the new Asian intelligentsia, Asian societies began to have a new look. Gone were the traditional social and political institutions, and with them many of the cultural and religious values and beliefs. The traditional role of elders as arbitrators in communal affairs was taken over by salaried government officials who could enforce new laws. The old system of education, intrusted to religious institutions, was replaced by the new public education system. The proud old aristocrats had to yield to the new rich who represented a hitherto unknown economic system. Even the sacred domain of religion was invaded by the new Westernized scholarship, which dared to investigate critically and historically the sacred scriptures and traditions of Eastern religions. The organic relationships among the different segments of society were scored as a legacy of the backward, feudalistic past. People were no longer evaluated by their status; they were regarded as individual human beings who had to fight for their own existence and social opportunity in a maddeningly competitive society.

Such radical social and cultural changes caused social and economic as much as mental and emotional upheaval for the traditional intelligentsia and the masses. All these modern institutions succeeded in destroying the old order of society without offering Asians a new sense of self-identity or a coherent view of life. In Burma, for example, "when the organic unity of the village was shattered, when external authority with penal sanctions was substituted for the authority inherent in a traditional way of life, the traditional guiding principle of social conduct was destroyed and there was nothing to take its place."[14] They felt as though they were foreigners in their own homelands. Their resentment, mixed with a certain amount of admiration, was directed against the new Asian intelligentsia, who exerted a direct influence on their lives. This situation threw the masses and the old intelligentsia into each other's arms. Both groups were torn between the new wants they felt in this strange new world and the sense of nostalgia for the old order they continued to idealize, much as the hero of the novel *How Green Was My Valley* felt caught between two worlds. The old order of society was gone, and they had to find some meaning in the new—but how? The only thing they could do was to envisage the restoration of past glory at some

---

[13] *The Jerusalem Conference of the I.M.C.*, Vol. I: *The Christian Life and Message in Relation to Non-Christian Systems of Thought and Life* (New York: International Missionary Council, 1928), p. 366.

[14] Margaret Mead (ed.), *Cultural Patterns and Technical Change* (New York: New American Library, "Mentor Edition," 1955), p. 33.

future time; the rememberance and the expectation thus became united in their minds, and they began to feel that history would "start tomorrow."

The period covering the two world wars was a turbulent era for the entire world, and Asians, who were more or less compelled to sit on the sidelines, were interested spectators. Long before the tension between America and Russia became accentuated, these two alternatives became real options in the minds of Asians, as exemplified by the emotional conflict that haunted the life of Sun Yat-sen. The Arabs, the Indians, and the Chinese felt that they were betrayed by Western nations at the Peace Conference, and the Japanese were incensed by the exclusion act of the United States govenment. Deeply hurt by, and disappointed in, both the Russian and the Western alternatives, Asians were compelled to re-examine themselves and their place in the world.

In China the leadership of the Kuomintang, which was the revolutionary party founded by Sun Yat-sen, was taken over by Chiang Kai-shek in 1928, and he immediately attempted to turn the clock backward. What he called the "New Life Movement" was in effect a movement to restore Confucian values, which were supreme because they were Chinese. Hu Shih and many other new intellectuals were warned about their iconoclastic views, and all books in conflict with the ancient doctrines of the "rites" were banned. The ultraconservative tendencies of the Kuomintang drove many young intellectuals with no real sympathy for communism into the Communist wing because of the lack of any practical alternatives. No doubt the Kuomintang's decline was accentuated by a prolonged warfare with Japan, but at the same time it was also due to the fact that Chiang Kai-shek's romantic nationalism, based on Confucian traditions, had no relevant message for the masses. In Japan the liberal trend of the 1920's was followed by the militant nationalism of the 1930's. The Japanese militarists were convinced that they could use cannon, bombers, battleships and other weapons of modern warfare to destroy the supremacy of the West. General Iwane Matsui, shortly before his execution as a war criminal at the Sugamo Prison in Tokyo, wrote: "Looking back, I have no regrets as I meet my death, nor have I anything to feel ashamed of before all creation, or before the Gods and Buddha. My deepest regret is that I was unable to realize Sino-Japanese Cooperation and a new life for Asia."[15] There is no question that Chiang Kai-shek and Matsui, as well as those who followed them, were sincere people, but they failed to understand the modern world in which their own people lived.

In India and other parts of Southeast Asia, the new intelligentsia, who had hitherto been regarded as faithful and useful citizens by the colonial administrators, began to demand political independence. They had little personal resentment or antagonism against Western civilization or Western

[15] Quoted in Shinsho Hanayama, *The Way of Deliverance*, trans. by H. Suzuki *et al*. (London: Victor Gollancz, Ltd., 1955), p. 256.

cultural values, but they were set against the continued exploitation of Asia by the colonial powers. They freely admitted the East's debt to the West. The West introduced not only modern technology but also new types of social and political institutions to Asia. They even admitted that the colonial administration introduced a sense of social justice, but it could not possibly provide political justice. And the new Asian intelligentsia were willing to die for political justice.

For that great cause of political justice, the new and old intelligentsia in Asia began to cooperate, and their combined effort was aimed at rectifying the political injustice imposed on them by Western colonial powers. Their temperaments were different, and they did not agree on many issues. But in their common struggle the old intelligentsia learned to use new methods and new learning as weapons, and the new intelligentsia began to rediscover in themselves their deeply rooted kinship with their own peoples. Many Westernized intellectuals like Nehru began to find a new sense of value in their ancestral cultures, which they had hitherto forgotten and scorned. "We are citizens of no mean country and we are proud of the land of our birth, of our people, our culture and traditions."[16] Both the old and new intelligentsia agreed on anti-Westernism as the goal and weapon of the mass movements. Anti-Westernism was not only a political slogan; it became a new gospel of salvation, and the masses found a meaning and a purpose for their lives in these movements. All the evils of society were blamed on the Western powers, and the masses in Asia were given a new sense of vocation as "collective suffering servants," as it were. They were not simply victims of greedy imperialists, mistreated and misunderstood, but they were, potentially at least, the bearers of a new gospel for the future, not only for their sons and grandsons, but also for the materialistic, warlike peoples of the West. We have no intention of belittling the genius and greatness of men like Gandhi, U Nu, and Sukarno; we only emphasize that their greatness was found in their ability to interpret the "messianic image" of the masses, so that the illiterate and the down-trodden would join forces with the intelligentsia in the struggle for political independence.

## THE INTELLIGENTSIA AND THE MASSES

Now that political independence has been achieved by most of the former colonial peoples in Asia, the situation has changed radically. During the period of the struggle for independence, the old and the new intelligentsia, republicans, Communists, socialists, democrats, Hindus, Muslims, Buddhists, Christians, rich and poor, were united toward a common goal. They were willing to endure hardships and difficulties because they had hope in the future. In a real sense the achievement of political independence meant the end of a dream. It was one thing for the prophets in exile to go into

[16] Jawaharlal Nehru, *The Discovery of India* (New York: John Day Co., 1956), p. 579.

ecstasy over the task of building a new Jerusalem. "Thus India gained her freedom but lost her unity," confessed Maulana Abul Kalam Azad.[17] The internal division cut deep into new nations in Asia.

At any rate, after World War II, many Asian nations gained independence—India, Ceylon, Burma, Indonesia, Vietnam, Malaya, the Philippines, and Korea. Mainland China emerged as a Communist state, and Japan was recently freed from Allied occupation. Each nation faces both internal and external pressures, politically, economically, socially, and culturally. The new nations in Asia, while rejoicing over their independence, realize that the era of a nation-state is over. Although none of them wishes to give up its national sovereignty, all of them feel the need of regional cooperation and collective security. This is the period of power blocs, and Asian nations, with the cooperation of African states, feel that they must develop some sort of unity to counterbalance the pressures of the Western and Communist blocs. Thus far, the AfroAsian bloc, often referred to as the "Bandung Front," has maintained its existence only as a non-Western and a non-Communist (with the exception of Communist China) bloc, with very little of a positive nature to inspire and guide the common life of its member nations. There are many reasons why this is so. For example, the new nations in Asia have been influenced by their former colonial ties far more than the spokesmen of the new governments are willing to acknowledge. To be sure, the historic insularity of various Asian cultures and societies was greatly broken down by the introduction of modern civilization. But each nation is jealous of its own existence, and is not emotionally open to the development of psychological fraternity with its neighbors.

By far the greatest problem for Asian nations is the internal unity of their own peoples. The difference along the political, economic, social, and cultural lines, as well as ethnic, religious, and linguistic differences, are obvious. Equally if not more persistent is the difference in mentality and outlook among the new intelligentsia, the old intelligentsia, and the masses. These categories, like all typologies, are naturally oversimplifications, and in reality there is more overlapping and further subdivision among them. Nevertheless, they may help us to clarify the existence of different images of the Asian peoples, crossing national, religious, and cultural boundary lines.

The "new intelligentsia" no longer play the decisively important role they did during the intitial encounter between the East and West. Then they were the creative minority, new "priests," dedicated to re-forming the backward Asian nations and to reshaping them after the models of modern Western nations. Now, however, they are "technicians," assigned to carry on their duties in government service, in business, in education, and in other spheres in the new nations. Although they were once caught in the whirlwind of the independence movement, they now feel stifled by the at-

[17] Maulana Abul Kalam Azad, *India Wins Freedom* (Bombay: Orient Longmans, 1959), p. 225.

mosphere of these nations which they helped to create. Some of them have
studied abroad; many were exposed to Westernized education at home. All
have the capacity to look at themselves and their own nations with a sense of
detachment,. They are at home in either the East or the West, but they feel
some distance from both of them. Both were learned and acquired cultures
for them, and they cannot reject either one; they are on the borderland
between the two. They may give lip service to their ancestral religious rites
and participate in their own neighborhood activities, but their hearts and
souls are not in them. In a sense, they envy their illiterate neighbors, who
can be comforted by old gods and superstitious rituals. They respect religions and mores, but they cannot believe in them. Most of them affirm
their faith in science and democracy. The sophisticated among them dream
of the eventual synthesis of Eastern and Western cultures; many of them are
interested in existentialism, depth psychology, Zen Buddhism, or Vedanta.
Their daily life is dictated by middle-class values and mores. They have
mixed feelings of admiration and fear for religiously oriented Pakistan or
Communist-oriented Red China, but they hope their own nations will remain neutral and uncommitted.

Some of the new intelligentsia cannot stand the strain of holding to both
Eastern and Western values, and they resort to submitting themselves to
authority, such as joining the Communist party or the Christian church or
embracing their ancestral faith. But an amazing number of these people find
it difficult to take such a step; they cling to the borderland, complaining
about the meaninglessness of life. Many of them confess their fears of
schizophrenia, high blood pressure, or ulcers. They are too proud to admit
that they have no clear sense of identity.

The "old intelligentsia," too, show their emotional strain. They suffer
from the discrepancy between their ideals and reality. Their grandfathers, be
it recalled, during the initial period of the encounter between the East and
West, categorically rejected new ideas and new ways introduced from the
West. However, since that time, the old intelligentsia— the guardians of
ancient religions and cultures—have been compelled to make a series of
concessions to the new order of society for the sake of their own survival. But
once they had installed telephones and radios in the temples and shrines,
and once they had started reading the Sacred Books of the East, translated
by Max Müller and others, they knew they were deviating from their ideas.
They could still sing the Lord's song but their tunes were contaminated by
the tunes of the strange new land. Nonetheless, the old intelligentsia found a
new incentive during the struggle for independence, and they commanded
the respect of the masses. In resisting the Western colonial powers, even
while utilizing Western technology, their inspiration had to be derived from
the traditional cultures and religions. The English-educated Gandhi advocated the importance of the spinning wheel, and the baptized Christian
Bandaranaike returned to the Buddhist fold. With the goal of political

independence in view, the old intelligentsia envisaged a glorious future for themselves and for the ideals they represented.

Now, however, they are horrified to realize that their own camp is not so solidly united as they thought it was. Some of the right-wing purists are under the happy illusion that history can be undone and that the pristine past can be realized. But how can they part with and forget all the experiences and the values accumulated in the meantime? And where can they find the pristine past? Denouncing modern inventions and modern misunderstandings of their past makes wonderful oratory, but it cannot be done in actual practice. The more progressive wing of the old intelligentsia, on the other hand, also suffer from a romantic illusion in claiming that their religions and cultures not only can cope with science and democracy but can also save the world from destruction and despair. The progressive elements of the old intelligentsia have all the marks of the new intelligentsia, except that they know which side of the fence they are on. They are afraid to look at themselves in the mirror for fear that they might find a very different (and Westernized) image. So they are on the defensive, although they appear on the surface to be taking a positive stand. For example, spokesmen of Eastern religions often claim that their religions are the most scientific, because, so they say, what is not scientific is not truly Buddhistic, Hinduistic, or Islamic, respectively. Today the old intelligentsia, both the conservative and the progressive wings, covet the position of leadership for the new cultures and societies in Asia.

The term "masses" is an ambiguous one, usually referring to the large body of people who do not have a self-conscious intellectual orientation, old or new, and who live close to nature. That they are not educated does not mean that they are not intelligent. Their culture is based on accummulated wisdom, handed down from generation to generation in their families, villages, and communities. The basic difference between the masses and the intelligentsia is that the former experience the meaning of life but do not reflect on it. Of course this pattern varies greatly in different parts of Asia. The situation in Japan, for example, with an almost complete literacy rate, cannot be compared with some of the Southeast Asian countries. But even in Japan the rural people preserve many of the mass qualities. Traditionally, the masses in Asia had their own small worlds. Political events had little direct meaning for them. The village was a social and residential unit, and it was the focus of their identification. Villagers lived together for many generations, and their time-honored way of doing things kept order and promoted orderly conduct in the village. R. Panikkar, a scholarly Roman Catholic priest who has a rare ability to feel the spirit of Hinduism, emphasizes that a man in traditional Hinduism feels a cosmic bond with the Cause, Principle, or Source of this very Cosmos. "His religion is a cosmic religion and his life a chthonic life. His actions are ultimately motivated by his ideas, not even by his human instincts, but by telluric forces, by the rhythm of the earth, by the dynamism of the whole world in which he simply plays a role."[18]

Masses in other parts of Asia share with traditional Hindus the attitude of accepting life as it is and also the belief that the whole process of the world, including their own destinies, is ordained by supraworldly forces of some kind. For the masses, religion pervades all dimensions of human life, because for them there is no difference between the sacred and the secular. "Fear is there and fascination also, but if you happen to believe in evil spirits and you see and hear them every day and you know that your headache of the last ten days is due to one of them, you continue to be careful, but not so much terrified."[19]

In the modern period the Asian masses experienced a number of shock treatments. The old order crumbled, and they had to make an adjustment to the new. Various spokesmen claimed that they were speaking for the masses, but they had little understanding of what the masses were really thinking. Although the masses were longsuffering and reluctant to voice their opinions, they learned by experience both the advantages and the disadvantages of the new type of social relations. For example, they were fascinated by the use of money, which was both a curse and a blessing to them. With money they could buy anything, and without money they could not maintain their self-respect. In the modern world, individuals and families had to look after themselves. "With the increase in population, and the breakdown of traditional patterns of behaviour, new lands which had been set aside for communal grazing or fuel or sanitary arrangements were appropriated by individual villagers, and individual villagers interfered, for instance, with the irrigation with a veiw to their own profit only, even when this caused damage to the whole village."[20]

The independence movements in various parts of Asia became powerful political forces when both the old and the new intelligentsia developed a rapport with the masses. Oppressed by colonial authorities, the intelligentsia identified their lot with that of the masses, whom they had hitherto looked down upon. In their rhapsody for the future the revolutionary leaders were inclined to promise the masses the pie in the sky and to demand from the masses in turn their wholehearted participation in the common struggle. The masses were no longer masses, blissful in their ignorance; the masses were people, comrades-in-arms, collective Messiahs. This view was dramatically worded by Sun Yat-sen in his "Three Peoples' Principles":

[18] R. Panikkar, "Some Phenomenological Aspects of Hindu Spirituality Today," *Oriental Thought* (n.d.), p. 183.

[19] *Ibid.*, p. 186.

[20] Mead, *op. cit.*, p. 33.

San Min Chu I (Three Peoples' Principles)
Our aim shall be
To found a free land;
World Peace be our stand.
Lead on, comrades;
Vanguards ye are!
Hold fast your aim
By sun and star!
Be earnest and brave
Your country to save.
One heart, one soul;
One mind, one goal![21]

Thus, during the struggle for political independence, temporarily at least, the masses had a clear image of who they were and what they were. This new sense of self-identity, coupled with their new economic needs and wants, was like an explosive charge put into their minds; it has exploded already in many parts of Asia, and it will continue to explode from now on.

## NATIONALISM AND RELIGIONS

It is difficult to appreciate the magnitude of the problems that confront the peoples of Asia today. There are two types of "priests" who feel the vocation to guide their people and provide them with a new image of themselves. They are the political leaders and the religious leaders. Parenthetically, political leaders sometimes include ecclesiastics, as in Ceylon; and religious leaders include many laymen, as in Burma. In times of crisis they have been able to work together, and in times of peace they try to complement each other, but not always with success. Both groups address themselves, on the one hand, to their own people, and on the other, to the world at large. To outsiders, nationalism and Eastern religions seem to be inseparable, and in some cases this is true. But, more often than not, there is a fine point of difference between them in the sense that political leaders tend to conceive religion politically, while religious leaders approach nationalism religiously. When their interests do not coincide, ecclesiastics may be silenced by the law, or the political leader may be shot by religious fanatics. Both groups know that they are dealing with the explosive dynamic power of the masses. "In Asia," says Adlai Stevenson, "the masses now count for something. Tomorrow, they will count for more. And, for better or for worse, the future belongs to those who understand the hopes and fears of masses in ferment. . . . The people want respect—and something to eat every day. And they want something better for their children."[22]

---

[21] Translated by Tu Ting-hsiu.
[22] *Chicago Sun-Times*, September 4, 1953.

Who can help the masses in ferment to realize this new vision? Understandably, political leaders, who have led the people through the painful struggle for independence, assume this role; their formula is nationalism. It is not only the problem of restoring national dress, national language, national monuments, and national economy; the whole national spirit, the pride and dignity of the people, is at stake. Religion, too, plays a significant role in this respect. For example, in the words of U Kyaw Thet: "Painfully aware that their national pride—even their continued existence—was manifestly debatable, the Burmese had to produce something tangible and traditional to justify their future as a separate entity. They found what they needed in Buddhism."[23] Many religious groups and institutions have benefited in this situation, even in Communist China, where some of the old monasteries have been restored as national monuments.

There are many religious leaders who for their part are keenly aware of the important role religion has to play in the formation of new nations. Adherents of religions are not citizens only, and as such have to do their share, but religion can provide the moral incentive which is so badly needed for the growth of national families. To be a Japanese means to be a Shintoist or a Buddhist, to be a Filipino means to be a Roman Catholic, to be Thai or a Burmese means to be a Buddhist, to be an Indian means to be a Hindu, and to be a Pakistani or an Indonesian means to be a Muslim. Such a simple equation between nation and religion, sanctioned by many political and religious leaders, has a powerful appeal to the masses in ferment. It was no surprise to me that several of the political leaders I met in Southeast Asia were most appreciative of religion as the moral and spiritual fabric of their national life.

The tragedy of Asia is that nationalism has emerged at a time when it is no longer adequate for guiding the explosive dynamics of the people in Asia. It is tragic, because nationalism alone was capable of liberating people from the yoke of colonialism, and yet beyond this goal it ran into a blind alley. For a decade or two after the independence, a residual prestige and inertia may enable nationalism to preserve its vitality, but the very problems which nationalism promised to solve for the masses cannot be solved solely on nationalistic terms.

The revolutionary presures go far beyond the matter of national independence to the issue of the whole social structure, relations on the land and between classes, the terms and methods of economic development . . . They are soluble no longer within the confines of separate

---

[23] U Kyaw Thet, "Continuity in Burma—the Survival of Historical Forces," *Atlantic*, CCI, No. 3 (February, 1958), 118.

national economies; a new world economy is wanted. Thus the great forces in motion move blindly toward some new coherence.[24]

Now that they have attained a new sense of national identity, for which they are grateful to nationalist ideology, people in Asia are beginning to demand a new social identity. They are no longer satisfied to stay at the bottom of the ladder, even if the top positions are held by their fellow nationals. They want to improve their lot; they insist on correcting unjust social relations, modernizing production, and securing equal opportunities. In this atmosphere, nationalism not only fails to give a vision of national unity but begets a "communalism" which further divides the national family. The Dravidians and the Scheduled Class (untouchables) in India, Tamils in Ceylon, Karens in Burma, and Tibetans in Communist China are but few examples of the disgruntled minority groups in Asia. Governments may pacify the people by promising miracles through a five-year plan or a ten-year plan, but the people are beginning to be dangerously impatient with such gradualism. Nehru is reported to have commented that "India's liberal Constitution will only last if the Indian economic plan can engender a sense of economic progress at least equal to that of China."[25]

Many of the Westernized Asian intelligentsia cling to democratic principles as the answer to the revolutionary situation in Asia. Hopefully, they point out the similarities between the independence of the young republic in North America and the independence of their own country. But the American Revolution was not the product of a nationalistic spirit or of a philosophy of democracy. The genius of American politics, says Professor Boorstin, is due to the "seamlessness" of its culture. Democracy in the American sense is not a philosophy; it is only a pragmatic, regulative principle which enables people and groups of different beliefs and persuasions to live together. "If we have learned anything from our history, it is the wisdom of allowing institutions to develop according to the needs of each particular environment; and the value of both environmentalism and traditionalism as principles of political life, as a way of saving ourselves from the imbecilities, the vagaries, and the cosmic enthusiasms of individual men."[26] As regulative principles, democracy is important for Asia, but the types of democracy which should develop depend largely on what contents are envisaged in their objectives; democratic means, however important, cannot create the image of the future for the people in Asia.

That Asians need a new sense of self-identity is well recognized. Many

[24] Harold R. Isaacs, "The Dimensions of the Crisis: Asia's Multiple Revolution," *Saturday Review of Literature*, XXXIV (August 4, 1951), 14.

[25] Quoted in the *Manchester Guardian*, December 28, 1954.

[26] Daniel J. Boorstin, *The Genius of American Politics* (Chicago: University of Chicago Press, 1953), pp. 185–86.

new nations in Asia subscribe to democratic principles as a means to regulate their political affairs, even though the meaning of democracy is interpreted differently in various countries. The crucial question is the creative vision of the future. Here the romantic conservatives, traditionalists, and rightists each make a bid, hoping to restore their peoples' past glory, and their proposals are supported by religious and cultural conservatives, medievalists, and classicists. The measures they are willing to employ in order to restore the past may be modern, that is, the use of mass media of communication, but they draw their inspiration primarily from the archaic, mythological past of their peoples. By separating ideals from history, and by ascribing eternal values, as it were, to the past, divorced from the contamination of the realm of history, these "prophets" of past glory can mercilessly denounce the present. We saw in the recent history of Japan how such "prophets" of past glory, when they secured political power and military weapons, were able to sway the imagination of disgruntled peoples. And, today, Asian nations are plagued by many religious, cultural, and political movements which are critical of the government and which want to restore the mythological past. Although they are harmless minorities in times of peace, these groups may quickly influence the masses in times of crisis.

Fortunately for Asia, as well as for the whole world, many of the first-generation revolutionaries, such as Sun Yat-sen and Gandhi, were world citizens as much as nationalist leaders. Under their leadership, the architects of the new nations in Asia committed their policies and constitutions to such principles as the social welfare state and the peaceful coexistence of all nations of the world. On the eve of the attainment of independence, Nehru stated in the Constituent Assembly:

> Long ago we made a tryst with destiny, and now the time comes when we shall redeem our pledge, not wholly or in full measure, but very substantially. At the stroke of the midnight hour, when the world sleeps, India will awake to life and freedom. . . . It is fitting that at this solemn moment we take the pledge of dedication to the service of India and her people to the still larger cause of humanity.[27]

In such a crucial turning point, which comes rarely in history, the nationalist leaders were able to superimpose very progressive measures and constitutions on their people, who had little understanding of what these constitutions meant. The irony is that people in Asia earned their political freedom, but they did not earn the liberal political principles which were given to them. Hence the emotional distance between the governments and their peoples. The situation is even further complicated in that the first-generation

[27] *Jawaharlal Nehru's Speeches* (New Delhi: Government of India, Publication Division, 1949), I, 25.

revolutionaries, who were oriented to the world community, are dying out, leaving a big question mark as to who, or what types of leaders, will take their places. Already President Sukarno makes it very plain that the democracy Asia has adopted is too Western; parliamentary democracy is not in harmony with the Indonesian atmosphere, and excesses are bound to occur—excesses such as the misuse of the idea of opposition in the political field, violation of discipline in the military field, and corruption in the socioeconomic field.

Events move quickly in Asia today. Border troubles, revolutions, and counterrevolutions will continue to occur. Urbanization, industrialization, and mass education will change the face of Asia as time goes on. On the other hand, millions of people still believe today that penicillin or quinine, for instance, cure diseases because of the presiding deity of each plant or because of the spiritual power of the person utilizing the remedies.[28] In this complex situation, in which various stages of human history exist side by side, revolutionary forces move around almost aimlessly, looking for a direction and a coherence. The old type of nationalism, which has guided Asians thus far, can no longer serve as a guiding principle for people who are looking for some sort of a new order or social fabric and yet are not willing to part with their spiritual and cultural traditions. The combination of religiously conceived nationalism and politically conceived religions may fill the need of the people for the time being, but not for very long. Romantic dreams of restoring the pristine past can spell out what is wrong with the present sociopolitical order, but they cannot give the people resources for interpreting their contemporary experiences and relating them to the vision of the future. For lack of alternatives, many Asian youths are attracted by communism.[29] One unforgettable moment for me was seeing the headquarters of the Nepalese Communist party right next to a lovely old Buddhist temple at Kathumandhu. What struck me was the contrast between the predominantly old worshipers at the temple and the predominantly young men and women who were going in and out of the party headquarters.

But nationalism is far from being dead, and Eastern religions certainly are not spiritually bankrupt. There are significant trends among some people in various parts of Asia toward grasping the meaning of their contemporary experiences. States Nehru:

> We seek no narrow nationalism. Nationalism has a place in each country and should be fostered, but it must not be allowed to become aggressive and come in the way of international development. Asia stretches her hand out in friendship to Europe and America as well as to

[28] Panikkar, op. cit., p. 185.
[29] Cf. Joseph M. Kitagawa, "Christianity, Communism, and the Asian Revolution," World Dominion, XXXIII (July–August, 1955), 199–206.

our suffering brethren in Africa. . . . The freedom that we envisage is not to be confined to this nation or to a particular people, but must spread out over the whole human race. That universal human freedom also cannot be based on the supremacy of any particular class. It must be the freedom of the common man everywhere and full opportunities for him to develop.[30]

Thus Nehru and many others like him try to reinterpret the meaning of nationalism, and they attempt to follow what might be termed a "dynamic neutralism" in international affairs. In the philosophical domain, Eastern philosophies are re-examined and reinterpreted from a world-wide perspective. Radhakrishnan, for example, reinterprets the Hindu doctrine of *maya* (usually translated as illusion): "The world of everyday events and things is not ultimate reality, to be sure, but neither is it unreality. He has defended the reality of the empirical world: it finds its basis in the Absolute."[31] Similarly, Professor Hajime Tanabe, rejecting the "as well as" of the speculative synthesis of Hegel and the "either/or" of the ethical earnestness of Kierkegaard, insists that the true dialectic is a "thoroughgoing negativity of our immediacy (the repentance of one's radical sin) by the mercy of the Absolute, who also negates Himself for the sake of Love and Mercy."[32] In the religious sphere a new spirit is observable in the world-wide missionary movements of Islam, the Ramakrishna Order of Hinduism, and Buddhism. Some of the younger Asian Christians are also trying to re-examine and reformulate their own beliefs and practices in the light of their contemporary experiences.

However, these new trends in various dimensions have not as yet related themselves to each other, nor have they related themselves to the revolutionary aspirations of the masses in Asia. Indian delegates may gain respect at the United Nations, but their government may lose votes at home. Radhakrishnans and Tanabes may influence college students, but they exert little influence on the actual life of the common people. Despite the much-publicized "resurgence" and "reformation" of Eastern religions, many religionists are not willing to face the present and the future. For example, reformers in Ceylon complain that

the Buddhist hides from the realities behind a barrier of well-meaning phrases, and concentrates so largely on the need for Love and Kindness that he ignores the inevitability of conflict with the reactionary ele-

[30] *Jawaharlal Nehru's Speeches*, I, 304–5.

[31] Radhakrishnan and C. A. Moore (eds.), *A Source Book of Indian Philosophy* (Princeton, N.J.: Princeton University Press, 1957), p. 610.

[32] Yoshinori Takeuchi, "Buddhism and Existentialism," in *Religion and Culture—Essays in Honor of Paul Tillich*, p. 301.

ments. The Buddhist is so entangled in the claims of tradition that he is a
stranger in the world of current politics.[33]

What is significant, though, is that there are creative and revolutionary
elements among the intellectuals, political leaders, religious leaders, and the
masses. Once, during the period of the political struggle for independence,
they were all united as comrades-in-arms and collective Messiahs. Can they
be united again in the near future? The collective suffering servants in Asia
today are paralyzed just as much by poverty and outmoded social relationships as by the lack of a central focus.

It is difficult to sort out numerous and diverse impressions and formulate
a coherent picture of the contemporary Asians. To whatever one says about
them, others can find contradictions and exceptions. One thing is clear,
however. They are passionately Asians in the messianic sense, even though
their message is still ambiguous and lacks cohesion. They are more articulate
in their criticisms of the West than about themselves. In 1956 the *New York
Times* stated that Christians are now "paying a price, not for their teaching,
but for not consistently practicing what they preach." That may be so; at least
many Asians still find it difficult to feel that the religion of the European
regiments of occupation during the colonial era could be their own faith.
Theoretically, one may argue this point. But it is not confirmed by Asian
experiences of the immediate past, of those years of humiliation and suffering. And, yet, Asians are by and large free from malice toward other peoples
and religions. Their anti-Westernism and anti-Christian attitude can be
traced to something much deeper, although they may not be conscious of it.
That is, the Asians' attitude toward the West—that strange combination of
resentment and admiration—is due to the fact that they are compelled to live
in a world which is no longer Asian in the traditional sense of the term. The
Western "oppressors" are gone, but they cannot throw away the "modernity"
which is reshaping Asian societies and cultures with a secular science and a
secular interpretation of state and law.[34] "Modernity," the legacy of the West,
has irresistibly permeated all aspects of their lives. On the other hand, what
are they contributing, or what can they contribute, to the West? Arts, poetry,
and spirituality, yes! But these reach only a tiny segment of Westerners.
They have not as yet found that unique quality with which Asia can confront
the West. They are certain that they have something, but not yet sure what it
is. Meanwhile, the Messiahs are frustrated because of the vagueness of their
message. This may account for their use of such generalities as the "spiritual
East" and the "materialistic West."

A spokesman at the Buddha Jayanti (1959) in Tokyo stated: "The modern-

[33] *The Revolt in the Temple* (Colombo: Sinha Publications, 1953), p. 604.
[34] William E. Hocking, *The Coming World Civilization* (New York: Harper & Bros., 1956), p.
4.

ization of the non-West is something beyond westernization and its process is very tortuous. If we are not creative, we may be assimilated to western civilization. But if we are vital and creative, we may have a narrow escape. We must find a creative way."[35] This sentiment is expressed in various other parts of Asia as well.

> The question is whether in the end the man of the East will have lost himself, whether he will be hopelessly subservient to the spirit of the West or whether he will emerge from the encounter a new man, who has found the way to a peculiar, creative reshaping of his life, as a nation and as a person. In this sense it is a question of life or death. Only as a new man can the man of of the East dominate the tremendous crisis which has come on him and which in breadth and depth is unparalleled in the history of mankind.[36]

This is not a problem for Asians alone, however. What happens in Asia will influence the course of history of the entire world. Will Asians find a creative way, a clear image of themselves, and a new sense of self-identity in this turbulent era?

[35] Shinn Yamamoto, "The Tragedy of Westernization" (Tokyo: Buddha Jayanti, 1959).

[36] Walter Freytag, *Spiritual Revolution in the East*, trans. L. M. Stalker (London: Lutterworth Press, 1940), pp. 18–19.

# 5

## CONVERGENCE AND PREJUDICE
## IN THE UNITED STATES

My "flirtation" with America started when I was in college in Tokyo during the early 1930's. Japanese students of my vintage were keenly interested in national and international affairs, for we all sensed that the old order was crumbling under our feet. We used to have heated discussions regarding various alternative ideologies that might provide Asia with guiding principles for the future. Some were attracted by American democracy, while others turned to the Russian form of economic democracy. Still others argued in favor of Sun Yat-sen's attempt to reconcile American and Russian elements with the indigenous national heritage by means of the "Three Principles of the People" (*San Min Chu I*): namely, people's rule (nationalism), people's authority (democracy), and people's livelihood (economic democracy). What inspired those of us who were attracted by American democracy was not the form of government, which we did not understand anyway, but the Wilsonian idealism which promised a universal program of peace, justice, and the liberation of peoples. I still remember Wilson's "Pueblo Speech," in which he described how a group of French women cared for the graves of American soldiers on the outskirts of Paris because those Americans died for the cause of French freedom. In Wilson's words: "France was free and the world was free because Americans had come!" Then, he continued: "I wish some men . . . could feel the moral obligation that rests upon us . . . to see it through to the end and make good their redemption of the world. For nothing less depends upon this decision, nothing less than the liberation and salvation of the world."[1] Understandably, this noble expression of American idealism impressed us as a gleam of hope for the future of the world. Our opponents in Tokyo were quick to point out, however, that Wilson's high-sounding words did not really represent America, which, according to them, was a new imperialist power, determined to dominate the rest of the world and persecute nonwhite peoples both at home and abroad. They cited many illustrations: Wilson's own program was rejected by Congress in 1920; in 1922 the

---

[1] Woodrow Wilson, WAR AND PEACE, II, in THE PUBLIC PAPERS OF WOODROW WILSON, Vol. III (New York: Harper and Bros., 1927), p. 414.

Supreme Court of the United States held that Japanese were ineligible for American citizenship; the 1924 Quota Act, passed by the Congress and signed by President Coolidge, excluded Japanese from immigration purely on the grounds of race.[2] Ironically, while the Japanese intelligentsia and college students were thus arguing the pros and cons of the American, Russian, and Chinese political systems, the Japanese government came to be dominated by ultranationalists and militarists who allied themselves with Hitler and Mussolini and subsequently led the nation down the fateful path to World War II.

Meanwhile, I came to this country in the spring of 1941. The contrast between life in Japan under the militaristic government and unregimented life in America was very marked. To the newcomer, the existence of the different ethnic groups that constituted America appeared to be a hopeful sign that peoples of diverse backgrounds, if given a chance, could live harmoniously in the world. Soon, however, I learned that the so-called melting-pot had many unreduced elements stubbornly preserved by prejudice, misunderstanding, and antagonism among the various groups. With the outbreak of war, my initiation into American society took a more radical form. Shortly after Pearl Harbor, I found myself eating canned beans in the Alameda County Jail, sandwiched between a thief and a smuggler. My brief contacts with them broadened my liberal education a great deal, especially in the choice and use of curse words. Then, after several months of "sojourn" in a detention camp in Santa Fe and the internment camp in Lordsburg, New Mexico, I was shipped to the War Relocation Center at Hunt, Idaho, which was a camp for American citizens and their parents who were victims of the mass evacuation of persons of Japanese descent from the West Coast. I stayed in this camp until October, 1945.

In retrospect, the period of "enforced seclusion," despite its many disagreeable features, induced me to reflect among other things on the nature of democracy and the interracial, intercultural, and interfaith problems that inevitably arise in a democratic society. To me, these questions were not simply academic. Every day, as the bright Idaho sun faded behind a skyline decorated with sagebrush, the old and the young sat around in the laundry room, the only place they could find, and shared their frustrations and problems as well as their meager happinesses. I listened to the endless tales of the older folks, those simple hard-working people, who had crossed the Pacific a few decades earlier with adventuring hearts. By the time I knew them, however, their dark hair had turned grey, and their hands were wrinkled; their faces, once youthful and proud, bore the creases of years of hardship. I also listened to the young people, who were mostly ambitious and industrious, willing to start life anywhere outside the camp if oppor-

[2] See Milton R. Konvitz, THE ALIEN AND THE ASIATIC IN AMERICAN LAW (Ithaca, N.Y.: Cornell University Press, 1946), pp. 22–25.

tunities should arise, but they were stymied, not knowing what the future would hold. Some blamed the government, some blamed their parents, and many suffered from internal anguish arising out of their ambiguous situation. The problem was equally serious for the young children. I could not get over the incongruity of seeing school children in the camp learning the principles and ideals of American democracy just a stone's throw from the gates watched by armed guards. Fortunately, they were young, and their innocent faces betrayed no bitterness. I admired the courage and patriotism of the young men who volunteered for the armed services, leaving their families behind barbed wire. Many of them were wounded at the front and some never came home.

My four years during the war, strange though it may sound, gave me some insight into the principles of democracy. I learned that, in order to function, democracy requires patience, compassion, hard work, and above all, "faith" on the part of everyone, especially those who belong to so-called minority groups. Furthermore, be it remembered, every one of us belongs to some kind of minority group—ethnic, cultural, religious, or what have you. Admittedly, this is not a particularly novel or profound insight, but it took me, at least, some painful experiences and years of reflection to come to the realization of this.

In more recent years, I have also become greatly concerned with the "image" of America, to use the current lingo. I have come to realize, in this connection, that there are actually at least three Americas. First, there is the image of Americans at home of what America is. This is something different from the second, which is what Americans abroad, whether consciously or unconsciously, attempt to present America to be. Third, there is the outsider's image of America, however distorted it may be. For example, during my recent visits to various countries in Asia (1958–59 and 1961–62), I was often cornered and questioned by different groups concerning the situation in America. Many of these persons were hostile, while some were friendly; surprisingly, none were indifferent to America. I frequently encountered the view, popular in Asia today, that, while Orientals are "spiritual," Americans are materialistic, oversexed, and gadget-happy. However, there were a few discerning souls who were genuinely interested in the social, cultural, and religious situation in America, and to them I tried to present not an apologia or propaganda line, but candid observation and diagnosis, as well as I could, of the promise and problems of present-day America. I realized then, and I realize now, even more acutely, how difficult, and yet how necessary, it is to articulate our understanding of democracy and its implications for the social, political, cultural, and religious spheres.

## A Vision of "One People"

Fortunately, or unfortunately, the term "democracy" means many things to many people. That it refers to the form of government in which the supreme power is retained by the people and exercised either directly or indirectly is generally accepted. However, whether democracy in the American sense is nothing but the pragmatic, regulative principle which enables men and groups of different beliefs and persuasions to live together, as Daniel Boorstin advocates,[3] or whether it embodies some normative doctrines based on certain cultural, philosophical, and religious assumptions and beliefs has not been resolved in my own mind. Rather, I follow the common-sense view that democracy boils down to at lest four basic fundamentals: namely (1) the dignity of the individual, (2) the right of the individual to seek a better life, (3) the guarantees of freedom of worship, of thought, of expression, of assembly, as well as of universal suffrage and of universal education, and (4) the principle that all men are born free and equal. The crucial problem, of course, is how to reinterpret these fundamentals in such a way that the rights of the individuals can be related to the rights of the groups. In our discussion, we are specially concerned with the problems of convergence and prejudice in relations between various ethnic, cultural, and religious groups.

It goes without saying that human society is made up of groups of persons each requiring certain social obligations on the part of the members of the group. American society is no exception in this respect. Furthermore, here as elsewhere all groups have portrayed different kinds and degrees of antagonism and prejudice against other parallel groups. Fortunately for America, the land was vast and natural resources were abundant, so that the various European settlers were spared from the more extreme forms of antagonism. Also, from the beginning the colonists took it for granted that English was the common language and English common law the framework for their common life. The various ethnic elements that settled in the new continent, Dutch, German, Scotch-Irish, and others, were quickly absorbed into the social, economic, and cultural life of the colonies that were Anglo-Saxon in temper and orientation. To be sure, many of them were adherents of the Protestant faith, and all of them were white Europeans. It is, nevertheless, a remarkable fact that by 1776 the people in the thirteen original states had developed a consciousness of being "one people," as stated in the Declaration of Independence.

On the other hand, the idea of "one people," like other noble concepts, was destined to remain perennially more a matter of aspiration than achievement. No one actually defined specifically what "one people" meant. The founding fathers simply affirmed as self-evident truths that all men are created equal and that all are endowed by their Creator with certain inalienable rights, but they never spelled out how a "one people" is to emerge in the course of human events. Rather, they were more concerned with the

---

[3] See Daniel J. Boorstin, THE GENIUS OF AMERICAN POLITICS (Chicago: The University of Chicago Press, 1953), pp. 184–189.

proper relationship that ought to exist between the government and the people. However, they had an overwhelming sense of the drama of a history in which free men, guided by the infinite wisdom of the Almighty, had the task of establishing a novel form of society based on democratic principles. Indeed, the Declaration of Independence was the expression of the founding fathers' affirmation of God, the free man, and the ever unfolding meaning of history. Thus, "for the support of this declaration," they said, "with a firm reliance on the protection of Divine Providence, we mutually pledge to each other our lives, our fortunes, and our sacred honor."

However, the events of the hundred years following independence fostered the development of sectional and group spirits which threatened the nebulous idea of "one people." Now that America was freed from the yoke of oppressive British rule, friction between states and between the colonial aristocracy and the working class, as well as between conservatives and radicals, became more apparent. Confronted by difficult issues which could not be adequately handled by the loosely knit Confederation government, the architects of the new nation drafted the Constitution of the United States as the supreme law of the land. In this document attempts were made to maintain an intricate balance between liberty and authority. While vast power was granted to the national government, the political structure was carefully designed to guard against either excessive centralization or decentralization of power. It is also to be noted that the seemingly conservative tenor of the Constitution was complemented by the more liberal ethos of the Bill of Rights.

In reading of the early development of America, one is struck by the fact that what guided the new nation was not a concrete model of society or of any set of arbitrary doctrines. Rather, the new forms of society and the new principles were hammered out of the historic experience of the American people. For example, initially, the idea of religious liberty was not a clearly defined abstract principle. Sidney Mead reminds us that during the colonial period each religious group aspired to the freedom to continue to press its absolute religious claims. "But what had become obvious to all by the end of the Revolution was that the only way to insure such freedom for itself was to grant it to others."[4] In other words, different religious groups had to learn to live together in relative peace before they came to accept religious liberty as a precious principle for the democratic society.

Similarly, Americans' understanding of racial equality, or rather their inability to understand it, was also strongly conditioned by their historic experience. While we are in no position to psychoanalyze the founding fathers in respect to their understanding of race questions, it is safe to assume that they never confronted the issue squarely. After independence,

---

[4] Sidney E. Mead, *The American People: Their Space, Time and Religion*, THE JOURNAL OF RELIGION, 34: 253, 1954.

the phenomenal population growth due to immigration, high birth rate, and territorial acquisition made Americans increasingly more cosmopolitan than Anglo-Saxon in ethos and ethnic affiliation. Even then old settlers, whose attitude toward newcomers was conditioned by previous experience, were inclined to believe that the absorption of immigrants from various parts of Europe into the American fold required nothing more than time. On the other hand, the general attitude of white Americans toward nonwhite peoples was conditioned by negative experience, chiefly the struggle against the native American Indians and their memory of Blacks as slaves. And, once their attitude toward Indians and Blacks was thus set, it was easy for them to transfer a similar attitude to all other nonwhite peoples, such as the Chinese, Japanese, and Hindus. In other words, the historic experience of the white Americans led them to develop a simple bipolar view in regard to race questions: namely, that descendants of Europeans constitute the dominant group and nonwhite groups are to be regarded as subservient to the dominant group. The gulf between these two groups resulted in institutional and other forms of bigotry. The American Union, which Lincoln called "a magnificent experiment in democracy," was nearly ruined by the civil conflict that centered around the question of Black slavery. And, notwithstanding Lincoln's Gettysburg Address and the Emancipation Proclamation, many Americans never quite believed that the proposition that all men are created equal was applicable in the full sense to people outside the so-called dominant group.

In a sense, the simple bipolar outlook of white Americans regarding the race question is inseparably related to their view of American culture which is also strongly colored by historical experience. It was but natural that men of letters in American colonies considered themselves members of the European intellectual class, more particularly of England. Understandably, college and private academies established in the new continent turned to England and Western Europe for cultural inspiration. There was a small minority of colonials who were not of British stock, but their cultural influence on colonial life was negligible. In this connection, it is a matter of great import for us to bear in mind that the American Revolution was primarily a "colonial rebellion," to use the favorite phrase of the Daughters of the American Revolution, without implying in any sense a "cultural break" with Great Britain. Boorstin rightly observes that "the American Revolution is notably lacking in cultural self-consciousness."[5] The American cultural tradition, which had been initially moulded primarily by Anglo-Saxon culture, continued to survive after the Revolution. To be sure, some of the nationality groups have preserved their own cultural traditions in certain sections of the country, and even today some of the big cities have sections occupied predominantly by the descendants of non-British stocks. Nevertheless, the

[5] Boorstin, *op. cit.*, p. 70.

majority of Americans have always taken it for granted that their culture, modified to be sure by the American experience, is Western European in ethos, contents, and orientation.

The dream of the founding fathers of establishing a democratic society for free men has been fulfilled to a great extent in the history of America. The principle of religious liberty has been securely established. Different cultural and nationality groups have enriched but not disrupted the continuity of American cultural tradition. American propagandists can boast that persons of various ethnic affiliations have found their places in the cabinet, Congress, and diplomatic service, to say nothing of culture, art, education, commerce, and sports. However, upon closer scrutiny, one sees many areas of tension and conflict within the democratic process which have to be dealt with before we come closer to the lofty ideal of "one people."

## PATTERN OF CONVERGENCE AND PREJUDICE

It has often been said that the unique quality of America might be explained to a great extent in terms of the "newness" of the nation. As early as 1782, J. Hector St. John de Crévecoeur characterized the American as a "new race of men." According to him, the American is a new man, "who, leaving behind him all his ancient prejudices and manners, received new ones from the new mode of life he has embraced, the new government he obeys, and the new rank he holds."[6] We must bear in mind, however, that newness does not always imply improvement. Moreover, very few things are really new; most things which we call new in human affairs are, in fact, transformations of the old. This is particularly true of our mental habits. Prejudice, suspicion, bigotry, and intolerance are as old as the history of the human race. While the American had left behind many of his old mental habits, he acquired new sets of prejudices and manners in the new society.

This is no place to compare American society with older societies in other parts of the world. We might mention, however, that each of the old societies is based on certain implicit regulative principles. For example, traditional Hindu society is based on the metaphysical assumption of cosmic hierarchy. Even Sarvepalli Radharkrishnan, who is critical of the rigidity and abuses of the traditional caste system, defends the hierarchical principle as a law of nature. He goes so far as to say that "if one who is of a lower nature desires to perform the social tasks of a higher class, before he has attained the answering capacities, *social order will be disturbed*."[7] Traditional English society was based on the premise, advocated by Richard Hooker, that the divinely ordained hierarchical principle joins individuals to each other in a

---

[6] J. Hector St. John de Crévecoeur, LETTERS FROM AN AMERICAN FARMER, ed. Ernest Rhys (New York: E. P. Dutton and Co., 1912), p. 43.

[7] See Paul A. Schlipp (ed.), THE PHILOSOPHY OF SARVEPALLI RADHAKRISHNAN (New York: Tudor Publishing Co., 1952), p. 775.

commonwealth which, in a subtle way, is identified with the established church. Similarly, all other societies are based on certain assumptions and principles that reflect accepted patterns of living and social behavior.

In sharp contrast to older societies, American society, at least in principle, has been based from its inception on the premise of the freedom and equality of individuals. The American creed, if we may use a tired phrase, rejects the notion that there is special virtue in ancestry. Instead, it affirms that all individuals of however diverse backgrounds, if given equal opportunity, can be assimilated into the new way of life to strengthen and enrich this "one nation, indivisible." However, in practice, the drive toward assimilation has brought about some strange results. For example, as Robert Maynard Hutchins reminds us, "the most striking paradox of American life is that this system, which must rest on individual differences, produces the most intense pressure toward uniformity. The fact that any boy can become President, instead of making every boy an individual, tends to make him a replica of everybody else."[8] Another side of the same paradox is that those who are not readily assimilable for reasons which are beyond their control tend to be excluded from full participation in national life. Such a double-edged pressure, which on the one hand drives men toward conformity and on the other hand discriminates against certain groups of people, developed in the course of time a "complex pattern of convergence and prejudice" which became, for all intents and purposes, the accepted principle of social control, exercising gentle tyranny over various segments of American society.

One of the most shocking and most persistent anomalies in American society has been its attitude to, and treatment of, first generation immigrants. America has always prided itself on welcoming new blood from various cultural, racial, and national groups, and some of the more fortunate or skilled people from other lands were, indeed, warmly welcomed. But many of the less fortunate immigrants have faced a number of serious hardships in this country. According to some testimonies, the experience of frustration and humiliation began as the boat entered the harbor of New York under the shadow of the Statue of Liberty. Shabby clothes, heavy foreign accents, strange manners, and lack of adequate funds have often made these would-be citizens the objects of ridicule and suspicion on the part of the descendents of earlier immigrants. Frightened by the unfriendly reception, these immigrants usually seek companionship and practical assistance in their own national or racial groups, which often congregate in certain sections, and this, in turn, makes them more unacceptable and unassimilable to American society. Thus, the vicious circle continues. The procedure of naturalization, simple though it is for the better educated, is not altogether easy for many older or less educated people. Besides, the process of natu-

[8] Robert Maynard Hutchins, NO FRIENDLY VOICE (Chicago: The University of Chicago Press, 1936), p. 1.

connection, it is to be noted that the thinking of the dominant group alone has been considered "public opinion" for a long time. It was the stereotypes of the dominant group that have kept alive the fictions that the Black is an inferior race and that the Indian is a savage.

The post-World War II period has propelled many new problems into the already complex racial situation. Today, the minority groups in America seem to share with all the oppressed peoples in the rest of the world an aspiration and demand for human dignity and social welfare. In an article entitled *Why the Mighty Fail to Prevail*, Walter Lippmann candidly observed the global situation as follows: "While the great powers have been making themselves infinitely stronger, the weak peoples have invented and are perfecting a method of warfare which enables them to elude and circumvent the great warfare of the great powers."[10] Similar observations may be made regarding the eruption of the Black Americans' discontent, whether their weapon is the nonviolence of the Martin Luther King variety or the militant Black racism of Malcolm X. However, despite success in their protest movements, the deeper issues of the race problem have yet to be faced squarely. By August, 1964, some Black leaders began to realize that the protest movement, especially in the North, would have to be replaced by political collective bargaining. While many of us realize that political bargaining is an effective means to bring about the legitimate demands of the Blacks, and of other minority groups for that matter, we are uneasy about the long-term implication of political bargaining. For example, some Black leaders demand not only civil rights but also compensatory and preferential treatment. To be sure, we are in full accord with Martin Luther King's argument that the principle of providing special measures for the deprived or the GI is in keeping with American tradition, and we admire his vision of a gigantic bill of rights for the disadvantaged, including both Blacks and poor whites. But when one translates such a demand into concrete terms for the purpose of political bargaining for special quotas or preference, we come uncomfortably close to the danger of communalism. In effect, what such a claim asserts is, as Daniel Bell points out, "that rights and opportunities should inhere to one on the basis of a [racial] group, not an individual, status."[11]

Another difficult issue before all ethnic, cultural, and nationality groups is how to develop effective and flexible community organizations to meet their own social problems to a certain extent, and yet to avoid the temptation of "separatism." Ironically, the middle class of various minority groups has been split between integrationists and self-appointed guardians of separate communities, with no other visible alternatives. The former envisage immediate integration of all individuals directly into the existing fabric of Amer-

---

[10] CHICAGO SUN-TIMES, August 20, 1964.

[11] Daniel Bell, *Plea for a "New Phase in Negro Leadership,"* THE NEW YORK TIMES MAGAZINE, May 31, 1964, p. 29.

ican society and avoid involvement in their own community affairs. The latter
feel that the identification of individuals with American society is possible
only through their own given communities, and thus stress the need of a
network of religious, social, cultural, economic, political, and philanthropic
organizations for each minority group. Both views have certain merits.
Unfortunately, the integration of any minority group into a larger society is a
painful process. Good will on both sides and resolutions by civic and church
groups, indispensable though they are, do not automatically solve complex
social, political, economic, and psychological problems involved in making
integration a reality. On the other hand, we have also seen in recent years the
danger of White and Black racist groups, notably the Ku Klux Klan and the
Black Muslims, which regard American society as a stage of perennial
conflict between races. In such a time as this, when emotions run high, we
should make every effort to seek out not only practical solutions for immediate issues, but, also, a more long range and visible alternative to the complex
problems of interracial relations. In this sense, the statement of Roy Wilkins
is worth noting: "Never before has the Negro been placed directly in such a
key role in the struggle to preserve the nation's tradition of freedom for the
individual. What rides here is democracy for white and black alike, for
Northerner and Southerner, for rich and for poor."[12]

No less difficult are the issues of interfaith and church-state relations.
Here again, double-edged pressures toward uniformity and separation have
been at work. Church historians tell us that as early as 1700 almost all the
major church groups found in America today were represented on American
soil. What developed gradually out of this background was the nebulous
principle of "religious liberty," which meant, according to Wilhelm Pauch,
that each church group "is enabled to act as if there were no other churches
in existence, but in so doing it concedes to other churches, which *do* actually
exist as its neighbors and rivals, the right to practice the same kind of
isolationism."[13] Thus, when the new national Congress decided to accept an
amendment on religious freedom to the Constitution, Madison proposed the
following draft for the First Amendment: "The civil rights of none shall be
abridged on account of religious belief of worship, nor shall any religion be
established, nor shall the full and equal rights of conscience be in any
manner, or on any pretext infringed," because he believed that "the people
feared one sect might obtain pre-eminence, or two might combine together,
and establish a religion to which they would compel others to conform."[14]
Such considerations led the Congress to adopt the famous wording of the
First Amendment which is known to all of us: "Congress shall make no law

[12] Roy Wilkins, *What Now?—One Negro Leader's Answer*, THE NEW YORK TIMES MAGAZINE,
August 16, 1964, p. 18.
[13] Mead, *op. cit.*
[14] Quoted in Anthony T. Bouscaren, *Church and State in America*, MEASURE, 1: 228, 1950.

respecting an establishment of religion, or prohibiting the free exercise thereof." This, indeed, was a sound, and probably the only possible, solution to the problem of religious pluralism in America. The acceptance of the principle of religious liberty by the Protestant, Catholic, and Jewish groups, however, had far-reaching implications for their subsequent development. Religious groups that had been either "national" churches or "sects" in Europe became what sociologists call "denominations" on the American scene. Even the Roman Catholic Church, which claims to be the only true church on earth, at least theologically, is no exception in this respect. Furthermore, the principle of religious liberty tends to undercut the very basis of monotheism, and thus all religious groups in America, despite their affirmation of the doctrine of monotheism, are compelled in practice to accept the basic tenet of "monolatry," and recognize the existence of other deities even though each group adheres to its deity as the only true God.

Understandably, the existence of religious pluralism in America presents many serious problems to church-state relationships. There are, no doubt, many religious groups that have never been convinced of the need for liberty of conscience except for themselves, and, as Alexis de Tocqueville once suspected, might be tempted to persecute others "if they found themselves the strongest."[15] Such discrepancy between the religious aspiration to become *the* religion and the reality of religious pluralism tends to foster religious communalism and/or religious bigotry. On the other hand, those who subscribe to the thesis of Locke that a church is a voluntary society of men joining themselves together of their own accord for the public worship of God tend to support either non-denominationalism or extreme forms of sectarianism, or even regard secularism or democracy as forms of religion. Former President Eisenhower once stated: "I am the most intensely religious man I know. That doesn't mean I adhere to any sect. A democracy cannot exist without a religious base. I believe in democracy."[16]

The crucial issue of church-state relationships has been viewed from all these different perspectives. There are some who interpret the "establishment of religion" clause in the Constitution in terms of "absolute separation of church and state," based on the conviction that religion is purely a private matter. In so doing, they virtually forfeit an important religious obligation to "judge the self-deification of nations," to use Reinbold Niebuhr's phrase. There are some, on the other hand, who interpret the First Amendment to mean that the state should be only neutral toward religious believers and nonbelievers, and argue in favor of equal protection of all religious groups based on the Fourteenth Amendment. These different interpretations of the

[15] Quoted by Joachim Wach, TYPES OF RELIGIOUS EXPERIENCE (Chicago: The University of Chicago Press, 1951), Chapter 8, *The Role of Religion in The Social Philosophy of Alexis de Tocqueville*, p. 182.

[16] Quoted in the CHICAGO DAILY NEWS, January 12, 1952.

church-state relationship have resulted in a series of serious controversies, such as those concerning the state support of parochial schools, the use of prayer in the public schools, and teaching of religion in state-supported educational institutions.

Obviously, there is no one solution to the problem of religious pluralism in America that is completely satisfactory to everybody. Certainly, no one group can coerce others to conform to its own interpretation of the First Amendment, nor is it advisable to erect such a complete wall between church and state that the only choice left will be either to uphold the new religion of "secularism" or to accept religious communalism and separatism. Basically, all religious groups in a democratic society must recognize government as a divine ordinance and must have "a decent sense of reverence toward the majesty of the law which coordinates the vitalities of a nation."[17] At the same time, I share the assumption of Wilbur Katz that "American religious pluralism is not so charged with hostilities that religious issues must be avoided by enforcing a rigid principle of separation."[18]

Ultimately, problems in a democracy cannot be solved by rigid conformity or anarchic separatism, for the fundamental issue is how to preserve freedom and liberty in a pluralistic society. There have been countless numbers of self-appointed guardians of the holy grail of Americanism who have attempted to impose a pattern of conformity, justifying the practice of racial, cultural, or religious prejudice under the guise of public order. Also, there are many of those who understand democracy as an accidental convergence of religious, cultural, and racial groups. Both of these views have greatly distorted the "image" of America both in other lands and at home.

Lastly, for those of us who are interested in the spiritual health of the nation, the most disturbing thing is the prevailing notion that religion is, at best, only a helpful supplement to democracy. While it is true that many Americans acknowledge the usefulness of religion, they feel that the basic processes of democracy must be constructed to get along without religion. And this is precisely how American democracy appears to people in other countries nowadays. However, I would like to believe with Alexis de Tocqueville that the democratic experiment in America is firmly based on combined loyalty to religion and to liberty, for, in his own words:

> Liberty regards religion as its companion in all its battles and triumphs as the cradle of its infancy, and the divine source of its claims. It considers religion as the safeguard of morality, and morality as the best security of law, and the surest pledge of the duration of freedom.[19]

[17] Reinhold Niebuhr, ESSAYS IN APPLIED CHRISTIANITY, ed. D. B. Robertson (New York: Meridian Books, 1959), p. 87.
[18] Wilbur Katz, *Religion in the Public Schools*, CHICAGO SUN-TIMES, June 16, 1963.
[19] Quoted in Wach, *op. cit.*, p. 186.

# 6

## THEOS, MYTHOS, AND LOGOS

*Then the eyes of both were opened, and they knew that they were naked; and they sewed fig leaves together and made themselves aprons.*

*And they heard the sound of the Lord God walking, . . and the man and his wife hid themselves from the presence of the Lord God among the trees of the Garden. But the Lord God called to the man, and said to him, "Where are you?"*

From the standpoint of many Christians the union or reunion of various branches of Christianity is a matter of utmost importance. To many people "ecumenicity" means simply "ecclesiastical consolidation" on the institutional level, which may be a desirable by-product but in itself cannot be equated with "ecumenicity." As I understand it, the ecumenical movement does not attempt to bring about the unity of Christendom. Rather it is a movement on the part of divided churches to dig down deep enough to discover the unity which exists already. In the words of James H. Nichols: "Our task is to so reshape the structure and practices of our several denominations that this actually existing unity shall be no longer obscured and hidden from the world, but manifest to all men."[1] And, if one accepts this understanding of ecumenicity, one is immediately confronted by a series of questions which cannot be easily evaded or solved. What is the nature of such a unity? How deep and how far does one have to go in the name of ecumenicity? More practically, what about the Seventh Day Adventists, Jehovah's Witnesses, and the Mormons, which claim to be the true heirs of Christianity? What about Judaism and Islam, which had obvious historic connections with Christianity? And how does one interpret the relationships among world religions, or more specifically, the relationships between Christianity and other religions? Obviously, there are no clear-cut answers which satisfy everybody concerning all these complex questions. Certainly, it is fairly easy to "prove" that one's position is right by carefully marshalling the facts and the historical silences, as it has been demonstrated all too often in

[1] James H. Nichols, "True and False Hopes for Evanston," *Pastoral Psychology,* Vol. 5, No. 45 (June, 1954), p. 15.

the so-called ecumenical and/or inter-faith conferences. But it is exceedingly more difficult to do justice to the views and positions of others, recognizing humbly that one's own position, however precious it may be to oneself, may not be the most adequate approach to such a complex issue as the relationships among different religions.

As for myself, I must candidly admit at the outset that I have no magical formula to deal with this question. But, having lived as I have on both sides of the Pacific Ocean and having been trained as a historian of religions, I have often reflected on the intricacy and the multi-dimensional character of the relations which exist among different religious systems and traditions. Thus, what I will present may be regarded as a sort of prolegomena to the question of the relations among world religions based on my reflections. I wish to make three points.

## WORLD OF MEANING

First, my own thinking is based on a simple premise that every individual, and every culture and people, lives not only in the geographical, physical world but also in what might be termed a "world of meaning." For the most part, we inherit what has been handed down to us—not only the language with its "magical circle of words" and ideas as well as values, but also the small intimate habits of daily life, such as the way of preparing food, putting on clothes, or of hushing a child to sleep. Thus, consciously or unconsciously, our own "world of meaning" approximates the world-view implicit in our cultural and religious traditions, which in turn exert decisive influence in patterning our behavior, beliefs and goals of life. This is another way of saying that our sensory perception and our mental and psychic reactions are guided into habitual channels by our cultural experiences. And this fact makes it very difficult for us to understand the depth of the "world of meaning" of other peoples who have been moulded by different kinds of historical, religious and cultural experiences.[2]

We must also bear in mind that the "world of meaning" of each person, culture and religion not only determines the priority of values but provides a characteristic mental outlook regarding the recollection of past experiences, the delineation of the meaning of present existence, and the anticipation of the future. These three foci are intricately interwoven in a sort of "mental prism," which sorts out significant items from a mass of data, relating historical realities to the realm of fantasy and imagination. It also has a built-in safety belt of forgetfulness and optical illusion. The tenacity of the power of the mental prism has been forcefully demonstrated by the recent Palestinian conflicts between the Jews and the Arabs, who are first cousins, so to

[2]This section of my paper is taken from my article, "The Asian's World of Meaning," contributed to *Glaube, Geist, Geschichte*—Festschrift für Ernst Benz—ed. by G. Müller and W. Zeller, Leiden, 1967, pp. 470–71.

speak, in terms of blood and religious heritage. Their conflicting views are based on two different ways of recollecting the presumably same historical event recorded in Genesis (XV:18), according to which Abraham received the divine assurance for the territory between the river of Egypt and the Euphrates as the promised land for his descendents. Fortunately or unfortunately, Abraham had two sons, Isaac, the ancestor of the Jews, and Ishmael, the legendary ancestor of the Arabs, who have been living in this territory for many generations. Ironically, seen through the Jewish prism, as I. F. Stone points out, "the establishment of Israel was a Return, with all the mystical significance the capital R implies, [whereas] for the Arabs it was another invasion."[3] Thus, it is not a question as to which group should occupy this small piece of real estate. The issue is that the sacred memories of the past, the very meaning of their present existence, and the hopes and fears for the future, of both the Jews and the Arabs, are centered and rooted in the land of Palestine. I cite this not to discuss the seemingly unsolvable Palestinian problem, but to point out that every group, be it ethnic, national, cultural, or religious, has its own mental prism which conditions the range of perception to a great extent. This implies that the task of thinking about other religions on the part of Christians, especially those of the West, involves the effort to comprehend the nature of the mental prisms of other religious groups and peoples, as well as the mental prisms through which the Christians in the West have been conditioned to view other religions.

## HISTORIC FACTORS

My second point, which is not a novel idea, is that such a complex issue as the relationships among religions must be considered not only on theoretical ground but also by recourse to full accounts of historic factors. One does not have to be a historic determinist, and I for one do not feel that we can write an unbiased, purely objective history. But there are certain things which can be understood only historically. Certainly, the tangled relationship between Christianity and other religions cannot be appreciated unless we make every effort to analyze the historic experiences of Christians and those of adherents of other religions soberly and honestly as much as we can.

As far as we know, the initial character of Christianity was found in its "Hebrewness," which was deeply imprinted in the life and teaching of Jesus. There is no reason to assume that he intended to found a new religion outside the religion of his forefathers. He worshipped regularly in the synagogues, and he was conscious of being sent to the "lost sheep of the house of Israel" (Matthew 15:24). To him, the history of the Hebrew community from the time of Abraham was a spiral development of the hidden drama of salvation, and he took with utmost seriousness the role that he and the remnant of the

---

[3] I. F. Stone, "Holy War" (review of "Le conflit Israelo-Arabe," in *Les Temps Modernes*, Paris, June, 1967), in *The New York Review of Books*, Vol. IX, No. 2 (August 3, 1967), p. 6.

household of Israel were destined to play in the history of salvation. But, in the eyes of his followers, it was Jesus himself who became the vehicle of "fulfillment" of prophecy of the Old Testament, and with this realization his words and deeds took on new significance. To the Christians, therefore, Jesus was not only the Messiah, who had been anticipated by the Jews, but "a light for the Gentiles," who will bring "salvation to the uttermost parts of the earth" (Acts 13:47). Clearly, a new religious movement was in the making.

Apparently, Christianity in its inception was not much different from many of the cultic movements which emerged in various parts of the Mediterranean world. The early church was no more than a small group of followers, mostly women, children, and slaves, looked down upon and despised by the elite, both in the Jewish and non-Jewish societies. But the followers of Christ were knit together with joyful anticipation of the coming of the end of the world when the Son of God would return as Redeemer and Judge. It was only when they began to feel that the end of the world was not impending, or perhaps had been partially realized in the Pentecost, that they had to come to terms with doctrinal, cultic and institutional problems. Inevitably, they had to define the relationship between the Christian faith and other religions, such as Judaism and the mystery cults, as well as Greek philosophical traditions. In this situation, the Christian apologists relied heavily on the motif of "fulfillment." That is to say, Christianity was proclaimed as the "fulfillment" of the religious aspirations of Jews and Gentiles. In so doing, the so-called Church Fathers appropriated Greek philosophical concepts, insights, and logic to substantiate their "fulfillment" theories. Even after Christianity became the religion of the Empire, Christians viewed the pagan religions of Europe through this prism. In short, all religions were regarded as "preparations" which were to be "fulfilled" in Christianity. In this respect, I am not debating whether the Christian understanding of other religions was right or wrong; I am suggesting that their historic experiences, starting from the time when the Christian movement was a minor segment of the Hebrew community to the time when it became the dominant religious force of the great Roman empire, reinforced the conviction of Christians that their faith was destined to "fulfill" the aspirations of all other religions. Besides, Christianity, which was eminently successful, was not threatened by other rival religions.

With the emergence of Islam in the seventh century, however, the Christian attitude toward other religions became hardened. Within ten years after the death of Muhammad, Syria, Iraq and Egypt were absorbed by the Muslim Empire. In less than a century, Islam conquered the Christian belt of North Africa, the home of St. Augustine and many other prominent Christian saints and patriarchs, and reached the Iberian peninsula. In the eighth century, the Muslim forces even threatened France. The intellectual life of the Muslims was greatly enriched by the translation of Greek philo-

sophical works and Persian and Indian scientific books into Arabic. The
Muslim universities in Cordova and Granada in Spain attracted Muslim as
well as Christian and Jewish scholars from other parts of Europe and Africa.
In fact, Christian Europe first became acquainted with the works of Plato and
Aristotle through the writings of Muslim scholars. The significance of Islam,
however, was not confined to its military, political and intellectual achievements. By its claim, Islam was the "fulfillment" of all religions of the Book,
including Christianity. Inevitably, the two religious communities, each
claiming to be the "fulfillment" of all religions, confronted each other in a
series of bloody Crusades from 1096 to 1291. Actually, the Crusades, in
which saints and scoundrels fought side by side with a mixture of spiritual
and mundane motives, failed to dislodge the Muslim power, although they
left unpleasant memories of European Christendom in the minds of the
Muslims. And "the false reports brought back to those who returned from
the wars filled the West with popular misinformation about Islam that
Western mass education has not yet been able to remove."[4] And once
European Christians came to regard Islam not as a "preparation" to be
fulfilled by Christianity but as their arch-enemy, the subsequent development in Europe, i.e., Reformation, Counter Reformation, and the rise of
Pietism, only added more fuel to the European Christians' antagonism
against non-Christian religions, and this in turn hardened the attitudes of the
Muslims, and other non-Western and non-Christian peoples for that matter,
toward "Christian" Europe.

Unfortunately, the belligerent attitude of European Christendom toward
other religions, cultures and peoples, which was accentuated by its historic
experience following the rise of Islam, was further reinforced by the colonial
expansion of Europe which began in the sixteenth century. For example,
"the early Spanish conquistadores considered themselves Christian
crusaders and brought over to the New World the ideas which had grown up
in the long wars which they had fought against the Moors in Spain, using the
same battle cries and evoking the same saints in the New World that had
served them in the old."[5] The Portuguese, with similar fanatic zeal, tried to
root out "infidels" in their colonies. Thus, under their rule, "Hindu temples
in Goa were destroyed and their property distributed to religious orders (like
Franciscans) in 1540, [and even] the Inquisition was established in 1560."[6]
In this respect, the colonial policies of the so-called Protestant nations in
Europe were not basically different from those of the Catholic nations.

[4] Edwin E. Calverley, "Islamic Religion," in T. Cuyler Young (ed.), Near Eastern Culture and
Society, Princeton, 1951, p. 103.
[5] William W. Sweet, "Christianity in the Americas," A Short History of Christianity, ed. by
Archibald G. Baker, Chicago, 1940, p. 227.
[6] K. M. Panikkar, Asia and Western Dominance, London, 1959, p. 280.

Furthermore, Western missionary societies, both of Catholic and Protestant groups, unconsciously if not consciously, cooperated with the aims and policies of the colonial rules.

In the course of time, the prosperity brought by colonial policies led many Westerners to feel that their culture, religion, and technology were superior because they belonged to a superior race. Thus, many came to accept an oversimplified formula that the European equals Christian equals superior race *versus* the non-Westerner equals pagan equals inferior race. Conversely, there developed a strong suspicion among the non-Westerners that the Westerners were aggressors and exploiters without any regard for human welfare. The question was not whether Western culture, Christianity and Europeans were right or wrong; it was the historic experiences of the Westerners which encouraged their illusion that they were a master race and that the non-Western world was destined to be Westernized and Christianized sooner or later. Similarly, the experience of non-Westerners during the past four centuries led them to react emotionally against the messianism of Christianity as much as of modern Western civilization, which had a "strange compound of genuine idealistic responsibility, blindness and hypocrisy, with a strong dose of will-to-power as the basic component."[7] Decades ago, a sensitive Vietnamese expressed the sentiment of the people toward their French rulers:

> In your eyes we are savage, dumb brutes incapable of distinguishing between good and evil. You not only refuse to treat us as equals, but even fear to approach us, as if we were filthy creatures . . . . There is a sadness of feeling and shame which fills our hearts during the evening's contemplation when we review all the humiliations endured during the day.[8]

Evidently, the initial Christian view of other religions as "preparation," to be "fulfilled" in Christianity, changed to a more belligerent view due largely to the historic factor, namely the encounter with the rival claims of Islam. Then, during the four centuries of the colonial era, which coincided with the period of Christian missionary expansion to various parts of the non-Western world, the Christian approach to non-Western religions, cultures and peoples came to "inhale" the messianism of Western civilization, coupled with the racial superiority complex of Europeans. In the words of Hendrik Kraemer, "it was not only the eye of faith, but also the eye of the Westerner, who subconsciously lived in the conviction that he could dispose of the destiny of the world, because the absorption of the Eastern by the

---

[7] William S. Haas, *The Destiny of the Mind—East and West*, London, 1956, p. 303.
[8] Panikkar, *op. cit.*, p. 166.

Western world appeared to come inevitably."[9] Unfortunately, these historic experiences of the Western Christians, and the reaction of adherents of other religions in the non-Western world toward Western Christendom, cannot be erased over night. And, unless we appreciate the tenacity of historic memories, which greatly color the "world of meaning" of Christians and non-Christians, we cannot even begin to understand the complexity of the relationship between Christianity and other religions in our time.

## RELIGIOUS UNDERSTANDING OF RELIGIONS

My third comment is that genuine relations among religions are possible only when the adherent of one faith tries to approach other religions as something "religious." Ironically, today many people think that relations among religions require primarily a sort of debating session, comparing respective doctrines, ethics and cultic practices of various religions. I have attended many such conferences, but it has become obvious that such an approach can barely scratch the surface of the issues involved. Useful and edifying though it may be, comparing notes on basic tenets of various religious systems does not enable us to understand how different religions have encountered each other historically, with certain decisive con sequences, and how religions color and shape the "world of meaning" of individuals as well as cultures and nations.

Actually it sounds very simple, but it is very difficult for most of us to try to understand religions "religiously." It is much easier to understand ethical, philosophical, psychological, sociological or political aspects of religions, and indeed many people suffer from such reductionistic thinking in regard to religion. Also, many of us tend to equate religions with something else, such as Protestantism with capitalism, Buddhism with Burmese or Ceylonese cultures, Islam with Arab or Pakistani nationalism. It is not surprising, therefore, that in the minds of many Americans, Christianity is equated with democracy. In the words of Former President Eisenhower: "I am the most intensely religious man I know. . . . That doesn't mean I adhere to any sect. A democracy cannot exist without a religious base. I believe in democracy."[10]

But how then shall we approach religions in order to understand them "religiously"? Here we run into a semantic trap, because our language implies that there is a domain of life called "religious," apart from other areas and activities such as commerce, politics, culture and art. Thus, we are inclined to depict more obviously indentifiable items, namely, doctrines, ritual practices, and ecclesiastical institutions, as components of the religious dimension, differentiated from the so-called "secular" dimension of life. In reality, however, religious man does not live such a compartmentalized life. The "world of meaning" of religious man defies the religious *vs.* secular

[9] Hendrik Kraemer, *The Christian Message in a Non-Christian World*, London, 1938, p. 36.
[10] Quoted in *Chicago Daily News*, Jan. 12, 1952.

dichotomy. Rather, politics, industry, commerce, culture, art, interhuman relations and all the rest are seen as interdependent parts of a unified life. We might say, resorting to the analogy of the iceberg, that what we usually refer to as "religious" components—doctrines, rituals, and ecclesiastical institutions—constitute that part of the iceberg which is above water, but that it is an integral part of the rest of the iceberg which is not readily visible. Or, to use a different analogy, the totality of life may be seen by religious man as a series of concentric circles, whose mid-point coordinates and integrates all aspects of life. Thus, for example, the ideal Muslim is the one who submits his whole being to the will of Allah and is not necessarily the one who attends the Mosque regularly. Similarly, the religious ideal for the Hindu is to order every step of his life from cradle to grave, as well as his past and future existences, in accordance with the Eternal Cosmic Law (*Sanatana Dharma*).

Many of us are puzzled, however, by the contradictory features of religions, especially the manner in which "universal" and "particular" dimensions are interwoven. Basically, all religions address themselves to human existence, and as such they share the concern with universal humanity. And yet, they address themselves not to human existence *in abstracto* but to man-in-a-particular-society-and-culture. It is taken for granted that one humanity has within it infinite possibilities which can be actualized in various historic forms of societies and cultures, each one of which has to be taken seriously. Hence the importance of symbols, rituals and myths, all of which embody both the universal and particular meanings. For example, the cross of Christianity, related to the particular event of Crucifixion "under Pontius Pilate", stands for the Cosmic Tree, situated at the center of the universe—the tree of life, rooted on both sides of the river, the leaves of which were "for the healing of the nations." (Revelation 22:1–2.) The Buddhist symbol of the wheel, related to Buddha's first sermon at Sarnath, stands for the Cosmic Wheel in motion which establishes the "Kingdom of Righteousness." Similarly, the rituals of the New Year festival in various cultures share the universal motif of repeating and celebrating the act of cosmic creation, although the forms of celebration are conditioned by the particular circumstances. Conversely, the celebration of the particular sacred events, such as the Exodus of the Jews, the Crucifixion of Christianity, and the Buddha's renunciation in the Buddhist tradition, for example, take on universal meanings.

Ironically, contradictory characteristics of religions have often resulted in the distorted views of religions. How easy it is to mistake symbols as sacred realities themselves, and how common it is to use rituals for purposes other than that for which they are intended! The distorted understanding of religions are particularly prevalent regarding the myth, which is the religious language *par excellence*, different from rational and scientific modes of language. It must be noted that the myth is not a fiction, legend or fairy tale; it is more like a picture painted with words, depicting certain sacred events which have saving (soteriological) significance. We must bear in mind that at the center of every religion there is the experience of sacral reality, however it is understood, god, holy, sacred, numen, *tao, nirvana* or divine, which is referred to as *theos* in the traditional Christian terminology. But the experience of the holy, *theos,* can be expressed only in terms of *mythos,* which is the language of faith, together with rituals and symbols. It is the human intellect which in turn discerns the pattern of meaning, *logos,* in the *mythos.* All *logos* concepts—theology, doctrine, dogma—are thus derived from *mythos,* which point to *theos.* And yet, in every religious tradition, once doctrines are formulated, they tend to exert gentle tyranny over the minds of adherents instead of allowing them to appreciate the rich imageries of the myths, which in turn point to the central religious experience of the holy, *theos.*

Even such telegraphic accounts of religions as I have attempted make it clear, I hope, that religious understanding of religions has to take it seriously that each religion "is an autonomous expression of religious thought and experience, which must be viewed in and through itself and its own principles and standards."[11] This means, among other things, that superficial comparisons, especially the best quality of one's own religious tradition with the worst features of others, have no place in genuine encounters among religions. On the other hand, we must recognize that seen through the prism of a partucilar religion the meanings of all other religions can be integrated into the concentric circle of that religion. Concretely, this means the possibility, at any rate, that Hinduism, Buddhism, Christianity or Islam, for example, can absorb the essential truth values of all others into their respective "worlds of meaning." Indeed the fact that Maritain, Tillich, Buber, Suzuki and Radhakrishnan have exerted profound influences on religious traditions other than their own indicates that dynamic interaction among religious traditions is more than a realm of possibility today. Nevertheless, I, for one, do not see that different religions will converge into a sort of super-Ba'hai system, as some people tend to think. I rather think that in the future diverse religious traditions, including Christianity, will continue to develop according to their own dynamics, crisscrossing on the face of the earth, which will involve inevitably certain kinds of conflicts and disagreements. But, if all religions learn to approach others "religiously," they will learn much from each other, without losing their own religious identities.

Admittedly, there will always be temptations to distort the religious character of religions, because religions have built-in demonic tendencies, as Paul Tillich used to remind us. According to the Old Testament myth, man from the time of Adam was looking for meaning beyond the confines of the givenness of human existence. And when their eyes were opened, Adam and

[11] H. A. R. Bigg, *Mohammedanism: An Historical Survey,* Oxford University Press, 1953, p. vii.

Eve were ashamed of their nakedness and sewed fig leaves and made themselves aprons. "And they heard the sound of the Lord God walking . . . , and the man and his wife hid themselves from the presence of the Lord God among the trees of the garden." (Genesis 37–9) In a real sense, all religions are integral parts of the religious search for the meaning of existence in the history of the human race and yet religions were also used by men and women to shield themselves from direct confrontation with the holy, sacred, or divine. Yet, so long as human beings or various religious and cultural traditions remain self-conscious about the genuine religious character of religions as well as their demonic tendencies, they may hear through the doctrinal, liturgical and ecclesiastical "forests," behind which they hide, the faint voice of the divine, calling: "Where are you?"

# 7

## EXPERIENCE, KNOWLEDGE AND UNDERSTANDING

Anyone teaching in theological schools or university departments of religion in the West should be struck by two related factors which seem to influence the attitude and thinking of today's students. The first is the preoccupation with 'experience', while the second is the openness toward Eastern religious insights as well as their meditation techniques. In this paper, the writer intends to reflect on these two factors both as the causes and the effects of the significant change that has taken place in Western man's world of meaning in our time.

### EXPERIENCE

It is safe to assume that all religions rest on three cornerstones, namely authority, tradition, and experience. The so-called 'religions of the book' hold their sacred scriptures as the primarly sources of authority, whereas in 'non-book' religions the source of authority may be attributed to myths or the teachings and life of the founder or the saints. But the primary source of authority in any religion is usually supported, amplified and elaborated by the tradition of that community. Even in Islam, which may be regarded as the religion of the book *par excellence,* the *Qur'an* is interpreted in the light of the *sunna* (custom), *hadith* (tradition) and a body of rules developed by legal experts *(fiqh).* In addition to the primary source of authority and tradition, all religions recognize the importance of the individual's own experience, as evidenced by the mystic's experiences which have been venerated in Western as well as Eastern religions. Ideally, all religions attempt to hold authority, tradition and experience in a proper balance, but not always successfully. All religions have their share of scriptural fundamentalists, staunch champions of tradition, and those who uphold experience above all else.

It should be stressed in this connection that throughout Western history it has been taken for granted that experiences of individuals were to be authenticated by authority or tradition or both. What is significant today is the fact, as Dean Inge astutely observed already fifty years ago, that "the center of gravity in religion has shifted from authority and tradition to experience,"[1] whereby the evidences of religion are now provided primarily

---

[1] William Ralph Inge, *Lay Thoughts of a Dean* (New York: G. P. Putnam, 1926), p. 323.

by experience and faith. That is to say, authority and tradition are no longer accepted just because they had given certitude and assurance to people of former generations. Authority and tradition are considered meaningful to the present generation only when they are tested by contemporary experience. Thus, according to Daniel Day Williams, the important question in the Christian world today is: "What is there in the Christian faith which gives us such an understanding of ourselves that we must assert our loyalty to the Holy God above all the splendid and yet corruptible values of our civilization?"[2] This way of asking questions indicates the extent to which even theological or philosophical reflection is grounded primarily in experience.

In retrospect, it becomes evident that the pre-modern world of meaning, in which authority and tradition restrained experience, is quickly becoming a thing of the past. Meanwhile, the historic foundations of culture and society have been badly shaken by the whirlwind of modernity. In the midst of today's uncertainty, many adherents of religions tend to look back toward previous eras with a sense of nostalgia, while antagonists often equate religions with outdated values and a pre-modern world of meaning. Here lies the double-edged distortion of the meaning of religion in our time. Accordingly, we are witnessing today a new vogue of faith-experience in various religious groups. In particular young people, expecially those who have been alienated from the faith of their forebears, are often lured by the mystique of Eastern religions and their meditation techniques.

## LURE OF EASTERN RELIGIONS

In the early 1950's Henri de Lubac shocked many Westerners by his observance that Europe was ripe for a spiritual colonization by the East.[3] This observation was shared by Hendrick Kraemer, a renowned scholar of Missiology. In Kramer's words:

> There is evident in the fields of practical art, of novels, of thinking and of depth-psychology, a kind of premonition. They manifest a spontaneous openness, *a readiness to be invaded*, to become "spiritually colonized" by the Orient. There are open "gates" for Eastern invasion, a *pénétration pacifique*, in the forms of dispositions and needs of mind, of intuition, which are transparently expressed in the thinking of the Orient. . . . this remarkable fact has not yet been appreciated in its true and profound significance.[4]

[2] Daniel Day Williams, *What Present-Day Theologians are Thinking* (New York: Harper, 1952), p. 12.

[3] Henri de Lubac, *La recontre du Buddhisme et de l'Occident* (Paris: Aubier, Editions Montaigne, 1952), p. 274.

[4] Hendrik Kraemer, *World Cultures and World Religions* (Philadelphia: Westminster, 1960), p. 18.

Today, no observing person can fail to see that an "Eastern invasion" has indeed taken place in Europe as well as in North America. To be sure, the Orient has had a mysterious spell on some Western minds from ancient times. Shortly after the invasion of Alexander the Great into India, one of the Greek kings in Bactria, Menander or Milinda, received instruction on Buddhism from a learned monk, Nagasena. In the third century A.D., Plotinus accompanied Emperor Gordian's Persian campaign in order to obtain direct knowledge of the philosophy of the Persians and the Indians. In more recent history, Voltaire, Leibniz and other European thinkers were fascinated by Oriental wisdom. It was reported that Sir Edwin Arnold's *Light of Asia*, published in 1879, went into sixty printings in England and eighty printings in America. Nevertheless, as Christy points out, until recently the real appeal of the Orient in the West was confined to a relatively small number of romantic thinkers or those who were interested in something "far away and long ago."[5] Since World War II, however, the Orient has come into the immediate experience of many more Westerners so that it is no longer something "far away and long ago."

Without accounting for all of the factors that have brought about the change in Westerners' perceptions of the Orient in our time, it is obvious that today many people in North America and Europe seem to feel quite at home with things Eastern—from art and literature to cuisine, movies, the arts of self-defense and flower arrangement. By far the most significant, from our perspective, is the widespread acceptance in the West of a variety of Eastern practices of meditation, such as Yoga, Zen and Transcendental Meditation. Ironically, such a massive invasion of Eastern meditation practices has created a one-sided impression among many people that meditation *is* an Eastern thing which is needed in the spiritually barren Western world, whereas historically meditation has been one of the most universally accepted religious practices, both in the East and the West.

## MEDITATION AND CONTEMPLATION IN THE WEST

While often associated with religion, meditation in its broad sense is not confined to a religious context. It is a common human behavior to meditate on various occasions in the course of ordinary daily life. However, in a religious context meditation takes on interior, spiritual connotations. Thus, it is not surprising that Webster's definition refers to meditation as "a form of private devotion or spiritual exercise consisting in deep, continued reflection on some religious theme," or "a discourse treating a theme meditatively or so as to lead to meditation." Understandably, each religion gives its own interior coloring and meaning to meditation, even though there are many

[5] Arthur E. Christy (ed.), *The Asian Legacy and American Life* (New York: John Day, 1942), p. 37.

similarities in external features of meditation—postures and forms—crossing religious lines.

It might be symptomatic of our time to find various forms of pseudo-religious meditation techniques which promise easy and quick attainment of Satori, Samadhi or Nirvana by utilizing drugs or do-it-yourself types of enlightenment kits. And it would be exceedingly difficult to differentiate these more popular meditation practices from more traditionally accepted religious forms of meditation on the basis of their external features. For instance, the celebration held in Chicago by the LSD cult group several years ago utilized all the symbols of traditional religious meditation with modern trappings. It began with two men on stage, one playing a guitar and the other a bongo drum. Huge figures of the Buddha and swirling gallaxies were projected by slides onto a larger screen. Then Timothy Leary led the group in meditation and prayer and told them he hoped to reproduce "some of the beauty, some of the meaning, some of the terror of the LSD experience." The celebraton was "designed to dramatise the mind of Buddha when he attained spiritual enlightenment five centuries before Christ."[6] Was this a form of Buddhist meditation or an LSD cult, or both? While opinions no doubt vary on this question, we suspect that Timothy Leary's celebration was at best peripheral to what is understood as Buddhist religious meditation.

We are told that historically in the West the subject of meditation has been closely related to contemplation, spiritual exercise and other forms of devotional practices and contemplative piety, especially those of the mystics. This term, contemplation, is defined by Webster as "meditation on spiritual things; narrowly, in mystical language, an experimental perception of God; a state of awareness of God's being and presence." We must remember, however, that contemplation with the transcendental diety as the supreme object was unknown to the ancient Greeks. For example, Plato defined *theoria* as "contemplation" or "intuitive knowledge," and, as Betty Heimann suggests, "this use of theoria [contemplation] . . . reveals Plato's general attitude, his humble openness towards the phenomena [of the world and cosmos rather than dieties] as objects of contemplation. . . ."[7] And, following this notion of contemplation, Plotinus went as far as to say:

> . . . the Nature-Principle produces by virtue of being an act of contemplation and a Reason-Principle; on this triple character depends its creative efficacy.
>
> Thus the act of production is seen to be in Nature as an act of contemplation; for creation is the outcome of a contemplation which

---

[6] Reported by William Braden in *Chicago Sun-Times*, January 8, 1967, p. 2.

[7] Betty Heimann, *Indian and Western Philosophy: A Study in Contrasts* (London: George Allen & Unwin, 1937), p. 28.

never becomes anything else, which never does anything else, but creates by simply being a contemplation.[8]

Understandably, most Christians as well as Jews and Muslims interpreted contemplation from their own respective theistic perspectives, which were different from that of ancient Greeks. Friedrich Heiler, reflecting a typical Western Christian orientation, states that "contemplation is the ancient word used by Western theologians for what the Greek theologians designated as *mysterion* and *mystike theologia*—the new current word 'mysticism,' an abbreviation of 'mystical theology,' has only quite recently gained full acceptance in the West."[9] Clearly, such an understanding of contemplation indicates the traditional Westerner's spiritual map, in which ultimate reality is conceived as the God who transcends the realms of man and nature. To be sure, they recognized the existence of the world of nature, but only to affirm the sovereignty of God over it. Western religious man's contemplation, therefore, was singularly directed toward God with the world of nature serving as a background. Thus the Psalmist, who begins a Song of Ascents by saying, "I lift up my eyes to the hills," immediately drops the reference to the hills and pays homage to the Almighty.

> I lift up my eyes to the hills.
>     From whence does my help come?
> My help comes from the Lord,
>     who made heaven and earth.[10]

Likewise in another Psalm we read:

> When I look at thy heavens, the works of thy fingers,
>     the moon and the stars which thou hast established;
> What is man that thou art mindful of him,
>     and the son of man that thou dost care for him?[11]

These Psalms provide a prototype of Western religious contemplation in which human beings seek the assurance of the abiding presence of God, who is the creator of heaven and earth and the Lord of history.

---

[8] *Plotinus* (Great Books of the Western World, Vol. 17) (Chicago: Encyclopaedia Britannica, 1952), p. 130.

[9] Friedrich Heiler, "Contemplation in Christian Mysticism," *Spiritual Disciplines: Papers from the Eranos Yearbooks*, ed. by Joseph Campbell (Bollingen Series XXX–4. New York: Pantheon, 1960), p. 186.

[10] Psalm 121: 1–2 (R.S.V.).

[11] Psalm 8:3–4 (R.S.V.).

## MEDITATION IN THE EAST

In contrast to the contemplation of Western peoples meditation in the East tends to be directed toward Sacred Reality present in the world of nature. This is due to the fact that unlike their Western counterparts, who believe themselves to be situated somewhere between God and the world of nature, Eastern people have always accepted the humble role of being a part of the world of nature. This does not mean that a human being has no value. A human being has value, but no separate destiny apart from nature. People in the East have never been regarded as sojourners in this world; they are certainly not the masters of this world, nor are they intruders or guests. They are an integral part of the cosmos with its seasons and changes. Thus the inner fabric of Eastern religions is characterized by the belief in the insep-arability of humankind and nature: "This Atman [the vital essence in man] is the same in the ant, the same in the gnat, the same in the elephant, the same in these three worlds . . . the same in the universe."[12] The close kinship which humans feel towards the world of nature was poignantly expressed by Rabindranath Tagore:

> Millions of years ago when the first dawn
> Appeared on this earth,
> Did you take the speck of the sun's rays
> to weave it into my life?
> Who knows how I came to be on that particular morn,
> What form you gave me, hidden from my knowledge,
> To blossom forth?
> O you ageless one, from time before memory,
> You have been moulding me anew throughout the ages,
> Abiding by me ever, you shall remain with me always.[13]

It is to be noted that according to such religious perception, the world was not created by someone or something other than itself. What is important is that the world *is*. Essentially, the world had no beginning, nor will it have an end. Accordingly, Eastern religious men never acknowledged the existence of a transcendental creator-diety in his perception of the monistic universe. Gods proliferated, but they, like human beings and other beings, were subservient to the regulative order or inner balance of the cosmos, variously known as *Rta, Dharma,* and *Tao.* The power of the immanent, hidden, cosmic order regulates the movement of the stars, and it creates and re-creates all life, be it milk in the cow's udder, water in the ocean, or flowers in the garden. So, the pious Asian is aware in meditation that:

[12] *Brhadranyaka-upanishad*, I, 3, 22.
[13] Indu Dutt (trans.), *A Tagore Testament* (New York: Philosophical Library, 1954), p. 9.

> If I were the soil, if I were the water,
> If I were the grass or fruit of flower,
> If I were to roam about the earth with beasts and birds,
> There would be nothing to fear.
> In never-ending ties wherever I go,
> It will be the limitless me.[14]

In the course of time, Eastern religions developed a rich variety of medita-
tion practices and devotional cults for deities and quasi-deities, such as Siva,
Visnu and Krisna in Hinduism, and Buddha, Maitreya and Amitabha in
Buddhism. But the basic structures of the great Eastern religions have never
lost the cosmo-centric orientation, as we read in the immortal phrases of the
*Tao Te Ching:*

> There was a formless actuality
> Before heaven and earth developed;
> Lonely, isolated,
> Independent, unchanging,
> Revolving unfailingly,
> Able to be mother of all things under heaven.
> Not knowing its name
> I call it "Tao."
>
> . . . . . . .
> Man follows the earth;
> The earth follows heaven;
> Heaven follows Tao;
> Tao follows its own nature.[15]

Even such a sketchy portrayal of the Eastern religious orientation makes
it evident that the meditation nurtured by Eastern religious soil has a very
different frame of reference from that of the Western man. Let us depict the
basic difference between them by comparing the Western understanding of
the body-soul relationship and the Eastern understanding of the spirit-
matter relationship. At the expense of oversimplification—and it has to be
that—we may say that Western religions tend to accept the superiority of
soul or spirit over body or matter, whereas Eastern religions tend to see
these two dimensions on equal footing.

[14] *Ibid.* p. 15.
[15] *Tao Te Ching*, Chap. 25. This is the translation by Constant C. C. Chang and William
Forthman, cited in James W. Dye and William Forthman, *Religions of the World: Selected
Readings* (New York: Appleton Century Crofts, 1957), pp. 247–8.

## Soul and Body

Obviously, there has never been single "Western" view on the soul-body relationship. Plato affirmed the immortality and divinity of the soul, which in life is controlled by the body. Similarly, Plotinus taught that the soul, "a divine being and a dweller in the loftier realms," becomes bitter and miserable when it descends into body, which is "its prison or its tomb."[16] The Hebrew creation myth, on the other hand, portrays God creating man's body from clay, into which he breathed the breath of life. If the Gospel account of the debate between the Sadducees and Jesus on the fate of the departed had any validity, it reflects the existence of different interpretations regarding the soul-body relationship among the Jews at the time of Jesus. But in the main, Hebrew thought affirmed that soul and body were co-essential, as expressed in the following prayer of Maimonides: "O God, Thou hast founded the body of man with infinite goodness; thou hast united in him innumerable forces incessantly at work like so many instruments, so as to preserve in its entirety this beautiful house containing his immortal soul. . . ."[17]

There is every indication that the original Jewish Christians inherited the Hebrew notion of the soul-body relationship, as reflected in the resurrection accounts in Matthew (27:51–3) and Luke (24:37–43). The Pauline Epistles lead us to the conclusion that on the one hand Paul affirmed the Hebrew anthropology as indicated in I Thessalonians, while on the other hand he sometimes appropriated Hellenistic categories in describing soul as an inner esential self dwelling in the "earthly tent" (body). "Here indeed we groan, and long to put on our heavenly dwelling. . . . For while we are still in this tent, we sigh with anxiety . . ." (II Corinthians 5:2–4). Following Paul, Christian thought generally attached higher values to soul or spirit and tended to equate body with the "desires of the flesh" (Galatians 5:19–20).

As to Islam, its original notion of the soul-body relationship was very simple and not dissimilar to Hebrew anthropology. Also, nowhere in the Qur'an did the Prophet mention anything like the soul's immortality. In the course of time, the ambiguity of the Prophet's notion of humankind resulted in heated controversies between the materialists, who viewed the soul as an accident of the body, and the spiritualists, who upheld the independent existence of the spirit as the power to govern the body. Meanwhile, the world of Islam came under the strong influence of Hellenism, although ironically it accepted, as von Grünebaum points out, "instead of Plato, Neo-Platonism, instead of Plotinus, Porphyry and Proclus, and Aristotle mostly as seen through the commentaries of the epigoni."[18] It was Sufism which, in part

---

[16] Plotinus, op. cit., pp. 202–3.

[17] Cited in Fred Gladstone Bratton, *Maimonides: Medieval Modernist* (Boston: Beacon, 1967), p. 81.

[18] Gustav E. von Grünebaum, *Medieval Islam: A Study in Cultural Orientation* (Chicago: The University of Chicago Press, 1946), p. 323.

under Hellenistic inspiration, articulated the notion of the soul as a spiritual entity distinct from the physical body. Moreover, the soul came to be interpreted as a spiritual substance derived from God, and as "it is of heavenly origin, it always tends to return to the source from which it emanated. It is only the sins and dross of the body that prevent the soul from attaining its end."[19]

Thus, Christianity and Islam, both of which had originally shared the historic Hebrew notion of the co-essentiality of soul and body, eventually came to accept the view, similar to the Hellenistic idea, that the soul or spirit is more essential than the corruptible body. Moreover, under Cartesian influence the soul and spirit were fused into one, so that the Pauline trichotomy of the spirit-soul-body (I Thessalonians 5:23) became for all intents and purposes the mind-body dichotomy in the Western Christendom, at least until the rise of modern psychology and psychiatry.[20] This may account in part for the one-sided stress in the West on the mental or spiritual aspects of meditation, contemplation and spiritual exercises, with very little attention given to the physical or bodily dimensions.

### Spirit and Matter

The question of the soul-body relationship is, of course, a universal problem, and as such it has concerned all Eastern religions. But, in the cosmic-oriented East, the issue of the soul-body relationship was usually raised in connection with that of spirit and matter. In the main, all the major religions in the East took it for granted that spirit and matter were equally primeval principles. In fact the Sankhya and Vedanta schools in India went so far as to affirm that "it is from Matter, not from Spirit, that all cosmic and specific psychic faculties are derived; Man's intellect (Buddhi) is also re-garded as an emanation of primeval Matter and not of Spirit."[21] Such a perception of the spirit-matter relationship fostered a belief, held widely from India to Japan, that deities were the inherent powers in everything in celestial and earthly spheres. In India, for example, prominent deities are believed to reside in the upper region of heaven, but there are also a countless number of earthly deities, such as the elephant-god, the monkey-god, and the snake-god. In Japan, the eighteenth-century Shinto theoretician, Motoori Noringa, affirmed that the word "kami" (god, deity, spirit) denotes heavenly and earthly deities. Furthermore, he says, "among all kinds of beings—including not only human beings but also such objects as

[19] Ibrahim Madkour, "The Concept of Man in Islamic Thought," in S. Radhakrishnan and P. T. Raju (eds.), *The Concept of Man: A Study in Comparative Philosophy* (London: George Allen & Unwin, 1960), p. 453.

[20] See William Temple, *Nature, Man and God* (New York: Macmillan, 1949), III: "The Cartesian 'Faux Pas,'" pp. 57–81.

[21] Heimann, *op. cit.*, p. 40.

birds, beasts, trees, grass, seas, mountains, and so forth—any being what-
soever which possesses some eminent quality out of the ordinary, and is awe-
inspiring, is called kami."[22]

As to the nature of human beings, all Eastern religions accept the
inseparability of man and nature, even though each religious system has its
own mode of interpretation on this subject. For instance, India has produced
a variety of philosophical and religious anthropologies. We learn from a Vedic
prayer—"May nothing of thy *manas* [faculty of mind], nothing of the *asu*
[psychic faculty], nothing of the limbs, nothing of thy vital fluid, nothing of
thy body here by any means be lost"[23]—that ancient Indians accepted man
as a psycho-mental-physical organism and a mortal being. At the same time,
the famous Vedic formula, "Thou Art That" *(tat tvam asi)*, affirms the
essential identity of individual man (*Ātman* or self) and the cosmic soul
(Brahman). In the words of Heinrich Zimmer: Brahman is "the highest,
deepest, final transcendental power . . . that turns into and animates everything in the microcosm as well as in the outer world; it is the divine inmate of
the mortal coil and is identical with the Self *(ātman)*—the highest aspect of
that which we in the West style (indiscriminately) the 'soul.' "[24] Following
this principle, Hinduism envisaged a hierarchical order on the cosmic level,
including the so-called "caste system" and the four stages *(āsrama)* of life.
India also developed one of the most thoroughgoing systems of meditation,
called Yoga, which enables man to be "liberated in this life" by recovering
"the original situation enriched by the dimension of *freedom* and *trans-
consciousness.*"[25] Such a lofty spiritual aim requires meticulous bodily training in "postures" *(asana)* and "respiratory discipline" *(pranayama).*[26] By
mastering physical as much as mental disciplines, according to Yoga, "man
creates the spiritual dimension of freedom, and 'introduces' it into the
cosmos and life—that is, into blind and tragically conditioned modes of
existence."[27]

As we turn to Buddhism, we realise how much it owes to Yoga, even
though Buddhist soteriology is quite different from that of Yoga. We are told
that one cool night, as the Buddha meditated under a Bodhi tree, he saw in a
trance a vision of his previous existence. In the second watch of the night he
saw another vision, which revealed to him how all beings pass away and are
reborn according to the moral law of cause and effect *(karma)*. Finally he

[22]Cited in Shigeru Matsumoto, *Motoori Norinaga, 1730–1801* (Cambridge: Harvard University Press, 1970), p. 84.

[23]*Atharvaveda* XVIII, 2–24.

[24]Heinrich Zimmer, *Philosophies of India*, ed. by Joseph Campbell (New York: Pantheon,
1951; Bollingen Series XXVI), p. 79.

[25]Mircea Eliade, *Yoga: Immortality and Freedom*, tr. by W. R. Trask (New York: Pantheon,
1958; Bollingen Series LVI), p. 99.

[26]*Ibid.* pp. 53–9.

[27]*Ibid.* p. 100.

gained piercing insight into the meaning of existence, and he experienced liberation. Indeed, from the night of the Buddha's emancipation experience until our own time, all Buddhists, divided though they have been along doctrinal and cultic lines, share the soteriological goal of attaining Nirvana. They all share the conviction that in the Buddhist path right conduct is the prerequisite for meditation and insight, both of which are in turn prerequisite for liberation.

The centrality of meditation in Buddhist soteriology is such that a number of different methods and techniques have been developed. Three are especially important. They are the meditation techniques of the Theravada tradition, the Tibetan Buddhist tradition, and Ch'an or Zen as practiced in China and Japan. All of them regard meditation as a discipline of the total person, combining mental, spiritual and bodily aspects, as evidenced in the "breath-and body-mindfulness" or "body-process-awareness" method of the Theravada,[28] the Tibetan tradition of *Mahamudra* (which may be characterized as the *Prajnaparamita* applied in its simplest and most practical form),[29] and *zazen* (sitting meditation) of Zen. In the words of the thirteenth-century Japanese Sōtō Zen master, Dōgen:

> *Zazen* is the most supremely important matter in Buddhism. Many persons in China attained enlightenment by practicing *zazen*. Even the illiterate, unintelligent, or mentally slow persons, if they devote themselves to *zazen*, will achieve more than the intelligent persons who spend years on sheer learning. Indeed the path of the Buddha is nothing but *zazen*. Nothing should interfere with its practice.[30]

### Some Observations

It is, of course, futile to try to evaluate the relative merits and demerits of the meditation practices in the West in comparison with those of the East. Perhaps it may be important to note that historically in the West meditation together with spiritual experiences and other devotional practices were developed and transmitted in cloisters. Considering the seriousness of the spiritual life, involving spiritual and psychic crises, we can readily understand why cloisters played such a decisive role in this respect. Inevitably, however, as John Gerson observed of the fifteenth century, contemplative life in the cloisters fostered spiritual pride. Moreover, there developed a widely-shared conviction that it was dangerous to expose the intricacies of spiritual

[28] See Winston L. King, *A Thousand Lives Away: Buddhism in Contemporary Burma* (Cambridge: Harvard University Press, 1964), Chap. VI, "The More Excellent Way," pp. 180–219.

[29] Chang Chen-chi, *The Practice of Zen* (New York: Harper, 1959), p. 170, fn. 1.

[30] See J. M. Kitagawa, "Religions of Japan," in W. T. Chan *et al.*, *The Great Asian Religions* (New York: Macmillan, 1969), p. 288.

life to uninitiated laity.[31] In the East, only the Theravada and Tibetan traditions of Buddhism regarded cloisters as guardians of meditation and spiritual life, whereas Mahayana Buddhism as well as Taoism encouraged meditation centered around individual Gurus and their disciples. Nevertheless, most Eastern religions for generations fostered a quietistic view of the end of spiritual life, i.e., moksha, samadhi, nirvana, satori, etc., as well as a static understanding of the givenness of human existence and a negative attitude toward life, world, and history.

The so-called resurgence of Eastern religions in our time may be seen as a reaction to the Westernisation of the East that lasted two or three centuries in our recent history. The current shift of accent in the thinking of many Easterners from a quietistic outlook to a more active participation in the affairs of this world inevitably brings religion closer to the everyday life of men and women. Even in Theravada Buddhism, which has been regarded by many as the most other-worldly among Eastern traditions, leaders are urged to "pursue not a will-o'-the-wisp Nirvana secluded in the cell of their monasteries, but Nirvana attained here and now by a life of self-forgetful activity."[32] It is not surprising, therefore, to see in various parts of Asia a variety of religious movements and activities, including meditation centers, sponsored and directed in many instances by laymen and laywomen. Another significant feature of contemporary Eastern religions is their missionary fervor to transmit the fruits of their spiritual culture, such as Yoga, Zen and Transcendental Meditation, to the Western world.

The current popularity of Eastern meditation practices in the West indicates, at least in part, that many Westerners, including some of those who participate in routinized church life, are looking for more direct and relevant ways to relate their life to a deeper level of spiritual foundation. It is as yet premature to predict whether the current vogue of things Eastern indicates a trend toward the "Easternization" of the West, as many Eastern Gurus and Rishis believe, or a trend toward spiritual revitalization of the West's own religious resources, as some of the advocates of Christian Yoga and Christian Zen seem to suggest. Also, it may be within the realm of possibility, as some self-styled pundits hold, that a new mode of spirituality, which is neither Eastern nor Western, may emerge out of a fusion between the two. Answers to these questions will have to be settled by future historians.

## Faith, Knowledge and Understanding

The current generation's preoccupation with experience, coupled with the popularity of various forms of meditation, leads us to reflect on the

---

[31] James L. Connolly, *John Gerson: Reformer and Mystic* (Louvain: Librairie Universitaire, 1927), pp. 259–60.

[32] *The Revolt in the Temple* (Colombo: Sinha Publications, 1953), p. 586.

perennial problem of faith and knowledge in a new way. It is worth noting that faith and knowledge are not exclusive religious categories in the West or in the East. In the main, here resorting to oversimplification again, we might say that the Western religions regard faith as the starting-point and a more primary category. Accordingly, many Westerners believe that faith leads to knowledge and informs knowledge. On the other hand, the Eastern religions regard knowledge as the starting-point—knowledge leads to faith and authenticates faith. Be that as it may, historically both in Western and Eastern religions, the precarious linkage between faith and knowledge has often been distorted in favour of one side or the other. Nevertheless, all religions in the West and in the East acknowledge that religious knowledge is not ordinary knowledge.

The intellectual climate of our time makes it all the more important for those of us teaching in universities and/or theological schools to articulate the multi-dimensional character of religious knowledge. First, religious knowledge, gained either by faith or in meditation, enables one to "recognize" that which had been previously "cognized," and thus it may be regarded as a form of "re-collection." In this sense, all the seers, prophets and holy men recognize what the human race had always known, however implicitly, about sacral reality from time immemorial. To be sure, what man perceived was often not theorized, and depended heavily on signs, symbols, myths, cults and works of art, through which the human spirit communicates itself. Secondly, religious knowledge, on the other hand, is not simply "re-collection" of something perceived vaguely at an earlier time. By the leap of faith, or in the depth of contemplative speculation and meditation, the human spirit reaches a level of understanding of the nature of sacral reality in its pristine character in such a way as "to free it of the accretions of time and of misunderstanding, to re-construct in its totality that which does not appear as a whole."[33] Thus, Abraham perceived that there was "the city which has foundations . . ." (Hebrews 11:10), and Moses recognized the existence of the Promised Land beyond the Jordan (Deuteronomy 3:23–27). Similarly, the Buddha in the depth of meditation understood the nature of the Chain of Causation and found the Way to be liberated from the endless cycle of rebirth. Thirdly, religious knowledge is basically soteriological in character; it does not provide information but rather orientation. That is to say, religious knowledge gives man understanding of the nature of existence in relation to the sacred source of reality, whereby one is able to chart the course of one's life.

Ironically, today man exalts experience above everything else, whereby he isolates himself from the source of religious authority and tradition. Thus, both inside and outside established religions, in the West as much as in the

---

[33] Joachim Wach, *Das Verstehen*, Vol. I (Tübingen: J. C. B. Mohr—Paul Siebeck, 1926), p. 178.

the East, experience is authenticated either by unrestrained feeling or by sentimental and artificial meditation. We readily acknowledge that we cannot turn the clock backward and return to the pre-modern world of meaning, in which authority and tradition authenticated the role of experience. But in rejecting the outdated world of meaning, modern man has lost touch with the source of knowledge, revealed or otherwise. This is particularly true with our current student generation. Thus, while many young men and women seem to experience a new sense of liberation, thanks to uninhibited expression of emotion or introspective meditation, they seem to have difficulties in realizing that religious orientation must be grounded in reflection and understanding, even when it demands the conversion of reflective thinking, through and within itself, toward the soteriological goal. This seems to be the basic dilemma in teaching religion(s) and theology in our time.

# 8

## OTHER RELIGIONS

There is today a general confusion and ambivalence among Christians, especially in the West, in regard to the problem of understanding other religions. Even those who are fairly well versed in the contents of the Scriptures and in the history of the church are often totally uninformed or greatly misinformed about the realities in religions outside their own. Though many of them come in contact with Jewish friends or neighbors, they are inclined to dismiss Judaism simply as a contempory form of the religion of the Old Testament. Until quite recently, Western education for the most part did not bother with the histories and cultures of non-Western peoples, to say nothing of their religions. To many Westerners, therefore, Islam, Hinduism, or Buddhism seemed to be as remote as, for example, the ancient Egyptian or Sumerian religions. Every once in a while, returned missionaries spoke of the customs and beliefs of peoples whom they tried to proselytize, but more often than not they painted gloomy pictures of other religions in order to promote missionary interests among the churches at home. Understandably, most Christians in the West had very little opportunity to learn anything about other religions. Many of them, to be sure, had heard of Mahatma Gandhi, who raised questions in the minds of some Christians, because they found in him not only utter dedication to truth and justice but also a saintly character. But then, many Westerners thought of him primarily as the political leader who almost singlehandedly had led the nonviolent resistance movement of the Indian masses against the mighty power of the British empire, and even those who thought of him as a religious man regarded Gandhi as being a Christian in all but name.

The situation has changed radically since the end of World War II. The postwar world situation has propelled many hitherto unknown leaders of Asian and African peoples to the forefront of international affairs, so that the names of Nehru, U Nu, Nasser, and Ben Gurion have become familiar to the West. These men not only play significant roles in making important decisions regarding the problems of the world, but also represent the hopes and aspirations of peoples in Asia and Africa who have been nurtured by their own religious and cultural traditions that are now being revitalized. Significantly, this development coincides with a vogue in the West for Eastern art, culture, and religions, as evidenced by the feverish publication of books in Western languages on the *Upanishads, Bhagavad Gita, Qur'an, Tao Te*

*Ching, Wisdom of Confucius, Dhammapada,* and Zen Buddhism. These two factors—the resurgence of religions in Asia and Africa and the penetration of Eastern religious and cultural influences into Europe and America—have caught many Christians off balance today, for they have not been prepared for this unexpected turn of events.

## THE PRESENT SITUATION

Since the end of World War II the problem of ecumenicity has become an urgent issue for Christendom. This does not mean, however, that the questions concerning relationships with other faiths have been overlooked. In fact, a number of theologians and missionary thinkers have attempted to re-examine these issues. With the combined efforts of the International Missionary Council and the World Council of Churches, Christian study centers for other faiths have been established in various parts of the world. These centers not only offer facilities to Christians for engaging in research concerning the other religions, but they also provide opportunities for Christians to meet and confer with the leaders and adherents of other faiths. It is encouraging to note that already some of the scholars of the younger churches together with Western Christians, though still very few in number, have begun to take seriously the study of non-Christian religions and cultures.

Equally important is the postwar Westerners' general attitude toward things Eastern, that marks a great change from the usual prewar attitude. Toynbee observes that although the West has exercised the predominant power over the rest of the world for the past four or five hundred years, recent events indicate that the East-West relationship has been altered. "The West's alarm and anger at recent acts of Russian and Chinese aggression at the West's expense are evidence that, for us Westerners, it is today still a strange experience to be suffering at the hands of the world what the world has been suffering at Western hands for a number of centuries past."[1]

Many Westerners, to be sure, realize intellectually that a new world order is in the making and that they have to understand the dynamics of peoples and events in non-Western parts of the world. And yet, Westerners for the most part are not prepared emotionally to encounter the "strangeness" of other peoples and cultures; as Mircea Eliade astutely observes, Westerners in their encounter with Easterners tend to depend on the more Westernized representatives of Eastern peoples or enter into relations with the East only in such external spheres as economics and politics. He goes so far as to say, "The Western world has not yet, or not generally, met with authentic representatives of the 'real' non-Western traditions."[2] This is especially true respecting the religions of non-Western peoples.

[1] Arnold Toynbee, *The World and the West* (New York: Oxford University Press, 1953), p. 4.
[2] Mircea Eliade, *Myths, Dreams and Mysteries,* Philip Mairet, trans. (New York: Harper & Brothers, 1960), pp. 8–9.

One may ask, then, how it is possible or Westerners, especially Western Christians, to understand the nature and ethics of other religions. This indeed is a complex problem. Even in the present oversimplified discussion, we are made to realize that there is no single correct approach to non-Christian religions. Moreover, there are different kinds and levels of understanding of other religions, depending on the motives and perspectives of those who deal with these problems.

Christians historically have approached other faiths from the single perspective of the Christian world mission, and have thus calculated their concern for non-Christians on the basis of making converts. Even the study of other religions has been undertaken with this motive. "Because as Christians," says Edmund Perry, "we are under mandate to proclaim the gospel to and make disciples of all peoples, we readily confess that our motive for studying their religion is ulterior or missionary."[3] Such an approach might enable a Christian to understand the nature of the Christian gospel in order to be sure of its relation to other faiths, but would throw very little light on the realities of other religions. Many of the so-called missionary scholars, who concern themselves with other religions, are in effect preoccupied with the Christian understanding of soteriology, that is, whether God's redemption is confined within the Christian community or not. It is true that this question cannot be bypassed altogether by any professing Christian. However, there are other kinds and levels of understanding involved in regard to other religions; so that starting with or being preoccupied with theological inquiry into soteriology alone fails to do justice to the task of understanding non-Christian religions. Ideally, it may be argued that theology is able "to produce that attitude of freedom of the spirit and of impartial understanding, combined with a criticism and evaluation transcending all imprisonment in preconceived ideas and principles as ultimate standards of preference."[4] Practically, however, all too hasty evaluation and judgment of other faiths, based on a rigid understanding of Christian theology, coupled with misguided passion and wishful thinking, tend to blind one's perception and capacity for understanding.

In a sense, the contemporary resurgence of Eastern religions and their apologetic self-assertion may be understood as part of a reaction against the exaggerated assertion of Christians about the religious and cultural universality and finality of their faith. It is well for us to recall that Christian expansion in Asia and Africa during the nineteenth and early-twentieth centuries coincided with the colonial expansion of Western nations in those parts of the world. In those days the political, economic, and military strength of the West was such that to Westerners Eastern civilization appeared to be stagnant, ready to crumble before the mighty power of the

---

[3] Edmund Perry, *The Gospel in Dispute* (New York: Doubleday & Co., 1958), p. 84.

[4] Hendrik Kraemer, *Religion and the Christian Faith* (Philadelphia: The Westminster Press, 1956), p. 53.

West. It was hard for most Westerners to imagine that "in Eastern cilviliza-
tion there is inherent a power that is no less remarkable than that of the West
because it operates in a subtler and less conspicious manner."[5] Likewise,
many Western missionaries took it for granted that Eastern religions were
disintegrating from within, so that they assumed the "cultural" as well as
"religious" superiority of Christianity.

Confronted with the relentless advance of Western civilization and religion, adherents of Eastern religions tended to accept the "cultural" superiority of Christianity, but not its "religious" superiority, for they believed that
their own traditional religions were sufficient to meet the spiritual needs of
Eastern peoples. As Dewick states, "So long as their continued existence was
not threatened, they showed little inclination to assert their own superiority
and were often quite ready to express admiration for the teachings of
Christ."[6] Many Eastern religious leaders hoped naïvely to be sure, that by
incorporating some of the Western forms and categories, and modernizing
and purifying their traditional cults and practices, their religions would be
received by Christianity in a partnership of genuine interreligious cooperation. In this hope and aspiration they were bound to be disappointed, for
Christianity continued to claim not only "cultural" but also "religious" superiority over all other religions. Also, Eastern religious leaders began to
realize that in the acceptance of Western ways and logic, Eastern religions
devaluated their own norms of belief and practice. For instance, D. T.
Suzuki remarks that whereas, formerly, Buddhists welcomed the Western
approach to the study of their religion, they are now resorting to the dialectic
of Buddhism, rejecting the Western approach and methodology. "There is a
growing conviction among the Buddhists that their philosophy does not
require the support of Western logic, especially modern science."[7] This, be
it noted, is not a unique development in Buddhism alone. Elsewhere, "there
is manifest in the Eastern world today, along with the general national
revitalization, a movement toward a heightening of religious group consciousness, embodying itself in movements for reform, reorganization, propaganda, consolidation, and converted opposition to Christian missions."[8]

What is significant today is that, just as many Christians approach other
religions from the standpoint of Christian faith, articulate Eastern thinkers
try to understand and evaluate all religions, including Christianity, from the
perspectives of their distinctive faiths. For example, Radhakrishnan asserts

[5] William S. Haas, *The Destiny of the Mind—East and West* (London: Faber & Faber, 1956),
pp. 57–58.
[6] E. C. Dewick, *The Christian Attitude to Other Religions* (Cambridge: Cambridge University Press, 1953), p. 14.
[7] Quoted in A. Eustace Haydon, ed., *Modern Trends in World-Religions* (Chicago: The
University of Chicago Press, 1934), p. 38.
[8] Kraemer, *The Christian Message in a Non-Christian World* (Grand Rapids, Mich.: Kregel
Publications, 1961).

that the fundamental teaching of Christianity is not knowledge of and faith in Jesus as a historic person; to him, Christianity is the continuation of the perennial religion of the human race. Seen from such a Hindu theological perspective, Gautama the Buddha as well as Jesus the Christ are "God-men," or the manifestations of the Spirit through human media. Accordingly, the Son—the second person of the Trinity—is "man universalized," whereas "Jesus Christ is God individualized."[9] Also, according to Radhakrishnan, this belief is not a monopoly of Christianity. "God-men are the precursors of the truly human. What is possible for a Gautama or a Jesus is possible for every human being. The nature of man receives its fulfillment in them. They are our elder brothers."[10]

Suzuki comments that Yahweh's disclosure of his own identity—"I am that I am"—is the most profound of utterances. "This is the same as Christ's saying, 'I am,' that is, he is eternity itself, while Abraham is in time, therefore, he 'was' and not 'is.' Those who live in the light of eternity are and are never subjected to the becoming of 'was' and 'will be.'"[11]

Reading these comments upon Christianity by non-Christian thinkers, Christians should not hastily conclude that these men have become partially Christianized, nor should Christians be disturbed by the presentation of a distorted understanding of the meaning of Christian faith. What these East-ern thinkers are doing is looking at Christianity through the eyes of their own faiths. They do not at the same time say that Christians should not approach other religions through the perspective of Christian faith;[12] they insist, however, that they too have every right to interpret Christianity from their own perspectives and to make theological judgments upon it. Thus, Radhakrishnan chracterizes the original teaching of Jesus as a typical Eastern spirituality, emphasizing intuitive realization, a nondogmatic attitude, the nonaggressive virtues, and a universalistic ethics. He considers that Western Christianity has distorted the original ethos of Christianity by placing "the emphasis on definite creeds and absolute dogmatism, with its consequences of intolerance, exclusiveness, and confusion of piety with Patriotism."[13] On the other hand, Sayyid Qutb considers Christianity as an individualistic and negative faith. "When it was embraced by Europe owing to specific historic circumstances, and when it proved incompetent to keep pace with life as it

[9] Sarvepalli Radhakrishnan, *Recovery of Faith* (New York: Harper & Brothers, 1955), p. 187.

[10] *Ibid.*, p. 179.

[11] D. T. Suzuki, *Mysticism, Christian and Buddhist* (New York: Harper & Brothers, 1957), p. 112.

[12] Cf. J. N. Farquhar, *The Crown of Hinduism* (1913); K. L. Reichelt, *Truth and Tradition in Chinese Buddhism* (1934); George Appleton, *Glad Encounter* (1959), and *On the Eightfold Path—Christian Presence Amid Buddhism* (New York: Oxford University Press, 1961); Kenneth Cragg, *The Call of the Minaret* (New York: Oxford University Press, 1956), and *Sandals at the Mosque—Christian Presence Amid Islam* (New York: Oxford University Press, 1959).

[13] Sarvepalli Radhakrishnan, *East and West in Religion* (London: George Allen & Unwin, 1933), p. 58.

developed then, Christianity confined itself to worship and to matters of individual conscience, ceasing to have any control over the practical affairs of life. . . ."[14]

To those Christians who hold that only they have a divine commission to witness for their faith, at the expense of other religions and without recognizing the same privilege for others, these statements by the adherents of non-Christian faiths may come as a shock. In much the same way that some Westerners forget that "the world has been suffering at Western hands for a number of centuries past," some Christians who resent the non-Christian criticism of Christianity forget that this is what Christians all these years have been doing respecting other religions. The crucial issue today, however, is not so much *whether or not* adherents of particular religions have the right to witness for their faiths as *how* they ought to do it. This is not to deny the importance of the contents and integrity of the faiths involved. As Pandit Nehru remarked recently, "Your manner of saying it—the mood you create, the kind of rapport you establish—all these are the most vital part of communication and have a great deal to do with the response you get."[15] This emphasis should not be interpreted as a preoccupation with the techniques or gimmicks of communications; what Nehru stresses is the basic attitude toward others who may or may not share the same views. Today, when the claims of Christianity confront both the rational and emotional rebuttals and countercharges of non-Christians, Christians are compelled to re-examine their basic attitudes toward other faiths and the people who adhere to them, for it will have a great deal to do with the response of others toward Christianity for years to come.

## THE PROSPECTS

In any area of life, one's attitude toward others is integrally related to one's attitude toward oneself; the Christian attitude toward other faiths must also be seen in this light. We must bear in mind, however, that one's own faith and the faiths of others require different kinds of understanding, even though the two cannot be separated. Utopians may equate the two, and confuse, for example, the comparative study of religions with theology. On the other hand, many Christians try to probe into the meaning of Christian faith alone and then attempt to communicate it to others, as though communication were a one-way street. How to maintain the necessary tension, while not losing sight of the internal relations, between the attempt to understand Christian faith and the effort to understand other faiths, is indeed a difficult problem in our time.

"In the past," says Adolph Keller, "Christian faith meant a certainty about life and its future, an assurance which gave a meaning to its continuous

[14] Quoted in Cragg, *The Call of the Minaret, op. cit.*, p. 247.
[15] Quoted in Norman Cousins, "Talk with the PM," *Saturday Review*, May 27, 1961, p. 13.

changes, an inner security which was a firm foundation from which the moving kaleidoscope of a whole world could be observed and judged."[16] Today, even convinced Christians are blinking and rubbing their eyes in a world that is changing and moving too rapidly for their comfort. Their image of a secure world has been destroyed; they have become sojourners in the world that is increasingly "alien" to them. Caught in this dilemma, some Christians try to retire to the citadel of the faith of their Fathers. For example, in a recent article, Dr. Cawley tells of his encounter with a Jewish scholar. "In your opinion," asked Cawley, "will the time come, near or remote, when the Jew will become a Christian?" To this his Jewish friend replied: "The Jew will become Christian when the Christian becomes Christian." In citing this experience, Cawley exhorts Christians to return to the unshakable Pauline faith in Christ: "Paul won his earlier day for Christ, for the simple reason that Christ held all there was in Paul, and shone his deathless light through him. That same principle of faith, of life, and of light wins today wherever it may be."[17]

Inspiring though Cawley's affirmation of faith is, his proposed solution fails to face the reality of the situation, for the difficulty with Asian religions that challenge Christianity today, as Tillich points out, "is not so much that they reject the Christian answer as answer, as that their human nature is formed in such a way that they do not ask the questions to which the gospel gives the answer. To them the Christian answer is not an answer, because they have not asked the question to which Christianity is supposed to give the answer."[18] This is the very problem that vexes Christianity today and will continue to do so tomorrow.

In today's world, where there is more than one religion that claims the truth as its own, the choice of attitude is limited. One may hold that different religions are fundamentally the same, as advocated by some of the extreme Christian liberals, some Buddhists and by Neo-Vedantists. Or one can stress, as indeed many adherents of different religions do, the exclusive value and unique meaning in a particular religious system. To the former the uniqueness of each religion is its disgrace, while to the latter universality implies the surrender of truth. Both of these fail to take adequate account of the dialectic relationship involved in the universal and particular dimensions of religions.

It must readily be admitted that in our divided world a common-sense appeal for humankind's unity cannot be dismissed as sheer sentimentality. The liberals in every religious tradition have made great contributions to

---

[16] Adolph Keller, *Christian Europe Today* (New York: Harper & Brothers, 1942), p. 4.

[17] F. Cawley, "Christ's Finality: A Lost Vision?" *Christianity Today*, Vol. 15, April 24, 1961, p. 17.

[18] Paul Tillich, *Theology of Culture*, Robert C. Kimball, ed. (New York: Oxford University Press, 1959), pp. 204–205.

understanding by emphasizing the common bond of humanity, crossing religious lines; this is a necessary emphasis that cannot be forgotten. However, in their eagerness to stress the universal aspect of religions, enthusiasts tend to ignore the tenacity and importance of differences that exist among the religions. These "doctrinaire liberals," in their adherence to a one-dimensional truth about the universal features of religions, naïvely assume that advocating this point of view will automatically bring about harmony and mutual understanding among the diverse religions. As Kraemer points out, some of the more aggressive advocates of universality of religions can be "exclusivists in a concealed way," in the name of inclusiveness, by claiming that interfaith relations are possible only when all religions drop at the outset their uniqueness and accept solely "the tenet of the one, universal religion, hidden in all religions" as the normative concept.[19]

On the other hand, advocates of the absoluteness of one faith face difficult problems as well. For example, if a Christian holds that all other faiths are "counterfeits" of the true religion and thus should be eliminated or displaced, he cannot help denying, unwittingly to be sure, God's freedom and the doctrine of creation. If he concludes that only the Christian apprehension of the truth is correct, without rejecting the availability of the Divine to others, he cannot escape "monolatry," which implies the sort of relativism that he tried to avoid in the first place. In either case, extreme exclusivists oversimplify the problem of understanding of their own faith as well as the faith of others. Actually, very few Christians have ever claimed that the Christian understanding of God is absolutely correct. Following Paul's testimony—"now we see in a mirror dimly . . . now I know in part. . . ." (I Corinthians 13:12)—most Christians would acknowledge that their manner of knowing, understanding, and even their mode of believing, are under the judgment of the redeeming God. One faces still greater problems in attempting to understand other faiths because of their unfamiliarity and because of one's own ignorance, together with mental and psychic attitudes that have been conditioned by particular experiences. "And when one has the will to overcome these barriers," says Meland, "there usually follows an overindulgent sense of identification and tolerance that both falsifies and sentimentalizes the factors involved."[20]

In rejecting extreme universalism and particularism, some Christian missionary thinkers are again emphasizing the historic motif of "fulfillment." Those who take this principle seriously stress the necessity of entering the religious life of non-Christians appreciatively and sympathetically, believing,

[19] Hendrik Kraemer, *World Cultures and World Religions* (Philadelphia: The Westminster Press, 1960), p. 364, footnote 1.
[20] Bernard E. Meland, "The Christian Encounter with the Faiths of Men," *The Resurgent Religions of Asia and the Christian Mission* (Chicago: University of Chicago Press, mimeo., 1959), p. 10.

however, that the religious quests of non-Christians will have to be answered in Christ. In the words of Canon Warren: "Our first task in approaching another people, another culture, another religion, is to take off our shoes, for the place we are approaching is holy. Else we may find ourselves treading on men's dreams. More serious still, we may forget that God was here before our arrival."[21] Cragg goes so far as to say that the church "exists to give, not to get; to preach, not to strive; to welcome, not to proselytize."[22] His chief concern, in regard to Muslims, is "the restoration to Muslims of the Christ Whom they have missed."[23] Such an attitude toward other faiths marks a great change from the attitude of many missionaries in the last century.

However conciliatory the fulfillment motif may seem, this principle alone will not resolve the intricate question of the relationship of Christianity to other faiths. To be sure, Cragg is interested not in "taking back cathedrals from mosques, but giving back the Christ."[24] But Muslims know that accepting Christ, in the way Cragg advocates, results in their ceasing to be Muslims. Likewise, despite Dr. Appleton's sympathetic interpretation of Theravada Buddhism, Buddhists would not accept his judgment that Buddhism is a magnificent preparation for the final vision but stops short, and that Christ alone leads men and women "through the veil of the temples to the presence of God himself."[25]

The irony of our time is that both Christians and non-Christians are making affirmations of faith by means of the fulfillment motif. When both sides know, or think they know, the ultimate answers, their encounter often degenerates into exchanges of platitudes or "the dialogue of the deaf" *(le dialogue des sourds)*, to use Dominique Pier's phrase. V. G. Sherburn of Rangoon aptly commented that "Christians and Buddhists have talked *at* each other in Burma, but they have not learned how to talk *to* each other as yet."[26] Kraemer, too, feels that a real dialogue among religions is bound to come in the future but that it has not taken place to date. What is implied by such dialogue is not the giving up of the uniqueness of each religion. All genuine religions cannot help witnessing for their own vision of ultimate reality, and inevitably each religion tries to relate its faith to other religions from its own perspective. This means, then, that Christianity, like other religions, must try to be true to its own faith and also to its missionary task. However, Christians must recognize that there is a path that leads them to participation in the religious quest of those outside the Christian community if they take both the universal and particular aspects of religion seriously. In

[21] Max Warren, "General Introduction," in *Sandals at the Mosque* by Kenneth Cragg (New York: Oxford University Press, 1959), pp. 9–10.

[22] *Ibid.*, p. 142.

[23] Cragg, *The Call of the Minaret*, op. cit., p. 246.

[24] *Ibid.*, pp. 256–257.

[25] Appleton, *op. cit.*, p. 139.

[26] Mentioned in a personal conversation with the writer in 1959.

other words, Christians have an obligation to enter into genuine conversation or dialogue with adherents of other faiths, not for the sake of Christian missionary outreach, but for the sake of understanding their own faith. To put it another way, the attempt of Christians to probe into the meaning of their own faith is not possible without a profound understanding of the religious quest and meaning of non-Western and non-Christian peoples and cultures. The same principle applies to adherents of other faiths as well.

It must be made abundantly clear, at this point, that the coming dialogue among great religions will not solve all the religious problems of the world. Such a dialogue is not meant to be a religious counterpart of the Rotary Club. In fact, as Professor Takeuchi remarks, "Where there is an enchanted possibility of mutual appreciation there is also the increased risk of misunderstanding."[27] Admittedly, those who participate in the coming dialogue will learn something from one another, and the chances are that their understanding of their own faiths will undergo changes. Those who feel that they have nothing to learn from others will have very little to contribute to such a dialogue. Though the problems in the coming dialogue are still a matter of conjecture, we can suggest some principles that are prerequisites for those who take this path seriously.

## A Meaningful Encounter

First, those who engage in the dialogue of religions must be willing to follow the principle that each religion is "an autonomous expression of religious thought and experience, which must be viewed in and through itself and its own principles and standards."[28] This does not mean that each religion is so different that it has no possibliity of relating itself to other religions. Morphologically at least, all religions manifest features in common, as expressions of man's experience of the Sacred, however differently the Sacred is apprehended and interpreted. To be sure, each religious faith provides a world of meaning that is self-evident to its adherents, to a degree that outsiders cannot share at the very depth of a tradition other than their own.

However, a dialogue implies that the meaning of the faith of one religious tradition is comprehensible, to a certain extent at any rate, to outsiders; hence there is an implied rejection of a thoroughgoing *Apartheid* principle in the religious domain. This realization demands that doctrines, cults, and institutions, as well as the modes of regulating human behavior and interpersonal relations in a particular religious tradition, must be viewed in their own context. This is easier said than done. For example, it is all too easy for an outsider to miss the "intention" of another religious tradition. Thus, though

---

[27] Quoted by Canon Warren in "General Introduction" to Appleton, *op. cit.*, p. 12.
[28] A. R. Hamilton Gibb, *Mohammedanism, An Historical Survey* (New York: Oxford University Press, 1953), p. vii.

acknowledging the existence of a certain element of world and life affirmation in the *Upanishads* and elsewhere, Schweitzer concludes that "world and life negation occupies a predominant position" in the Indian religious tradition.[29] Many other writers, viewing Hinduism from this perspective, interpret the concept of *māyā* simply as "illusion" and conclude that Hinduism is a faith of world-negating asceticism. However, the "intention" of this concept of *māyā* in the sacred tradition of India, as seen in the *Bhagavad Gita,* is not that men should be urged to renounce the world and history. As Eliade rightly insists, the meaning of *māyā* is a warning against the idolatry of history: "that the state of ignorance and illusion is not that of *living* in History, but of *believing in* its ontological reality."[30] Those who engage in a dialogue cannot help becoming aware of the shortcomings of all religious traditions in carrying out their "intention." This being the case, one must not fall victim to the common temptation of comparing the worst in other religions with the best in one's own. Rather, as Sir Hamilton admonishes us, "while the practice of every religion to some extent falls short of its own highest ideals, the exposition of an outside observer should lay more stress upon the ideals which it strives to realize than upon the failings of our common humanity."[31]

Second, there must be a recognition on the part of the participants in the dialogue that each religion has its own history and that each religion views history from its particular perspective. This means, on the one hand, that Buddhism and Christianity, for instance, are not to be understood solely in terms of the teachings of Gautama and of Jesus, respectively; and, on the other hand, it must be acknowledged that one's mode of apprehending the meaning of history, to say nothing of the history of salvation, is conditioned by a particular religious and cultural tradition to a greater extent than is readily admitted. The recognition of this double-edged principle spares one from making an overeasy comparison of the type that leads to the distorted conclusion that what appears to be similar in different historic contexts or in different religious and cultural traditions has the same meaning. There is no such thing as completely objective historical data, for all data are to some extent interpreted data. This implies, then, that the horizontal dimension of history cannot be understood without reference to the vertical dimension of values in every tradition. This is another way of saying that there is no vantage point from which one can observe all religions objectively. Rather, this concept of dialogue implies participation and an effort to come to some level of mutual understanding through mutual participation. Realization of this fact places special burdens on the scholars of all religious traditions, for

[29] Albert Schweitzer, *Indian Thought and Its Development,* Mrs. Charles E. B. Russell, trans. (New York: Henry Holt & Co., 1936), p. 3.

[30] Eliade, *Myths, Dreams and Mysteries, op. cit.,* p. 242.

[31] Gibb, *op. cit.,* p. vii.

as W. C. Smith succinctly points out, "In addition to their academic standards they may adopt as a new criterion the capacity to construct religious statements that will be intelligible and cogent in at least two different traditions simultaneously."[32]

Third, a dialogue of religions presupposes that the meaning of a religion can be understood only if it is studied as something religious. Kraemer is equally emphatic in stating that those who are involved in religious dialogue "should be themselves sincerely religious and, above all, have a readiness to take a candidly self-critical view of the empirical reality of their own religions."[33] Without such a self-critical attitude, the appreciation of other traditions, and a sensitivity to the religious meaning of religion, his own as well as others, one should not even attempt to engage in the dialogue of religions.

Fourth, in a religious dialogue overemphasis on and preoccupation with doctrines and dogmas should be avoided. A religion is not primarily a system of doctrines, coherently constructed for the purposes of an interfaith debating society; a religion is a "community" with its beliefs, laws, customs, and traditions, penetrating not only what is usually associated with the "religious" domains but also the "profane" realms of communal and individual life. For example, to understand the Sermon on the Mount is not the same thing as understanding Christianity. At the same time, any description of a religion based solely on observable factors is quite misleading; "it would be like the description of a man founded only upon his public behavior and leaving out of account his secret passions, his nostalgias, his existential contradictions and the whole universe of his imagination, which are more essential to him than the ready-made opinions that he utters."[34]

These are but a few examples of the most obvious principles involved in the coming dialogue of the great religions. It must be pointed out that although this article has been addressed primarily to Christians in the West, and thus has placed emphasis upon the dialogue between Christians in the West and the adherents of Eastern religions, this is only one aspect in the religious world situation. We should not overlook the fact that Christians in Asia and Africa have already become deeply involved in the dialogue of religions in an existential way. It is simply a fact that many Asian and African Christians, born and reared in Christian communities in traditionally non-Christian cultures, have experienced and are experiencing serious social, psychological, and religious tensions, especially in the face of the recent reassertions of Eastern religions and the whirlwinds of nationalism. As the Indian Christians admit: "Having never been in the habit of concerning itself

[32] Wilfred Cantwell Smith, *Islam in Modern History* (Princeton, N.J.: Princeton University Press, 1957), p. vi.

[33] Kraemer, *World Cultures and World Religions, op. cit.*, p. 356.

[34] Eliade, *Myths, Dreams and Mysteries, op. cit.*, p. 107.

with contemporary social affairs, and therefore not having been educated to relate its message to contemporary events . . . [the younger church] stands today as an ineffective spectator of the contemporary scene."[35] Happily, the picture is improving today with an increasing number of Asian and African Christians taking an active part in the social and political affairs of their own lands as well as participating in a self-conscious dialogue with fellow nationals of other faiths. Whether or not there is adequate mutual understanding between the Christians in the West and Christians in Asia and Africa is a related but distinctive problem that cannot be discussed here.

In his recent book Kraemer posits the difference between the pragmatic and the fundamental aims of the dialogue among religions. The pragmatic aim, according to him, is the preliminary step, which is that of "removing mutual misunderstandings and serving common human responsibilities." All too often advocates of interreligious cooperation stop here without moving on to work toward a fundamental aim, which is an "open exchange of witness and experience, cross-questioning and listening."[36] Serious adherents of all religions ought to recognize the necessity of working toward this lofty aim. Whether we like it or not, diverse religions will continue to develop according to their own dynamics, crisscrossing on the face of the earth. Facing such a prospect in the future, Christians have yet to learn to probe simultaneously into the meaning of Christian faith while sharing in the religious quests of those outside the Christian community.

There are, no doubt, some Christians who might fear that participation in a dialogue of religions is a betrayal of their Christian commitment to proclaim the gospel. But the proclamation of the gospel is not meant to be a one-way street; it requires both listening and witnessing. Only through constant dialogue and sharing in the serious religious quests of peoples of diverse religious and cultural backgrounds can Christians come closer to the mystery of their own faith, which is rooted both in particularity and universality. Admittedly there is no clear formula or blueprint for the coming dialogue of religions. We can only say at this point, echoing the statement of Gamaliel, made nearly 2,000 years ago, that "if this plan or this undertaking is of men, it will fail; but if it is of God, you will not be able to overthrow them" (Acts 5:38–39).

[35] *The Indian Journal of Theology*, I, 2, November, 1952, p. 48.
[36] Kraemer, *World Culture and World Religions, op. cit.*, p. 356.

PART III: MY MENTORS

# 1

## JOACHIM WACH

Joachim Wach (1989–1955), German-American historian of religions, was born in Chemnitz, Saxony, and died while vacationing in Orselina, Switzerland. A descendent of Moses Mendelssohn, his lineage affected his life and career both positively and negatively. His paternal grandfather, the noted jurist-consult Adolph Wach, married Lily, the daughter of Felix Mendelssohn, the composer. His father, Felix, married Katherine, granddaughter of the composer's brother, Paul. Young Wach was early exposed to music, literature, poetry, and both classical and modern languages. After two years of military service (1916–18), Wach enrolled in the University of Leipzig, but in 1919 and early 1920 he studied with F. Heiler at Munich and with E. Troeltsch at Berlin. He then returned to Leipzig to study the history and philosophy of religion and Oriental languages. For a time he came under the spell of the enigmatic poet Stefan Georg, whose heightened sense of "experience," through which one perceives the multiple threads of the tapestry of life as a transparent whole, fascinated him. He received a Ph.D. in 1922 from Leipzig with a thesis on "The Foundations of a Phenomenology of the Concept of Salvation," published as *Der Erlösungsgedanke und Seine Deutung* (1922).

When Wach started teaching at Leipzig in 1924, the discipline of the history of religions *(Religionswissenschaft)*, still in its infancy, faced serious dangers. On the one side, its right to exist was questioned by those who insisted that whoever knows one religion (i.e., Christianity) knows all religions; on the other, its religio-scientific methodology was challenged by reductionist psychological and social scientific approaches. Thus in his *Habilitation* thesis, *Religionswissenschaft: Prolegomena zu ihrer wissenschaftstheoretischen Grundlegung* (1924), Wach insisted on the integrity and autonomy of the history of religions, liberated from theology and the philosophy of religion. He emphasized that both historical and systematic dimensions are necessary to its task, and he argued that the discipline's goal was "understanding" *(Verstehen)*: "The task of *Religionswissenschaft* is to study and to describe the empirical religions. It seeks descriptive understanding; it is not a normative discipline. When it has understood the historical and systematic aspects of the concrete religious configurations, it has fulfilled its task" (p. 68). His *Religionswissenschaft* is still regarded as a small classic in the field.

Wach's agenda centering on understanding led him to produce a three-volume work on the development of hermeneutics in the nineteenth century (*Das Verstehen* [1926–33]). The first volume traced the hermeneutical theories of such major figures as Schleiermacher, Ast, Wolf, Boeckh, and von Humboldt. The second volume dealt with theological hermeneutics from Schleiermacher to Hofmann, while the third volume examined theories of historical hermeneutics from von Ranke to historical positivism. Understandably, Wach felt it absolutely necessary to establish solid hermeneutical foundations for the history of religions.

Wach was convinced that the history of religions (*Religionswissenschaft*) should not lose its empirical character. He felt that C. P. Tiele and Chantepie de la Saussaye had failed to make an adequate distinction between the history of religions and philosophy of religion. He was critical both of those who started with philosophy and developed science and of those who started with science and moved toward philosophy. In his view, the history of religions lay rather precisely between the two. In this respect he followed Max Scheler, who posited a "concrete phenomenology of religious objects and acts" between a historical study of religions (a positive *Religionswissenschaft*) and the essential phenomenology of religion (*die Wesensphänomenologie der Religion*). According to Scheler, this intermediate discipline aims at the fullest understanding of the intellectual contents of one or more religious forms and the consummate acts in which these intellectual contents have been given. It was Wach's conviction that an inquiry such as Scheler envisaged could be carried out only by employing the religio-scientific method of *Religionswissenschaft*.

Wach's reputation for erudition attracted many students to Leipzig. However, his productive career there came to an abrupt end in April 1935. The government of Saxony, under pressure from the Nazis, terminated Wach's university appointment on the ground of his Jewish ancestry, even though his family had been Christian for four generations. Fortunately, through the intervention of American friends, Wach was invited to teach at Brown University in Providence, Rhode Island, where he stayed until 1945. His adjustment to the new environment was by no means easy. He was especially anxious about his mother, sister, and brother, who were suffering under the Nazi tyranny. From 1946 until his death ten years later, Wach taught the history of religions at the Divinity School of the University of Chicago.

Wach always asserted that the method of the history of religions must be commensurate with its subject matter, i.e., the nature and expressions of the religious experience of humankind as that experience has been unfolded in history. Following his mentor, Rudolf Otto, Wach defined religious experience as the experience of the holy. Throughout his life, he never altered his views on the basic structure of the discipline: its twin tasks (historical and theoretical); the centrality of religious experience and its three-fold expressions (theoretical, practical, and sociological); and the crucial importance of hermeneutics. But Wach emphasized three different methodological accents in three successive phases of this career.

During his "first" phase, Wach was preoccupied with the hermeneutical basis for the descriptive-historical task of the discipline. He was greatly influenced by the philological hermeneutics of August Boeckh, who defined the hermeneutical task as "re-cognizing" that which had previously been "cognized," that is, as articulating what has been recognized in its pristine character, even to the extent of reconstructing in its totality that which does not appear as a whole. Accordingly, Wach insisted that the historian of religions must first try to assimilate that which had been recognized as a religious phenomenon and reproduce it as one's own. Then he must observe and appraise that which has become one's own as an objective something apart from oneself.

During his "second" phase, Wach attempted to develop the systematic dimension of the history of religions by following the model of sociology. In Wach's view, the systematic-sociological task of *Religionswissenschaft* had two main foci: (1) the interrelation of religion and society, which requires both an examination of the sociological roots and functions of myths, doctrines, cults, and associations, *and* research on the sociologically significant function and effect of religion in society; and (2) the study of religious groups. In dealing with religious groups, and especially with the variety of self-interpretations advanced by these groups, Wach employed the typological method. As he stated in his *Sociology of Religion* (1944), he was convinced of the need to develop a closer rapport between *Religionswissenschaft* and other disciplines, especially with the social and human sciences. In this sense, his *Sociology of Religion* was an attempt to bridge "the gulf which still exists between the study of religion and the social sciences" (p. v). Yet the ultimate aim of his sociological-systematic study of religion was "to gain new insights into the relations between the various forms of expression of religious experience and eventually to understand better the various aspects of religious experience itself" (p. 5).

During the "third" phase, Wach's concern for an *integral understanding* of the various aspects of religious experience and its expressions led him to reassess not only the relationship of *Religionswissenschaft* with the social sciences but also its relationship with normative disciplines such as philosophy of religion and the various theologies. After Wach's sojourn to India, where he delivered the Barrows Lectures at various universities in 1952, this concern became more pronounced. It was, in fact, one of the key motifs of his Lectures on the History of Religions sponsored by the American Council of Learned Societies in 1954. Increasingly the vocabulary of "explaining" (*Deuten, Erklären*) came to be used side by side with that of "understanding" (*Verstehen*) in his lectures. He shared his dream of pursuing a new grand synthesis for the study of the human religious experience, a sequel to earlier works such as *Religionswissenschaft* and *Das Verstehen*, with friends during the Seventh Congress of the International Association for the History of Religion, held in Rome in the spring of 1955. But death came that summer and robbed him of this venture.

# BIBLIOGRAPHY

Selected writings of J. Wach: *Der Ehrlösungsgedanke und seine Deutung* (Leipzig, 1922). *Religionswissenschaft: Prolegomena zu ihrer wissenschaftstheoretischen Grundlegung* (Leipzig, 1924). *Das Verstehen: Grundzüge einer Geschichte der hermeneutischen Theorie im 19. Jarhundert* (Tübingen), Vol. I (1926), II (1929), III (1933). *Sociology of Religion* (Chicago, 1944). *Types of Religious Experience, Christian and Non-Christian* (Chicago, 1951).

Posthumous publications of J. Wach: *The Comparative Study of Religions* (New York, 1958)—also available as *Vergleichende Religionsforschung* (Stuttgart, 1962) and *El Estudio Comparado de las Religiones* (Buenos Aires, 1967). *Understanding and Believing* (New York, 1968).

Works on J. Wach: J. M. Kitagawa, "Joachim Wach et la sociologie de la religion," *Archives de Sociologie des Religions*, I, No. 1 (Paris, 1956). Kurt Rudolph, "Joachim Wach," *Bedeutende Gelehret in Leipzig*, Bd. I (Leipzig, 1965). J. M. Kitagawa, "Verstehen and Erlösung: Some Remarks on Joachim Wach's Work," *History of Religions*, Vol. 11, No. 1 (1971). Rainer Flasche, *Die Religionswissenschaft von Joachim Wach* (Berlin, 1978).

# JOACHIM WACH AND SOCIOLOGY OF RELIGION

## INTRODUCTION

With the untimely death of Joachim Wach in August, 1955, we lost one of the most articulate spokesmen of the sociology of religion.

Although he never occupied a chair of sociology of religion as such either in Germany or in the United States, this subject fascinated him early in his life and remained close to his heart until the end. In all fairness to him, however, we cannot label him as a sociologist of religion per se. Rather, his understanding of sociology of religion must be seen as a part of his comprehensive system of *Religionswissenschaft*.

## RELIGIONSWISSENSCHAFT[1]

To Joachim Wach, Religionswissenschaft is an empirical science and not a philosophic discipline. He is critical of C. P. Tiele, who erased the boundaries between Religionswissenschaft and the philosophy of religion.[2] Similarly, Wach feels that Chantepie de la Saussaye equated Religionswissenschaft with the philosophy and history of religion.

Turning to philosophers of religion, Wach notes that his own teacher, Ernst Troeltsch, not only erased the boundaries between philosophy of religion and Religionswissenschaft but was never clear as to the essence and the task of the latter. Troeltsch maintained that one cannot speak of a "universal position, a common universal possession of the science of religion."[3] To him Religionswissenschaft was a normative discipline; for example:

---

[1] I am indebted to Mr. F. Dean Lueking, who made available his translation of part of Wach's *Religionswissenschaft*.

[2] Joachim Wach, *Religionswissenschaft* (Leipzig: J. C. Hinrichs, 1924), p. 119. Wach disapproves Tiele's statement that "ist [die Religionsphilosophie] nichts anderes als Religionswissenschaft im engeren Sinne des Wortes; denn Wissenschaft ist die philosophische Bearbeitung des gesammelten und geordneten, klassifizierten Wissens."

[3] *Ibid.*, p. 121.

Die Religionsphilosophie ist zur Religionswissenschaft geworden. Aus einem Zweige der Metaphysik zu einer selbständigen Untersuchung der Tatsachenwelt des religiosen Bewusstseins, aus der höchsten Generalwissenschaft zu einer neuen Wissenschaft.[4]

After Troeltsch, Wach observed two trends in Religionswissenschaft, one starting from philosophy and developing a science, the other starting from science and leading into philosophy. However, it was Wach's conviction that between these two extremes lies the independent task of Religionswissenschaft.[5]

Among recent religious philosophers, Wach depicts Max Scheler as the single individual who is clear on the distinction between philosophy and Religionswissenschaft. Scheler inserts between a positive Religionswissenschaft (and history of religion) and the essential phenomenology of religion ("die Wesensphänomenologie der Religion") a broader discipline as a unifying theme. He calls it "concrete phenomenology of religious objects and acts" ("konkrete Phänomenologie der Religionsgegenstände und Akte").[6] According to Scheler, this inquiry aims at the fullest understanding of the intellectual contents of one or more religious forms and the consummate acts in which these intellectual contents have been given.[7] Thus Scheler clearly views the religio-scientific task from an expressly religio-scientific viewpoint. It is a task which can be carried out only religio-scientifically with the decisive methodological means of Religionswissenschaft.

Wach maintains that the point of departure of Religionswissenschaft is the historically given religions. While the philosophy of religion proceeds from an a priori deductive method, Religionswissenschaft has no speculative purpose. However, it is not purely descriptive, though description has a basic importance in the discipline. Wach holds that the effort of the inquirer into religion must always be directed toward the *Deutung* of phenomena.[8]

In comparison with other disciplines, Religionswissenschaft has special difficulties with *Bedeutung* because of the nature of its subject matter. For instance, Wach argues that the scholar of the arts deals with a more objective structure in art than the student of religion deals with in manifestations of religion. In the study of the arts there is a greater possibility of agreement between the lower "interpretations," which seek to establish the *Bedeutung* of an expression, and the higher *Verstehen*, which seeks to relate the phenomenon in its total context. In Religionswissenschaft one starts with an inquiry into the meaning of religious phenomena. At this point the philo-

[4] Quoted *ibid.*, p. 123.
[5] *Ibid.*
[6] *Ibid.*, p. 128.
[7] *Ibid.*, p. 129.
[8] *Ibid.*, p. 130.

sophical and metaphysical questions are raised, questions which Religionswissenschaft leads to but is not called upon to deal with.[9]

In the philosophy of religion the idea of religion must come first, and the
phenomenon of religion follows, because its problem concerns the *Wesen* of
religion and its place in a system of values and in the processes of the spirit.
Thus it is always a difficult problem for the philosophy of religion to determine how much of the empirical-historical ought to be appropriated in the
religio-philosophical task. Even when such an appropriation takes place, it
remains an application of philosophy to the date of religion. That which
comes from above cannot do justice to the empirical-historical inquiry which
works from below upward.[10]

The task of Religionswissenschaft is the comprehension, treatment, and
*Deutung* of historical data, and its methods and procedure are conceived
accordingly. In this context its systematic task must rely solely on empirical
data. And both historical and systematic concerns are necessary to Religionswissenschaft in its quest to "understand" religions.[11]

It is Wach's conviction that, while the theologian and the philosopher of
religion are entitled to defend and advocate a definite doctrine, the student
of Religionswissenschaft cannot make value judgments. In principle, at least,
dead religions and historic religions can be treated alike.[12] Subjectively,
however, an empirical inquirer is not free from philosophical presuppositions, and one must be aware of the danger of subjectivism and speculation.[13]

In three ways, according to Wach, the philosophy of religion can help
Religionswissenschaft: (1) by sharpening the methods of the discipline (the
logic of Religionswissenschaft), (2) by articulating the procedure of inquiry
and the philosophic determination of its object, and (3) by the philosophic
ordering of phenomena in the whole of knowledge (historico-philosophy and
the metaphysics of religion). This relationship in no way nullifies the clear
distinction between empirical and philosophical inquiries, however. Also,
Wach disagrees with historians who derive universally valid norms from
empiricism,[14] even though he acknowledges that religio-scientific inquiry
shares the principles and methods derived from universal history.[15]

In the systematic inquiry of Religionswissenschaft, Wach, like Simmel,
utilizes a hermeneutical theory of the "relative a priori," which mediates
between the one who seeks to understand and the object to be understood.[16]

[9] Ibid., pp. 130–31.
[10] *Ibid.*, pp. 131–32.
[11] *Ibid.*, p. 132.
[12] *Ibid.*, p. 133.
[13] *Ibid.*, p. 136.
[14] *Ibid.*, pp. 136–37.
[15] *Ibid.*, p. 138.
[16] *Ibid.*, p. 143.

Wach's assumption is the fact of a universal human nature. Hence the importance of Wach's typological method, which stands between what he calls the *ewig-menschliche* and the historically distinct phenomena.[17]

In short, Wach divides the study of religion into two dimensions—the normative disciplines of theology and philosophy of religion, on the one hand, and the empirical discipline of Religionswissenschaft, on the other. Furthermore, Religionswissenschaft is divided into historical and systematic subdivisions. Under the heading of "historical" come the general history of religion and the history of specific religions. Under the heading of "systematic" comes his typological concern—both historical and psychological types.

One of the most imaginative ideas developed by Wach is the "concept of the classical."[18] Wach believes that the concept of the classical enables one to bridge the gap between the descriptive and the normative aspects of the study of religion. It is, in his own words, a *"relative norm* which does not need to do violence to heterogeneous phenomena from a preconceived point of view."[19] Thus he states:

> What do we mean by "classical" . . . ? Negatively, we do not mean those out of a multitude of phenomena which merely happen to be familiar to us. . . . The phenomena which we designate as classical represent something typical; they convey with regard to religious life and experience more than would be conveyed by an individual instance. We may consider Meister Eckhart, Al Ghazzali, and Shankara as classical mystics because something typically mystical is to be found in their devotion and teaching. However, the notion of the classical does not denote only the representative character which inheres in a phenomenon, but also implies a norm. Out of the multitude of historical personalities, movements and events . . . some are chosen because we deem it possible to ascribe to them potentially an illuminating, edifying, paradigmatic effect by which they may influence our own religious life.[20]

In short, the concept of the classical is Wach's attempt to walk between absolute relativism and a view which starts uncritically with any particular theological or philosophical standpoint. In this attempt, Wach finds affinities with Gerardus van der Leeuw's phenomenology of religion and Mircea Eliade's religious morphology. Wach is convinced of the necessity of the principle of relative objectivity, as exemplified in the concept of the classical,

[17] *Ibid.*, p. 147.
[18] "Der Begriff des Klassischen in der Religionswissenschaft," in *Quantulacumque*, November, 1937; "The Concept of the 'Classical'" in his *Types of Religious Experience* (Chicago: University of Chicago Press, 1951), pp. 48–57.
[19] *Ibid.*, p. 51.
[20] *Ibid.*, pp. 51–52.

"if we want to escape an anarchical subjectivism which would make all 'Wissenschaft' impossible."[21]

At any rate, the impressive superstructure of Wach's Religionswissenschaft is grounded in his three main areas of concern: (1) hermeneutics, (2) inquiry into the nature and expression of religious experience, and (3) sociology of religion.

## HERMENEUTICS

Wach's great concern with hermeneutics is well evidenced in his massive three-volume work, *Das Verstehen: Grundzäge einer Geschichte der hermeneutischen Theorie im 19. Jahrhundert*.[22] Although Wach was not yet thirty years old when he wrote this work, *Das Verstehen* is a brilliant and comprehensive treatment of the main features of the history of hermeneutical theory in the nineteenth century. This fact may also explain why, as Bultmann rightly observes, the study reveals very little of "the position he himself takes up—one which might illuminate history from the critical standpoint."[23]

Following the insight of Dilthey, Wach regarded hermeneutics as a connecting link between philosophy and the *Geisteswissenschaften*. In Volume I of *Das Verstehen*, Wach treats the hermeneutical systems of *(a)* the classical philologists—Wolfs, Ast, Boeckh; *(b)* Schleiermacher; and *(c)* Wilhelm von Humboldt. Wach follows with keen sensitivity the interdependent relationship between the individual scholar's hermeneutical theories and his philosophical orientation. In Volume II the author deals with the theological hermeneutics of fourteen well-known theologians. Following Schleiermacher and others, Wach in his Introduction asks whether there can be such a thing as a general hermeneutics adequate to the understanding of religion, as well as of the arts and literature. Also, if religious scriptures, being *sui generis*, require a special hermeneutics, in what sense can a discipline dealing with Scripture be called a science? Volume III is devoted to the hermeneutical theories of well-known historians, notably Ranke and Droysen.

His interest in hermeneutics was not confined to external rules and principles of interpretation but extended to an "integral understanding" of religion itself. Those of us who were fortunate enough to study under him will remember very well the four cardinal principles of the late master: (1) a comprehensive description of the facts, (2) a historical and sociological explanation, (3) a technical process of classification, and (4) the necessity of psychological understanding.[24]

---

[21] *Ibid.*, p. 57.

[22] Vol. I (1926), Vol. II (1929), Vol. III (1933) (Tübingen: J. C. B. Mohr).

[23] Rudolf Bultmann, *Essays, Philosophical and Theological*, trans. James C. G. Greig (New York: Macmillan Co., 1955), p. 235.

[24] *Ibid.*

Early in his life, Wach struggled with the hermeneutical problems involved in Religionswissenschaft. Following Söderblom, he asked whether it is possible to inquire into a religion from a point outside. Can its *Wesen* be disclosed to one who does not belong to it? Can an Islamic scholar make the Christian religion an object of scientific research? And how far can he hope to judge these strange phenomena?[25]

In *Das Verstehen*, Wach starts with the assumption that there can be no understanding without human corporateness *(Zusammenleben)* and that there is a primordial phenomenon of understanding prior to communication. Thus understanding is a social fact. And no single discipline has a monopoly on the problem of understanding. For instance, philosophy is interested in logic and epistemology; it considers the presuppositions as well as the effects of understanding and its metaphysical foundation. Psychology asks the place of understanding in the over-all life of the psyche. It explores the development of the person in order to relate understanding to the experience of life.[26]

But most important of all is the study of language, because language is the decisive vehicle in direct intercourse between human beings, and it is the most faithful medium of communication extending beyond space and time. Wach goes so far as to say that to understand someone means to understand his or her language. In his understanding of hermeneutics, Wach owes much to Wilhelm von Humboldt, who had profound insights into the nature of speech, the structure of language, its psychological and sociological problems, its typology and function in the development of human civilization.[27] Following Von Humboldt, Wach regarded language as a creative act of the mind. Indeed, speech can be defined as "das bildende Organ des Gedankens," and language is the outward manifestation of the *Geist* of the people who created it. Hence the importance of philology. Furthermore, Wach, following Von Humboldt and Dilthey, insists on the importance of the understanding of individuality.

Significantly, Wach points out that the problem of understanding is a problem of limitations or grades of understanding. In this connection, Wach writes:

> . . . In all understanding . . . two factors combine: the subjective interpretation, which intends to make sure the psychological meaning of an expression by relating it to its author, and the objective interpretation, which takes it as an entity in itself and tries to unfold its meaning. The objective exegesis consists of three different procedures: the technical interpretation, analysis of the material or elements of expression

[25] *Religionswissenschaft*, p. 138.
[26] "Einleitung," *Das Verstehen*, Vol. I.
[27] *Das Verstehen*, I, 227 ff.

. . . the generic interpretation, asking for the genre or GENOS, type or form of work; the historical and sociological interpretation, which attempts to elucidate the socio-historical background and the development of the phenomenon. . . .[28]

. . . In the interpretation of art, interpretation and appreciation or evaluation are closely connected, more so than in the interpretation of laws. And in the interpretation of religion, it is doubtful whether the meaning of a religious message can be understood without any reference to its historic character. That is how the early Protestant theologians conceive of understanding: *Primum perceptio, deinde cogitatio de illa percepta notitia in praxim, tertio velle, quarto perficere.*[29]

Wach advised his students of the four prerequisites for the task of understanding religions other than their own: (1) the most extensive information available, (2) an adequate emotional condition, (3) a right volitional preparation, and (4) personal experience of the holy. Thus the author of *Das Verstehen* holds that the aim of Religionswissenschaft must be an integral comprehension of religion, even though an absolutely objective understanding is not attainable.

## RELIGIOUS EXPERIENCE

Wach holds that the method of Religionswissenschaft must be adequate to its subject matter, the nature and expression of religious experience. Following his master, Rudolf Otto, Wach defines religious experience as experience of the holy.[30] Wach paid warm tribute to this great Marburg scholar in his articles.[31] According to Wach, Otto stood in a philosophical tradition which was concerned with the epistemological question "What constitutes experience?" Otto was convinced of the specific character of religious experience. "To this task he brought, besides a gift for conceptual analysis, an unusual depth and intensity of religious feeling."[32] Wach accepts Otto's starting point:

Religious experience differs from other kinds, moral, aesthetic, etc., though it appears in interrelation with them. It is a specific category

---

[28]"On Understanding," in *The Albert Schweitzer Jubilee Book*, ed. A. A. Roback (Cambridge: SCI-ART Publishers, 1946), p. 137.

[29]*Ibid.*, p. 138.

[30]Rudolf Otto, *The Idea of the Holy*, trans. J. W. Harvey (London: Humphrey Milford, Oxford University Press, 1923).

[31]"Rudolf Otto and the Idea of the Holy," in *Types of Religious Experience*, pp. 209–27; and "Rudolf Otto und der Begriff des Heiligen," in *Deutsche Beiträge*, ed. A Bergsträsser (Chicago: Henry Regnery Co., 1953), pp. 200–217.

[32]*Types of Religious Experience*, p. 218.

("Bewertungs-Kategorie"), for which [Otto] conceived the term *numinous*, derived from the Latin word *numen*. The religious realm is the realm of the Holy. This statement is not, as one might think, tautological. However, it is not the final word. Some mistakes might have been avoided if [Otto] had started . . . with the demonstration of the objective quality of the reality of which we become aware in religious experience.[33]

Unfortunately, Otto's analysis of the feeling of creatureliness and "numinous *Unwert*" caused some critics to believe that his concept of the holy was too psychological. However, Wach feels that Otto's first proposition in *The Idea of the Holy* is grounded in an objective quality of *mysterium*. Tillich makes a similar point when he states:

The phenomenological description of the holy in Rudolf Otto's classical book *The Idea of the Holy* demonstrates the interdependence of the meaning of the holy and the meaning of the divine, and it demonstrates their common dependence on the nature of ultimate concern. When Otto calls the experience of the holy "numinous," he interprets the holy as the presence of the divine. When he points to the mysterious character of holiness, he indicates that the holy transcends the subject-object structure of reality. When he describes the mystery of the holy as *tremendum* and *fascinosum*, he expresses the experience of "the ultimate" in the double sense of that which is the abyss and that which is the ground of man's being. This is not directly asserted in Otto's merely phenomenological analysis, which, by the way, never should be called "psychological." However, it is implicit in his analysis, and it should be made explicit beyond Otto's own intention.[34]

Significantly, Wach observes that Otto in his last two decades struggled with two problems, one of a philosophical, the other of a theological, nature. The first is the question of the relation of religion and ethics. Wach states:

Nearly all critics agree that the weakest point in Otto's analysis of religious experience is his concept of schematism ("Gefühlsgesellung"). The word he took from Kant, but he changes its meaning. Religious experience becomes schematized in entering into relationships with other modes of experience or of judgment. The central religious notions of sin and of redemption, even that of the Holy, have moral associations. A phenomenological demonstration of the foundation of moral values was the aim of the last endeavours of Rudolf Otto.[35]

---

[33] *Ibid.*, p. 219.
[34] Paul Tillich, *Systematic Theology* (Chicago: University of Chicago Press, 1951), I, 215–16.
[35] *Types of Religious Experience*, p. 222.

The second problem which confronted Otto was "What think you of Christ?" This great theological issue was discussed by another of Wach's masters, Ernst Troeltsch, in his *Die Absolutheit des Christentums*, which appeared in the same year (1902) that Otto's *The Life and Work of Jesus* was published. Wach quotes approvingly Otto's statement that "this new religion of Jesus does not grow out of reflection and thinking. . . . It breaks forth from the mysterious depth of the individuality of this religious genius."[36] According-ing to Otto, this religion of Jesus centers on the preaching of the Kingdom of God. This view is also expressed in his book *The Kingdom of God and the Son of Man*, subtitled *An Essay in the History of Religions*. However, Otto's conclusion is that the answer to the question "Was Jesus the Christ sent by God?" can be decided only by faith and thus does not fall within the competence of history.[37] It might be added in this connection that Wach wrestled with the same theological question toward the end of his life.[38]

While Wach was seriously concerned with the analysis of the nature of religious experience, his great contribution was made in the systematic formulation of the expression of religious experience in three main areas—theoretical, practical, and sociological.[39] Methodologically, Wach suggests the following four formal criteria of religious experience:

1. Religious experience is a response to what is experienced as ultimate reality. . . ,

2. Religious experience is a total response of the total being to what is apprehended as ultimate reality. . . .

3. Religious experience is the most intense experience of which man is capable. . . .

4. Religious experience is practical, that is to say it involves an imperative, a commitment which impels man to act. . . .[40]

Concerning the "theoretical expression" of religious experience, Wach states:

A minimum of theoretical expression is always already present in the original religious intuition or experience. This intuition is often repre-sented in symbolic form, which in itself implies elements of thought or doctrine. This first perception is formulated in more or less well-defined and coherent theoretical statements.[41]

---

[36] *Ibid.*, p. 223.

[37] *Ibid.*, p. 225.

[38] Cf. Wach's article. "Radhakrishnan and the Comparative Study of Religion," in *The Philoso-phy of Sarvepalli Radhakrishnan*, ed. P. A. Schilpp (New York: Tudor Pub. Co., 1952), pp. 443–58; "Redeemer of Men," in *Divinity School News* (University of Chicago), November, 1948; and "General Revelation and the Religions of the World," in *Journal of Bible and Religion*, April, 1954.

[39] *Types of Religious Experience*, pp. 38–47.

[40] *Ibid.*, pp. 32–33.

[41] Wach *Sociology of Religion* (Chicago: University of Chicago Press, 1944), p. 19.

The *content* of the intellectual expression of religious experience revolves about three topics of particular importance—God, the world, and man. In other words, theological, cosmological, and anthropological conceptions are continuously being evolved in terms of myth, doctrine, and dogma. . . .[42]

. . . In the original experience, however, or in its primary expression, it is difficult to differentiate between theory and practice, between theology and ethics. . . .[43]

Although Wach rightly holds that what is formulated in the theoretical statement of faith is done in religiously inspired acts, and thus, "in a wider sense, all actions which flow from and are determined by religious experience are to be regarded as practical expression or *cultus*,"[44] he nevertheless narrows his definition of the "practical expression" of religious experience to worship. He says in part:

Religion as such has been defined as worship; experiences of the holy are in all religions expressed in acts of reverence toward the numen whose existence is intellectually defined in terms of myth, doctrine, and dogma. . . . Underhill, to whom we are indebted for some of the most significant contributions to the study of worship, divides these acts into (1) ritual (liturgical pattern), (2) symbols (images), (3) sacraments (visible things and deeds), and (4) sacrifice.[45]

While Wach did not take sides in the controversy as to whether myths are derived from ritual or vice versa, he took a keen interest in the interplay between compulsion and tradition, on the one hand, and the constant drive for individual liberty, on the other hand, in the historic development of the cult.[46]

Among the three areas of the expression of religious experience, Wach was most keenly interested in the "sociological expression," which motivated him to publish *Einführung in die Religionssoziologie*,[47] *Sociology of Religion*,[48] *Religionssoziologie*,[49] and *Sociologie de la religion*.[50] Let us now turn to Wach's understanding of the sociology of religion.

---

[42] *Ibid.*, p. 23.
[43] *Ibid.*, p. 25.
[44] *Ibid.*
[45] *Ibid.*
[46] *Ibid.*, p. 27.
[47] Tübingen, 1931.
[48] Chicago, 1944; London, 1947.
[49] Tübingen, 1951.
[50] Paris, 1955.

## Sociology of Religion

Wach views sociology of religion as one subdivision—albeit an important one—of Religionswissenschaft. It is the offspring of two different scholarly pursuits—the study of society and the study of religion:

> In addition to the problems which the sociology of religion inherits from the two parental disciplines, it has its own peculiar difficulties and tasks. That is to say: sociology of religion shares with the sociology of other activities of man certain problems and, in addition, has its own which are due to the peculiar nature of *religious* experience and its *expression*.[51]

Briefly stated, the task of sociology of religion is the individual, typological, and comparative study of religious grouping, religious fellowship, and religious association.[52] Before the emergence of the sociology of religion as a recognized discipline, a great deal of material was gathered, "particularly in the course of the nineteenth century, and periodically grouped and reviewed from theological and philosophical, psychological and sociological viewpoints."[53] However, until the beginning of the twentieth century there was no sociology of religion as such, with categories with which to organize the vast materials assembled and "its own methodology based on an unbiased examination of the nature of its subject matter."[54]

While Wach acknowledges his indebtedness to sociologists of religion in the United States, Great Britain, the Netherlands, France, and Scandinavian countries, he stands, by temperament and by training, in the German tradition of "die verstehende Soziologie." Among the forerunners of this school were Max Weber, Ernst Troeltsch, Werner Sombart, and Georg Simmel. Wach was personally influenced by Dilthey and says that "the philosophical and historical work of Wilhelm Dilthey, himself averse to establishing an independent sociological discipline, proved to be important systematically and epistemologically."[55] Indeed, House's account of a basic concept of Dilthey can be used to describe Wach's own view:

> Society . . . is a stream of socio-historical happening, constituted through the interaction of individuals. This interaction is infinitely complex and far-reaching; the comprehension of it and the formulation of the

---

[51] Wach, "Sociology of Religion," in G. Gurvitch and W. E. Moore (eds.), *Twentieth Century Sociology* (New York: Philosophical Library, 1945), p. 406.

[52] *Sociology of Religion*, p. 2; also cf. "Religionssoziologie" by J. Wach in Franz König (ed.), *Religionswissenschaftliches Wörterbuch* (Freiburg: Verlag Herder, 1956), pp. 749–52.

[53] *Twentieth Century Sociology*, p. 407.

[54] *Ibid.*

[55] *Ibid.*, p. 412. Wach's devotion to Dilthey is seen in his dedication of *Das Verstehen*, Vol. III, to this master.

laws that govern it are attended with great difficulties. Nevertheless, the
phenomena of social interaction are known to the individual as a participant, by direct inner perception. We stand outside nature and can
comprehend its working only to a limited extent, through the power of
imagination. The world of society, on the contrary, is our own; we
experience the interaction that goes on in it. The other individuals in
society are like me, and I can conceive the workings of their inner life. I
understand (verstehen) the life of society.[56]

Wach shares Richert's conviction that "understanding social phenomena
does not involve adherence to any particular system of values . . . but the
behavior of human beings in society can be understood only with reference
to the meaning of things (Sinn)."[57] From his master, Max Weber, Wach
learned that human conduct alone, unlike all other phenomena, is "understandable" (verständlich), but that "the understandable had fluid limits for
the empirical sciences."[58]

On the whole, however, [human] conduct that can be rationally
interpreted often serves best, in sociological analysis, the purpose of an
"ideal type"; sociology, like history, interprets its data, pragmatically, in
terms of the rationally understandable interconnection of human acts.[59]

Wach considers Weber the first formulator of a systematic sociology of
religion.[60] He laments the fact that only Weber's work in Calvinism is widely
acclaimed, "leaving in the dark the major portion of his contribution to the
systematic sociology of religion."[61] Nevertheless,

Max Weber left much to be done. In his scheme of religions he neglected to include the entire group of so-called "primitive" religions as
well as Mohammedanism and other important faiths. In addition, the
great scholar's understanding of religion was somewhat impaired by his
critical attitude toward it. The categories under which he classified
religious phenomena are not entirely satisfactory, because not enough
attention is paid to their original meaning.

In many respects Weber's work was complemented by the ex-
haustive studies of his friend, Ernst Troeltsch, which were, unfor-

[56] Floyd Nelson House, The Development of Sociology (New York and London: McGraw-Hill
Book Co., 1936), p. 396.

[57] Ibid., p. 397.

[58] Ibid., p. 399.

[59] Ibid.

[60] Cf. Wach's Einführung in die Religionssoziologie (Tübingen: J. C. B. Mohr, 1931), esp. "Max
Weber als Relgionssoziologie" (Appendix).

[61] Sociology of Religion, p. 3.

tunately, limited exclusively to Christianity. . . . It is regrettable that the commendable precedent set by the two German scholars—one a social scientist, the other a theologian and philosopher—in refusing to allow personal metaphysical and other theories and conceptions to interfere with the impersonal task of analyzing and describing social phenomena of religious significance has not always been followed.[62]

Basically, Wach maintains that the methdology of the sociology of religion must be impartial and objective. Certain principles must be observed, however:

> The first requirement is an appreciation of the vast breadth and variety of religious experience. This implies that the basis for all sociological treatments of religion must be found, in the first place, in a wide range of phenomenological and psychological types . . . and, second, in the multifarious historical types of religion experience. In other words, any attempt to limit the scope of our study to one religion . . . is bound to lead to insufficient and perverted conclusions. . . .[63]

> The second requirement . . . is an understanding and appreciation of the nature and significance of religious phenomena. The inquirer must feel an affinity to his subject, and he must be trained to interpret his material with sympathetic understanding.[64]

Elsewhere he asserts that "objectivity does not presuppose indifference."[65] Can there be one sociology of religion, then? Wach thinks so, "though there is a Catholic and a Marxian philosophy of society, there can be only *one* sociology of religion which we may approach from different angles and realize to a different degree but which would use but one set of criteria."[66] This does not imply, however, that sociology of religion must rely on the traditional "comparative method" and seek only analogies of religious concepts, rites, and organization. Rather, "individual features have to be interpreted as part of the configuration they form."[67] The sociologist of religion must follow hermeneutical principles and attempt to understand the *intention* of religious ideas, rites, and forms of organization within their context.[68]

Because each religious group has its own self-interpretation of "intention," the question naturally arises as to how the sociologists of religion can

---

[62] *Ibid.*, pp. 3–4.
[63] *Ibid.*, pp. 8–9.
[64] *Ibid.*, p. 10.
[65] *Twentieth Century Sociology*, p. 418.
[66] *Ibid.*
[67] *Ibid.*, p. 419.
[68] *Ibid.*

deal with a variety of such interpretations. Wach tries to answer this difficult question by relying on Max Scheler's "relationism"[69] (sociology of knowledge) and utilizing the "typological method"[70] (methodology of the sociology of religion). Characteristically, Wach suggests that the student of religion must acquaint himself with the research of the sociologist, while he can supply the sociologist with a working theory of religious life and its manifestations. Cooperatively the student of religion and the student of society can articulate specific categories of the sociology of religion. For this task Wach emphasizes the importance of hermeneutical principles to determine

> first, the actual meaning of any word and concept, sometimes obscured by tradition and age; secondly, the religious implications of terms like sin, repentance, grace, redemption, etc.; thirdly, the concrete, individual "theological" interpretation given to the term in a religious community. . . . There is no hope of grasping the spirit and of understanding the life, symbolism, and behavior of religious group so long as no serious attempt is made to correlate the isolated traits (concepts, rites, customs) observed with a notion of the central experience which produces them.[71]

What are the main tasks of the sociology of religion? In Wach's formulation there are two main areas of study. The first is "the interrelation of religion and society." This may be subdivided into (a) an examination of the sociological roots and functions of myths, doctrines, and dogmas, of cultus and association in general and in particular and (b) research on the sociologically significant function and effect of religion in society.[72]

The second main area of study is "the religious group." Obviously, there are many approaches to the study of religious groups. In the main, however,

> it is the task of general sociology to investigate the sociological significance of the various forms of intellectual and practical expression of religious experience (myth, doctrine; prayer, sacrifice, rites; organization, constitution, authority); it falls to the *specific sociological* study to cover sociologically concrete, historical examples: a Sioux (Omaha) Indian myth, an Egyptian doctrine of the Middle Kingdom. . . . Such studies should be carried out for the smallest conceivable units (one family or clan, a local group at a given period of time, the occasional following of one cult leader, etc.). There is no danger of this task turning

[69] *Ibid.*, p. 420.
[70] *Sociology of Religion*, pp. 9–10.
[71] *Twentieth Century Sociology*, pp. 424–25.
[72] *Ibid.*, pp. 425–28; *Sociology of Religion*, pp. 13–17 and 54–109.

into a historical, psychological, anthropological, theological undertaking, because the sociological viewpoint will be the decisive one.[73]

Ideally, Wach maintains, a systematic sociology of religion must take into account all religious groups, Christian and non-Christian, past and present, in their relation to ethnic divisions, cultures, and societies throughout the world.[74] In the Preface to *Sociology of Religion,* he says:

> The author, a student not of the social sciences but of religion, is convinced of the desirability of bridging the gulf which still exists between the study of religion and the social sciences. . . . He considers his contribution more as a modest attempt at a *synthesis* than an inventory with any claim to completeness.[75]

Similarly, in his conclusion, he goes on to say:

> Yet the fact that this study is limited to a descriptive sociological examination of religious groups need not be interpreted as an implicit admission that the theological, philosophical, and metaphysical problems and questions growing out of such a study of society have to remain unanswerable. They can and most certainly should be answered, but it is not the task of this inquiry to do so. Our purpose has been to present materials . . . to readers of different religious and philosophical convictions and persuasions who are interested in a study of the interrelation of religion and society.[76]

Although cognizant of the importance of the sociological method, Wach does not regard this method as the universal key to an understanding of religious phenomena. He maintains that the inquiry into the social origin, the sociological structure, and the social efficacy of religious groups cannot deal with the questions of meaning, value, and truth which are so essential in religion. While recognizing the limitations of the sociological method, Wach insists that a sociological approach to the study of religious groups can shed much light on how religious experience is expressed in religious fellowship. In this sense, his short study of "Church, Denomination, and Sect"[77] reveals most clearly his method and synthetic perspective.

As stated earlier, Wach was not a sociologist of religion per se. His

[73] *Twentieth Century Sociology,* p. 434.
[74] *Ibid.,* pp. 435–36.
[75] *Sociology of Religion,* p.v (my italics).
[76] *Ibid.,* pp. 374–75.
[77] *Types of Religious Experience,* pp. 187–208.

sociology of religion must be seen in the total context of Religionswissenschaft and in relation to his other concerns, namely, hermeneutics and the inquiry into the nature and expression of religious
experience.

> Through this approach [sociology of religion] we hope not only to
> illustrate the cultural significance of religion but also to gain new insight
> into the relations between the various forms of expression of religious
> experience and eventually to *understand* better the various aspects of
> religious experience itself.[78]

Wach's own words, written in tribute to Albert Schweitzer, are equally
appropriate to Wach himself:

> [He] is a master of understanding. Without a great natural talent—
> or shall we say genius—no amount of acquired skill and knowledge
> would have enabled him to interpret so profoundly and comprehensively
> as he has done personalities of the past, distant periods and peoples,
> great religious documents and works of art, the thoughts, feeling, and
> emotions of human beings. . . . Yet, like all masters of a craft, he never
> relied on the inspiration of his genius but perfected his talents consist-
> ently and methodically by experience and study over a long period of
> years. His understanding, moreover, has proved to be deep and fruitful,
> because it is the result not only of a great and inclusive mind, but of an
> equally great and cultivated heart.[79]

---

[78] *Sociology of Religion*, p. 5 (my italics).
[79] *The Albert Schweitzer Jubilee Book*, p. 133.

# WACH'S MAJOR STUDIES

### 1922

"Grundzüge einer Phänomenologie des Erlösungsgedankens. Unpublished Ph.D. dissertation (April 5, 1922), University of Leipzig. Excerpts were printed in *Jahrbuch der philosophischen Fakultät Leipzig*, II (1922), 14–16.
*Der Erlösungsgedanke und seine Deutung*. ("Veröffentlichungen des Forschungsinstituts für vergleichende Religionsgeschichte an der Universität Leipzig," No. 8.) Leipzig: J. C. Hinrichs.

### 1924

*Religionswissenschaft: Prolegomena zu ihrer wissenschaftstheoretischen Grundlegung*. ("Veröffentlichungen des Forschungsinstituts für vergleichende Religionsgeschichte an der Universität Leipzig," No. 10.) Leipzig: J. C. Hinrichs.

### 1925

*Mahayana, besonders im Hinblick auf das Saddharma-Pundarika-Sutra: Eine Untersuchung über die religionsgeschichtliche Bedeutung eines heiligen Textes der Buddhisten*. ("Untersuchungen zur Geschichte des Buddhismus und verwandter Gebiete," No. 16.) Munich-Neubiberg: Schloss.
*Meister und Jünger: Zwei religionssoziologische Betrachtungen*. Tübingen: J. C. B. Mohr.

### 1926

*Das Verstehen: Grundzüge einer Geschichte der hermeneutischen Theorie im 19. Jahrhundert*, Vol. I: *Die grossen Systeme*. Tübingen: J. C. B. Mohr (P. Siebeck). This volume became the dissertation for the theological Doctor's degree at the University of Heidelberg in 1930.
*Die Typenlehre Trendelenburgs und ihr Einfluss auf Dilthey: Eine philosophie- und geistesgeschichtliche Studie*. ("Philosophie und Geschichte," No. 11.) Tübingen: J. C. B. Mohr.

### 1929

*Das Verstehen: Grundzüge einer Geschichte der hermeneutischen Theorie im 19. Jahrhundert*. Vol. II: *Die theologische Hermeneutik von Schleiermacher bis Hofmann*. Tübingen: J. C. B. Mohr (P. Siebeck).

### 1931

*Einführung in die Religionssoziologie*. Tübingen: J. C. B. Mohr (P. Siebeck).

### 1932

*Typen religiöser Anthropologie: Ein Vergleich der Lehre vom Menschen im religionsphilosophischen Denken von Orient und Okzident*. ("Philosophie und Geschichte," No. 40.) Tübingen: J. C. B. Mohr (P. Siebeck).

1933

*Das Verstehen: Grundzüge einer Geschichte der hermeneutischen Theorie im 19. Jahrhundert.* Vol. III: *Das Verstehen in der Historik von Ranke bis zum Positivismus.* Tübingen: J. C. B. Mohr (P. Siebeck).

1934

*Das Problem des Todes in der Philosophie unserer Zeit.* ("Philosophie und Geschichte," No. 49.) Tübingen: J. C. B. Mohr (P. Siebeck).

1942

*Johann Gustav Droysen.* ("Heimatklänge," Vol. XIX.) Treptow a.d. Rega.

1944

*Sociology of Religion.* Chicago: University of Chicago Press.

1946

*Church, Denomination, and Sect.* Evanston: Seabury-Western Theological Seminary.

1947

*Sociology of Religion.* ("International Library of Sociology and Social Reconstruction.") London: K. Paul, Trench, Trubner.

1955

*Types of Religious Experience: Christian and Non-Christian.* Chicago: The University of Chicago Press.

# 3

## DAISETZ TEITARŌ
## SUZUKI
### (1870–1966)

With the death of Daisetz Teitarō Suzuki on July 12, 1966, the world lost one of its most eminent Buddhist scholars and a great human being. Although his writings made his name widely known in various continents, he never wrote much about himself. Consequently, only those who had personal contacts with him know about his independent and indomitable mind, his passion for and dedication to learning and the search for truth, and his profound love and appreciation of nature and of his fellow human beings. Yet, these were the marks of the man whose life extended nearly a century.

Suzuki was born in the city of Kanazawa only three years after the inauguration of the Meiji regime. It was the period of transition from the feudal to the modern phases in Japanese history, characterized by restlessness and uncertainty caused by the decline of the old order and the penetration of influences of modern Western civilization. He also experienced a personal tragedy in the death of his father when he was five years old. It was during his brief student career at the Junior College at Kanazawa, which had to be terminated for financial reasons, that he came to know a fellow student named Nishida Kitarō (1870–1945), who later became the foremost philosopher in modern Japan. The friendship between Suzuki and Nishida, which lasted until the latter's death, was very close, and they stimulated each other's thinking a great deal. In 1889, Suzuki began to teach English in a local junior high school, but following his mother's death in 1890 he resumed his own education, first at Tōkyō Semmon Gakkō (which subsequently became the Waseda University) and later at Tōkyō Imperial University. He was then studying English literature and was greatly influenced by Emerson, among others. Meanwhile, his own sense of spiritual restlessness led him to the discipline of Zen under the tutelage of two great Zen masters, Imakita Kōsen and Shaku Sōyen. It was Shaku Sōyen and Paul Carus, a freelance philosopher and editor of the *Monist* and the *Open Court*, who were instrumental in bringing Suzuki to the Western world.

In a rare personal reminiscence, which he made as a part of his tribute to Paul Carus, Suzuki stated:

My relationship with Dr. Paul Carus started through my teacher, Shaku Sōyen, who attended the Parliament of Religions in Chicago in 1893. . . . . I had the task of translating the message of my teacher into English, and my friend Natsume Sōseki, a great Japanese novelist, improved my translation. After the Parliament Shaku Sōyen and another Buddhist priest were invited to spend about a week with Dr. Carus and his father-in-law, Mr. E. C. Hegeler, at LaSalle, Illinois. Both Dr. Carus and Mr. Hegeler were great advocates of the religion of science. . . . At any rate, soon after the Parliament, Dr. Carus must have collected all the available books on Buddhism written in English, German, French and other languages. . . . After working nearly two years on *The Gospel of Buddha,* Dr. Carus sent the proof-sheets of the book to Japan for the inspection of Shaku Sōyen. In turn, Shaku Sōyen, who did not read English, turned them over to me, so that I might read them for him in Japanese. This task prompted me to translate *The Gospel of Buddha* into Japanese, and my translation, which was endorsed by Shaku Sōyen, was published not long after the appearance of the English edition. . . . When *The Gospel of Buddha* was finished, Dr. Carus continued to be interested in things Oriental, and he began to translate the *Tao Te Ching* of Lao-tzu. For this task he needed someone who could read Chinese with him, and he wrote to Shaku Sōyen, asking him to recommend someone. That is how I came to LaSalle in 1897 [and] I remained with Dr. Carus for about twelve years in LaSalle, working with the Open Court Publishing Company. [D. T. Suzuki, "Introduction: A Glimpse of Paul Carus," in J. M. Kitagawa (ed.), *Modern Trends in World Religions* (LaSalle: Open Court, 1959), pp. ix–xi.]

Thus began D. T. Suzuki's long and distinguished scholarly career away from his homeland. Energetically he worked on the publications of *Asvaghosha's Discourse on the Awakening of Faith in the Mahayana* (1900); *T'ai-Shang Kan-Ying P'ien: Treatise of the Exalted One on Response and Retribution* (1906); *Yin Chin Way: The Tract of the Quiet Way* (1906; the above three were translated from Chinese); *Sermons of a Buddhist Abbot* (1906; translated from the Japanese manuscript of Shaku Sōyen); *Amida-butsu* (1906; Japanese translation of Paul Carus' *Amitabha*); as well as his own book entitled *Outlines of Mahayana Buddhism* (1907). In 1908, he visited various parts of Europe, partly as a guest of the Swedenborg Society.

Upon his return to Japan in 1909, he was offered a chair of English literature at the Peers' School, Tokyo, and two years later married Beatrice Lane. He was, for a period of several years, under the spell of Emanuel Swedenborg, the eighteenth-century Swedish scientist, philosopher, and theologian. Not only did he visit England in 1911 by the invitation of the Swedenborg Society, but he translated Swedenborg's four major works into

Japanese and wrote a biography of Swedenborg. At the same time, he became interested in the True Pure Land doctrine of Buddhism which, he felt, was a necessary complement to Zen. Also, his continued interest in Chinese philosophy resulted in his publication of *A Brief History of Early Chinese Philosophy* (1914).

In 1921 Ōtani University, Kyōto, persuaded Suzuki to accept a chair, which he kept until his retirement. It was this university which conferred the D. Litt. degree on Suzuki when he was sixty-three years old. In a sense, the 1920's and 1930's were the best years of his life. Although Ōtani University was an institution affiliated with one of the True Pure Land schools, it offered considerable freedom to him. He founded an English journal, *Eastern Buddhist*, which he edited single-handedly for twenty years. He traveled widely in Korea, Manchuria, and China (1934), and Europe and America (1936–37). He wrote numerous articles and books, both in Japanese and English. Among his English publications were: *Essays in Zen Buddhism,* 3 vols. (I, 1927; II, 1933; III, 1934); *Studies in the Lankavatara Sūtra* (1930); *An Index to the Lankavatara Sūtra* (1933); *The Training of the Zen Buddhist Monk* (1934); *An Introduction to Zen Buddhism* (1934); the critical edition of *The Gandavyuha Sūtra* (with H. Idzumi, 1934–36); *Manual of Zen Buddhism* (1935); *Buddhist Philosophy and Its Effects on the Life and Thought of the Japanese People* (1936); *Japanese Buddhism* (1938); and *Zen Buddhism and Its Influence on Japanese Culture* (1938)

Toward the end of the 1930's, however, the national and international situation as well as the failing health of his wife concerned him deeply. In the summer of 1939, Beatrice Lane Suzuki, his companion and co-worker, died at St. Luke's International Medical Center, Tōkyō. The hospital chaplain performed the Anglican rite for her by the request of Suzuki. After the loss of his wife, followed by the outbreak of World War II, he kept rather much to himself, reflecting on the meaning of religion, especially Zen, not only as an intellectual but also as a more practical, soteriological problem. The emphasis on experience as the foundation of religious life runs through all the works (more than twenty in number) written by him in Japanese during the war. In his words:

> To study Zen means to have Zen-experience, for without the experience there is no Zen one can study. But mere experience means to be able to communicate it to others; the experience ceases to be vital unless it is adequately expressible. A dumb experience is not human. To experience is to be self-conscious. Zen-experience is complete only when it is backed by Zen-consciousness and finds expression in one way or another. [D. T. Suzuki, "Interpretation of Zen-Experience," in Charles A. Moore (ed.), *Philosophy—East and West* (Princeton, 1946), p. 110.]

When the war ended, Suzuki, now 75 years of age, established the Matsu-ga-oka ("Pine Hill") Library at Kamakura, where he planned to retire. Little did he realize that another phase of his career was then just beginning! At that time, he wrote most books in Japanese, with the exception of *The Essence of Buddhism* (1947), although he also started an English journal, *Cultural East,* with a collaborator. In 1949, he was made a member of the Japan Academy of Sciences and was decorated with a Cultural Medal by the Japanese government. In the same year, he participated in the second "Philosophy—East and West" conference in Hawaii. In 1950, at the age of 80, Suzuki was invited by the Rockefeller Foundation to deliver lectures at various universities in America, and except for intermittent visits to Europe and Japan he stayed in America, teaching, for the most part, at Columbia University, New York, until 1958. Although much of his time was given to classroom and public lectures, he gave generously of his time to a countless number of scholars, students, and seekers who came to him for counseling and advice. It was the measure of his true greatness that he was willing to take even a very naïve question seriously, though he himself never claimed to be an effective teacher. Rather, he regarded all others as his fellow seekers and fellow students. His own intellectual curiosity was insatiable even at his advanced age. With keen interest, he approached new thoughts. He read and reread the writings of Eckhart, Berdyaev, Tillich, Fromm, and a number of existentialists. He made every effort to write simply and concisely in his later years, as seen in his *The Zen Doctrine of No-Mind* (1949); *A Miscellany on the Shin Teaching of Buddhism* (1949); *Living by Zen* (1949); *Studies in Zen* (1955); *Mysticism: Christian and Buddhist* (1957); *Zen and Japanese Buddhism* (1958); *Zen and Japanese Culture* (1959); and (with Erich Fromm and Richard De Martino) *Zen Buddhism and Psychoanalysis* (1960).

One of the most heart-warming experiences in his later years, according to Suzuki, was his "homecoming" to LaSalle, Illinois—which indeed was his home from 1897 to 1908—as the guest of honor and the featured lecturer at the Paul Carus Memorial Symposium. This was not just another conference to him. He was warmly welcomed by the children of Paul Carus, who were youngsters when young Suzuki knew them. He recalled how he used to accompany Carus in his motorboat up the Illinois River to Starved Rock, and he was gratified to see that the natural beauty of Starved Rock had been preserved so well. He also related that he used to agree with Carus and his father-in-law, Hegeler, that religion must stand on scientific foundations, but added:

> If it were possible for me to talk with them now, I would tell them that my ideas have changed from theirs somewhat. I now think that a religion based solely on science is not enough. There are certain "mythological" elements in every one of us, which cannot be altogether lost in favor of science. This is a conviction I have come to. By this I do not

mean that a religion is not to undergo a rigorous purging of all its "impure" elements. [D. T. Suzuki, "Introduction: A Glimpse of Paul Carus," *op.cit.*, p. x.]

The participants of the Symposium, which incidentally gathered together many historians of religions in America probably for the first time in recent history, were greatly impressed to see Suzuki sitting in the front seat at every session, listening to every discussion with the help of Mihoko Okamura, who by that time was his constant companion and secretary. We also discovered that he had an uncanny sense of catching other persons' ideas even when his hearing aid was not plugged in!

In 1959, he attended the third "Philosophy—East and West" conference at Honolulu. In 1960, after returning from India where he lectured at the request of the Indian government, he remained in Japan where he continued his research and writing. As late as May, 1966, when Jerald C. Brauer of the University of Chicago Divinity School paid him a visit, he found Suzuki perfectly alert, carrying on an animated discussion on sundry subjects. He even recollected vividly for the benefit of Brauer the conversation he had had with William Rainey Harper (1856–1906), the first president of the University of Chicago.

Standing so close to his death, it is still very difficult for us to assess the real significance of D. T. Suzuki's contribution to the world. There is no question that he dedicated his life to scholarship. However, he realized early in his life that knowledge which does not seek higher wisdom is meaningless, and that higher wisdom cannot be attained without compassion. "The Wisdom flows from the Compassion and the Compassion from the Wisdom, for the two are in fact one though from the human point of view we have to speak of it as two" (D. T. Suzuki, *The Essence of Buddhism* [1948], p. 50). This synthesis of wisdom and compassion, which he endeavored to achieve throughout his life, enabled him to see the meaning of humanity transcending ethnic, cultural, national, philosophical, and, above all, religious boundaries.

A few years ago, when the writer bade farewell to him in Kyōto, he said: "Well, at my age I never know how long I will live." And, with a twinkle in his eyes, he added: "But, for me, any day is a good day to go!" This was his way of saying that each day fully lived is worth living for and dying for. Suzuki led such a life!

# 4

## G. VAN DER LEEUW AND "WORSHIP"

Worship, like taboo, is an all-pervasive phenomenon. Because of its nebulous character and the central position it holds in religion, it presents a serious challenge to the student of the History of Religions. The term "worship" is an almost untranslatable English word with many meanings. According to Webster, "worship" as a noun refers to "courtesy or reverence paid to merit or worth," "that which is praiseworthy," "devotion," or "an object of worship." As a transitive verb, it means "to treat with reverence; to respect," "to pay divine honors to; to reverence with supreme respect and veneration; to perform religious exercise in honor of; to adore; venerate;" and as an intransitive verb, it means "to perform acts of homage or adoration, especially to perform religious service." While worship usually signifies the active side of religion, including cult and taboo, sacramental and ascetic rites, devotion, feasts, and penance, it can also refer to inner attitudes, such as fear, love, or awe, which promote the act of worship.

Ironically, the study of worship has been neglected by many historians of religions. Until recently, the "conversation partners" of the History of Religions have been philosophy and theology. Thus, many scholars in the discipline have been influenced by philosophers' and theologians' interests in doctrine, philosophy, and ethics at the expense of praxis-oriented worship. In recent decades, however, historians of religions have turned to sociology, anthropology, psychology, and the other social sciences for new "conversation partners." Understandably, many social scientists are interested in religion primarily as a "cultural system," and as such they are concerned with ritual, myth, and symbol. Yet they exhibit little interest in worship, a phenomenon related, but not identical, to ritual. Thus, many scholars in the History of Religions who are familiar with the social scientific literature tend to elucidate the "cultural meaning" of rituals without concerning themselves with the "religious meaning" of worship. In short, the neglect of serious inquiry into worship as a scholarly subject in the History of Religions reflects the ambiguous understanding of the discipline itself on the part of those who claim that they are engaged in it.

## THE HISTORY OF RELIGIONS

Since there is no adequate English translation for *Religionswissenschaft* (to be more exact, *Allgemeine Religionswissenschaft*), the discipline has come to be known variously in the English-speaking world as the History of Religions, the Science of Religions, Comparative Religion, or the Comparative Study of Religions. Each of these expressions is open to misunderstanding. Friedrich Max Müller (1823–1900) preferred the nomenclature of the Science of Religions; however, it is not clear whether this German-English scholar had in mind the German sense of "Wissenschaft" or the English usage of "science." The second refers more usually to a model of "natural science" characterized by a predictive connotation. The meaning of "science" has remained ambiguous to this day, and in some quarters scholars are still debating whether or not a "science of religion" in the English sense of "science" is possible at all.[1] We detect similar ambiguities in Japanese nomenclature.

*Shūkyō-gaku*, for example, might signify an "area" of religion approached from any one of the various disciplinary perspectives, while *Shūkyō-shi* implies a purely historical study of religions. Although I acknowledge the fact that scholars in British academic circles, for example, continue to use "Comparative Religion,"[2] I will adopt in this article the term "History of Religions" with capital "H" and capital "R"—following the usage of the International Association for the History of Religions (IAHR)—to designate *Religionswissenschaft*, and the term "history of religions" with small "h" and small "r" to indicate the historical dimension of the study of the History of Religions.

Although it is a truism, it is nevertheless worth mentioning that the task of the History of Religions differs from that of the studies of particular religious traditions. Whereas these studies deal with precivilized religions or any one of the contemporary primitive religions, ancient Near Eastern religions, religions of Greece and Rome, Christianity, Islam, Hinduism, Buddhism, and Chinese and Japanese religions, for example, the subject matter of the History of Religions is more inclusive. The task of the History of Religions is to investigate the nature and structure of the religious experience of the human race and its diverse manifestations in history, through the integration and "significant organization" (van der Leeuw) of diverse kinds and forms of religious data. Although many historians of religions are engaged in research in one, two, or three religious traditions, it is humanly impossible for a historian of religions to acquire technical competence in the vast variety of religious traditions; therefore, a historian of religions has to depend on the researches of experts in these various religions.[3]

From the perspective of the History of Religions, all particular religious

[1] Donald Wiebe, "Is a Science of Religion Possible?" *Sciences Religieuses/Studies in Religion*, Vol. 7, No. 1 (1978), pp. 5–17.

[2] See, for example, A. S. Geden, *Comparative Religion*, 2nd ed. (London, 1922); E. M. Pyre, *Comparative Religion* (Newton Abbott, 1972); and Eric J. Sharpe, *Comparative Religion: A History* (London, 1975).

[3] See J. M. Kitagawa, "The Making of a Historian of Religions," *Journal of the American Academy of Religion*, Vol. XXXVI, No. 3 (September 1968), pp. 191–202.

traditions are "parts" of the "whole" religious experience of the human race. As such, all of the diverse religious data (i.e., the "parts") must be seen from the perspective of the whole. Thus, for example, in comparison with the Islamicist, the Indologist, the Buddhologist, and the scholar of Christianity, who view *salāt, pūja, sūtra*-recitation and the Eucharist solely as expressions of Islamic, Hindu, Buddhist, and Christian religious experience, the student of the History of Religions should approach these forms of worship from a larger, more comprehensive perspective, in order to discern the general meaning of worship. This broad perspective in turn will illumine the significance of worship in the life of the *homo religiosus*.

The principle of the "priority of the whole", as well as other methodological procedures of the History of Religions, makes it clear that this discipline is a child of the Enlightenment. Like other *Geisteswissenschaften*, the History of Religions affirms that the task of *Wissenschaft* is to bring into view the whole of all knowable particulars. This task involves the act of recognition, that is, the "re-cognizing" of that which has been previously cognized, and the reconstruction in its totality of that which does not appear as a whole. The History of Religions also inherited Dilthey's concern with the relationship between "experience, expression, and understanding (*Erlebnis, Ausdruck,* and *Verstehen*); the interdependence of self-knowledge and knowledge of other persons; and . . . the understanding of social groups and historical processes," as well as the principle of comparative method.[4] All these concerns have been woven into the hermeneutical framework of the History of Religions.

## HISTORICAL AND SYSTEMATIC DIMENSIONS

One of the most difficult problems for the History of Religions has been to maintain a balance between its historical and its systematic dimensions. The historical dimension has been emphasized by some scholars who see the main task of the History of Religions to be the collection and classification of the empirical historical data of various religious traditions. The meaning of this data, they maintain, is to be judged not by the History of Religions, but by a related but once-removed discipline which they call "comparative religion," conceived as a normative discipline with theological or philosophical concerns.[5] This approach to the study of religions, with its emphasis on the historical dimension to the exclusion of the systematic, appeals to certain philosophers of religion as well as to those whose understanding of religion is informed by normative concerns. In fact, those who are engaged today in inter-religious dialogue (which is often erroneously confused with the com-

---

[4]See H. A. Hodges, "Dilthey, Wilhelm," *Encyclopaedia Britannica* (1971 ed.), Vol. 7, p. 439, and Rudolf A. Makkreel, *Dilthey: Philosopher of the Human Sciences* (Princeton University Press, 1975), pp. 270–71.

[5]This position was clearly stated by Morris J. Jastrow, Jr. in *The Study of Religion* (New York, 1902).

parative study of religions) often turn to the History of Religions to perform precisely this type of descriptive historical task in preparation for their dialogue.

Conversely, there have been historians of religions who have emphasized the systematic dimension of the discipline to the exclusion of the historical. Some of these scholars have engaged in systematic, phenomenological, or morphological analyses of the vast amount of religious data without doing the requisite historical research. Some have even imposed interpretive schema borrowed from other disciplines (e.g., psychology, sociology, anthropology, art history, literature, linguistics) onto the data in the name of inter-disciplinary cooperative inquiry. This practice is a common temptation in today's academia where many social scientists are inquiring about the "cultural meaning" of myths, symbols, and rituals from their own disciplinary perspectives. It goes without saying that the History of Religions must be informed by and learn from other disciplines; but psychological, sociological, ethnological and other inquiries cannot substitute for the systematic task of the History of Religions.

Understandably, many leading figures in the History of Religions have given serious attention to the relationship between the historical and the systematic dimensions of the discipline. One of the most articulate was Raffaele Pettazzoni (1883–1959), whose name is well-known in Japan because he presided at the International Association for the History of Religions during its Congress in Tokyo and Kyoto in 1958. Since he devoted much of his scholarly career to a study of the development of the historical forms of monotheism, Pettazzoni is usually regarded as the spokesman for the historical dimension of the History of Religions.

According to Pettazzoni, the historical task of the discipline is not simply a descriptive, chronological inquiry but an attempt to coordinate religious data, to establish relations, and to group the facts according to those relations in such a way that the events in time correspond to the internal development of religious history. Thus, according to him, the History of Religions

> aims first of all at settling the history of the various religions. Each separate religion is studied . . . in its own environment, in its development within that environment, and in its relations with the other cultural values belonging to the same environment, such as poetry, art, speculative thought, social structure and so on. [The historical dimension of the History of Religions] therefore studies religious data in their historical connections not only with other religious data but also with those which are not religious, whether literary, artistic, social or what not.[6]

[6] See his "History and Phenomenology in the Science of Religion," in R. Pettazzoni, *Essays on the History of Religions*, trans. by H. J. Rose (Leiden, 1954), p. 216.

Pettazzoni believed that the historical inquiry of the History of Religions can only elucidate what happened and how the facts came to be; systematic inquiry is necessary to elucidate the meaning of what happened. Yet he recognized both the importance and the danger of the systematic task, exemplified especially by the so-called "phenomenological study" of religion. On the positive side, he recognized the value of phenomenological study, which delineates the universal structure and meaning of religious phenomena "independently of their position in time and space and of their attachment to a given cultural environment." On the negative side, he recognized the possible danger that occasionally phenomenological understanding runs a risk of "ascribing a like meaning to phenomena whose likeness is nothing but the illusory reflexion from a convergence of developments different in their essence; or, on the contrary, of not grasping the similar meaning of certain phenomena whose real likeness in kind is hidden under an apparent and purely external dissimilarity,"[7] unless the phenomenological inquiry constantly checks its understanding with historical inquiries. In short, Pettazzoni was persuaded that the relationship between historical and systematic inquiries must be reciprocal and mutually interdependent, and that these two dimensions are in reality two interdependent instruments or dimensions of one and the same discipline of *Religionswissenschaft* (History of Religions), "whose composite unity corresponds to that of its subject, that is to say of religion, in its two distinct components, interior experience and exterior manifestations."[8]

We have cited Pettazzoni's view of the reciprocal relationship between the historical and the systematic dimensions of the History of Religions not only because he was one of the towering figures in the discipline in our time but because his view has influenced many contemporary scholars in the discipline. The crucial methodological question, however, remains: how should a scholar bring both the historical and the systematic dimensions of inquiry in the History of Religions together in such a way that the variety of the religious experiences of human history on the one hand, and the basic structure and meaning of religion and religious experience on the other, can be unified within a single coherent framework? In addition to this question, there is the issue of the elements of "foreunderstanding" and "prejudgment" that necessarily belong to any act of interpretation. That is to say, no matter how much a scholar tries to be "neutral" and "objective", all investigation into religious phenomena is inevitably influenced and conditioned by the scholar's cultural background, religious commitment (or the lack of religious commitment), temperament, and unconscious assumptions or conscious philosophical and theological views about the world and human destiny. What is necessary, then, is that these hidden assumptions and presupposi-

---

[7] *Ibid.*, pp. 217–18.
[8] *Ibid.*, p. 218.

tions be made self-conscious and explicit in order that the procedures followed and the meanings uncovered in the work of each scholar can be more adequately critiqued by the larger community.

## G. VAN DER LEEUW'S SCHEMA

Among the various approaches proposed in the History of Religions, the interpretive schema of Gerardus van der Leeuw (1890–1950) is one of the most serious and viable. The so-called phenomenology of religion advocated by van der Leeuw[9] was not derived from Edmund Husserl's philosophical phenomenology, although the former appropriated the Husserlian concepts of intellectual suspense (*epochê*, "holding back" or "bracketing") and *eidetic* vision (visionary or intuitive perception of the essense of a phenomenon). Briefy stated, van der Leeuw divides religious data into (1) the Object of religion: "power"; (2) the Subject of religion: (a) "the sacred man," (b) "the sacred community," (c) "the sacred within man: the soul"; and (3) Object and Subject in their reciprocal operation: (a) outward action and (b) inward action. He makes it clear that "the Subject of religion is, in the sense of religion itself, the Object, and its Object the Subject," and thus the expressions of "the reciprocal relationship between Subject and Object . . . are to be understood only in their figurative meaning." He goes on to say: "Nor must the designation of the actions performed by the subject, as either 'external' or 'internal,' be taken to imply any essential distinctions, for . . . any 'external' activity can always be understood as 'internal.'"[10]

In accordance with these principles, van der Leeuw develops the following schema:

(a) *Outward Action*
Conduct and Celebration
Purification
Sacrifice
The Sacrament
Service
Divination
Sacred Time
Festivals
Sacred Space
The Sacred Word

(b) *Inward Action*
Religious Experience
The Avoidance of God
Servitude to God
The Covenant with God
Friendship with God
Knowledge of God
The Fellowship with God
Being filled with God
Mysticism
The Love of God

[9] One of the most helpful essays on van der Leeuw's approach is "Gerardus van der Leeuw as a Theologian and Phenomenologist," in Jacques Waardenburg, *Reflection on the Study of Religion* (The Hague, 1978), pp. 187–247.
[10] G. van der Leeuw, *Religion in Essence and Manifestation*, tr. by E. J. Turner (London, 1938), p. 339.

The Word of Consecration
Myth
The Story of Salvation: The Word of
  God
The Word of Man: Magical Formula
  and Prayer
Praise, Lallation and Silence
The Written Word
Endowment with Form in Worship
Endowment with Form in Custom

Children of God
Enmity of God
Conversion, Rebirth
Faith
Adoration

These items are not self-evident and independent "things," for according to van der Leeuw's phenomenological principle, a phenomenon is "what appears" in the object-subject reciprocal operation, and thus the essence of the phenomenon is given only in its appearance to *someone*. In its relation to that "someone," the phenomenon appears on three levels: (1) its (relative) concealment; (2) its gradually becoming revealed; and (3) its (relative) transparency.[11]

At this point, van der Leeuw proposes a five-step hermeneutical procedure. First, "what has become manifest," that is, the phenomenon, must be given a name (e.g., sacrifice, sacrament, service, worship, etc.). Second, we must "interpolate" the phenomenon into our own lives, because " 'reality' is always *my* reality, history *my* history." Third, we must apply the principle of *epochê* and thus suspend our own value judgment. Fourth, we must classify what has been observed into types. Fifth, in following these procedures, we find that "the chaotic and obstinate 'reality' thus becomes a manifestation, a revelation. The empirical, ontal, or metaphysical *fact* becomes a *datum*; the object, living speech; rigidity, expression." While van der Leeuw affirms the formula of *Geisteswissenschaften*, namely, "experience, expression, and understanding," he reminds us that "the intangible experience in itself cannot be apprehended nor mastered, but that it manifests something to us, an appearance."[12] Accordingly, his systematic enterprise begins with the phenomenological examinations of "manifestations" *(Erscheinungen)* with the aim of achieving the "understanding" *(Verstehen)*—via *eidetic* vision—of the "essence" *(Wesen)* or *logos* of religion that provides the foundation and framework for the "experience" *(Erlebnis)* of the *homo religiosus*. It should be noted that "experience" to van der Leeuw includes all past experiences of the human race which are grounded in the primal experience. Accordingly, he states that his experience of writing a few lines a moment ago is no nearer to him "than is the experience of the

---

[11] *Ibid.*, p. 671.
[12] *Ibid.*, pp. 674–676.

Egyptian scribe who wrote his note on papyrus four thousand years ago. That he was 'another' than myself makes no difference whatever . . . "[13]

In van der Leeuw's systematic schema, the central *phenomenon* of object-subject reciprocal operation is "worship," which is *manifested* in various forms of "rituals." That is to say, he is interested in rituals as *manifestations* in order to explore the meaning of the *phenomenon* of worship as such, which is the heart of religion. This decision was based in part on his view of man. Like Heidegger's notion of being-in-the-world, van der Leeuw holds that human beings not only exist in the world but also participate in it and care for it. Human beings also do not accept the "givenness" of the world, which appears alien or strange:

> Man therefore . . . does not immediately and straightway find himself at home therein: he experiences a foreignness that can all too readily deepen into dread or even into despair. He does not resignedly assent to the world given to him, but again and again says to it: "No!" This saying "No!" is indeed the very basis of his humanity; it proves that he has spirit . . . In life, then, man sees far more than givenness: he perceives possibility also.[14]

This possibility motivates various human activities, including one's conduct and celebration in relation to the Powerful which reveals itself to him. One has to be alert—as expressed in the word *religio*, which implies alertness—in order to seize upon the possibilities concealed in the world by shaping life into a fixed course of activity.

Van der Leeuw illustrates how man may act *vis-à-vis* Power with his story of a child from a strict pietist family. This child enjoyed pushing a barrow around, but was told that such a meaningless act of pleasure was sinful. Then the child imagined that the infant Jesus was in the barrow, so that the childish conscience was pacified by the thought of pushing the barrow not for his own little pleasure but for the enjoyment of the infant Jesus. Thus, according to van der Leeuw:

> from the game a rite has arisen . . . For a game bound by rules is, as such, always a rite, conduct, dominance; and the rite gained control over life, and drew power therefrom, long before thought could do so: "man was a ritualist before he could speak." The rite also discovered the way of worship far in anticipation of thought. Like the child, then, man pushes his barrow, but his sense of alienation causes him to apply some fixed standard to his activities, so that dread may be silenced and he may feel

[13] *Ibid.*, pp. 671–672.
[14] *Ibid.*, pp. 339–340.

at home therein. Then he places his god in it: and now he pushes Power itself! But he can also pause, and kneel before the God in the cart of his life.[15]

Of course, this is not a historical explanation as to how worship came about but an account based on van der Leeuw's view of human nature. To him, as Waardenburg astutely points out, phenomenological experience and understanding were matters of a "preeminently human attitude, a human characteristic which has been given neither to God nor to the animals. Consequently, van der Leeuw saw phenomenology as not only a scholarly method . . . but in the first place as a way of existing, being, and knowing that is given with human life as such."[16] Also, according to Waardenburg, van der Leeuw tried to locate the religious substrata—or the religious possibility inherently given to humankind, e.g., the structure of participation, mythical thinking and magical behavior—in psychic and cultural life, as exemplified by the prominent place he assigned to *mana* and Power in religion. "*Mana* indicates the experienced reality of power, and the concept of Power as a constituent element of religious experience, with a (later) sacramental background, is the fundamental category"[17] in van der Leeuw's schema, which follows the ascending movement of meaning structures.

In his view of the ascending movement, the object-subject reciprocal operation, which begins with the simple perception and negotiation with *mana*, culminates in worship, which "assembles together the scattered and sporadic feelings, and transforms an indefinite religious sentiment into an individual, and at the same time collective religious consciousness."[18] He goes on to say:

> In worship, therefore, man seeks to give form not only to individual and to collective experience, not only to the conduct of himself and his community, but also to the activities of Power, indeed to its very existence. In worship the being of man and the Being of his God are comprehended within one actual "being-thus . . . In worship, the form of humanity becomes defined, while that of God becomes the content of faith, and the form of their reciprocal relation experienced in action."[19]

In other words, worship is the very link between Subject (human person) and Object (Power), between human community and cosmos, and between a human being and other human beings. Worship not only defines

[15] *Ibid.*, p. 340.
[16] Waardenburg, *op. cit.*, p. 224.
[17] *Ibid.*, p. 221.
[18] Statement by R. Will, cited in van der Leeuw, *op. cit.*, p. 447.
[19] *Ibid.*, p. 447.

the nature of relationships but also defines reality itself in its various levels, including the level of ultimate reality. In short, worship reflects an interconnection of meaning (structure) or reality significantly organized.

Lastly, worship is the link between two dimensions of religion in van der Leeuw's schema, namely, "religion as experience," which can be studied phenomenologically, and "religion as revelation," which is incomprehensible and thus can only be studied theologically. The distinction between these two dimensions of religion enables, or rather requires, van der Leeuw to pursue both the phenomenological study of religion and the study of theology simultaneously. For the same reason, he never claimed that his phenomenological study was empirical, because to him empirical research is needed only to control and correct what has been understood phenomenologically.[20] Other scholars may disagree with him on this point, but on his part van der Leeuw has made his methodological assumptions and theological views explicit throughout his systematic endeavor.

Whether we agree with him or not, and I am one of those who takes issue with him on several key points, all of us are greatly indebted to van der Leeuw for his grand vision and academic integrity as well as for reminding us of the importance of worship as a serious scholarly subject for the History of Religions. He has set a high standard for all of us to follow.

[20] See Waardenburg, *op. cit.*, p. 232.

# 5

## TILLICH, KRAEMER, AND THE
## ENCOUNTER OF RELIGIONS

In 1960 two prominent Western Christian scholars visited Japan—Paul Tillich in the spring, and Hendrik Kraemer in the autumn. Their visits aroused unusual interest among Japanese scholars and religious leaders—certainly among Christians, as might be expected, but also among Buddhists and Shintoists as well, Although Tillich and Kraemer had never visited the Far East before, some of their published works had been widely read in Japan. Understandably, both the visitors and their Japanese hosts appreciated the opportunity to learn from each other through their personal encounter.[1]

What fascinated the Japanese scholars were certain similarities and sharp contrasts that they found in the two visitors. Tillich (1886–1965) and Kraemer (1888–1965) were contemporaries. Both were products of European culture, and both had experienced the devastation of World War I with the subsequent erosion of the foundation of the religious, cultural, social, and political fabric of Europe. Moreover, as committed Christians both were concerned with the encounters among various religions, more particularly between Christian and Eastern religious traditions.

On the other hand, their differences were striking. Tillich had always lived, according to his own account, on the "boundaries," between philosophy and theology, between religious and social and political issues, between religion and culture, and between his native Germany and America. Also, while he kept in close touch with people in various circles, his base of operation was always the academy. Even his connection with the Christian church was primarily through his theological reflections. In reference to Buddhism, he was particularly intrigued by the mental and spiritual training of Zen, which aims at "enlightenment." In sharp contrast to Tillich, Kraemer, who had been trained in Oriental languages and the history of religions, was an advocate of "biblical realism." He had served as an adviser to the Dutch Bible Society in Java, as professor of the history of religions at

---

[1] See Robert W. Wood, "Tillich Encounters Japan," and L. Newton Thurber, "Hendrik Kraemer and the Christian Encounter with Japanese Buddhism," *Japanese Religions* 2 (May 1961); 48–71, 76–90.

Leiden, and as Director of the Ecumenical Institute of the World Council of Churches in Switzerland. Also, while earlier he had been interested in Islamic mysticism in Java, he became deeply interested in the "salvation" experience of the Pure Land School of Buddhism.

It is not surprising, therefore, that despite Tillich's and Kraemer's professed keen interest in a meaningful "dialogue" between Christian and Eastern religious traditions, their perspectives had very little in common. More important, perhaps, for our present discussion is the fact that their respective approaches to Eastern religions may be regarded as two important options that are still viable today for the enterprise called a "theological history of religion," or a theological approach to comparative religions.

## Encounters Among Religions

Such designations as the theological history of religion and a theological approach to comparative religions are new, but their underlying concerns are very old. It is significant that this age-old question regarding the meaning of the encounter among religions has become a serious intellectual and existential problem in our time, especially among Christians.

As far as we can ascertain, various religious thinkers and philosophers throughout history have attempted to resolve the mystery regarding the division of humanity into various religious, ethnic, linguistic, and cultural groups. For example, Zoroastrianism affirmed the eventual resolution of the chaos and division of humankind in Ahura Mazda's eschatological war against the forces of evil and urged men and women to join this war in order to establish on earth the righteous and peaceful Kingdom of God. Ancient Hinduism taught the appearance of a just and virtuous world monarch, the Cakravartin, whose coming would be marked by the end of strife and division of the world. And, like the Cakravartin, the Buddha also was believed to turn his wheel—the Buddhist *dharma*— to unify the whole universe. Equally significant was the ancient Chinese vision of the grand commonwealth. "From the age of Confucius," says Fung Yu-lan, "the Chinese people in general and their political thinkers in particular began to think about political matters in terms of the [whole] world."[2]

In the West, the Greeks envisaged the unification of peoples in the "oikoumene" by means of Hellenistic civilization and Greek language. While Alexander's dream to establish a universal empire was doomed to failure, Oriental-Hellenistic culture, consolidated further by Rome, remained for centuries the broad framework for cultural development in the Mediterranean world. Meanwhile, the once-tribal religion of the Hebrew community in the Middle East developed an ethical universalism under the influence of the prophetic movement, whereby the God of Israel came to be conceived of

---

[2] Fung Yu-lan, *A Short History of Chinese Philosophy*, ed. Derk Bodde (New York: Macmillan, 1950), 181.

as the divine ruler of all humankind.[3] While Christianity and Islam developed within the orbit of Oriental-Hellenistic culture, both inherited their beliefs of the unity of humanity from the Hebrew example. Accordingly, the early Christian community considered itself the new Israel; Pentecost signified the reversal of the Tower of Babel in that the scattered and divided human race was now reunited, potentially at least, as the one true humanity. Similarly, Islam, which accepted the human division to be the inscrutable divine decree, nevertheless affirmed that all those who surrender to Allah are to be included in the universal congregation *(Ummah)* of Allah.[4]

In Asia neither the Hindus with their cosmic orientation nor the Chinese with their universal outlook propagated their beliefs outside their respective spheres of influence. However, the Buddhist King Asoka in the third century B.C. initiated an energetic missionary expansion beyond his empire, whereby the Buddhist community came to be understood as potentially a worldwide community, embracing peoples and nations outside India, uniting all humanity by means of Buddhist *dharma*.

It is interesting to note that Christianity, which also emerged as a missionary religion, had to come to terms with the traditions of pre- and non-Christian religions and philosophies in the West—just as Buddhism had to do earlier *vis à vis* other traditions in the East. In this task, some of the early Christian apologists affirmed the truths of other religions and philosophies as the *praeparatio evangelica*—a natural revelation by the *Logos spermatikos*—which were to be fulfilled by Jesus Christ, the *Logos-incarnate*. The appropriation of the Logos doctrine and the fulfillment theory enabled apologists to relate *Heilsgeschichte* directly to the general history of religions of humankind. Meanwhile, the Christian community gradually developed canons, orders, and creeds to consolidate the faith and practice of the community.

The emergence of Islam in the seventh century A.D. successfully confined the core of Christianity to Europe until the sixteenth century. Confronted by Islam's claim to be the fulfillment of all previous revelations, Christian dogmatists responded by portraying Islam as the "fulfillment" of the coming of the false prophet prophesied in the Johannine apocalypse. Although European culture benefited greatly from the Muslims, the attitude of Christendom toward Islam became fiercely antagonistic, as exemplified by the bloody Crusades. Moreover, subsequent religious developments in Europe—the Reformation, the CounterReformation, and the rise of Pietism—added more and more fuel to Christians' prejudice against Islam as well as other non-Christian religions and cultures.[5] A remarkable exception in

[3] See R. G. Collingwood, *The Idea of History* (Oxford: Clarendon Press, 1946), 17.

[4] See "Umma or Ummah," *Shorter Encylcopaedia of Islam* (Leiden: E. J. Brill, 1953), 603–4.

[5] See J. M. Kitagawa, ed., *Understanding Modern China* (Chicago: Quadrangle Books, 1969), 24–26.

Christendom was Nicholas of Cusa, a cardinal and a "renaissance man," who affirmed the existence of diversity of religions as a part of the divine plan, while acknowledging the Christian revelation as the fullest expression of divine truth and love. His irenic view of non-Christian religions, however, was not shared by the official church.[6]

The phenomenal colonial expansion of Iberian Catholic powers during the sixteenth and seventeenth centuries was marked by blatant economic exploitation mixed with fanatic motivation for religious conquest. These were residues of the Iberian Christians' campaign against Muslims. Meanwhile, in Europe the foundation of the Corpus Christianum was undermined by the Renaissance, which now equated the development of civilization with *Heilsgeschichte*, thus making in effect "civilization" a pseudoreligion of secularized salvation.[7] Many Europeans came to regard themselves as a new chosen people in the sense of being the inventors and transmitters of true civilization, which was to be propagated for the edification of the "backward" and "unenlightened" people in the non-Western world. This motivation was implicit in the second wave of Western colonial expansion in the eighteenth and nineteenth centuries.

It should be noted that the Pietists rejected this secularized view of the human being and of civilization. Thus, the initial ethos of Christian foreign missions, inaugurated by the continental Pietists and British evangelicals to "save the poor heathens from damnation," ran counter to the secular spirit of colonial policies. During the nineteenth century, however, Christian missions in Asia and Africa unwittingly cooperated with European colonialism, whereby Christianity was propagated as one—albeit an important one—of the constituents of Western civilization. While missionaries contributed much to education and philanthropy in the non-Western world, they viewed non-Christian religions, for the most part, as unenlightened paganism.

Ironically, while Christian missionaries were trying to save souls from pagan religions, English Deists and philosophers of the Enlightenment discovered the religious and ethical values of non-Western religions. For example, Voltaire praised China as the bearer of the true religion of Nature: "Worship God and praise justice—this is the sole religion of the Chinese literati. . . . O Thomas Aquinas, Scotus, Bonaventura, Francis, Dominic, Luther, Calvin, Canons of Westminster, have you anything better?"[8] The rejection of the Christian claim to be the sole bearer of the highest and absolute religious truth by the European intellectuals led to a new understanding of *Heilsgeschichte*, articulated by German idealism, that the whole

[6] Ernst Benz, "The Theological Meaning of the History of Religions," *The Journal of Religion* 41, no. 1 (January 1961): 7–8.

[7] William S. Haas, *The Destiny of Mind—East and West* (London: Faber and Faber, 1956), 298–305.

[8] Quoted in Arthur E. Christy, ed., *The Asian Legacy and American Life* (New York: The John Day Co., 1942), 22.

history of humankind was the evolutionary history of the self-realization of natural religion. "Here the idea of the absoluteness of Christianity was retained; however, it did not stand over against the remaining religions in the sense of negation but in the sense of crowning of a historical, developmental process."[9]

Significantly, the enormous body of data concerning the languages, customs, and religions of non-Western peoples made available to Europeans during the nineteenth century through the accounts of travelers, colonial officials, and Christian missionaries were devoured by the scholars of languages, ethnology, arts, philosophy, and religions. E. B. Tylor, James G. Frazer, E. Burnouf, F. Max Müller, Andrew Lang, E. Durkheim, and James Legge, to name only a few, pioneered the scholarly studies of primitive and Eastern religions and philosophies. Following the establishment of the first chair of the history of religions in Geneva in 1873, similar chairs were instituted in other European universities. And the first full-scale Congress of the History of Religions was held in 1900 in Paris.

It is to be noted, as G. van der Leeuw suggested, that the scholarly study of religions came under the impact of three phases of romanticism: first, romantic philosophy, which regarded diverse religious manifestations as symbols of a primordial natural religion; second, romantic philology, which, while rejecting unfettered speculation, still viewed religion as "the expression of a universal mode of human thinking"; and third, romantic positivism, which sought "to comprehend the objective appearances of religion in the light of subjective processes."[10] Understandably, because of their philosophical assumptions—whether rationalistic or romantic—pioneers of *Religionswissenschaft* dealt with religio-scientific data "philosophically." Even today the distinction between the history of religions and the philosophy of religion is not clearly understood in some quarters.

This is not the occasion to delineate the complex development in our century of the history of religions *(Religionswissenschaft)* as a nonspeculative religio-scientific discipline that deals with religious phenomena. It is pertinent, however, to point out that both the method and the data of the history of religions have come to be appropriated by other disciplines for their respective purposes, especially by Christian missionary thinkers and theologians who are concerned with the relationship of Christianity and non-Christian religions.

## MISSIONSWISSENSCHAFT AND THE ENCOUNTER OF RELIGIONS

Before the emergence of modern *Missionswissenschaft*, medieval Christendom felt no need for scholarly studies of missions or non-Christian

[9] Benz, "The Theological Meaning of the History of Religions," 10.

[10] G. van der Leeuw, *Religion in Essence and Manifestations*, trans. J. E. Turner (London: George Allen and Unwin, 1938), 691–94.

religions. The Roman Catholic dogma, *extra ecclesiam nulla salus*, explicated in the 1442 Council of Florence, was followed almost verbatim by Luther's statement that those who are outside Christianity, "be they heathens, Turks, Jews or false Christians," will remain in "eternal wrath and damnation."[11] Calvin, who felt that "the kingdom of God is neither to be advanced nor maintained by the industry of man,"[12] was not interested in missions or in non-Christian religions. It is commonly agreed that the father of *Missionswissenschaft* was Gustav Warneck (1834–1910) of Halle. Since his time many scholars, especially the members of the *Deutsche Gesellschaft für Missionswissenschaft*, have made valuable contributions to the study of non-Christian religions as a part of the agenda for their discipline.

The first international program of the scholarly study of missions was undertaken for the 1910 World Missionary Conference at Edinburgh. At the 1928 Jerusalem Conference of the International Missionary Council, which marked a second landmark of missiology, no other than Hendrik Kraemer insisted that while the missionary ought to proclaim the Gospel, "he must have an intense longing to discover the spiritual values of other religions." The council in the end concluded that "we rightly study other religions in order to approach men wisely, yet at the last we speak as men to men, inviting them to share with us the pardon and the life that we have found in Christ."[13] Thus, in effect the conference accepted the data and methods of the history of religions in their study of non-Christian religions for the service of *Missionswissenschaft*. The conference also expressed a native optimism about the future of Christian missions based on the "fulfillment" theory.

In 1931 the so-called "Laymen's Inquiry," comprised of laity from seven American Protestant denominations, evaluated missionary work in India, Burma, China, and Japan. Although this unofficial inquiry was not undertaken by scholars of missions, the prominence of the group headed by a Harvard philosopher, William Ernest Hocking, gave a special aura to its findings, entitled *Re-thinking Missions*. Among other important observations and recommendations, the findings called for a reappraisal of the relationship between Christianity and Eastern religions, since both were threatened by the spread of secularism, and also because of changes that were taking place in non-Christian religions. Thus, *Re-Thinking Missions* recommended a "creative relationship" that asked missionaries first to gain a knowledge and understanding of other religions, and "then to recognize and associate itself with whatever kindred elements there are in them." Moreover, the mission-

---

[11] See *Large Catechism*.

[12] Charles H. Robinson, *History of Christian Missions* (New York: Charles Scribner's Sons, 1915), 42–43.

[13] See the proceedings of the Jerusalem Conference of the I.M.C., vol. 1, *The Christian Life and Message in Relation to Non-Christian Systems of Thought and Life* (New York and London: I.M.C., 1928), 284, 410–12.

ary aim was defined as follows: "to seek with people of other lands a true knowledge and love of God, expressing in life and word what we have learned through Jesus Christ, and endeavoring to give effect to his spirit in the life of the world."[14]

Not unexpectedly, a strong rebuttal against *Re-Thinking Missions* came from Hendrik Kraemer, who wrote *The Christian Message in a Non-Christian World* for the 1938 World Missionary Conference held at Tambaram, India. The main thesis of the book appeared in a later article, "Continuity or Discontinuity," in which he stated: "the Christian revelation as the record of God's self-disclosing revelation in Jesus Christ is absolutely *sui generis*." As such, Kraemer saw only discontinuity between the world of spiritual realities defined by "biblical realism" and the whole range of other religious experiences and human endeavors. He insisted that the sole standard of reference for religion was revelation in Christ, and not a general idea about the essence of religion.[15] Accordingly, he felt that *Re-Thinking Missions* confused apostolic obligations with the noble human desire to respect other religions, which amounted to "the subversion of Christianity into a noble this-worldly idealism." Kraemer was convinced that the relation between Christianity and other religions was one of the gravest problems that "the Christian Church all over the world and the missionary cause have to face at the present time." As a trained historian of religions Kraemer acknowledged the legitimacy of the scientific study of religions. However, as a scholar of *Missionswissenschaft*, he resorted finally to a theological "dialectic" approach that was based on the affirmation that the revelation in Christ was the only way to acquire a true insight into the meaning of all human existence.[16]

Unfortunately, many of the serious and important issues raised at the Tambaram conference regarding the relation between Christian and other religions were not followed up during World War II; and when some of the same concerns were raised again after the war, the situation had changed radically.

## EASTERN RELIGIONS SINCE WORLD WAR II

Historians tell us that the decline of Asia during the past four centuries was caused initially by an internal cultural erosion, which in turn encouraged

[14] William Ernest Hocking, *Re-Thinking Missions: A Laymen's Inquiry After One Hundred Years* (New York: Harper & Brothers, 1932), 33, 59. Parenthetically, Hocking further delineated his own philosophical reflections on the future of relations between religions in his *Living Religions and a World Faith* (New York: Macmillan, 1940); and *The Coming World Civilization* (New York: Harper & Brothers, 1956). His famous theory was the "Way of Reconception."

[15] Hendrik Kraemer, *The Christian Message in a Non-Christian World* (London: The Edinburgh House, 1938); idem, "Continuity or Discontinuity," *The Authority of the Faith*, vol. 1 (New York and London: I.M.C., 1939), 1, 2, 21.

[16] Kraemer, *The Christian Message*, 45, 48, 102, 146.

commercial, political, and cultural encroachment by the West. Thus, Asian peoples' historic confidence in the autonomy and superiority of their cultures was rudely shattered by the technologically superior Western civilization, which was presented as a pseudoreligion of secularized salvation. In the course of time there developed a core of Asian intelligentsia with westernized education who endeavored to reform the stagnant Asian cultures and societies of their time. Some of them accepted the secular values of modern Western civilization, while others embraced Christianity or Marxism, although in their minds they were passionately Asians.

With this historical background in mind, we can appreciate the fact that the end of World War II signified to Asians not only the end of Western colonial imperialism but more basically a momentous redefinition of their destiny, their sense of dignity, value, and freedom. Confronted by such an enormous burden, Asians have been trying to come to terms with such issues as modernity and tradition, secularity and spirituality, liberation and freedom. We must understand recent religious developments in Asia in this broader context.

Already before the war, the "Laymen's Inquiry" team observed that contemporary Hinduism, Islam, and Buddhism were not those of a hundred years ago.[17] Hendrik Kraemer, too, noted that there was "along with the general national revitalization, a movement towards a heightening of religious group consciousness, consolidation and concerted opposition to Christian missions."[18]

After the war many religious leaders cooperated with political leaders in rebuilding a spiritual fabric for a new Asia with the firm conviction that their cultural tradition had resources that were no less remarkable than those of the West. Also noteworthy was the fact that, like their Christian counterparts, theoreticians of Eastern religions advocated their own versions of "fulfillment" theories by appropriating the data and methods of the history of religions.

Sarvepalli Radhakrishnan, for example, felt that studies in comparative religion reveal not only the bewildering variety of religious beliefs and practices but also show common features, such as ideas about incarnation, miracles, and festivals among different religions. To him, Christianity is the continuation of the perennial religion of the human race. Seen from his Hindu theological perspective, Gautama the Buddha as well as Jesus the Christ were "God-men," or the manifestations of the Spirit through human media. As such, they are the precursors of the truly human: "The nature of man receives its fulfillment in them. They are our elder brothers."[19]

---

[17] Hocking, *Re-Thinking Missions*, 32.
[18] Kraemer, *The Christian Message*, 46.
[19] Sarvepalli Radhakrishnan, *Recovery of Faith* (New York: Harper & Brothers, 1955), 13, 179.

Similarly, D. T. Suzuki tried to show how Jewish and Christian insights could be "fulfilled" in Zen.

During the immediate postwar era, leaders of Eastern religions expressed a jubilant optimism that their faiths were the way of the future not only in Asia but also in the materialistic West. For example, U Nu during his tenure as prime minister attempted to establish in Burma an earthly Nirvana, a Buddhist socialist state, with a firm confidence that it would permit "a maximum observance of the Dhamma to the point of perfection, making possible man's sublimation into future Buddhahood."[21] Similar endeavors elsewhere sought to actualize historic religious ideals in concrete programs. Pakistan, for example, was created in order to enable Muslims "to order their lives in the individual and collective spheres in accord with the teachings and requirements of Islam. . . ."[22] India, too, tried to synthesize its time-honored sacramental view of life and the ideal of socialist commonwealth by establishing a modern "secular" state in which religious freedom and the equality of opportunity were to be assured. Notwithstanding the apparent failures of these schemes, the fact that such attempts were seriously made was a matter of great significance.

By far the most serious challenge to postwar religions—including Roman Catholicism in the Philippines and other indigenous Christian groups elsewhere called the "younger churches"—came from communism. The emergence of communist states in China, North Korea, Vietnam, and more recently in Kampuchea, Laos, and Afghanistan confirms Hans Morgenthau's notion that Asian communism—unlike European communism, which was initiated by Soviet power—developed out of social revolution.[23] This does not mean that communism occasioned the social revolution in Asia. "What the communists claim to do is to explain the revolution and to have the right of leading it to a successful end." Equally important is the pseudoreligious appeal of communism in Asia where "the impact of the West has destroyed old religions and family and village loyalties, and robbed life of its spiritual comfort and purpose. People [now] ask a new code, a new certainty, a new religion, and some of them find it in communism."[24] In the course of time various modes of relationship, from hostility to submission, developed between religions and communism. In this respect, the common weakness of Eastern religions thus far seems to have been their failure to articulate to today's Asians the visions of their religious ends—for which the establish-

[20] See D. T. Suzuki, *Living by Zen* (New York: Rider, 1950), especially p. 13.

[21] E. Sarkisyanz, *Buddhist Backgrounds of the Burmese Revolution* (The Hague: Martinus Nijhoff, 1965), 225.

[22] Stated in the "Objective Resolution" (1949).

[23] Hans J. Morgenthau, *In Defense of the National Interest* (New York: Knopf, 1951), 201–2.

[24] P. D. Devanandan and M. M. Thomas, eds., *Communism and the Social Revolution in India* (Calcutta: Y.M.C.A. Publishing House, 1953), 7; W. MacMahon Ball, *Nationalism and Communism in East Asia* (Melbourne: Melbourne University Press, 1952), 198.

ment of a social utopia is a precondition—in relation to viable concrete social or political theories.[25]

It is a great irony that today Eastern religions, which are threatened by antireligious humanism and communism in Asia, are gaining converts in the West. For the most part, constituents of Eastern religions in the West belong to three types—ethnic-cultural, intellectual, and cultic. The fact that Asian residents or their descendants hold their ancestral religious traditions is nothing new. What is new today is the phenomenal rise in the second and third groups.

Intellectual interest in Eastern religions is illustrated by a recent survey that lists 1,653 professors who teach Asian religious traditions in colleges and universities in Canada and the United States.[26] A wide variety of cultic groups—not only the established ones like Vedanta and Zen, but a whole series of new groups, for example, Hare Krishna, Transcendental Meditation, Nichiren Shōshū, and the Unification Church (known as the Moonies)—now are present in the West. Whether or not the presence of Eastern religions implies the spiritual colonization of the West by the East, it adds complexity to the encounter of religions in our time.

## THEOLOGICAL HISTORY OF RELIGION AND THE INTERRELIGIOUS DIALOGUE

The last three decades have brought new modes of interreligious or interfaith relations, most notably the "dialogue" between Christian and non-Christian religious leaders and scholars. This dialogue has arisen primarily from the new mood of Eastern religions, coupled with new social and political realities in the non-Western world, and equally significant changes in religious outlook as well as in social, economic, and political spheres in the West. What is new on the Christian side is that the encounter among religions, as a serious scholarly and existential problem, has captured the imagination not only of enlightened church leaders and scholars of missions but also of leading theologians.

Not surprisingly, the original impulse for the dialogue came from the indigenous Christian ("younger") churches in the non-Western world. Controlled for decades by churches in the West, these younger churches were an insignificant minority within global Christendom and were ineffective spectators of the social and political events in their own lands. The leaders of the younger churches were embarrassed by the denominational divisions of the church, and had a different approach from that of the Western church in the

---

[25] See Ernst Benz, *Buddhism or Communism: Which Holds the Future of Asia?*, trans. Richard and Clara Winston (Garden City, N.Y.: Doubleday, 1965), 217–94.

[26] See *Professors in the United States and Canada Who Teach the Religious Traditions of Asia* (Hamilton, N.Y.: Colgate University, Fund for the Study of Great Religions, 1980).

development of a meaningful relationship to the non-Christian religions to which the majority of their fellow citizens belonged. Hence their push for "ecumenical movement" and "dialogue."[27] The 1938 World Missionary Conference at Tambaram made a profound impression on the younger churches concerning the need for the scholarly study of non-Christian religions. The younger churches were also greatly affected by Asian political events, especially the national independence of former European colonies, and by the Chinese Christian churches' declaration of self-help after the establishment of the People's Republic of China. Thus, instead of returning to the prewar pattern of heavy dependence on the financial and theological resources of the Western churches, they redefined their relationship with the older churches in the West in terms of "mutual dependence" or "partnership in obedience."

One concrete outcome of the partnership of the younger and older churches was the establishment of the World Council of Churches' committee for a research program entitled "The Word of God and The Living Faiths of Men." A document of this committee, released in 1958, states that "each individual religion is *sui generis* and complete in itself. . . . This denies the concept that Christianity is the fulfillment of other religions," based on the ground that all religions, including Christianity as a religion, are "distorted responses" on the part of men to the works of God.[28] The committee envisaged the development of a continuing dialogue with other living faiths and ideologies, including Marxism, in order to listen to what they had to say "about their understanding, their vision, their hope of salvation."[29]

The notion of "dialogue" was not accepted universally by Western churches. There were many differences in motivation, procedure, and objective, even among scholars of missions who accepted it. For example, one group of scholars, represented by those who contributed to the "Christian Presence Series,"[30] accepted coexistence with other faiths as an existential reality and dialogue as an expression of their deepest loyalty to the Christian Gospel's real content.[31] Thus, feeling that God had been in Asia and elsewhere before missionaries arrived, Max A. C. Warren suggested that "we must try to sit where [the adherents of other faiths] sit, to enter sympathetically into the pains and griefs and joys of their history and see how those

---

[27] See J. M. Kitagawa, "Divided We Stand," *Religion in Life* 27, no. 3 (Summer 1958); 335–51.

[28] Cited in Masatoshi Doi, *Search for Meaning Through Interfaith Dialogue* (Tokyo: Kyo Bun Kwan, 1976), 92.

[29] S. J. Samartha, ed., *Living Faiths and Ultimate Goals: A Continuing Dialogue* (Geneva: World Council of Churches, 1974), xiv.

[30] The "Christian Presence Series," under the general editorship of Max A. C. Warren, included Kenneth Cragg, *Sandals at the Mosque;* George Appleton, *On the Eightfold Path;* Raymond Hammer, *Japan's Religious Ferment;* and William Stewart, *India's Religious Frontier.*

[31] See for example, Max A. C. Warren, "General Introduction," in William Stewart, *India's Religious Frontier: Christian Presence Amid Modern Hinduism* (Philadelphia: Fortress Press, 1964), 13.

pains and griefs and joys have determined the premises of their argument. We have, in a word, to be 'present' with them."[32]

On the other hand, Hendrik Kraemer and others considered the coexistence of religions as the foreshadowing of a future meeting of religions as well as of an "interpenetration and *Auseinandersetzung* of cultural attitudes and orientations contained in [Eastern and Western] civilizations." Kraemer felt strongly, as he told Buddhist scholars in Japan, that "the great responsibility of all thinking people . . . who belong to the great religions is that such a dialogue take place in a really worthy form." As a scholar of missions and the history of religions, Kraemer shared J. H. Gunning's critique of the narrow horizon of an orthodox theology that passed its value judgments on other religions without knowing them. But he also shared Gunning's conviction that "only theology, if rightly understood, is able to produce that attitude of freedom of the spirit and of impartial understanding."[33] Therefore he was persuaded that Christian participants in the coming dialogue needed the training in what might be called a "theological" science of religion or history of religion.

The concern for "dialogue," however, has not been confined to missionary circles or to the younger churches. Vatican II's "Declaration on the Relation of the Church to Non-Christian Religions"[34] also gave cautious encouragement to such a dialogue. In addition, a number of interfaith conferences have been held in recent decades in Europe and North America under different auspices. Moreover, the notion of "dialogue" as a principle for the academic study of religions has been promoted by the Union for the Study of the Great Religions in Great Britain, and has been implemented in North America by such programs as McGill University's Institute of Islamic Studies. McGill's policy is that half of the teachers and half of the students be Muslims. According to its founder, Wilfred Cantwell Smith, "it is the business of comparative religion to construct statements about religion that are intelligible within at least two traditions simultaneously." Smith hopes that "comparative religion may become the disciplined self-consciousness of man's variegated and developing religious life."[35]

Equally significant is the fact that the encounter and "dialogue" of religions have concerned many Christian theologians in our time. A prominent example was Paul Tillich who, as a systematic theologian concerned

---

[32] Ibid., 15.

[33] Hendrik Kraemer, *World Cultures and World Religions: The Coming Dialogue* (Philadelphia: Westminster Press, 1960), 14; Thurber, "Hendrik Kraemer and the Christian Encounter," 82; Kraemer, *Religion and the Christian Faith* (Philadelphia: Westminster Press, 1956), 53.

[34] Cited in John Hick and Brian Hepplethwaite, eds., *Christianity and Other Religions: Selected Readings* (Glasgow: Collins-Fount Paperbacks, 1980), 81–82.

[35] W. C. Smith, "Comparative Religion: Whither—and Why?" in *The History of Religions: Essays in Methodology*, ed. M. Eliade and J. M. Kitagawa (Chicago: University of Chicago Press, 1959), 52, 55.

with the encounter of religions, attempted to develop a theoretical formula
for the theological history of religion. Convinced that the Bible, church
history, and the history of religions and cultures were legitimate sources of
systematic theology, Tillich asked: "How are these contents made available
for use in a way parallel to the method by which the biblical theologian
makes the biblical materials available and the historian of Christian thought
makes the doctrinal materials available?"[36]

Tillich acknowledged the following presuppositions in his theological
history of religions: first, "revelatory experiences are universally human";
second, "revelation is received by man in terms of his finite human situation"; third, not only are there particular revelatory experiences throughout
human history, but also "there is a revelatory process in which the limits of
adaptation and the failures of distortion are subjected to [the mystical, the
prophetic, and the secular forms of] criticism"; fourth, there may be "a
central event in the history of religions" that "makes possible a concrete
theology that has universalistic significance"; and fifth, "the history of religions . . . does not exist alongside the history of culture. The sacred does
not lie beside the secular, but it is its depth."[37] It is worth noting that as early
as 1919 Tillich wrote on a "theology of culture,"[38] in a theological attempt "to
discover the ultimate concern in the ground of a philosophy, a political
system, an artistic style, a set of ethical or social principles."[39] The theological history of culture or theology of culture, in his view, provided an important framework for the theological history of religion.

According to Tillich, the orientation for the theological history of religion
is that of the history of salvation. The crucial task is to inquire whether there
are great symbolic movements and moments (kairoi) in the general history of
religions, here including prereligious and religious traditions. It is interesting to note in this connection that his earlier formulation of the theological
history of religion pointed more directly to the Christian solution. In his own
words: "A theological history of religion should be carried through in the light
of the missionary principle that the New Being in Jesus as the Christ is the
answer to the question asked implicitly and explicitly by the religions of
mankind."[40] However, as he gave more thought to Eastern religions, Tillich
acknowledged that "to them the Christian answer is not an answer, because
they have not asked the question to which Christianity is supposed to give

[36] Paul Tillich, *Systematic Theology*, vol. 1 (Chicago: University of Chicago Press, 1951), 39.
[37] Paul Tillich, "The Significance of the History of Religions for the Systematic Theologian," in
*Essays in Divinity*, gen. ed. J. C. Brauer, vol. 1., *The History of Religions: Essays on the
Problem of Understanding*, ed. J. M. Kitagawa (Chicago: University of Chicago Press, 1967),
242–43.
[38] See Tillich's "Ueber die Idee einer Theologie der Kultur," in *Religions philosophie der
Kultur* (Berlin: Reuther und Reichard, 1919).
[39] Tillich, *Systematic Theology*, 1:39.
[40] Ibid.

the answer."[41] Thus, he began to stress the importance of a "dialogue" with other religions, especially those in Asia, rather than a missionary encounter or an indirect cultural contact with them, provided such a dialogue presupposed that "both partners acknowledge the value of the other's religious conviction," "each of them is able to represent his own religious basis with conviction," there is "a common ground which makes both dialogue and conflicts possible," and there is "openness of both sides to criticisms directed against their own religious basis."[42]

In many ways Tillich's visit to Japan in 1960 was an eye-opening experience for him. For example, he was most curious about the nature of Shinto and asked many questions, but candidly admitted that his "categories simply are not sufficient to grasp the situation" of Shinto. He also found difficulties in establishing common grounds for discourse with Buddhists. For instance, his question as to how Buddhist leaders deal with popular piety, especially in countering the dangers of mechanization, superstition, and demonization, was summarily dismissed by a leading Zen scholar, Shinichi Hisamatsu, on the ground that even the most primitive piety "could be the way of awakening the Buddha spirit in every human being." He had, however, a more fruitful exchange of ideas with Buddhist scholars. Tillich felt that the task of Christianity in its encounter with Japan was to show that people had to make existential decisions by giving "their ultimate concern to the really Ultimate." He expressed the conviction that the Kingdom of God "is fighting in the tremendous spiritual experiences of the Buddhists" and adherents of other religions, "but the *criterion* is lacking." And while he affirmed that for him "Jesus as the Christ" was the criterion for the Kingdom, he did not pursue the question of the adequacy of the symbol of the Ultimate—"why Christ (not Jesus) and not Buddha?"[43]

Discussing "A Christian-Buddhist Conversation" (written after he returned from Japan), Tillich used a dynamic typology of telos formula in characterizing the typical structures of Christianity and Buddhism: "In Christianity the telos [is] of every*one* and everything united in the Kingdom of God; in Buddhism the telos [is] of every*thing* and everyone fulfilled in the Nirvana." It was his contention that "the decisive point in a dialogue between two religions is not the historically determined, contingent *embodiment* of the typological elements, but these elements themselves." Significantly, his earlier notion of the theological history of religion—to subject Christianity and other religions to "the criterion of final revelation"—gave way to his new approach based not on antitheses but on polarities, and "not

[41] Paul Tillich, *Theology of Culture*, ed. R. C. Kimball (New York: Oxford University Press, 1959), 204–5.

[42] Paul Tillich, *Christianity and the Encounter of the World Religions* (New York: Columbia University Press, 1963), 62.

[43] See Wood, "Tillich Encounters Japan," 57, 60, 63, 66, 71.

conversion, but dialogue." According to his hopes for the dialogue, each religion would find in its depth "a point at which the religion itself loses its importance, and that to which it points breaks through its particularity, elevating it to spiritual freedom and with it to a vision of the spiritual presence in other expressions of the ultimate meaning of man's existence." In his very last lecture, given a few days before his death, Tillich used the expression "the religion of the concrete spirit" to refer to such an idealized feature of religion, an ideal that cannot be identified with any particular religion—not even Christianity—and yet can be found in the depths of every concrete religion.[44]

It is clear that Tillich was willing to encounter other religions as well as determined to remain an authentic Christian. Ironically, his earlier formulation of a theological history of religion based on his well-known theories of a "theological center," the "principle of correlation," "critical phenomenology," and the "latent church," was too formal to deal with concrete historical religious data and was too Christological to deal adequately with the motives and meanings of non-Christian religious expressions. To be sure, it was a useful tool against the scientific and philosophical criticisms of Christianity, but it was not entirely able to clarify the issues involved in the dialogue situation. Although he abandoned some of his formal categories in his conversations with non-Christian thinkers, he had definite ideas about the universality of religion lying in the depths of concrete religions. Thus, his approach to a dialogue was to compare, on his own terms, the typical structures of a unique form of historic religions with the typical structures appearing in Christianity as a historic religion. Therefore, when a Buddhist asked a prior question, such as why he chose as basic religious categories "being rather than nonbeing, life rather than death,"[45] it was difficult to continue the dialogue.

Also, as Mircea Eliade pointed out, Tillich was concerned not with *Historie* but with *Geschichte*, the existential meaning of history. In dealing with various religions, he was interested primarily in "their historical concreteness and immediacy, not in their modifications or changes or in the results of the flowing of time."[46] Nevertheless, Tillich's openness to engage in serious conversations with adherents of other religions opened new possibilities for Christianity to judge "itself in the light of its encounter with the world religions." This, of course, is a prerequisite for a meaningful dialogue.

---

[44] Tillich, "A Christian-Buddhist Conversation," in idem, *Christianity and the Encounter of World Religions*, 64, 65; idem, *Systematic Theology* 1:221; idem, *Christianity and the Encounter of World Religions*, 95, 97; idem, "The Significance of the History of Religions," 249, 255.

[45] See Langdon Gilkey, "The Mystery of Being and Nonbeing: An Experimental Project," *Journal of Religion* 58, no. 1 (January 1978): 2.

[46] Mircea Eliade, "Paul Tillich and the History of Religions," in Paul Tillich, *The Future of Religions*, ed. Jerald C. Brauer (New York: Harper & Row, 1966), 33.

### Notes on "Public Monologue" and "Dialogue"

Since the publication of the first volume of Tillich's *Systematic Theology* (1951), a number of Protestant and Catholic theologians and their counterparts in Jewish and non-Western religions have addressed the issue of the encounter of religions. Since all religions define the nature of reality, including ultimate reality, from their own "theological/religious center," any encounter of religions involves each participant's "public monologue" regarding this issue. Of course, each participant must realize the presence of others who also are engaged in similar public monologues. Thus, the encounter of religions compels each religious tradition not only to acknowledge the existence of others but also to try to make sense—here again from the perspective of each "theological/religious center"—of the sum total of a reality that includes the existence of other religions. Accordingly, each religious tradition must develop its own way of absorbing the data of alien religions into its own image of total reality. Such absorptions might be exemplified by historic Christian apologia of the Logos doctrine, the fulfillment theory, true versus false religions, *Heilsgeschichte* versus the history of empirical religions, and the Christian revelation versus historic religions. They are similarly represented by more recent proposals, such as Tillich's "latent church," Karl Rahner's "anonymous Christians," and Hans Küng's "ordinary and extraordinary [Christian] ways of salvation." All these proposals have helped to articulate the Christian "public monologue," which takes into account the relation of other religions to the Christian faith.

Ironically, the phenomenal expansion of Western colonial powers and civilization in the modern period has misled many Western Christians: some feel that their "public monologue" was the most decisive factor involved in the encounter of religions. Fortunately, in recent decades an increasing awareness has developed that other religious traditions, too, have been engaged in similar efforts to absorb the existence of alien religions into their image of reality. Thus, in their efforts to develop a theological history of religions, Christians must recognize their non-Christian counterparts in people like Radhakrishnan and Suzuki. Only a mutual recognition will transform a series of "public monologues" into a "dialogue." In this connection, Eliade astutely observes that, in their encounter with Easterners, Westerners have tended to depend on the more westernized representatives of Eastern peoples and religions: "The Western world has not yet, or not generally, met with authentic representatives of the 'real' non-Western traditions."[47]

Each religious tradition in a dialogue must alternately talk and then listen, reflect and then observe, and articulate self-affirmations and then self-criticisms. Thus far, the encounter of religions has meant, for the most part,

---

[47] Mircea Eliade, *Myths, Dreams, and Mysteries*, trans. Philip Mairet (New York: Harper & Brothers, 1960), 8–9.

theoretical discussions of doctrines and ethics. But each religious tradition is not simply a stereotyped system of doctrines, cults, and ecclesiastical institutions; rather, each is a dynamic and ever-growing organism that defines total reality and provides its adherents with the meaning of life as well as guidance for their actions. Similarly, in recent encounters of religions, each religious tradition often has been presented as a unified system without due recognition of the diverse strands represented within it. Unfortunately, because of their overindulgent sense of identification with and tolerance of others, participants of many well-meaning interfaith conferences underestimated the difficulties in understanding other faiths presented by what Tillich called "offenses."[48]

It is sobering to realize that a dialogue among religions is not the solution to religious problems. Besides, as Yoshinori Takeuchi astutely remarks, "Where there is an enhanced possibility of mutual appreciation, there is also the increased risk of misunderstanding."[49] Even so, interreligious dialogues are some of the best ways to enhance religious persons' self-understanding as well as to encourage a mutual understanding among religious traditions in a time when humanity is divided not only along ethnic, cultural, and political lines but also along religious lines as well.

[48] While in Japan, Tillich tried to differentiate "justified" and "unjustified" offenses of the Christian Gospel. "I would, for instance, say it is unjustified to claim that one must accept the doctrine of the Trinity or the doctrine that Jesus was the Son of God and to throw them as stones at the heads of people, for both are completely misunderstood even by theologians. Now that is not the right offense. But the right offense is to accept the demand of ultimate seriousness of the Ultimate, as it is seen in the picture of Jesus in the Gospels. . . ." See Wood, "Tillich Encounters Japan," 69.

[49] Quoted by Max A. C. Warren in his "General Introduction" to George Appleton, *On the Eightfold Path* (New York: Oxford University Press, 1961), 12.

# 6

## ELIADE AND TILLICH

### A REFLECTION ON THEIR ENCOUNTER

In his *Journal* Eliade writes most appreciatively of his experiences teaching joint seminars with Paul Tillich in the 1960's.[1] When Tillich accepted the John Nuveen Professorship in Philosophical Theology in the Divinity School of the University of Chicago in 1962, he was very eager to work with Mircea Eliade, whose works he had read and admired. On his part, Eliade enthusiastically responded to this proposition. Thus began an exciting two-year encounter of two creative minds, each stimulating and learning from the other. In his very last lecture, given only ten days before his death, Tillich stated:

> I now want to return my thanks . . . to my friend Professor Eliade for the two years of seminars and the cooperation we had in them. In these seminars I experienced that every individual doctrinal statement or ritual expression of Christianity receives a new intensity of meaning. And in terms of a kind of apologia, yet also a self-accusation, I must say that my own *Systematic Theology* was written before these seminars . . . But perhaps we need a longer, more intensive period of interpenetration of systematic theological study and religious historical studies. Under such circumstances, the structure of religious thought might develop in connection with another or different fragmentary manifestation of theonomy or of the religion of the concrete spirit. This is my hope for the future of theology.[2]

It was indeed interesting to watch how these two scholars, despite their difference in academic training, temperament and background, developed

---

[1] The exact wording is as follows. "Although my knowledge of depth psychology was rather precarious, these conversations with Jung impressed me in the highest degree. (The only comparable experience for me was the series of joint seminars I taught with Paul Tillich at the University of Chicago in the sixties.)" Mircea Eliade, *No Souvenirs: Journal, 1957–1969*, trans. Fred H. Johnson, Jr. (New York: Harper & Row, 1977), p. xiii.

[2] Paul Tillich, "The Significance of the History of Religions for the Systematic Theologian," in J. M. Kitagawa (ed.), *The History of Religions: Essays on the Problem of Understanding* (Chicago: The University of Chicago Press, 1967), p. 252.

meaningful modes of discourse as they probed together the nature of humanity's religious experience.

*   *   *

Those who have come to know Eliade and Tillich are no doubt aware that they share some significant qualities—their enormous erudition, extraordinary intellectual gifts, insatiable curiosity, unusually good memories, and capacity to relate themselves to a wide circle of friends in diverse fields. As young men, both Eliade and Tillich were well grounded in the cultural legacy of their homelands. This instilled in them passion not only for knowledge (learning) but also for culture *(paideia)* in the Greek sense of the term. Later, both of them underwent several radical changes caused by world events that had changed the destinies of their respective homelands. Tillich, who was born two years before Eliade, was profoundly influenced by his experience of World War I. According to his biographers:

> At the beginning of the war Tillich was . . . a German patriot, a proud Prussian, as eager to fight for his country as anyone else, but politically naive. When he returned to Berlin four years later he was utterly transformed. The traditional monarchist had become a religious socialist, the Christian believer a cultural pessimist. . . . These years represent *the* turning point in Paul Tillich's life . . .[3]

After the war, Tillich—then a young academic—devoted much of his energy to the renewal of his homeland and western civilization with firm conviction that the end of World War I was indeed the *kairos* "for a general cultural reformation in accordance with the *vision of a new humanism* that was intended to be true to the requirements of modern life as well as to the inherited ideals of Jewish, Greek, and Christian origins."[4] However, the rise of the Nazis changed the course of his life again. Dismissed from his professorship in Frankfurt, he began a new life in America. "Emigration at the age of forty-seven," he wrote, "means that one belongs to two worlds: to the Old as well as to the New . . ."[5]

Tillich's involvement in the ecumenical movement provided him with an opportunity to visit Europe in 1936, his first return since his emigration. He noted in his diary his profound love for the landscape and people of his native country, but detested the state of Germany under the Nazis: "Dead, de-

---

[3] Wilhelm & Marion Pauck, *Paul Tillich: His Life and Thought, Vol. 1: Life* (New York: Harper & Row, 1976), p. 41.

[4] Wilhelm Pauck, "The Sources of Paul Tillich's Richness," in Jerald C. Brauer (ed.), *Paul Tillich: The Future of Religions* (New York: Harper & Row, 1966), pp. 23–30, esp. pp. 26–27. (My italics.)

[5] Paul Tillich, *My Search for Absolutes* (New York: Simon & Schuster, 1967), p. 50.

stroyed; barbed wire and Gestapo."[6] Understandably, during World War II Tillich had high hopes for the early defeat of the Nazis and longed for a just peace in Europe and elsewhere. But the end of the war did not bring about peace; it only marked the beginning of the cold war. Disappointed but without losing hope, Tillich then poured his energy into the completion of his *Systematic Theology* which, according to Wilhelm Pauck, "bears the marks of having been written by one who on passing with utmost consciousness through great historical changes had never ceased to think of plans of action for himself and his fellowmen through which a *true humanity would be realized* . . ."[7] In my own view, another prominent feature of Tillich's enterprise is the fact that history of religions and cultures are included, together with Bible and church history, as legitimate sources of Systematic Theology. According to him, "a theological history of religion," grounded though it is in a particular religious tradition, "should interpret theologically the material produced by the investigation and analysis of the pre-religious and religious life of mankind. It should elaborate the motives and types of religious expression, showing how they follow from the nature of the religious concern and therefore necessarily appear in all religions, including Christianity in so far as it is a religion."[8]

Tillich's biographers tell us that he was keenly conscious of the incompleteness of his *Systematic Theology* and after his trips to Greece and Japan stated that "his entire system had to be rewritten in the light of his new visions of the ancient and Eastern worlds."[9] His trip to Japan in 1960 in particular made a special impact on him. In his own words: ". . . I know that something happened: no Western provincialism of which I am aware will be tolerated by me from now on in my thought and work . . ."[10] Thus, one can readily understand how eager he was to pursue his inquiry with Eliade when he arrived at Chicago campus in 1962.

*    *    *

Like Tillich, Eliade too was destined to experience the upheavals of world events throughout his life. Born in Bucharest in 1907, he witnessed the German occupation of his homeland when he was nine years old.[11] While in lycée he began to be fascinated not only by literature, which he had

---

[6] Paul Tillich, *My Travel Diary: 1936—Between Two Worlds*, ed. by Jerald C. Brauer (New York: Harper & Row, 1970), p. 72.

[7] Pauck, "The Sources of Paul Tillich's Richness," *op. cit.*, p. 28. (My italics.)

[8] Paul Tillich, *Systematic Theology*, Vol. I (Chicago: The University of Chicago Press, 1951), p. 39.

[9] Wilhelm and Marion Pauck, *op. cit.*, p. 245.

[10] *Ibid.*, p. 261.

[11] Mircea Eliade, *Autobiography, Vol. 1: 1907–1937, Journey East, Journey West*, trans. by Mac L. Ricketts (New York: Harper & Row, 1981), chap. 2, "The War at Age Nine," pp. 20–36.

always loved, but also by philosophy, Oriental studies, alchemy, and history of religions. Also, he had already published his one hundredth article by the time he entered the university. For his thesis at the university he pursued Italian Renaissance philosophy, which counterbalanced, unconsciously to be sure, his "passion for transcendence, mysticism, and Oriental spiritualism."[12] Keenly aware of being one of the "young generation" that had grown up during World War I, Eliade felt that, while the previous generation had the historic mission of reintegrating the Romanian people and consolidating Romania's national identity, his generation had no ready-made ideal. "We were the first Rumanian generation unconditioned in advance by an objective to be realized in history. In order not to slumber in cultural provincialism or spiritual sterility, we had to know what was happening everywhere in the world, in our own time."[13] Significantly, in one of the articles addressed to the younger generation he advised the reader "to imagine the coming year, 1928, as *his last year*, and to strive to do, during those twelve months ahead, everything he had promised himself to do in his life"[14]—the advice which Eliade himself has been following each year since then. In hindsight his sense of urgency proved to be correct by the events that followed. "Actually," he wrote later, "our generation had only about ten or twelve years of 'creative freedom.' In 1938 the royal dictatorship was established; then came the Second World War; and in 1945 the Russian occupation—and total silence."[15]

As might be expected, Eliade was nothing but idle during the all too short period of "creative freedom." Strange as it may sound, his dedication to the study of the Italian Renaissance further strengthened his sense of vocation as an Orientalist, especially in Indian studies, because to him Orientalism was a new version of the Renaissance. "Perhaps," he says, "without knowing it, I was in search of a *new, wider humanism*, bolder than the humanism of the Renaissance, which was too dependent on the models of Mediterranean classicism . . . . a provincial image of man didn't satisfy me. . . . ultimately, I dreamed of rediscovering the *model of a 'universal man.'*"[16] By chance, as though to fulfill his pre-ordained destiny, the Maharaja of Kassimbazar offered Eliade financial help to study for a few years with philosopher Surendranath Dasgupta in Calcutta. India beckoned him not only as a field of research. He had an uncanny sense that the unknown mystery was waiting for him somewhere in India, and it was for him to decipher and that, in his own words, "in deciphering it I would at the same

---

[12] *Ibid.*, p. 128.

[13] *Ibid.*, p. 132. He further stated that, for a part of the younger generation, "the Orthodox heritage could constitute a total conception of the world and existence, and that this synthesis, if it could be realized, would be a new phenomenon in the history of modern Rumanian culture."

[14] *Ibid.*, p. 135.

[15] *Ibid.*, p. 136.

[16] Mircea Eliade, *No Souvenirs: Journal, 1957–1969, op. cit.*, p. 17. (My italics.)

time reveal to myself the mystery of my own existence; I would discover at last who I was and why I wanted to be what I wanted to be, why all the things that had happened to me had happened to me . . ."[17] Thus, shortly after receiving his Licence es lettres in 1928 Eliade, at the age of twenty, left for India where he studied for three years Indian philosophy and the practice of Yoga, the subject on which he made significant scholarly contribution subsequently. He also continued his literary productivity during his stay in India.

Obviously, Eliade was profoundly impressed by Indian philosophy and asceticism because they show man how to exist as a free being by abolishing or transcending the conditions of existence.[18] Another aspect of the mystery which Eliade deciphered in India was the significance of the peasant roots of Romanian culture "that compelled us to transcend nationalism and cultural provincialism and to aim for 'universalism.'" He came to be convinced that "the common elements of Indian, Balkan, and Mediterranean folk culture proved to me that it is *here* that *organic universalism* exists, that it is the *common history* (the history of peasant cultures) and not an abstract construct."[19] Thus, anticipating that oppressed people of Asia and elsewhere soon would take their rightful place in world history, he felt that Romanians could serve as a bridge between the West, Asia and cultures of the archaic folk type.

Eliade returned to Bucharest in 1932 and began his teaching career in the following year. He also plunged into scholarly as well as literary writings like a driven person. The publication in 1936 of his *Yoga*—in which he attempted a "new interpretation of myth and symbolism, of archaic and Oriental religions"[20]—attracted the attention of a number of prominent Orientalists, ethnologists, and historians of religions. By that time the future of Europe was threatened by Hitler, while political stability was steadily eroding in Romania. When Eliade visited Berlin in the summer of 1936 — unbeknown to Tillich who also was visiting Europe then—a fellow Romanian predicted the coming of war in a few years, and said: "then we Rumanians would have one great problem: to find a way to 'hibernate,' to survive this new cataclysm."[21] This sentiment was shared by many Romanians, including Eliade himself.

In one sense Eliade was able to escape the cataclysm of World War II, because he was serving as cultural attaché, first in London and then in

---

[17] Eliade, *Autobiography, op. cit.*, p. 153.

[18] Eliade, *No Souvenirs, op. cit.*, p. 122: "Even better than Christianity, Hindu spirituality has the merit of introducing freedom into the cosmos. A *jivanmukta*'s mode of being is not given in the cosmos; very much to the contrary, in a universe dominated by laws, absolute freedom is unthinkable. India has the merit of having added a new dimension to the universe: that of existing as a free being."

[19] Eliade, *Autobiography*, p. 204. (My italics.)

[20] *Ibid.*, p. 314.

[21] Eliade, *No Souvenirs, op. cit.*, pp. x–xi.

Lisbon. After the war, he settled in Paris, and thus began the life of a self-imposed exile away from his homeland. "It was," he recalls, "a trying experience to start a new career in another, great country at the age of thirty-eight and to begin writing in a foreign language."[21] On the other hand, living in Paris enabled him to meet a host of scholars, utilize excellent libraries, teach and lecture both in Paris and in other European universities, attend various scholarly conferences, and above all publish a series of important scholarly as well as literary works. Although he confesses that he was not then aware of the structural analogy between the scientific and literary imaginations, he was fascinated by the fact that "in the same way as the writer of fiction, the historian of religions is confronted with different structures of sacred and mythical space, different qualities of time, and more especially by a considerable number of strange, unfamiliar, and enigmatic worlds of meaning."[22] Little did Eliade realize that his chance meeting with Joachim Wach—who like Tillich had been driven out of Germany by the Nazis and was then teaching History of Religions in Chicago—at the 1955 International Congress of History of Religions in Rome would result in his being invited to deliver the Haskell Lectures in Chicago the following year,[23] which in turn opened the way for his accepting a professorship at the University of Chicago.

Eliade's move to Chicago at the age of forty-nine meant a second migration for him, but he and his wife Christinel made excellent adjustment to the new environment. Not only were they warmly welcomed by faculty and students at Chicago, but his books were eagerly read in many quarters of North American academic communities. Meanwhile, his paper on "The Structure of Religious Symbolism"[24] was enthusiastically received at the International Congress of History of Religions held in Tokyo in 1958—two years prior to Tillich's visit to Japan. On his part, Eliade was greatly impressed by two features of Japanese religious life:

> The first is the cosmic dimension of the Japanese religious experience. The fact that the sacred and divine manifest themselves through nature or, more exactly, through the beauties of nature. . . . there is no break between the divine, human and the world of nature. The sacred is

---

[22] *Ibid.*, p. ix.

[23] The Haskell Lectureship on Comparative Religions was established in 1895 by the gift of Mrs. Caroline Haskell who, inspired by the World's Parliament of Religions (held in Chicago in 1893), proposed that the newly established University of Chicago invite renowned scholars in comparative religion and history of religions from Asia and Europe. Eliade's lectures were entitled "Patterns of Initiation"—published as *Birth and Rebirth: The Religious Meanings of Initiation in Human Culture* (New York: Harper & Row, 1958).

[24] *Proceedings of the IXth International Congress for the History of Religions* (Tokyo & Kyoto, 1958) (Tokyo: Maruzen, 1960), pp. 506–512.

manifested by the cosmic creations as well as by the most noble spiritual experiences . . . .

The second . . . is the fact that the archaic element of religion coexists with the most recent, and that they coexist sometimes in symbiosis, sometimes apart. . . . here in Japan, one finds still living and creating religious forces that have long been extinguished in other parts of the world.[25]

Eliade's growing reputation was such that students from various parts of North America as well as those from Europe and Asia began to find their ways to Chicago from the early 1960's. Understandably, his students were as curious as he was about the proposed joint seminars between Eliade and Tillich.

*  *  *

The Eliade-Tillich seminars were intended to provide occasions for an interpenetration between History of Religions and Systematic Theology. Equally significant from our point of view was the fact that it meant a fascinating encounter between these two creative minds, their thoughts, their histories and their visions. Both of them embodied within themselves rich and varied heritages and experiences, which they remolded and gave new forms. Both were willing to ask daring questions and discern religious meanings and human values in all dimensions of life. By holding these joint seminars they of course did not expect to arrive at any new synthesis between History of Religions and Systematic Theology, but they had hopes that both historians of religions and theologians, enriched by their encounter, would be stimulated to ask more fundamental questions, transcending disciplinary myopia, provincialism and timidity.

Undoubtedly, Tillich was an unusual theologian in many respects. As a child—so we are informed by Pauck—Tillich absorbed Evangelical-Lutheran piety in his father's parsonage and continued subsequently to derive "his pristine sense for religion" from this heritage, even though in his philosophical and theological development he was greatly influenced by, besides Luther, the pre-Socratics, Plato, Plotinus, Stoics, Augustine, Eckhart, Cusanus, Boehme, Kant, Schelling, Hegel, Schleiermacher, Kierkegaard, Nietzsche, Marx, and Freud.[26] As a theologian and a philosopher of religion as well as a humanist and a modern man, Tillich came to be concerned with the problem of the encounter between Christianity and world religions as well as with what he calls quasi-religions, e.g., liberal humanism, fascism, and communism.

In dealing with the phenomena of the encounter of religions and of

[25] *Ibid.*, p. 839: Mircea Eliade, "Impression of Japan."
[26] Pauck, "The Sources of Paul Tillich's Richness," *op. cit.*, pp. 25–26.

quasi-religions, Tillich in his 1962 Bampton Lectures poses two alternative approaches—either to "draw the panorama of the present situation as factually as possible" as an "outside observer," or to "*select* facts according to his judgment of their relative importance, *interpret* these in the light of his own understanding, and *evaluate* them" as an "inside participant" in the dynamics of the situation.[27] Although he acknowledges that an "outside observer" is always an "inside participant," at least in one part of his being, because of his "confessed or concealed answers" to the questions involved in every form of religion, Tillich maintains this type of methodological dichotomy in principle much as he suggested previously in his *Systematic Theology*, according to which the descriptive task was assigned to History of Religions, whereas the task of interpreting the data derived from History of Religions was assigned to Theology, or more precisely to Theological History of Religion.[28] Thus, reiterating this formula again in his Bampton Lectures, Tillich states that it is the task of the theologian, grounded as he is consciously in a particular religion, "to grasp the facts as precisely as is humanly possible, and to show that there are elements in human nature which tend to become embodied in symbols similar to those of his own religion."[29] As to the task of comparing, contrasting and evaluating religious data, Tillich advises the theologian to start with the question of the intrinsic aim of existence *(telos)* that underlies the movement of history generally, and more particularly the history of religion. Thus, for example, he discusses the Christian-Buddhist dialogue in terms of the two *telos*-formulae, namely, that of the Kingdom of God in Christianity and that of Nirvāna in Buddhism.[30] Realizing his own provincial orientation, which became evident to him after his visit to Japan, Tillich wanted to delve into what to him was unfamiliar data from the field of History of Religions for his further systematic theological inquiry. Thanks to Eliade's influence, Tillich quickly discovered that, contrary to what he earlier had thought, History of Religions was not simply a descriptive study of religious data.

\* \* \*

Working with Tillich was undoubtedly a moving experience for Eliade. "It was not just the amazing spectacle of a 78-year-old master being, after three hours of discussion, more alert and more resourceful than many members of the seminar . . . . it was refreshing to see how the immense and heteroclite materials brought forward by the historians of religion would disclose [to Tillich] their structures and by this very fact become susceptible

[27] Paul Tillich, *Christianity and the Encounter of the World Religions* (New York: Columbia University Press, 1963), p. 2. (My italics.)
[28] Tillich, *Systematic Theology*, Vol. I., *op. cit.*, p. 39.
[29] Tillich, *Christianity and the Encounter of the World Religions, op. cit.*, p. 3.
[30] *Ibid.*, p. 64.

of classification and analysis."[31] Those who know Eliade will testify to the
similar intellectual passion and sense of mission that characterize his own life
and work. He himself admits that even when he was still in lycée he was
obsessed by what he had to do: he had thousands of books to read and many
disciplines to study before time ran out. "This time, it was no longer a
question of myself alone. I felt responsible for the entire 'young generation,'
that I imagined called to grand destinies."[32] His study in India, too, was
motivated by the sense of duty he felt as a mentor of the young generation of
Romanians; he felt the need to expand their cultural horizon and to open for
them windows "toward [the] spiritual universe that until then had been
inaccessible." Thus, Eliade demanded from himself "a superhuman effort to
learn and to do everything that our forebears had not had the leisure to learn
or to do."[33] Once he was in India, he wrote rhapsodically about the spiritual
universe which he found there—"a certain atmosphere of renunciation, . . .
of control of consciousness, of love . . . . an extraordinary belief in the reality
of the verities, in the power of man to know them and to live them by an
interior realization, by purity, and above all by meditation."[34] Eliade, the
advocate of a modern Renaissance, however, admitted later that it took him
"ten years to understand that the Indian experience alone could not reveal to
me the *universal man* I had been looking for since my adolescence." And,
since that time, he has become oriented more toward the two spiritual
universes which have preserved "an inexhaustible wealth of human situations"—the world of the "primitives" and the universe of folklore.[35]

It is apparent that all the works of Eliade, both scholarly and literary,
have the marks of a spiritual geography which he has been deciphering. They
are records of situations in which he has exercised what he calls the her-
meneutic of religious creations. This, however, has not been a simple intellectual enterprise for Eliade. He makes the following poignant remarks as he
recalls:

> These thirty years, and more, that I've spent among exotic, barbar-
> ian, indomitable gods and goddesses, nourished on myths, obsessed by
> symbols, nursed and bewitched by so many images which have come
> down to me from these submerged worlds, today seem to me to be the
> stages of a long initiation. . . . An infinite series of intellectual adven-
> tures . . . . These were not only bits of knowledge acquired slowly and

[31] Mircea Eliade, "Paul Tillich and the History of Religions," in Jerald C. Brauer (ed.), *Paul
Tillich: The Future of Religions, op. cit.*, pp. 31–36, esp. pp. 32–33.

[32] Quoted in Virgil Ierunca, "The Literary Work of Mircea Eliade," *Myths and Symbols:
Studies in Honor of Mircea Eliade*, ed. by J. M. Kitagawa & C. H. Long (Chicago: The
University of Chicago Press, 1969), p. 349, n. 24.

[33] Eliade, *Autobiography, op. cit.*, p. 136.

[34] Quoted in Ierunca, *op. cit.*, p. 344.

[35] Eliade, *No Souvenirs, op. cit.*, p. 17. (My italics.)

leisurely in books, but so many encounters, confrontations, and temptations. I realize perfectly well now all the dangers I skirted during this long quest . . . the risk of forgetting that I had a goal, that I was heading toward something, that I wanted to reach a "center."[36]

Through it all, Eliade has attempted to decipher the hidden meanings impregnated in these encounters, confrontations, and temptations. Like the protagonists in many of his novels, to whom situations and places, daily existence in the midst of historical times in Bucharest, India, London, Lisbon and Paris unfold signs of reality in another plane, Eliade has caught the glimpse of the sacred in the profane, the fantastic in the real, the eternal in the temporal, and the lost paradise in the banal existence of the present. For Eliade, therefore, History of Religions is a crucially important way to attain a deeper knowledge of humanity and of the meaning of human existence, a knowledge which to him is destined to play a decisive role in the development of "new humanism" in our time. This sense of mission prompted him to found in 1938 an international journal—significantly entitled *Zalmoxis*, the name of a popular god in Rumanian folklore. The same sense of mission led him to found another international journal, *History of Religions*, in 1961.

\* \* \*

In reflecting on the experience of teaching with Tillich, Eliade makes three pertinent observations. First, it was a "unique experience" for him to follow Tillich's mind as the theologian confronted unfamiliar religious acts— such as a cosmogonic myth, an initiation ritual, an eccentric divine figure— and was amazed by Tillich's ability to see in each case a specific encounter with the sacred. Second, Tillich was always interested in the existential meaning of history; for him history was *Geschichte*, not *Historie*. When confronted with archaic, traditional, and oriental religions, Tillich was primarily interested in deciphering their meaning by grasping their structures. Third, Tillich, who had earlier addressed himself to the question as to "what it means to be a religious man, and especially a Christian, in a world without God," was then most eager to encounter non-Christian and non-religious realities because, to him, "they were part and parcel of his historical moment."[37]

Tillich on his part was fascinated by the theological implications of Eliade's interpretation of history of religions, especially his notion of the *deus otiosus*. According to Eliade:

. . . myths and religions, in all their variety, are the result of the vacuum left in the world by the retreat of God, his transformation into *deus*

[36] *Ibid.*, pp. 74–75.
[37] Eliade, *"Paul Tillich and the History of Religions,"* op. cit., p. 34.

*otiosus*, and his disappearance from the religious scene . . . in the religious experience of primitive humanity. He was supplanted by other divine forms—divinities which were active, fertile, dramatic, etc.[38]

Tillich came to be interested in the repetition of the similar phenomenon of the withdrawal and passivity of God in the religions of the ancient East and in Greece. Eliade states that both he and Tillich,

> . . . wonder whether the same process isn't confirmed in Judaism. Yahweh becomes more and more transcendent in later Judaism. Intermediaries take his place. The power of Yahweh appears hypostatized: his "Wisdom," his "Glory," or his "Spirit," his "Word." In the image of the Messiah, the Son of Man, we have the "intermediary Power" *par excellence*.
>
> Tillich goes further: for him the theology of the Enlightenment represents a deistic form of the withdrawal of God from the world. As for American Protestant theology of the last fifty years, Tillich considers it "Unitarian in Christ." God is reduced to the second person of the Trinity. The demoniac elements of Yahweh disappear. God becomes the moral law.[39]

Tillich's negative judgment of the current theological and religious scene in the West, however, did not discourage him. Rather, it heightened his sense of urgency for the renewal of his systematic theology which now takes most seriously—to quote the title of his very last lecture—the "significance of the History of Religions for the systematic theologian." In such a task Tillich as a Christian theologian felt called to decipher the "inner *telos*" of the history of religions, which would break through particularities and elevate it "to spiritual freedom and with it to a vision of the ultimate meaning of man's existence."[40] In his last lecture he gave a tentative designation of "the religion of the concrete spirit" to refer to the inner aim of religion which lies in the depth of every concrete religion. Tillich was careful not to identify the "religion of the concrete spirit" with any specific world religion, not even Christianity. He saw the whole history of religions "as a fight for the religion of the concrete spirit, a fight of God against religion within religion."[41] Toward the very end of his last lecture, Tillich expressed his expectation that the historian of religions, in turn, will "place the reinterpreted concepts into the framework of the dynamics of religious and secular history and especially into the framework of our present religious and cultural situation."[42]

---

[38] Eliade, *No Souvenirs, op. cit.*, p. 74.
[39] *Ibid.*, p. 210.
[40] Tillich, *Christianity and the Encounter of the World Religions, op. cit.*, p. 97.
[41] Tillich, "The Significance of the History Religions . . . " *op. cit.*, p. 249.
[42] *Ibid.*, p. 254.

Those who have followed Eliade's works may be struck by the amazing parallels between his and Tillich's perceptions of current religious and cultural situations, although their vocabularies are different. Both thinkers share a futuristic orientation with Teilhard de Chardin. As Eliade sees the religious and cultural scene in the West, it was Christianity that emptied the cosmos of the sacred by emphasizing personal religious experience. Modern science "would not have been possible without a nature which was desacralized and emptied of gods." Actually, Christianity did not have to desacralize nature, because "the cosmos remains no less the creation of God." However, he continues:

> . . . from the moment that historical time and irreversible duration triumphed, the religious charm of the cosmos was dissipated. There was also something else: nature had been inhabited by pagan gods that Christianity had converted into demons. Nature, as such, could no longer interest Christians existentially. [43]

In spite of his negative judgment of the legacy of Christianity in the West, Eliade sees a happy exception in the peasant tradition in eastern Europe which preserves the cosmic dimension of Christianity. For example, he points out that Romanian peasants are Christians but they also practice a "cosmic Christianity," which has been lost elsewhere. "The peasant believes that the world is good, that it returned to that state after the incarnation, death, and resurrection of the Savior." [44] He also deciphers a similar "cosmic orientation" in archaic and Oriental religions. Parenthetically, Eliade refutes the accusation that he "idealizes" only the primitives. He recognizes the significance of historical situations and their usefulness for understanding religious creations. He is persuaded, however, that the West must rediscover the presence of the transcendent in human experience and in this respect learn much from the primitive, archaic, and Oriental religions.

Eliade's sense of urgency is derived from his perception, which has been confirmed by his scholarly reflection and experience, that the people of the West are no longer the only ones to "create" history, and that "their spiritual and cultural values will no longer enjoy the privileged place, to say nothing of the unquestioned authority, that they enjoyed some generations ago." The people of Asia have already re-entered history, and the so-called "primitive" peoples are now coming into the horizon of greater history. In this sense, Eliade shares with Tillich a belief in the supreme importance for humanity of the role played by authentic religious orientation for the realization of true humanity. They also share the sense of urgency for Western culture to be "deprovincialized." It was no doubt a rewarding experience for Eliade to

[43] Eliade, *No Souvenirs, op. cit.*, p. 71.
[44] *Ibid.*, p. 189.

learn that the projected renewal of Tillich's systematic theology took most seriously the significance of the History of Religions.

> . . . the History of Religions is destined to play an important role in contemporary cultural life. This is not only because an understanding of exotic and archaic religions will significantly assist in a cultural dialogue with the representatives of such religions. It is more especially because, by attempting to understand [them], the history of religions will inevitably attain to a deeper knowledge of man. It is on the basis of such a knowledge that a new humanism, on a world-wide scale, could develop.[45]

[45] Mircea Eliade, "History of Religions and a New Humanism," *History of Religions*, Vol. 1, No. 1 (Summer 1961), p. 3.

# 7

## MIRCEA ELIADE

Eliade Mircea (1907–1986) was a Romanian-born historian of religions, humanist, Orientalist, philosopher, and creative writer. He served as editor-in-chief of *The Encyclopedia of Religion* (1987). Since this article can give only a brief, general introduction, those who wish to know more of his life and work are referred to the Bibliography.

Born in Bucharest and the son of an army officer, Eliade witnessed the German occupation of his homeland when he was only nine years old. His lifelong fascination with literature, philosophy, Oriental studies, alchemy and the history of religions began when he was still in the lycée. An early article entitled "The Enemy of the Silkworm" reflects the boy's intense interest in plants, animals, and insects. In fact he had already published his one hundredth article by the time he entered the University of Bucharest in 1925. At the university, he became a devoted disciple of the philosopher, Nae Ionescu, who taught him the importance of life experience, commitment, intuition, and the spiritual or psychological reality of mental worlds. At the university Eliade became particularly interested in the philosophy of the Italian Renaissance, especially in Marsilio Ficino's rediscovery of Greek philosophy.

Eliade was blessed with the happy combination of an unusually keen mind, strong intuition, fertile imagination, and the determination to work hard, and much of the structure of his later thought, and some of the paradoxes of his life, were foreshadowed then. Simultaneously he was both a Romanian patriot and a world citizen. He was proud of Western civilization, although he lamented its provincial character, particularly its will to "universalize" Western ideas and values into the norm for all of humankind. Looking back he could see that in his country previous generations had had no cause to question their historic mission to consolidate Romania's national identity. His own generation, though, had experienced World War I and seemed to have no ready-made model or mission for themselves. Eliade's plea was that his fellow countrymen should exploit this period of "creative freedom" from tradition and try to learn from other parts of the world what possibilities for life and thought there were. His ultimate concern was the revitalization of all branches of learning and the arts, and his great hope was to decipher the message of the cosmos, which to him was a great repository of hidden meanings. Judging from his diaries and other writings, it would seem that Eliade had a strong sense of destiny, from his youth until his last day in Chicago, calling him from one phase of life to the next, though he felt he was not always conscious of what lay in store for him along the way.

Concerning his preoccupation with the Italian Renaissance in his college days, Eliade later stated, "Perhaps without knowing it, I was in search of a new, wider humanism, bolder than the humanism of the Renaissance, which was too dependent on the models of Mediterranean classicism. . . . Ultimately, I dreamed of discovering the model of a 'universal man'" (*No Souvenirs*, 1977, p. 17). As though to fulfil his pre-ordained destiny, the Maharaja of Kassimbazar offered Eliade a grant to study Indian philosophy with Surendranath Dasgupta at the University of Calcutta, 1928–1932. He also spent another six months in the *ashram* of Rishikesh in the Himalayas. To him, India was more than a place for scholarly research. He felt that a mystery was hidden somewhere in India, and deciphering it would disclose the mystery of his own existence. India indeed revealed to him the profound meaning of that freedom which can be achieved by abolishing the conditions of human existence indicated in the sub-title of his book on Yoga: "Immortality and Freedom."

The stay in India also opened his eyes to the existence of common elements in all peasant cultures, e.g., in China, Southeast Asia, pre-Aryan aboriginal India, the Mediterranean world, and the Iberian peninsula, the elements from which he would later derive the notion of "cosmic religion." In fact, the discovery of pre-Aryan aboriginal Indian spirituality (which has remained an important thread in the fabric of Hinduism to the present) led Eliade to speculate on a comparable synthesis for Dacians, whose culture formed the "autochthonous base" of present-day Romanian culture. Dacian culture was reconstructed by a Romanian philosopher-folklorist, B. P. Hasdeu. Moreover, Eliade came to believe that the substratum of peasant cultures of southeastern Europe has been preserved to this day underneath the cultural influences of the Greeks, the Romans, the Byzantines, and Christianity, and he went so far as to suggest that the peasant roots of Romanian culture could become the basis of a genuine universalism, transcending nationalism and cultural provincialism, in today's world where the oppressed peoples of Asia and elsewhere might take their rightful place in world history: "We, the people of Eastern Europe, would be able to serve as a bridge between the West and Asia." As he remarked in his autobiography, "A good part of my activity in [Romania] between 1932 and 1940 found its point of departure in these intuitions and observations. . ." (*Autobiography*, Vol. I, 1981, p. 204).

In 1932 Eliade returned to Romania and was appointed to assist Nae Ionescu at the University of Bucharest in the following year. His publication of *Yoga. Essai sur les Origines de la Mystique Indienne* (1936), in which he attempted a new interpretation of the myths and symbolism of archaic and

Oriental religions, attracted the attention of such eminent European scholars as Jean Przyluski, Louis de La Vallee Poussin, Heinrich Zimmer, and Giuseppe Tucci. He also plunged feverishly into literary activities. Many people were under the impression then that Eliade thought of himself primarily as a novelist, although he was strongly motivated to engage in scholarly activities as well. Eliade had made his literary debut in 1930 with *Isabel si Apele Divolului* (Isabel and the Devil's Water), which was obviously colored by his Indian experience. According to Matei Calinescu, most of Eliade's fiction inspired by India was written between 1930 and 1935, and his earlier Indian novels, e.g., *Maitreyi*, were strongly autobiographical. He also points out that Eliade's later novellas with Indian topics, such as *Secretul Doctorului Honigberger* (The Secret of Dr. Honigberger) and *Nopti la Serampore* (Night in Serampore), "deal with the major problem of the fully mature Eliade, that of the ambiguities of the sacred and the profane in their characteristical relationship." He concludes that "Eliade had discovered the 'ontological' signification of narration" by 1940 ("'Function of the Unreal': Reflections on Mircea Eliade's Short Fiction," in N. J. Giradot & M. L. Ricketts, ed., *Imagination & Meaning*, 1982, p. 142).

Once Eliade stated that young Romanians had a very short period of creative freedom, and that sense of fear of foreboding compelled him to work against the clock. Accordingly, he published not only literary works but also a series of important scholarly studies on alchemy, mythology, Oriental studies, philosophy, symbology, metallurgy, and the history of religions. In 1938 he founded the journal, *Zalmoxis: Revue des Etudes Religieuses*. (Unfortunately, circulation ceased after 1942.) Eliade was also active in the so-called Criterion group, consisting of male and female intellectuals, a significant collective manifestation of the "young generation," which sponsored public lectures, symposia and discussion on important contemporary intellectual issues as a new type of Socratic dialogue. Eliade said: "The goal we were pursuing was not only to inform people; above all, we were seeking to 'awaken' the audience, to confront them with ideas, and ultimately to modify their mode of being in the world" (*Autobiography, op cit.*, p. 237). Meanwhile, Romania could not help but be touched by the political whirlwind that was blowing in Europe, manifested in the conflicts and tensions between communism and democracy, fascism and nazism. Following the assassination of Romanian Prime Minister Duca in December, 1933, Eliade's mentor, Nae Ionescu, was arrested for suspicion of being an anti-royalist rightist. Also arrested were the leaders of the pro-Nazis Legion of the Archangel Michael, commonly known as the Legionnaires or the Iron Guard, and some of Eliade's friends in the Criterion group. Of course the Criterion experiment ceased to function because it was impossible for Legionnaires, democrats, and communists to share the same platform. Thus, Romania entered a "broken-off era," as Eliade called it, with fear and trembling. The tense political atmosphere, the cruelties and excesses of all sorts, find their echoes in Eliade's *Huliganii* (The Hooligans), although he wants us to know that the hooligans in his novel were very different from the actual Romanian hooligans of the 1930's—those "groups of young antisemites, ready to break windows or heads, to attack or loot synagogues. . ." (*Autobiography, op. cit.,* p. 301). What concerned Eliade was not only the sad political reality of his homeland. According to him: "I had had the premonition long before . . . that we would *not have time.* I sensed now not only that time was limited, but that there would come a terrifying time (the time of the "terror of history")" (*ibid.,* p. 292). In 1938 the royal dictatorship was proclaimed; then came World War II.

\* \* \*

In 1940 Eliade was appointed cultural attaché at the Royal Romanian Legation in war-torn London. In the following year he became a cultural counselor in neutral Lisbon. When the war was over in 1945, Eliade went directly to Paris, thus starting the life of self-imposed exile. Although he could write or lecture in French, starting a new life in a foreign country at the age of thirty-eight required considerable adjustment. On the other hand, by that time he was already a highly respected, mature scholar. "It took me ten years to understand," he says, "that the Indian experience alone could not reveal to me the universal man I had been looking for. . ." (*No Souvenirs, op. cit.,* p. 17). For this task he acknowledged the necessity of combining the history of religions, Orientalism, ethnology and other disciplines. In his own words:

> The correct analyses of myths and of mythical thought, of symbols and primordial images, especially the religious creations that emerge from Oriental and "primitive" cultures, are . . . the only way to open the Western mind and to introduce a new, planetary humanism. . . Thus, the proper procedure for grasping their meaning is not the naturalist's "objectivity," but the intelligent sympathy of the hermeneut. *It was the procedure itself that had to be changed. . .* This conviction guided my research on the meaning and function of myths, the structure of religious symbols, and in general, of the dialectics of the sacred and the profane (*ibid.,* p. xii).

In 1946 he was invited to serve as a visiting professor at the Ecole des Hautes Etudes of the Sorbonne. He then proceeded to publish such famous works as *Techniques du Yoga* (1948), *Traité d'historie des religions* (Patterns in Comparative Religion), *Le mythe de l'éternel retour* (The Myth of the Eternal Return) (1949) and *Le chamanisme et les techniques archaïques de l'extase* (Shamanism: Archaic Techniques of Ecstasy) (1951), etc. He was also invited by many leading universities in Europe to deliver lectures, and he appeared in a number of seminars and conferences, e.g., the one at Ascona, Switzerland.

In retrospect, it becomes clear that during his stay in Paris, 1945–1955, Eliade solidified most of his important concepts and categories, such as *homo religiosus, homo symbolicus,* archetypes, *coincidentia oppositorum,* hierophany, *axis mundi,* cosmic rope, nostalgia for Paradise, androgyny, initiatory scenario, etc., all of which became integral parts of a coherent outlook or system that aimed at what Eliade later called a total hermeneutics. This may account for the impossibility of divorcing, or even criticizing, any part of his system without disturbing the entire framework. Side by side with this development, one notices the shift in his personal orientation. Before World War II his scholarly and literary activities had focused very much on Romania. Then he affirmed that "the orthodox heritage could constitute a total conception of the world and existence, and that this synthesis, if it could be realized, would be a new phenomenon in the history of modern Romanian culture" (*Autobiography, op. cit.,* p. 132). After the war, he continued to regard himself as a Romanian writer, but something new was added, in the sense that his experience suggested the paradigm of the homeless exile as a symbol of religious reality for modern, secularized humankind. In this situation, his literary works, too, took on the coloring of a "*redeeming force (forta recuperatoare),*" to quote Eugene Simion (*Imagination & Meaning, op. cit.,* p. 136).

*    *    *

Like many other historians of religions, e.g., Raffaele Pettazzoni (1883–1959) and Joachim Wach (1898–1955), Eliade held that the discipline of the history of religions (Allgemeine Religionswissenschaft) consisted of two dimensions, historical and systematic. Characteristically, he worked initially on the systematic dimension (using the "morphological" method, inspired by Goethe), as exemplified by his *Traité* or *Patterns in Comparative Religion,* which presents a bewildering variety of religious data and their basic "patterns." The book starts with certain "cosmic" hierophanies ("manifestations of the sacred"), such as the sky, waters, earth, and stones. Analyses of these manifestations are based on his notion of the dialectic of the sacred in order to show how far those hierophanies constitute autonomous forms. He goes on to discuss the "biological" hierophanies (from the rhythm of the moon to sexuality), "local" hierophanies such as consecrated places, and "myths and symbols." Throughout the book, Eliade examines both the "lower" and "higher" religious forms side by side instead of moving from lower to higher forms, as is done in evolutionary schemes. He takes pain to explain that "religious wholes are not seen in bits and pieces, for each class of hierophanies . . . forms, in its own way, a whole, both morphologically . . . and historically . . ." (*Patterns in Comparative Religion,* 1958, p. xiv).

It is not surprising that Eliade's morphology of religion, which is his version of the systematic aspect of the history of religions, has much in common with the phenomenology of religion of Gerardus van der Leeuw (1890–1950), a Dutch historian of religions, theologian, ethnologist, and a phenomenologist. Eliade wrote a very positive review of van der Leeuw's *Religion in Essence and Manifestation* in *Revue d'Histoire des Religions* 138 (1950): 108–111). Although Eliade is uneasy with van der Leeuw's starting point, he praises the book because it shows that human beings can and do find religious meaning even in the most banal physiological activities such as eating and sexuality, and the book portrays the entire cosmos with its most humble parts serving as grounds for the manifestation of the sacred. It should be noted that religion has two dimensions in van der Leeuw's scheme, namely, "religion as experience," which can be studied phenomenologically, and "religion as revelation," which is basically incomprehensible and thus can be studied only theologically. Furthermore, van der Leeuw never claimed that his phenomenological study was empirical, because to him empirical research is needed only to control what has been understood phenomenologically. Similarly Eliade never claimed that the history of religions, including its systematic task, was empirical in a narrow scientific sense, even though it certainly has empirical dimensions.

Eliade always felt a need for the alternating modes of the creative spirit—the "diurnal," rational mode of scholarship, expressed in French, and the "nocturnal," mythological mode of imagination and fantasy, which he continued to express in Romanian. In 1955, the French translation of his major novel, *Forêt interdite*, appeared. According to Mac L. Ricketts, who translated this novel into English, Eliade felt it would be for this work and other fiction that he would be remembered by later generations, more than for his erudite scholarly works. *The Forbidden Forest* is in a sense a historical novel, dealing with the events and activities of the protagonist and his lovers, friends, and foes during the turbulent twelve years from 1936 to 1948, in Romania, London, Lisbon, Russia and Paris. In another sense it is an original novel. Eliade skillfully creates characters, all of whom are caught by "destiny," as people often are in his other stories. All of them try to escape from the network of historical events and from destructive "time," which is the central theme of this novel. The tangled story begins on the summer solstice in a forest near Bucharest. After twelve years, again on the summer solstice but in a French forest near the Swiss border, the protagonist encounters his long lost girl friend, and he finds salvation, which is "a kind of transcendental love for a girl—and death" (*Imagination and Meaning, op. cit.,* p. 105). To be sure, the novels were not meant to be literary illustrations of Eliade's theories, but he admits there are some structural analogies between the scientific and literary imaginations, such as the structure of sacred and mythical space, and more especially "a considerable number of strange, unfamiliar, and enigmatic worlds of meaning" (*No Souvenirs, op. cit.,* p. ix).

In 1956 Eliade was invited by the University of Chicago to deliver the Haskell Lectures, which were published under the title, *Birth and Rebirth.* In the following year, he joined the Chicago faculty and continued to live in that city after his retirement. At the time of his death in 1986, he was the

Sewell L. Avery Distinguished Service Professor Emeritus. His move to the United States at the age of forty-nine meant a second migration for him, but he made an excellent adjustment to the new environment. The University of Chicago had traditionally been an important center for the study of the history of religions and graduates trained by Eliade's predecessor, Joachim Wach, were scattered in many parts of North America and on other continents. Eliade's appointment at Chicago coincided with the sudden mushrooming of departments of religion or religious studies as part of the liberal arts in various colleges and universities in North America. Fortunately, his books and articles—mostly scholarly ones and not the literary works—were beginning to be translated into English, and the reading public devoured them. Eliade made a deep impression on young readers with such works as *Cosmos and History; The Sacred and the Profane; Myths, Dreams and Mysteries; Images and Symbols; Myth and Reality; Mephystopheles and the Androgyne; Zalmoxis; The Forge and the Crucible; The Quest;* etc. He also exerted a tremendous influence on more advanced students with *Yoga, Shamanism,* and *Australian Religions.* The fact that Eliade was willing to use nonphilosophical and nontheological terms in an elegant literary style to discuss religious subjects attracted many secularized youths.

There were three new factors which helped Eliade's cause enormously. The first was the founding of a new international journal for comparative historical studies called *History of Religions* in the summer of 1961. Wisely Eliade suggested making it an English language journal instead of a multilanguage one. For the opening issue, Eliade wrote the famous article entitled "History of Religions and a New Humanism." In it, he expressed his sympathy with young scholars who would have become historians of religions but who resorted to becoming specialists in one religion or even in a particular period or a single aspect of that religion in a world which exalts "specialists." Historians of religions, he felt, are called to be learned "generalists." He recognized the danger of "reductionism" in the history of religions as much as in the interpretation of art and literary works. He insisted that a work of art, for example, reveals its meaning only when it is seen as an autonomous artistic creation and nothing else. In the case of the history of religions he realized that the situation is complex because there is no such thing as a "pure" religious datum: human datum is also historical datum. But this does not imply that, for historians of religions, a historical religious datum is in any way reducible to a nonreligious, economic, social, cultural, psychological, or political meaning. And, quoting the words of Raffaele Pettazzoni, he exhorted readers to engage in the twin (systematic and historical) tasks of the history of religions. But, ultimately to him, the history of religions was more than merely an academic pursuit. In his own words:

> . . . the History of Religions is destined to play an important role in contemporary cultural life. This is not only because an understanding of exotic and archaic religions will significantly assist in a cultural dialogue

with the representatives of such religions. It is more especially because
. . . the history of religions will inevitably attain to a deeper knowledge
of man. It is on the basis of such knowledge that a new humanism, on a
world-wide scale, could develop. (*ibid.*, pp. 2–3).

Secondly, Eliade took an active part as a member (and President for a
term) of a small group of North American scholars called the American
Society for the Study of Religion (ASSR), established in Chicago in 1958. It
was through this group that much of Eliade's personal contacts with fellow
historians of religions and scholars in related fields in North America were
made.

Thirdly, Eliade, who had previously worked either on "systematic"
endeavors or on studies of "particular" religious forms, e.g., yoga,
shamanism, Romanian folk religion, or Australian religion, always from the
perspective of the history of religions, embarked during his Chicago days on
a new genre, namely, a "historical" study of the history of religions. Initially
he worked on a "thematic source book" entitled *From Primitive to Zen*,
dealing with religious data from nonliterate, ancient, medieval, and modern
religions. Then he envisaged the publication of four volumes (though his
health prevented his working on the fourth volume himself) entitled *A
History of Religious Ideas*. Although the scheme of the series follows manifestations of the sacred and the creative moments of the different traditions
more or less in chronological order, readers will recognize that these books
reflect faithfully his lifelong conviction about the fundamental unity of all
religious phenomena. Thus, in his "historical" studies as much as in his
"systematic" endeavors, he was true to his hypothesis that "every rite, every
myth, every belief or divine figure reflects the experience of the sacred and
hence implies the notions of *being*, of *meaning*, and of *truth*" ("Preface," Vol.
1, p. xiii).

During the latter part of his stay in Chicago, fame and honor came his
way from various parts of the world. By that time, many of his books,
including his literary works, had been translated into several languages. He
had his share of critics. Some people thought that he was not religious
enough, while others accused him for being too philosophical and not
humanistic enough, historical enough, scientific enough, or empirical
enough. But, as hinted earlier, he held a consistent viewpoint which penetrated all aspects of his scholarly and literary works, so that it is difficult to be
for or against any part of his writings, without having to judge the whole
framework.

Eliade's last major undertaking in his life was *The Encyclopedia of
Religion*. As he stated himself, what he had in mind was not a dictionary but
an encyclopedia—a selection of all the important ideas and beliefs, rituals
and myths, symbols and persons, that played a role in the universal history of
the religious experience of humankind from the paleolithic to our time. It is

to his credit that various scholars from every continent cooperated on the encyclopedia to produce concise, clear descriptions of a number of religious forms within the limits of our present knowledge. As soon as he had completed the major portion of his work as editor-in-chief of the encyclopedia, he was already thinking of several new projects, among them ones that would develop the themes of "cosmos," "humankind," and "time." Throughout his life, Eliade never claimed that he had the answer to the riddle of life, but he was willing to advance daring hypotheses.

Once Eliade paid a high tribute to his friend and colleague, Paul Tillich, at the latter's memorial service in Chicago, and if we replace the name of Eliade for that of Tillich, it portrays him admirably:

"Faithful to his vocation and his destiny [Eliade] did not die at the end of his career, when he had supposedly said everything important that he could say . . . Thus, his death is even more tragic. But it is also symbolic. . ." (*Criterion*, 5, no. 1, 1968, p. 15).

# BIBLIOGRAPHY

Both as a scholar and as a writer, Eliade was prolific throughout his life, and his works have been translated into many languages. Thus, it is virtually impossible to list all his books and articles, even the major ones, although efforts were made to include the major titles in the above text. Fortunately, there are some Eliade bibliographies in English, which are readily available to readers, such as the one included in *Myths and Symbols, Studies in Honor of Mircea Eliade*, ed. by J. M. Kitagawa and C. H. Long (1969), and a more up-to-date one by Douglas Allen and Dennis Doeing, *Mircea Eliade: An Annotated Bibliography* (1979). One of the best introductions to Eliade's thought is his *Ordeal by Labyrinth: Conversations with Claude Henri Rocquet* either in its French original (1978), or in its English translation (1982). This book has the virtue of unfolding Eliade's own mature views about himself, and it includes "A Chronology of Mircea Eliade's Life," which calls attention to his major writings. There are also many articles and books in various languages on Eliade's scholarly and literary works, critical, sympathetic, and favorable. The third section of the above-mentioned *Myths and Symbols*, N. J. Girardot & M. L. Ricketts, eds., *Imagination and Meaning, The Scholarly and Literary Worlds of Mircea Eliade* (1982), and D. Carrasco & J. M. Swanberg, eds., *Waiting for the Dawn: Mircea Eliade in Perspective* (1985) make helpful references to his creative writing, although his scholarly side inevitably comes into the picture too.

There are many other works (mentioning only monographs) that readers should find useful. See Douglas Allen, *Structure and Creativity in Religion:*

*Mircea Eliade's Phenomenology and New Directions* (1978); Thomas J. J. Altizer, *Mircea Eliade and the Dialectic of the Sacred* (1963); Guilford Dudley, *Religion on Trial: Mircea Eliade and His Critics* (1977); J. Z. Smith, *Map is not Territory: Studies in the History of Religions* (1978); Ioan P. Culianu, *Mircea Eliade* (1978); and Antonio B. de Silva, *The Phenomenology of Religion as a Philosophical Problem: An Analysis of the Theoretical Background of the Phenomenology of Religion, in General, and of M. Eliade's Phenomenological Approach, in Particular* (1982).

# APPENDIX

## THE 1893 WORLD'S PARLIAMENT OF RELIGIONS
## AND ITS LEGACY

I have often wondered why the Parliament of Religions, which has been all but forgotten here in Chicago, has remained so vivid in the memories of many religious people in other parts of the world. I have also been intrigued by the fact that such an unprecedented affair as the Parliament of Religions was held as a part of the Columbian Exposition, which marked the 400th anniversary of Columbus' discovery of America.

Admittedly, there are many different ways to deal with these questions. I would like to share with you my reflections on the significance of, first, the unlikely convergence of two very different undertakings, that is, the Columbian Exposition and the Parliament of Religions; second, the encounter of Western Christendom and Eastern religions in the nineteenth century as reflected in the Parliament; and third, the mixed legacies of the Parliament which we have inherited.

Historically, Columbus's discovery of America signified the ascendency of the Western powers, which by the end of the nineteenth century dominated the entire world politically, economically, and culturally. There is much truth in Toynbee's well-known observation that "in the encounter between the [non-Western] world and the West that has been going on . . . for four or five hundred years . . . it is the [non-Western] world that has been hit—and hit hard—by the West."[1] The enormous vitality of the West during the past five centuries has been made apparent in the cultural domain through the phenomena of modern nation-states, economic nationalism, a new social structure, and the Renaissance, and in the religious domain through the Reformation and the Counter Reformation.

It was the Renaissance which gave birth to the new conception of "civilization"—that is, Western civilization—as a pseudoreligion of secularized salvation. Rejecting the medieval notion that civilization was subservient to the church, modern Europeans came to regard themselves as the

Parts of this material were presented as the 75th Anniversary Lecture of the Haskell Lectureship at Oberlin College and as the Stewart Lecture at Princeton University.
[1] Arnold Toynbee, *The World and the West* (New York: Oxford University Press, 1953), pp. 1–2.

inventors and transmitters of true civilization. The phenomenal expansion of the West, coming as it did after Europe's centuries-old struggle against the world of Islam, convinced many Europeans of the superiority of their culture, their technology, and their socio-economic and political systems. They came to be persuaded that "biology and sociology point to the superiority of . . . the white races over the coloured races of the earth. Superiority in physical and mental constitution, together with superiority in civilization and organization, entail responsibility as well as privilege."[2] This notion is what Kipling called "the white man's burden"—the underlying, motivating force implicit in the colonial expansion of the modern West over the non-Western world.

Significantly, Pietist Christians in the eighteenth century rejected the secular view of the human being as the creator of cultural values. Thus the initial ethos of the Christian foreign missions, inaugurated by the continental Pietists and English Evangelicals, ran counter to the spirit of secular European civilization and of colonialism. During the nineteenth century, however, the Christian missionary enterprise in Asia and Africa unwittingly cooperated with European colonialism, and Christianity was propagated for all intents and purposes as one—albeit an important one—of the constituents of Western civilization. The combined forces of Western civilization, Christian missionary activities, and colonial expansion brought about social, political, economic, cultural, and religious changes in much of the non-Western world by the end of the nineteenth century.

The self-confidence of the nineteenth-century West was extravagantly displayed in a series of large-scale exhibits and fairs held in Europe and America, starting with the 1851 Exhibition at the Crystal Palace in Hyde Park, London. The nineteenth century also witnessed the emergence of the United States onto the world stage as a new Western power, whereby eager Americans sponsored their own Crystal Palace exposition in New York in 1853 and a more successful Philadelphia Centennial exposition in 1876. (By the way, the eight million visitors who poured into Philadelphia were fascinated not only by the old Liberty Bell, but also by such new inventions as Alexander Graham Bell's telephone, the Westinghouse air brake, Edison's duplex telegraph, the typewriter, and the sewing machine.) This event was followed by the Paris exhibition of 1889, which lured the curious multitudes to the newly built Eiffel Tower. Then, in 1893, the Columbian Exposition, the last major exhibition of the nineteenth century, was held in Chicago as the crowning symbol of the achievement of Western civilization during the great century.

The Columbian Exposition was held in Jackson Park and the adjoining

[2] Allan John Macdonald, *Trade Politics and Christianity in Africa and the East* (London: Longmans, Green and Co., 1916), p. 270.

Midway. The expansive grounds, far larger than the space occupied by the Philadelphia Exposition, held a series of white buildings with classic façades, one of which was later remodelled as the Museum of Science and Industry. The Exposition grounds also had large plazas, lagoons with floating gondolas, and a playground with the first ferris wheel, from which visitors could catch a glimpse of the infant University of Chicago. The designers of the "White City" made full use of electricity, and the great Allis engine in Jackson Park was dramatically started by President Cleveland in the White House at the touch of a magic button.[3]

The more I think about it, the idea of holding such an unprecedented assembly of representatives of the various religions of the world in connection with the Columbian Exposition is not so outrageous after all. As far as we can ascertain, the underlying link between the two events was the motif of "progress"—an idea that was shared by many American civic, government, business, and religious leaders in the nineteenth century. In this regard, we might recall Paul Tillich's distinction between the "concept" of progress, which is just a theoretical abstraction, and the "idea" of progress, which is an interpretation of our historic existence in terms of progress.[4] Religiously, the Jewish and Christian "idea" of progress is traced to the Hebrew scripture, according to which God had chosen a nation and a people and would fulfill his promise to move history toward a specific end. It is significant that the biblically oriented American pioneers interpreted the birth of the new republic in biblical terms. Moreover, many Americans felt that their experience in the nineteenth century of transforming landscape and overcoming frontiers confirmed their faith in progress. In this situation, progress became "not only conscious doctrine but also an unconscious dogma."[5] This dogma was eloquently stated by Charles C. Bonney, an influential lawyer, a civic leader, and a devout Swedenborgian, who first proposed that the Parliament of Religions be held as an integral part of the Columbian Exposition. In his words:

> The coming glory of the World's Fair of 1893 should not be the exhibit . . . of [only] the material triumphs, industrial achievements, and mechanical victories of man, however magnificent that display may be. Something higher and nobler is demanded by the progressive spirit of the present age. . . . [What is needed is] a congress of statesmen, jurists, financiers, scientists, literati, teachers, and theologians, greater

[3] For a description of the physical designs of the Columbian Exposition, see *The White City (As It Was)* (Chicago: White City Art Co., 1894).
[4] Paul Tillich, *The Future of Religions*, ed. Jerald C. Brauer (New York: Harper & Row, 1966), p. 64.
[5] Ibid., p. 68.

in numbers and more widely representative of all peoples and nations and tongues than any assemblage which has ever yet been convened.[6]

The organizers of the Columbian Exposition accepted Bonney's proposal, and decided to hold the Parliament of Religions with the following charter:

> To unite all Religions against all irreligion; to make the Golden Rule the basis of this union; to present to the world . . . the substantial unity of many religions in the goods deeds of the Religious life; to provide for a World's Parliament of Religions, in which their common aims and common grounds of unity may be set forth, and the marvelous *Religious progress* of the Nineteenth century be reviewed. . . ."[7]

The Parliament was held from September 11 through 18, primarily at two assembly halls in the present Art Institute on Michigan Avenue. Each hall accommodated 3,000 people, and both were full at every session.

In retrospect, it is evident that the Parliament had several layers of meaning. First, in spite of its designation as a "World's Parliament of Religions," it was predominantly an assembly of Christians, and more particularly of American Christians, who constituted the majority of the 400 delegates. Although the Parliament was not an official church assembly, it brought face-to-face representatives of various Christian groups, Roman Catholics, Orthodox, and many Protestant denominations, as well as those of smaller, splinter groups. Moreover, the programs of the Parliament, though liberal, had a definite Christian flavor, with the singing of hymns and the recitation of the Lord's Prayer.

Second, the Parliament signified the pluralistic religious reality of North America, epitomized by the presence of many articulate Jewish leaders, who took their rightful place beside Protestant and Roman Catholic leaders. The Parliament also demonstrated the growing influence of laymen and laywomen in American religious life.

Third, the Parliament presented a Christian theological rationale for inviting representatives of other religions to a common assembly. In the words of Charles Bonney, it was "a friendly conference [based on] the golden rule of Christ: a royal feast to which the representatives of every faith were asked to bring the richest fruits and rarest flowers of their religion."[8] No representative was asked to surrender any conviction he or she believed to

[6] Cited in Walter R. Houghton, ed., *Neely's History of the Parliament of Religions and Religious Congress' World's Columbian Exposition* (Chicago: F. Tennyson Neely, 1893), pp. 15–16.

[7] The World's Religious Congress, *Programme of the World's Religious Congresses of 1893* (preliminary edition, Chicago: Rand, McNally & Co., n.d.), p. 19, italics mine.

[8] Cited in George S. Goodspeed, ed., *The World's First Parliament of Religions: Its Christian Spirit, Historic Greatness and Manifold Results* (Chicago: Hill & Shuman, 1895), p. 56.

be the truth, nor was anyone asked to participate in any part of the program of the Parliament which might compromise his relationship to his own religion. Yet even then, some influential leaders, notably the Sultan of Turkey, strongly opposed the idea of the Parliament; as a result of such opposition, Islam was represented only by an American convert to Islam and some Western scholars and missionaries who worked among Muslims. Fortunately, though, the Parliament was able to attract articulate spokesmen of modern-day Hinduism, Buddhism, and other Eastern religions who came to Chicago in spite of the opposition of their conservative coreligionists at home. In a sense, the Parliament dramatically acknowledged the general interest in Eastern religions that was developing among many Americans, an interest that was evidenced by the disproportionate degree of attention given to Eastern representatives by the daily presses; and as might be expected, this aspect of the Parliament was condemned by some and praised by others among the Christian leaders and missionaries.

Fourth, while the Parliament was an assembly of religious representatives and not a gathering of scholars, it nevertheless called attention to the need for scholarly approaches and resources in dealing with the fact of religious pluralism on the global scene. It is worth mentioning in this regard that Friedrich Max Müller, a leading spokesman of the new discipline of the science of religion *(Religionswissenschaft)*, had enthusiastically endorsed the idea of the Parliament but could not attend; nor could another leading scholar, C. P. Tiele, whose paper was presented at the Parliament by another representative.[9] But the presence of other important scholars from Europe and North America aroused keen interest among enlightened educators and religious leaders.

As we turn our attention to the encounter between Western Christendom and Eastern religions as reflected in the Parliament of Religions, it is worth recalling that the historic patterns of Christian outreach to the non-Western world, initiated by Iberian maritime kingdoms in the sixteenth century, had already deteriorated by the end of the eighteenth century. This deterioration was due in large part to the decline of Spain and Portugal and to the dissolution of the Society of Jesus. During the nineteenth century, Protestantism, which had been a minority movement in northwest Europe, took the initiative in the overseas missionary enterprise. By the end of the nineteenth century, almost every Christian group "and almost every country, from the Lutheran Church of Finland . . . to the newest sects in the United States, had its share in the missionary enterprise overseas."[10]

Initially, European colonial authorities were hostile to Christian mission-

[9] See C. P. Tiele, "On the Study of Comparative Theology," in John Henry Barrows, ed., *The World's Parliament of Religions* (Chicago: Parliament Publishing Company, 1893), 2 vols., 1:583–590.

[10] Stephen Neill, *The Christian Society* (London: Nisbet, 1952), p. 203.

ary work. For example, the British East India Company followed the policy that "to hold India in subjugation Christian missionaries must be excluded."[11] Yet, colonial officials soon began to favor Christian missionary work, especially its educational and philanthropic activities. This development resulted in the conscious and unconscious cooperation of Christian missionaries with colonial administrators who reinforced each other in transmitting Western civilization to the non-Western world.

The massive penetration of Western civilization into the East greatly accelerated the disintegration of Asian societies, cultures, and religions during the nineteenth century. Inevitably there developed a deep chasm between the traditional Asian elites, who resented anything new and Western, and the new, Western-educated elites, who scorned old customs and values as a legacy of the backward, feudalistic past. With the passion of new converts, they were determined to interpret their own people's contemporary experiences not with the accumulated values and wisdom of Asia, but with the new gospel of Western civilization: liberty, equality, fraternity, democracy, science, and technology. As might be expected, some of the new Asian elites embraced Christianity.

In addition to, or rather, in between the old and the new elites, there emerged a third type of Asian elite, who for lack of a better designation may be called simply "modern religious reformers." Although they were small in number and often criticized, attacked, and ridiculed by both the old and the new elites, these modern religious reformers had the unshakable conviction that their inherited religious and cultural traditions had sufficient resiliency to come to terms with the serious issues raised by modernity. They had been influenced by Western education and Western thought, but they were proud of the languages, cultures, and religions of their homelands. While not engaging in political activities, they were all patriots without being narrow Nationalists. None of these figures were scholars by temperament, but they were religious and social reformers, keenly aware of the welfare of their own peoples. They were leaders and practitioners who possessed an astute understanding of their own religious traditions. Moreover, all of them had a global vision. Significantly, it was these modern religious reformers in Asia, and not the old elites or the traditional religious leaders, who responded to the invitation to participate in the Parliament of Religions.

Among those modern Asian religious reformers at the Parliament, three are especially important for our consideration: Vivekananda of India (1863–1902), Dharmapāla of Ceylon, now Sri Lanka (1864–1933), and Shaku Sōyen of Japan (1859–1919). All of them were relatively young then—Vivekananda was 30, Dharmapāla was 29, and Shaku Sōyen was 34 years of age. They were eager to come to Chicago, not only because they all subscribed to the principle of interreligious understanding and cooperation, but also because

[11] Macdonald, *Trade Politics*, pp. ix–x.

they saw in the Parliament an opportunity which they had never had: a platform from which to address the whole world. Even though their own homelands were under the strong influence of Western civilization, these three young men had the audacious dream of reversing the tide of history and beginning the Easternization of the West.

Much has been written about Swami Vivekananda, the founder of the Ramakrishna Order. In his time, India was under the rule of the British Crown. English was already the *lingua franca* of the multilingual Indian subcontinent, and the educated Indians who were exposed to Western social and political philosophies wanted a greater share in the government of their own country. Great famines, such as the ones in Bihar from 1873 to 1883 and in South India from 1876 to 1878, continued to haunt India from inside, while Russian intrigue and Afghan wars threatened her from outside. Articulate, educated youths, dissatisfied with both the general state of unemployment and racial discrimination in government services, were attracted to political activities such as the Indian National Congress, while those more religiously motivated were lured to Hindu reform movements such as Keshub Chunder Sen's Brahmo Samaj and Dayanand Sarasvati's Arya Samaj.

Meanwhile, Vivekananda, who had studied law at the University of Calcutta and was about to sail to England for further study, abruptly changed his course and became the disciple of the saintly mystic, Sri Ramakrishna (1836–1886). Under Ramakrishna, he endeavored to translate his master's teaching into concrete measures for the reformation of Hinduism and of Hindu society. Vivekananda's neo-Vedantic belief is based on the eternalness of the human soul, which is capable of becoming divine. His message to the world, as presented at the Parliament, concerned the supremacy of the eternal principle (*sanatana dharma*) of the Hindu tradition as separated from its metaphysico-social principle and as exemplified by the caste *dharma* (*svadharma*), which is above all creeds and religions, Eastern or Western. He never asked whether such a separation of the eternal *dharma* from the Hindu religious and social tradition was legitimate, he simply preached: "Do not care for doctrines, do not care for dogmas, or sects, or churches, or temples; they count for little compared with the essence of existence in each man which is spirituality. . . ."[12] Understandably, his message at the Parliament for religious toleration,[13] although reflecting his neo-Hindu perspective, was well received. After the Parliament, he spent four years preaching his gospel in America and England, and upon his return to India, founded the Ramakrishna Mission, which now has branches in India as well as in various Western cities.

Dharmapāla—or more precisely, Anāgarika Dharmapāla, "the celibate servant of the *Dharma*" (David Hewavitarane)—was a child of Ceylon, the

---

[12] *Speeches and Writings of Swami Vivekananda* (Madras: n.d.), p. 31.
[13] Barrows, *Parliament*, 1:102.

proud homeland of Pali Buddhism, but a homeland that had been occupied successively since the sixteenth century by the Portuguese, the Dutch, and the British. Early in the nineteenth century, the British had guaranteed the protection of Buddhism, but all education was controlled by Christian missionaries. In addition, the introduction of the planting of coffee resulted in the importation of a sizeable number of South Indian Hindu Tamil laborers, who settled in the northern section of Ceylon. With the opening of the Suez Canal in 1869, Colombo became a prosperous center of international trade. Understandably, the growing middle class in Ceylon became heavily westernized in orientation and in daily habits.

Amidst this mixed cultural milieu, through his numerous writings and speeches, the young Dharmapāla advocated the importance of the Buddhist heritage, Buddhist education, and the Singhalese language and culture. In addition, in 1891, two years before the Parliament, he founded the Mahā Bodhi Society, originally the Bodhgaya Mahābodhi Society, in Colombo. One of the purposes of this society was to work towards the restoration of the sacred city of Bodhgaya in India as the site for a monastery and college, to be staffed by scholars from various Buddhist nations in Asia. In both of his projects, Dharmapāla was greatly aided by the Buddhist Theosophical Society, founded in Ceylon by Colonel Henry Steel Olcott and Madame Blavatsky; and it was through the activities of the Mahā Bodhi Society in its publications and its educational and evangelistic works that important contributions were made to both the rejuvenation of Buddhism in Ceylon and India and the expansion of Buddhism to the West.

At the Parliament, Dharmapāla presented the main tenets of Buddhism with a touch of Theosophy, stressing that "Buddhism is a scientific religion, inasmuch as it earnestly enjoins that nothing whatever be accepted on faith. . . . Buddhism is tantamount to a knowledge of other sciences."[14] Understandably, the scientific nature of Buddhism, an important aspect of modern Buddhism, caught the attention of many people at the Parliament. Dharmapāla also offered advice to the Christian missionaries: ". . . if you want to establish Christianity in the East, it can only be done on the principles of Christ's love and meekness. Let the missionaries study all the religions; let them be a type of meekness and lowliness and they will find a welcome in all lands."[15]

Little is known in the West about Shaku Sōyen other than that he was instrumental in bringing D. T. Suzuki to the West; but he was a remarkable person in his own right. He was born shortly after Commodore Perry's expeditions, which forcibly opened Japan's doors to the West. During Sōyen's childhood, the feudal regime declined and the Meiji imperial regime began its reign. Under the pro-Shinto policy of the imperial regime, Bud-

[14] Ibid., 2:878.
[15] Ibid., p. 1093.

dhism lost many of its traditional prerogatives. Moreover, Buddhism now faced the massive impact of Western civilization and the newly introduced Christianity. Under these circumstances, the morale of Japanese Buddhists reached its lowest ebb. Fortunately, there were a small number of enlightened Buddhist leaders, including Sōyen's own master, Imagita Kōsen (1816–1892), who were determined to reform Buddhism for the new age. Thus Sōyen, unlike other Buddhist clerics of his time, studied at Keiō Gijuku, the center of the Japanese enlightenment movement, and also spent two years studying in Ceylon and visiting Thailand and China. In 1892, at the age of 33, Sōyen became the chief abbot of the prestigious Engaku-ji, Kamakura, and attracted many serious–minded lay disciples, including D. T. Suzuki.

At the Parliament, Sōyen pleaded for world peace and mutual assistance: ". . . let us, the true followers of Buddha, the true followers of Jesus Christ, the true followers of Confucius and the followers of truth, unite ourselves for the sake of helping the helpless and living glorious lives of brotherhood under the control of truth."[16] After the Parliament, he made two more visits to the West, accompanied by his disciple, D. T. Suzuki, also preparing the ground for Zen Buddhist activities in the West. True to his convictions, when he returned to Japan he was instrumental in organizing the Buddhist-Christian conference of 1896, then known as the "Little Parliament of Religions," against strong opposition from both sides. Parenthetically, at its second meeting in 1897, the main speaker was John Henry Barrows, the permanent chairman of the Chicago Parliament of Religions, about whom I will speak presently.

Even such brief portraits of these three modern religious reformers from the East make it clear, I hope, that what they had expected from the Parliament was slightly different from the intent of the organizers. To Charles Bonney and his colleagues, the Parliament was an "extended Christian feast" to which the representatives of other religions were asked to bring the richest fruits and rarest flowers of their faiths. What the religious reformers from Asia expected to find was a genuine parliament of religions, in which representatives of all religions would share their insights and wisdom as to how each faith could cope with the issues raised by modernity, and how "all religions [could] be united against all irreligion," to use the phrase of the preliminary program of the Parliament.

Undoubtedly the most important leader and spokesman of the Parliament was the then 46-year-old John Henry Barrows, pastor of the First Presbyterian Church in Chicago, who served as the permanent chairman of the Parliament. A graduate of Olivet College, Yale University, Union Seminary, and Andover Seminary, Barrows had had pastorates in Kansas, Massachusetts, and Paris. He was a relative newcomer to Chicago, and he liked

---

[16] Ibid., p. 1285.

the city, which was then rebuilding from the devastation of the Great Fire. He quickly made the acquaintance of civic leaders, many of whom supported both the Parliament and the new University of Chicago. He was also a great admirer of William Rainey Harper, the energetic first president of The University of Chicago, who held a vision of the "second Reformation" of Christianity through scholarship. It was reported that over 1,000 members were added to Barrow's parish during the first two years of his pastorate. His personality comes through vividly in a letter he wrote a few years after the Parliament during his tenure as president of Oberlin College. The letter was addressed to the newborn son of Professor J. Ross Stevenson of McCormick Theological Seminary. It reads:

My dear William:

I have just heard of your alighting on this planet and hasten to welcome you to the land of William McKinley and the speech of William Shakespeare. I am sorry that you cannot vote against William Bryan, but your father will do that for you.

As a Republican, a Presbyterian, an American, a Chicagoan, and as the son and heir of such a father and mother your prospects are bright. Be good to your father. Kindly tell them how happy I am for them. Believing that you are "the bright, consummate flower" of the vanishing century and with all high hopes, I remain, with loving congratulations to your jubilant parents. . . .[17]

The letter was dated November 1, 1900. Incidentally, the baby in question, William Edward Stevenson, later followed Barrows as the eighth president of Oberlin College.

Both as an American and as a Christian, Barrows shared the optimism of his generation. He lived at a time when America was internally recovering from the effects of the Civil War and externally emerging as a new world power. His was also the time when many idealistic young men and women took up evangelistic, educational, and philanthropic activities in far-off lands. Their vision was exemplified by the motto of the Student Volunteer Movement: "The evangelization of the world in this generation."

During the Parliament, the tall and genial Barrows, combining learning, rhetorical gifts, and a sense of humor, won the admiration of participants and the press for his intelligence, ability, tact, skill, and courage. He perceived the meaning of the Parliament in terms of three concentric circles, with the Christian assembly at its center. Indeed, to him the Parliament was the first modern parliament of Christendom and marked an important step toward the prophecy of a united church. In his words: "The solemn charge which the

---

[17] Printed in Oberlin College *Alumni Magazine* (December 1958). I owe this information to Professor Grover Zinn, Jr.

Parliament preaches to all true believers is a return to the primitive unity of the world. . . . The results may be far off, but they are certain."[18]

Next to the Christian center was the circle of the American religious assembly. Following the American principle of religious liberty, this circle demonstrated both a genuine cooperation between Jews, whom he called Old Testament Christians, and Christians, whom he called New Testament Jews, and the growing leadership of women in American religious life.

Third and last came the outer circle comprising all the religions of the world, and on this level, Christianity was one among many faiths "competing for the conquest of mankind."[19] To Barrows, the plurality of religions was a genuine mystery, but he was certain that the deity whom Jews and Christians worship had something to do with all these religions of the world. He asked, "Why should not Christians be glad to learn what God has wrought through Buddha and Zoroaster—through the sages of China, and the prophets of India and the prophet of Islam?"[20]

For Barrows, therefore, what united these three circles of the Parliament was the religious quest, the hope, and the longing of the children of the one God, the Christians and the Jews, and adherents of other faiths. As he stated in his opening address:

> We are met as religious men, believing here [meaning Chicago] in this capital of material wonders in the presence of an Exposition which displays the unparalleled marvels of steam and electricity, that there is a *spiritual root of all human progress*. We are met in a school of comparative theology . . . in the temper of love, determined to bury, at least for the time, our sharp hostilities, anxious to find out wherein we agree, eager to learn what constitutes the strength of other faiths and the weakness of our own.[21]

It is interesting to note that Barrows' search for "a spiritual root of all human progress" led him to turn not to theology but to "comparative religion" for illumination. Untrained in any aspect of comparative religion, he had nevertheless an immense admiration for Friedrich Max Müller, that ardent spokesman for the emerging discipline of the science of religion, although Barrows' understanding of comparative religion was much more simplistic and pragmatic than his mentor's explications. For example, Barrows cites the work of Max Müller solely to make his point that the same sun "which shone over Bethlehem and Calvary has cast some celestial illumina-

[18] See Goodspeed, *World's First Parliament*, p. 60.
[19] Cited in ibid., p. 53.
[20] Barrows, *Parliament*, 1:75.
[21] Ibid., italics mine.

tion and called forth some devout and holy aspirations by the Nile and the Ganges, in the deserts of Arabia and by the waves of the Yellow Sea."[22]

Barrows was entirely clear, however, about the concrete objectives of comparative religion in his time. These objectives were: (1) to present to the West the religious reality of the world, especially undistorted accounts of non-Christian religions, in order to combat general ignorance and prejudice in "Christian lands" concerning other religions; (2) to present to the non-Western world the best available views on the relations of Christianity and other religions; and (3) to probe more deeply into the ancient Near Eastern religious roots which had culminated in the Bible and Christianity. He did not see any fundamental tension between being both a seeker of universal religious truth and a Christian. Accordingly, he was able to welcome openly and warmly the representatives of the many different religions who had gathered together at the Parliament; and in his address at the closing session, he stated quite as sincerely: "I desire that the last word which I speak to the Parliament shall be the name of Him to whom I owe life and truth and hope and all things, who reconciles all contradictions, pacifies all antagonisms, and who from the throne of His heavenly kingdom directs the serene and unwearied omnipotence of redeeming love—Jesus Christ, the savior of the world."[23]

One can readily understand that the Parliament provoked both extremely positive and intensely negative reactions in its contemporaries. Yet as we look back from today's vantage point after ninety years, we can probably assess without undue emotionalism the mixed legacies of the Parliament.

First, it is important to point out that, contrary to popular views, the Parliament did not initiate comparative religion in America. It did, however, provide such a strong stimulus for the wide acceptance of the study of comparative religion in American colleges, universities, and theological seminaries that in the minds of many Americans comparative religion and the cause of the Parliament of Religions became inseparably related. To be sure, there were some positive results from such an identification. For example, Barrows' contagious enthusiasm for comparative religion, which he called "the highest study to which the human mind can now devote its energies,"[24] caught the imagination of one of his parishioners, Mrs. Caroline Haskell, the widow of the wealthy businessman, Frederick Haskell. In 1894, she established the Haskell Lectureship in Comparative Religion at the infant University of Chicago, expressing herself "in hearty agreement with the conviction that the immense interest awakened by the wonderful Parliament of Religions makes it eminently desirable that the students in the University of

[22] Ibid., pp. 74–75.
[23] Ibid., pp. 184.
[24] Cited in Godspeed, *World's First Parliament*, p. 14.

Chicago, and the people generally, shall be given wise instruction on this most important of all subjects."[25] Barrows was named the first Haskell Lecturer of this lectureship, which has since brought many prominent scholars from Asia and Europe, including Professor Mircea Eliade, who subsequently stayed at Chicago.

Later in that same year, Mrs. Haskell offered to The University of Chicago a second endowed lectureship, with the request that this one bear the name of John Henry Barrows. The purpose of this lectureship was the presentation of lectures on "the relations of Christianity and other religions," to be given in India and, if deemed best, in other parts of Asia. Again Barrows became the first lecturer of this series, even though it meant resignation from his pulpit. It is worth noting that this lectureship sent many scholars to India from The University of Chicago, including Dean Charles Gilkey and Professors Bernard E. Meland and James M. Gustafson. Moreover, it was this same Mrs. Haskell who donated to the University Haskell Hall, which for many years housed The Divinity School, the office of the University president, and the Haskell Oriental Museum. At its dedication, Professor George S. Goodspeed spoke on Mrs. Haskell's behalf, expressing the hope that "there will go forth from these halls enlightenment, inspiration, and guidance in that learning which has come from the East and which, culminating in the Book of Books and in the teaching and life of the Son of Man, will ever abide as our most precious possession."[26] The cornerstone of Haskell Hall bears inscriptions in three languages: in Greek, "He was the true light, that, coming into the world, enlighteneth every man"; in Latin, "Light out of the East"; and in Hebrew, "The entrance of thy words giveth light." I am sure that our colleagues in the Anthropology Department, the present inhabitants of Haskell Hall, have some appreciation of these inscriptions.

In 1898, when Barrows became president of Oberlin College, Mrs. Haskell designated funding for another Haskell Lectureship to be based at Oberlin for the promotion of scholarship in oriental literature and its relation to the Bible and Christianity. Like its Chicago forerunner, Oberlin's Haskell Lectureship has brought a number of eminent scholars to this country, including Rudolf Otto, Adolf Deissman, Gunther Bornkamm, and Yihard Yadin.

In addition to the three lectureships established by Mrs. Haskell, around this time a group of scholars on the East Coast were forming the American Committee for Lectures on the History of Religions. The chief advocate of this lectureship was Morris Jastrow of The University of Pennsylvania, who is considered to be the "father" of what is today called "religious

[25] President's Papers, 1889–1925, The University of Chicago Archives, box 35, folder 2.
[26] Cited in *The Biblical World*, n.s. 5 (February 1895):132–134, reprinted in Goodspeed, *World's First Parliament*, pp. 12–13.

studies" in America. This lectureship brought T. W. Rhys Davids, Karl Budde, J. J. M. de Groot, Franz Cumont, C. Snouck Hurgronje, and other leading scholars to the United States. In 1937, the lectureship was taken over by the American Council of Learned Societies and has come to be known as the ACLS Lectures on History of Religions.[27] Professor Peter Brown served as the 1982–83 ACLS Lecturer.

Despite—or possibly because of—its lack of clarity as a discipline, the popularity of comparative religion during the first quarter of our century was greatly aided by the spirit of religious liberalism predominant at that time, a spirit which affirmed the oneness of humanity and which had an optimistic vision of social progress. Later, in the 1930s, the sudden decline of comparative religion was accelerated by the impact of neoorthodox theology, the depression, and the impending war.

Ironically, the Parliament of Religions and its advocacy of comparative religion had a very different effect upon Eastern religions than it had upon the American religious scene. Actually, what modern religious reformers from the East, for example, Vivekananda of India, Dharmapāla of Ceylon, and Shaku Sōyen of Japan, learned at the Parliament was not comparative religion à la Barrows but the Christian formula of "fulfillment" implicit in Barrows' understanding of comparative religion, according to which all the religious quests of the human race, including those of the other great religions, would be "fulfilled" in the Christian gospel. These modern religious reformers in Asia quickly appropriated this "formula" for themselves and reversed the Christian claim, developing "fulfillment" theories from their own faith perspectives.

Following the lead of these early modern religious reformers, many articulate spokesmen of Eastern religions in our time have refined their "apologetics." They do not suggest that Christianity is wrong; rather, they insist that they can embrace Christianity within their particular religious frameworks, much as Barrows and his colleagues tried to do from a Christian perspective at the Parliament. Thus, Sarvepalli Radhakrishnan states:

> The saving knowledge of God is not knowledge and faith in Jesus as a historic person portrayed in the Gospels. . . . Christ is the spirit of the Supreme, the Eternal Word. . . .
>
> Christian religion is the continuation and restoration of the ancient religions, of something eternal, the Law which Christ came to fulfill but not to destroy. . . . To be a Christian is not the profession of an outward creed but the living of an inward life.[28]

---

[27] See D. H. Daugherty, "Committee on the History of Religions," *ACLS Newsletter* 15 (November 1964); 11–13.

[28] Sarvepalli Radhakrishnan, *Recovery of Faith* (New York: Harper, 1955), pp. 159–160.

Likewise, Shaku Sōyen's disciple, D. T. Suzuki, gives the Zen commentary on the Genesis account of creation:

> When God saw the light which came out of his command, he said, "It is good." This appreciation on the part of God is the first awakening of consciousness in the world; in fact the beginning of the world itself. The mere separation of light and darkness does not demonstrate the beginning. The world starts only when there is a mind which appreciates, viz., a mind critically conscious of itself. This is also the eating of "the fruit of the tree which is in the midst of the garden." The eating means "knowing good and evil," appraising the light and darkness, and in this appraisal, in this knowledge, there is the secret of living by Zen.[29]

In retrospect, it becomes clear that what the Parliament contributed to Eastern religions was not comparative religion as such. Rather, Barrows and his colleagues should receive credit for initiating what we call today the "dialogue among various religions," in which each religious claim for ultimacy is acknowledged.

Another important fact which those of us interested in religion often forget is that the Parliament of Religions was but one of twenty congresses held as part of the Columbian Exposition, including those on women's progress, the public press, medicine and surgery, temperance, moral and social reform, commerce and finance, music, literature, education, engineering, art, government, science, and philosophy. However successful or unsuccessful they may have been, we cannot help being impressed by the bold vision of the planners of the Columbian Exposition for the "establishment of a universal fraternity of learning and virtue" coupled with the firm affirmation of the human capacity to move forward.[30] Yet in their organizational overkill they viewed religion as a single dimension, however important and colorful, of human activities. In so doing, despite the best of intentions they trivialized the very nature of religion itself. This pigeon holing of religion into one aspect of human life is what Paul Tillich later criticized as the "*Time Magazine* approach to religion," the allocation to it of a small space between sections on theater and sports. Accordingly, many people now take it for granted that if the pope were shot, it would be a religious matter, whereas Hindu-Muslim conflicts in India or Christian-Muslim conflicts in the Philippines are either international or domestic political matters. Be that as it may, we can ill afford to forget the Parliament and its mixed legacies which we have inherited, directly or indirectly.

Not so long ago I was showing a Buddhist visitor from Japan around the campus, and as we walked along the Midway, I explained to him that it was

---

[29] D. T. Suzuki, *Living by Zen* (New York: Rider, 1950), p. 13.
[30] Barrows, *Parliament*, 1:186.

the site of the lagoon during the Columbian Exposition. Then I told him that one evening, so the story goes, some leaders of the Parliament were aboard a gondola floating over the illuminated waters. Stunned by the beauty of the White City, the Ceylonese Dharmapāla said with a smile, "All the joys of heaven are in Chicago," to which an English delegate replied, "I wish I were sure that all the joys of Chicago are to be in heaven." In reporting this conversation, John Henry Barrows added his comment: "But surely there will be a multitude there, whom no man can number, out of every kindred and people and tongue, and in that perpetual parliament on high the people of God will be satisfied."[31]

Now all of these leaders have joined the heavenly parliament, leaving behind precious memories of a grandiose vision, an undaunted spirit, and a profound dedication to the search for truth in religion—indeed, noble legacies that we are proud to inherit.

[31] Reported in ibid., p. 183.

# INDEX

Abe, Masami, 52
Abegg, Lily, 193
Abel, Professor, 119n
academic specialization, 107–109
Acts, Book of, 234
Adams, Henry, 103
Ahlström, Gösta, 144
Ainu:
 bear festival, 33, 47–99
 chieftains, 49–50
 conception of sacred, 72–76, 79–80
 epics, 49
 folklore, 47–99
 (see also Batchelor, 48n)
 funerary rites, 80–82
 grammar, 48n
 initiation rites, 76n–77n
 in Japanese history, 57–66
 language, 56
 prehistory, 50–59
 racial characteristics, 50–51
 revolt, 63–66
 shamanism, 69–70, 69n
 Tokugawa attitude toward, 63–66
 village life, 75–77
 witchcraft, 69–70
Alger, William R., 5
Al Ghazzali, 280
Allen, Douglas, 353
*Allgemeine Religionswissenschaft*, 14,
 25, 128, 152, 301–303
Altizer, Thomas J.J., 353
America, 218–230
Anesaki, Masaharu, x
Angelis, Girolamo de, 47n
*apartheid*, 264
Appleton, George, 263
Aristotle, 39
Arnold, Edwin, 103

Ashby, Phillip H., 103n, 133
Asia:
 anti-Westernism, 203
 democracy in, 211
 communism in, 319–320
 meditation in, 246, 254
 nationalism, 208–215
 religion since WWII, 317–320
 self-identity, 191–215
 Western imperialism in, 179–190
 Westernisation of, 252–254
Asians in American law, 218–219
Asian studies, 127–128
Augustine, 335
*Ausdruck*, 303
Azad, Maulana Abul Kalam, 204

Baelz, Erwin, 50
Barrows, John Henry, 5, 316–367
Batchelor, John, 47, 47n, 48n, 51, 57n,
 62n, 71n, 73–75, 81, 84–85, 87, 89n,
 92, 93n, 94, 98
bear ritual, 47–99 (see also Iyomante,
 Ainu, Hallowell)
*Bedeutung*, 278
Bell, Alexander Graham, 113
Bell, Daniel, 227
Bellah, Robert N., 44n
Benz, Ernst, 314n, 320
Berdyaev, Nikolas, 298
Berger, J., 5
Bergson, Henri, 116
Berkeley, G., 16
Bertholet, Rene, 117
*Bhagavad Gita*, 255
Bigg, H.A.R., 239
Black America, 226–230
Bleeker, C.J., 118, 119n
Boardman, George Dana, 5

theological history of religions, 124–
131 (see also Tillich)
Wach's view of, 139–141
Hitchcock, Romyn, 47, 53, 56n, 65
Hitler, Adolf, 333
Hocking, William Ernest, 12, 25n, 112,
214, 317–318
Hodges, H.A., 153
Holbrook, Clyde A., 107
*homo neanderthalensis*, 30
*homo religiosus*, 27, 39, 303, 347
Hopkins, Edward Washburn, 4
Hori, Ichiro, 60, 79
Horton, Douglas, 109
House, Floyd Nelson, 288n
Hume, David, 16
Hurgronje, C. Snouck, 368
Husserl, Edmund, 306
Hutchins, Robert Maynard, 106, 224

Idzumi, H., 297
Imakita, Kosen, 295
imperialism, 179–185
Inge, William R., 241
integral understanding, 110, 271–274
(see also Wach)
interfaith dialogue, 311–327, 329–341
internment camps, 219–220
Irwin, William, 35n
Isaacs, Harold, 170–171, 210
Iyomante (Ainu bear festival) 33, 47–99
bear as sacred, 82–84, 88–89
description of ritual, 88–99
speculated outside influences, 82

Jacobsen, Thorkild, 35n, 37
Jastrow, Morris J., 154, 303n, 367
Job, Book of, 15
Johnson, Samuel, 4
Jōmon culture, 52
Jones, Jenkin Llyod, 5
Jordan, Lewis Henry, 4, 6n, 114, 135,
150

Kan, Enkichi, xi
Kant, Immanuel, 335
Kasahara, Kenju, xi
Keller, Adolph, 261

Keller, Helen, 161
Kellog, Samuel Henry, 4
Kierkegaard, Sōren, 335
Kincheloe, Samuel, 18
Kindaichi, Kyosuke, 48, 48n, 50n, 62n,
68, 69n, 76–77, 81, 84, 87, 87n, 88,
93, 98
King, Winston, 257
Kishimoto, H., 143
Konvitz, Milton R., 184, 218
Kraemer, Hendrik, 12, 13, 13n, 115,
141, 169, 172, 237, 242, 257–258,
262, 266, 267, 311–327
Krasheinnikoff, 47
Kristol, Irving, 115, 163, 170
Kroeber, A.L., 50
Kuomintang, 202

Lach, Donald F., 185
La Farge, John, 103
Lane, Beatrice, 296
Lang, Andrew, 315
Lawrence, William M., 5
Leeuw, Gerardus van der, 3, 16, 17n, 22,
28n, 33n, 40, 110, 143, 347
on history of religions, 301–306
methodological schema, 306–310
worship, 301–310
Legge, James, 315
Leibniz, G.W., 16
Lessa, William A., and Evon Z. Vogt,
166
Leuking, F. Dean, 277n
liberalism, 6
Lin Yutang, 195, 197
Linton, Ralph, 51
Lippman, Walter, 190
Littlefield, Henry W., 180
Locke, John, 16
*logos* (vs. *mythos*), 35, 231–240, 313
Long, Charles H., 32, 119n, 144, 353
LSD, 244
Lubac, Henri de, 242

*ma'at*, 35
Macdonald, A.J., 181, 356
Madkour, Ibrahim, 249
Mahatma Gandhi, see Gandhi